10B

'20 52

£4,99

INTERPRETATION AND CULTURAL HISTORY

Also by Joan H. Pittock

ABERDEEN AND THE ENLIGHTENMENT   (*co-editor*)
THE ASCENDANCY OF TASTE: The Achievement of
Joseph and Thomas Warton

Interpretation and Cultural History

Edited by

Joan H. Pittock
Senior Lecturer in English
University of Aberdeen

and

Andrew Wear
Lecturer in History of Medicine
Wellcome Institute for the History of Medicine, London

M
MACMILLAN

First published 1991

Published by
MACMILLAN ACADEMIC AND PROFESSIONAL LTD
Houndmills, Basingstoke, Hampshire RG21 2XS
and London
Companies and representatives
throughout the world

Typeset in 10/12 pt Palatino by
TecSet Ltd, Wallington, Surrey

Printed in Hong Kong

British Library Cataloguing in Publication Data
Interpretation and cultural history.
I. Pittock, Joan H. II. Wear, A. Andrew
352.556094
ISBN 0–333–52494–2

Contents

List of Plates

Section I

1 *Descartes' Nervous Man*. 1662. French edition, facing titlepage.

2 *The Third Vision of Christoph Haizmann which Occurred while He was Most Seriously Ill*. Source: Oesterreichische Nationalbibliothek, MSS 14,084. Date: 1677. The Bavarian man Christoph Haizmann was seized in August 1677 with nervous convulsions and acute mental illness. The record of his derangement survives in a diary, nine paintings showing his visions while afflicted, and in dozens of statements made by priests and holy men, medics and lay people who observed his derangement. This is the third of the nine paintings and contains these words (translated from the German): 'The third time he [the Devil] appeared after one and a half years in this loathsome guise, with a book in his hand, which was full of sorcery and black magic. I was able to amuse myself with it, and drive away melancholy.' Haizmann's case was studied by Richard Hunter and Ida Macalpine in *Schizophrenia 1677* (London, 1956).

3 Thomas Rowlandson, engraving of *Justice, Philanthropy and Sensibility*. ca. 1780. Notice *'Sensibility'* on the right, personified with a haggard look and wracked by nervous illness. Tearful and sullen and possessed of straggly hair, she has mounted a candle on a muff on her left hand and holds a copy of a book by Jean-Jacques Rousseau in her right. Her left foot is wrapped up for the gout.

4 *Thomas Rowlandson's Anatomy of Melancholy*. 1808. Caption: 'Tis a Misery to be born, a pain to live, a trouble to die.' The old melancholic is seated in his chair before his fire on the right. Above are his pills and potions and three important signs adorn the walls: the skeleton portending imminent death; the portrait of Democritus referring to Burton (whose title-page of *The Anatomy of Melancholy* reads 'by Democritus

vii

Junior'); and a painting or drawing above the fireplace with snakes at the top containing an inscription reading 'Sorrow and grief,' and a dagger held by disembodied hands with another inscription reading 'in suffering is all.' A sheet titled 'Remedies against Discontents – Cure of jealousy' is pinned to the wall. At the table behind him are a man and woman enjoying wine and song, suggesting that lechery is the cure-all and the poor man's antidote to melancholy.

littered with pills and potions and uneaten food, and his servant and the physician (identified by his wig and cane) mourn his sorry state in the right hand corner. The tetrameter verse attached underneath reads:

The Mind distemper'd – say what potent charm,
Can Fancy's Spectre – breeding rage disarm?
Physics prescription, art assails in vain,
The dreadful phantoms fleating cross the brain!

Until with Esculapian skill, the sage M.D.
Finds out at length by self taught palmistry
The hopeless case – in the reluctant fee:
Then, not in torture such a wretch to keep.
One pitying bolus lays him sound asleep.

The box next to his chair may be filled with his important belongings and papers.

9 *The Hypochondriac* by John Atkinson (1775–1831), drawn at the end of the eighteenth century. Atkinson, like Rowlandson and Gillray, was one of the best-known caricaturists of the day. Here the male hypochondriac is viewed sitting in his parlor, having converted it into a sick man's ward, his bed near by and dressed as a hospital invalid. His hands clasped, he is cold and sick and praying, his eyes shut, and his mouth chewing on a pill whose identity is not clear in the engraving. A sheet of paper hangs over the table; he has been writing something and let it go. His dog's bone is on the floor but there is no dog; perhaps in his anxiety over his ailments he has let the dog die.

10 *Lunatic in a Cell.* ca. 1770. Engraving in the Huntington Library. The eyes suggest that he is a madman, the mouth, lips and teeth anguish and delusion. The position of his hands is significant, with his left hand holding his chest/intercostal diaphragm area and the right clutching his genital area. He has removed his breeches or undergarment, which now lies on the rack.

11 *Madwoman in Terror*, 1775, Mezzotint by W. Dickinson after a painting by Robert Edge Pine. Engraving in the Wellcome

Institute in London. The portrait illuminates the female iconography of madness, in this instance a young woman of perhaps twenty or so whose wild hair is strung with straw, and whose eyeballs flash with terror and fear. A bandana is wrapped around her head; in fury she has torn the garment from her breast which now lies bare. A feathery or animal garment clings loosely around her, and she is chained and roped, evidence that she poses a threat to others and is dangerous to herself. Window high up in the left corner makes clear that this is a cell where she has been incarcerated.

12 *Lavater's Physiognomy*. An iconography of the male from the Holcroft 1793 translation, plate 4, n.p. No nervous figure here but notice the melancholic male at the bottom, especially when he is aligned with the madman and lunatic. His eyes and lips are crucially expressive, as in the iconography of the humours or temperaments.

13 Early nineteenth-century engraving of the temperaments, derived in part from LeBrun: *lymphatic; sanguine; bilious; nervous*. The expression of the eyes and lips provide the clue and the cheeks reflect the degree of passion. All are male because the temperaments generally were iconographically understood as masculine. The nervous male resembles a minister of state: driven, engrossed, professional, perhaps a statesmen or aristocrat who has been idolised and romanticised.

The above illustrations are reprinted by kind permission of the Wellcome Institute for the History of Medicine.

Section II

1 *Galileo's Objective Lens with Ivory Mount of 1677 by Vittorio Croster*, Florence, Museo di Storia della Scienza.

2 Girolamo della Volpaia, *Armillary Sphere*, 1564, Florence, Museo di Storia della Scienza.

3 Giovanni Bologna, *Astronomy*, 1573, Vienna, Kunsthistoriches Museum.

Acknowledgements

The editors wish to acknowledge the generous sponsorship of the British Academy, of Waterstone's Ltd, and of BP, which enabled the Cultural History Group of the University of Aberdeen to hold its 1987 symposium.

JOAN H. PITTOCK
ANDREW WEAR

Notes on the Contributors

Jonathan Barry is a lecturer in the Department of History and Archaeology at the University of Exeter. He has published several articles on early modern Bristol, based on his doctoral dissertation, *The Cultural Life of Bristol, 1640–1775,* which he is currently revising for publication. He has edited the Tudor and Stuart volumes in the series *Readers in Urban History* and is currently editing a book on the middling sort, 1550–1800, for Macmillan. He is General Editor of *Exeter Studies in History* and active in Exeter's Centre for South-Western Historical Studies.

Peter Burke taught at the University of Sussex from 1962 to 1978 and is now Reader in Cultural History at the University of Cambridge and Fellow of Emmanuel College, Cambridge. His publications include *Culture and Society in Renaissance Italy; Venice and Amsterdam; Popular Culture in Early Modern Europe;* and *Historical Anthropology of Early Modern Italy.*

Paul Dukes is Professor of History at the University of Aberdeen where he has taught since 1964. He is the author of a wide range of books and articles on Russian, European and Comparative History. His most recent publication is *The Last Great Game: USA versus USSR: Events, Conjunctures, Structures.* Together with John Dunkley he has edited *Culture and Revolution,* a collection of essays drawn largely from the 1988 Aberdeen Cultural History Group Conference.

Peter Hulme was educated at the Universities of Leeds and Essex. Since 1979 he has taught in the Department of Literature at Essex, where he was involved with the Essex Sociology of Literature Conferences (1976–84) and the publication of their proceedings. His articles have appeared in *Literature and History; Forum for Modern Language Studies; Critique of Anthropology; New Formations* and he is the author of *Colonial Encounters: Europe and the Native Caribbean, 1492–1797.*

Ludmilla Jordanova is Senior Lecturer in History at the University of Essex, where she has taught since 1980. She is the author of *Lamarck* and *Sexual Visions: Images of Gender in Science and Medicine between the Eighteenth and Twentieth Centuries*. She edited and contributed to *Languages of Nature: Critical Essays on Science and Literature*. Among her current interests are the cultural history of the biomedical sciences and the family in eighteenth-century Europe. She is presently writing a book on the latter.

Martin Kemp has been, since 1981, Professor of the Department of Art History at the University of St Andrews. He was educated at the University of Cambridge and the Courtauld Institute, University of London. He has been a lecturer at Dalhousie University, Nova Scotia and at the University of Glasgow. He was Slade Professor at the University of Cambridge, 1987–8 and Visiting Professor at the Institute of Fine Arts, New York University in 1988. His publications include *Leonardo da Vinci: The Marvellous Works of Nature and Man*, for which he won the Miller Prize, and *The Science of Art: Optical Themes in Western Art from Brunelleschi to Seurat*. He is the current Chairman of the Association of Art Historians.

Lawrence Lipking is Chester D. Tripp Professor of Humanities at Northwestern University, a post he has held since 1979. Previously he taught at Princeton University. His teaching and professional interests include eighteenth-century English Literature, Comparative Literature, Women's Studies and Romantic Poetry. His publications include *The Ordering of the Arts in Eighteenth-Century England; The Life of the Poet*, for which he won the Christina Gaus Award; and *Abandoned Women and Poetic Tradition*.

Joan H. Pittock is Senior Lecturer in English at the University of Aberdeen and is Convener of the Cultural History degree. She was founder-editor of the *Journal of the British Society for 18th Century Studies* in 1978 and President of the British Society for 18th Century Studies 1980–2. Her publications include *The Ascendancy of Taste*. She has recently written on Chatterton, Boswell and the Scottish Enlightenment and is currently completing her account of the Oxford Chair of Poetry.

Roy Porter is Senior Lecturer at the Wellcome Institute for the History of Medicine, London and was, 1988–9, William Andrews

Clark Professor at the University of California, Los Angeles. He is the author of, among others, *A Social History of London; English Society in the Eighteenth Century*; and *Mind Forg'd Manacles*. He is currently working on a history of Bethlem.

George Rousseau is Professor of Eighteenth-Century Studies at the University of California, Los Angeles, having been Professor of English 1970–9. Among his many books are *English Poetic Satire: Wyatt to Byron* (with Neil Rudentine); *Organic Form: The Life of an Idea; The Ferment of Knowledge: Studies in the Historiography of Science* (with Roy Porter); *Sexual Underworlds of the Enlightenment* (with Roy Porter). He has been Osgood Fellow in Literature at Princeton University, 1965–6, Senior Fulbright Research Professor at the Sir Thomas Browne Institute at Leiden, The Netherlands, 1983; and Clark Library Professor at the University of California 1985–6.

William Scott is Senior Lecturer in History at the University of Aberdeen and a member of the University's Cultural History Group. A specialist in French History, especially the Enlightenment and the French Revolution, he is the author of *Terror and Repression in Revolutionary Marseille* and has recently finished a work on attitudes to certain key problems of reform as expressed in the unpublished essays submitted for the *concours* of French provincial academies in the period 1774–93.

Andrew Wear lectures in the History of Medicine at University College, London, and the Wellcome Institute. He has written on renaissance medicine and early modern social history.

Introduction

Joan H. Pittock and Andrew Wear

Like the rest of human activity, the discipline of history is always changing and transforming itself. Cultural history has been written for centuries, but in recent years it has presented novel facets of itself to the world. It was in an attempt to capture the new spirit of cultural history that a colloquium was held in the University of Aberdeen in July 1987. The papers given at that meeting form the basis of the chapters in the present volume. The aim of the colloquium, and now of the book, was to bring together scholars who had what the organisers took to be the key to the new type of cultural history, an eclectic and cross-disciplinary approach. Although the contributors often differed in methodology and aim, they were all united in their willingness to cross academic boundaries in order to throw light on particular aspects of culture. (Indeed, in some cases, one felt that they were creating and mapping out a new cultural history in order to free themselves from what they felt were the limitations to historical insight produced by established ways of writing history.) The organisers asked the contributors not merely to discuss their approaches but to base their chapters around particular historical examples and problems. This British emphasis on an empirical grounding to historiography has a twofold advantage: the reader can see how a particular interpretative approach works in practice and benefit from the contributors' historical research.

The provinces of cultural history lie open now to countless definitions. The gap between the phenomena – the institutions, signs, mentalities – and the discipline becomes relatively insignificant when we consider how all those ideological assumptions which seemed to hold firm the ideas of unity, homogeneity and progress on to the twentieth century crumble in the political and social upheavals of the last decade. We are back to the power of human energies moving with less certain direction and more racial and national force along unpredictable paths.

1

Perhaps, also, the term 'culture' itself is too amorphous, polyvalent, even self-justifying in its ampler significances. It can be taken in its historical aspects as consciousness, self-awareness, a sense of past achievements prov:ding a shape, a tradition, an identity.

Despite such ambiguities, approaches to cultural history are today increasingly sophisticated and interconnected. No longer is the subject content to focus upon the 'Kultur-objekts' of elite art and of rich civilisations, but sociology, anthropology, modern literary criticism, linguistics, psychology and the various newer disciplines of history such as historical demography, family history, feminist history, the history of science and medicine all now inform cultural history. There is a danger that all this may merely produce undiscriminating and unreflective writing, but it is unlikely when the practitioner is as skilled as a Simon Schama, a Peter Burke or a Natalie Zimon Davies.

The diversity and mix of academic disciplines in cultural history is mirrored by the wide rar ge of topic upon which cultural history focuses. The wish to see cultural history as all embracing (though ironically, and sadly, political history is often ignored) is not an eccentric aberration, but reflects developments in cognate fields. Structuralism and poststructuralism have viewed the texts (that are to be semiotically understood) as unlimited: they are documents, revolutions, institutions, scientific and industrial developments and the arts themselves. The works of Shakespeare, the idea of the family, the media, are alike objects of scrutiny; concerns which any location of authority whether academic, social, political or aesthetic, must take account of. The hegemonies of traditional disciplines seem to break down under the power of this new critical approach and new cartographies are drawn in ever expanding and intersecting circles. The implications of de-coding and de-constructing, of contextualising and locating difference establishes new boundaries, alters modes of perception and reforms analyses. The recognition of achievement and of values within a tradition is something that, nevertheless, must be retained as inherent in culture.

The differences between history, literature, art often become illusory when cultural historians analyse topics like the representation of the nerves or the body (as George Rousseau and Roy Porter do in their chapters). Indeed, it is precisely because they can, as cultural historians, bring to bear on their topics a variety of historical and other disciplines that we can speak of a cultural rather than a medical history of the nerves or of the body. Again, the culture of towns, whether civic or revolutionary, and of regions can also be reconstructed by historians who have been released from disciplinary boundaries and can use different disciplines at will (as Jonathan Barry does for eighteenth-century Bristol, William Scott for revolutionary Marseilles and Paul Dukes for the north-east of Scotland).

Yet the individual and his or her intentions when creating art, rather than 'society' or social significance, have traditionally been the objects of study in cultural history in the past (an approach which has the merit of a rigorous use of historical evidence). Martin Kemp's chapter on how to interpret instruments of art argues like the other contributions for a cross-disciplinary approach, but rejects the new semiology of literary and historical critics for an interpretation based on people's perception at the time of the function of the instruments under discussion. Again, although Lawrence Lipking uses the modern concept of the literary canon as the theme of his chapter, he bases his work on the sense of authority as it was created and perceived by writers and readers in the past rather than by the interpretations of deconstructionists today. Cultural history has space for different interpretations and schools of thought.

A central issue concerns the place of culture in a society: what culture does to or for a society. Ludmilla Jordanova and Peter Hulme show how culture can be critically interpreted as reinforcing the status quo, justifying a hierarchy and the domination of some people in it. On this reading culture helps to shape the internal relationships within a society.

In contrast, Paul Dukes shows how a sense of a continuous culture, and its intrinsic worth, has survived in the isolated north-east corner of Scotland. Cultures are often shaped and perpetuated by geography as much as by people. Colonies, towns, cities, villages all have distinctive cultures, and so do regions. In a world where commercial culture makes recognition of a Coke bottle unsurprising in the smallest village in Asia or Norway; where communications are swift, population exchange common and where, to be trite yet truthful, the pace of change makes other periods appear almost stationary, it becomes difficult to find regional cultures where there still exists the sense of the past blending with present – the *longue durée* of slow change. Geographical isolation, or a shared dialect or language (for instance, the

Celtic languages of Breton, Welsh and Gaelic) allow such communities still to exist.

The retention of a minority culture often requires political action, especially as in this case one is discussing a minority culture within a minority culture – the latter being Scotland in relation to England. What can make such action worthwhile is the sense, present also in the past, that there is value in the culture, that the culture is integral to a people's sense of identity.

The possibilities of cultural history remain largely underdeveloped: the contributions in this book suggest some directions. We feel that the openness of a new cultural history to interpretation and subject matter will provide fresh knowledge of what we have made of ourselves.

2

Reflections on the Origins of Cultural History

Peter Burke

In this chapter Peter Burke lays down historical perspectives for the volume. He shows that an awareness of cultural history existed long before the term *Geschichte der Kultur* was being used in late eighteenth-century Germany. Starting with the Renaissance humanists, and with an awareness of classical antecedents, Burke discusses how histories of language and literature were written in the context of the Renaissance framework of classical glory, the darkness of the middle ages, and new dawn of the Renaissance. More surprisingly, because of art's less learned image, the lives of artists and of art became the subject of histories, beginning with Vasari's *Lives of the Painters, Sculptors and Architects* and continuing with writers intent on boosting the artistic reputation of their particular cities. The histories of individual intellectual disciplines and doctrines also came to be written in the period spanning the Renaissance and Enlightenment. The Reformation stimulated the history of religious institutions and doctrines, whilst at a secular level the history of philosophy was being attempted by Otto Heurn in his *The Philosophy of the barbarians* (1600) and by his successors. From the history of philosophy there naturally came a series of histories of specific disciplines such as mathematics and medicine.

When Burke comes to the seventeenth and in particular the eighteenth century it is clear that the origins of culture assume a greater significance. Burke shows that scholars went beyond the 'Lives' and the specific subject format to consider the modes of life and thought of peoples in other countries and times. Locke, Montesquieu, Warton and others predicated much of their interpretative work upon a relativistic approach in which the ability to empathise with the alien thought or mentality of another culture was most important. The eighteenth century, according to Burke, also saw the view develop that a culture was a totality of interconnected parts, so that one period could be distinguished from

5

another; general terms such as 'esprit général', 'the spirit of the age', 'Geist' became common, leading to the view of 'Kultur' in Germany in the 1780s. In a sense, the eighteenth century had a concept of cultural history which, although lacking in, say, modern quantitative or class-based analysis, stretches out its hand to the present and shares with it an eclectic, multidisciplinary approach. Burke's discussion of how historians after 1800 became professionalised and influenced by Ranke, limited to 'the documents' and political narrative, whilst cultural history was left to the amateur, shows why it is that cultural history until recently has had to fight an establishment view of history, and reminds us that the recent orthodoxies as to the proper subject matter of history were not verities founded upon the rocks of time, but shifting sands hiding the recent ancestors of today's cultural history.

What is cultural history? Whether or not is was easy to answer this question in the age of Jacob Burckhardt or Johan Huizinga, it is certainly difficult now, just as it is increasingly difficult to answer the question, 'What is culture?' We no longer use the term in its 'opera-house sense', as one anthropologist calls it, but include popular culture as well as elite culture, and everyday attitudes and practices as well as images, texts and music.[1] It is increasingly difficult to discover anything which is not described by someone as part of culture.[2]

Is all history cultural history, then, or does the adjective still describe a distinctive approach (if not a distinctive 'field')? In this search for our subject it may be appropriate to adapt the existentialists' definition of man and say that cultural history has no essence, but it does possess a history. But how does one write a history of something which lacks a fixed identity? It is rather like trying to catch a cloud in a butterfly net. However, Herbert Butterfield and Michel Foucault have taught us, in their very different ways, that all historians face this problem. If we wish to avoid the anachronistic attribution of our own intentions, interests and values to the dead, we cannot write the continuous history of anything.[3] On one side we face the danger of 'present-mindedness', and on the other the risk of inability to write anything at all.

Perhaps there is a middle way, an approach to the past which asks present-minded questions but refuses to give present-minded answers, which concerns itself with traditions but allows for their continual reinterpretation; and which notes the importance of unintended consequences in the history of historical writing as well as in the history of political events. That is, at any rate, the aim of this essay, which is concerned with the history of culture before the term 'culture' came into general use at the end of the eighteenth century.[4] It thus ends where it might reasonably be expected to have started – yet it will shortly be clear that there is no shortage of material to discuss.

In this case the present-minded questions are the following: how old is cultural history, and how have conceptions of cultural history changed over time? The difficulty to be avoided is that of giving these questions equally present-minded answers. The problem is a slippery one. We are not the first people in the world to realise that culture, as we now call it, has a history. The term 'cultural history' goes back to the late eighteenth century, at least in German (*Geschichte der Kultur*).[5] However the idea that litera-ture and philosophy and the arts have histories is much older, as I shall try to show. This tradition deserves to be commemorated. The difficulty is to do this without falling into the Whig error of imagining that what we have defined (and indeed in some places, such as Aberdeen, institutionalised) as a 'subject' or 'sub-discipline' existed in the past *in this form*.

In some respects the most historically-minded manner of approaching the problem would be to tell the story backwards from today, showing how Huizinga's conception of cultural his-tory differs from that of the 1980s, how Burckhardt's differed from Huizinga's, and so on. But in liberating us from assumptions of continuity, this backward narrative would obscure the ways in which practical, partial and short-term aims and motives (such as civic pride and the search for precedent) contributed to the development over the long term of a more general study pursued for its own sake. The best thing to do is perhaps for the author to share the difficulties with the reader in the course of the narrative. In other words, I shall try, like some contemporary novelists and critics, to tell a story and at the same time to reflect on it and even, perhaps, to undermine it.

Whenever one begins the story, it can be argued that it would have been better to have started earlier. I shall begin with the humanists of Renaissance Italy, whose attempt to undo the work of what they were the first to call the 'Middle Ages' and to revive the literature and learning of classical antiquity implied a view of three ages of culture: ancient, medieval and modern. In fact, as the humanists well knew, the idea that language has a history, that philosophy has a history, that literary genres have a history, that the life of mankind has been changed by a succession of inventions, all these ideas go back to ancient Greece and Rome, and can be found in Aristotle's *Poetics*, for example, in Varro's treatise on language, in Cicero's discussion of the rise and fall of oratory, and in the account of the early history of man given in the poem of Lucretius on the nature of things (so important for Vico, among others).[6]

THE HISTORY OF LANGUAGE AND LITERATURE

However, the humanists had a more dramatic story to tell about language and literature than had their ancient models: a story of barbarian invasions and of the consequent decline and destruction of classical Latin, followed by an account of revival, the work (of course) of the humanists themselves. In other words, an age of light was followed by the 'Dark Ages', followed in turn by the dawn of another age of light. This is the story which emerges from Leonardo Bruni's lives of Dante and Petrarch, for example, or from the historical introduction to Lorenzo Valla's Latin grammar, the *Elegantiae*.[7]

In the fifteenth and sixteenth centuries, debates about the relative merits of Latin and Italian as a literary language, and the best form of Italian to use, generated a good deal of research into the history of language by Leonardo Bruni, Flavio Biondo and others, who tried to discover, for example, what language the ancient Romans had actually spoken: Latin or Italian. In the early sixteenth century, one humanist produced a history of Latin divided into four periods – 'very old', 'old', 'perfect' (the age of Cicero) and 'imperfect' (ever since). Pietro Bembo, who did as much as any man to freeze Italian at a particular point in its development, allowed one of the characters in his famous dialogue on the vernacular to point out that language changes 'like fashions in clothes, modes of warfare, and all other manners and customs'.[8]

Northern humanists, at once imitators and rivals of their Italian predecessors, amplified the story by drawing attention to literary and linguistic developments in their own countries. In England in the 1580s, a discussion of English poetry from Chaucer onwards can be found in the treatise attributed to George Puttenham.[9] In later sixteenth-century France, we find two humanist lawyers, Etienne Pasquier and Claude Fauchet, chronicling and celebrating the achievements of French writers from the thirteenth century to the age of François I and the Pléiade.[10] A history of Castillian was published at the beginning of the seventeenth century.[11] The Germans had to wait until the late seventeenth century for an equivalent of the poets of the Pléiade, but the history, when it came, was more elaborate and comparative. Daniel Morhof placed the history of the German language and German poetry in a comparative European framework.[12]

Building on these foundations, a number of eighteenth-century scholars produced large-scale multi-volume histories of national literature, notably those of France, by a research team of Maurists (Benedictine monks) headed by Rivet de la Grange, and of Italy, compiled single-handed by Tiraboschi.[13] In Britain there were similar plans afoot. Alexander Pope put forward a 'scheme of the history of English poetry'; Thomas Gray amended it. Meanwhile the history had been undertaken by Thomas Warton. Warton never went beyond the early seventeenth century, but his unfinished work remains impressive.[14]

Monographs were written on the history of particular literary genres. Dryden, following the learned Casaubon, wrote an essay on the origin and progress of satire from what he called the 'rough-case, unhewn' extempore satire of ancient Rome to the polished productions of the period when the Romans 'began to be somewhat better bred, and were entering, as I may say, into the rudiments of civil conversation.[15] Again, the rise of the novel in the seventeenth and eighteenth centures was accompanied by investigations of its oriental and medieval origins by the polymath bishop Pierre-Daniel Huet, for example, and by Thomas Warton.[16]

THE HISTORY OF ARTISTS, ART AND MUSIC

It is hardly surprising to find men of letters devoting attention to the history of literature. Art was a less obvious object for a historian's attention, even in the Renaissance. Learned men did not always take artists seriously, while artists generally lacked the kind of preparation necessary for historical research. When, in fifteenth-century Florence, the sculptor Lorenzo Ghiberti sketched the history of art in his *Commentaries*, he was doing something rather unusual.[17]

We ought not to take Vasari for granted either. He was remarkable in his own day because he had a double education, not only a training in an artist's workshop but a humanist education sponsored by Cardinal Passerini.[18] Vasari's *Lives of the Painters, Sculptors and Architects* was written, so the author tell us, in order that young artists might learn from the example of their great predecessors, and also (one may reasonably suspect) for the greater glory of his adopted city, Florence, and his patrons the Medici (it was in fact published by the Grand Duke's press).[19]

However Vasari's book is much more than a work of propaganda. It is also, of course, a good deal more than a biographical collection. The prefaces to the three parts into which the work is divided include an account of the development of art: its rise in antiquity, its decline in the Middle Ages, and its revival in Italy in three stages, culminating in Vasari's master Michelangelo (it should be clear from this example that Whig history long antedates the Whig party). What is more, this concern with art rather than artists is stronger in the second edition (1568) than in the first (1550).[20] It has been shown by Ernst Gombrich that Vasari's developmental scheme was adapted from Cicero's account of his history of rhetoric. Without Vasari's double education this adaptation would have been virtually inconceivable, even if we allow for the fact that Vasari was helped by a circle of scholars who included Gianbattista Adriani, Vincenzo Borghini and Paolo Giovio.[21]

Vasari's book was treated as a challenge. Artists and scholars from other parts of Italy compiled lives of local artists in order to show that Rome, Venice, Genoa and Bologna were worthy rivals to Florence.[22] However they paid much less attention than Vasari had done to general trends in art. The same goes for responses to Vasari outside Italy, in the Netherlands and Germany in the seventeenth century. It was only in the mid-eighteenth century that Horace Walpole's *Anecdotes of Painting*, intended as an English equivalent of Vasari, found room not only for biographies but also for chapters on the 'state of painting' at different periods, the equivalent of the chapters on economic, social and literary history in Hume's *History of England*.[23]

The rise of what it is retrospectively convenient to call the history of art as opposed to the biography of artists took place earlier in studies of classical antiquity, for a sufficiently obvious reason. Despite the famous anecdotes of Greek artists told by Pliny (and adapted by Vasari), little was known about Apelles, Phidias and the rest, so that biographies could not be used to frame a study of ancient art. Yet ancient art, like other aspects of antiquity, fascinated the humanists, and important studies were made. One of them was the work of the Florentine scholar Giambattista Adriani, who composed a brief history of ancient art to help Vasari in his second edition of the *Lives* and organised it around the idea of artistic progress. Other studies were made by the Dutch humanist Junius, and by André Félibien, the first official historian of art.[24] Félibien's essay on the origin of painting and Huet's on the origin of romances were written in France in the same decade, the 1660s, as if expressing a more general change in historiographical taste. The outstanding achievement in this area, Winckelmann's great *History of Ancient Art*, should be considered not as a radically new departure but as the culmination of a trend.[25]

In this respect the history of art makes a dramatic contrast with the history of music. Some sixteenth- and seventeenth-century scholars, such as Vincenzo Galilei (father of the scientist) and Girolamo Mei, were well aware of changes in musical style over the long term and indeed discuss them in their treatises.[26] However, their aim was to attack or defend particular styles, not to write histories of music. At the end of the seventeenth century, a 'historical description' of music through the ages was published in Germany.[27]

However, systematic histories of music were published only in the eighteenth century. In Italy, Gianbattista Martini published an important study of the music of antiquity. In France, one major study was published by the Bonnet-Bourdelot family, and another written, but not published, by P. J. Caffiaux, a learned Maurist who was, appropriately, doing for music something like what his colleague Rivet was doing for literature. In Switzerland, another Benedictine, Martin Gerbert, made an important contribution to the history of church music. In England, Charles Burney and John Hawkins were contemporaries and rivals. In Germany, Forkel of the university of Gottingen, whose importance for cultural history will be emphasised later in this chapter, summed up the work of the century in his *General History of Music*.[28]

THE HISTORY OF DOCTRINE

The histories of language, literature and the arts seem to have begun as side-effects of the Renaissance. The Reformation also had its historical by-products. As the humanists defined their place in history by dividing the past into ancient, medieval and modern, so did the reformers, who saw themselves as going back behind the Middle Ages and reviving Christian antiquity or the 'primitive church'.[29] Histories of the Reformation begin with the Reformation itself: among the most famous are the *Commentaries* of Johann Sleidan and the *Acts and Monuments* of John Foxe. They tend to be histories of events or histories of institutions, but some of them find a place for the history of doctrines. This concern can be seen with still greater clarity in some seventeenth-century histories of the Reformation, by Raemond, for example, by Maimbourg and by Bossuet.[30] These three works are not exactly examples of the study of the past for its own sake; they are highly polemical. The books of Maimbourg and Bossuet were written for a political purpose, to support Louis XIV's anti-Protestant policies at the time of the Revocation of the Edict of Nantes. However their central idea that doctrines (at least false doctrines) have a history, an idea developed most fully, brilliantly and destructively by Bossuet, was one which would come, in the nineteenth century, to have a considerable appeal outside the polemical context in which it was developed.[31] As early as the end of the century it was deployed by an apologist for unorthodoxy, Gottfried Arnold, for whom church history was essentially the history of heresies, some of which hardened into official doctrine (as Luther's had done), only to be challenged by later generations.[32]

THE HISTORY OF PHILOSOPHY

From the history of religious doctrine it is no great step to the history of secular doctrine, or philosophy, in a wide sense of that term which includes natural philosophy, indeed much of the 'history of ideas' (the phrase was re-launched by Arthur Lovejoy in the 1920s but it had already been employed by Vico two hundred years earlier).[33] It seemed appropriate to delay discussion of it until this point because (unlike art history in the age of Vasari or the history of literature and language in the age of Pasquier) there seem to have been few significant developments before the year 1600. Perhaps the need to assess past achievements was a by-product of the scientific revolution of the seventeenth century, in which the 'new' mechanical philosophy, as it was often called, became a matter for debate.

The classical model for these histories of philosophy is, of course, the *Lives of the Philosophers* by Diogenes Laertius. However, from Otto Heurn's treatise on *The Philosophy of the Barbarians* onwards, attempts were made to tell a story as well as to collect biographies and also to write the history not only of the ancient Greeks but also of the Chaldeans, Persians, Indians and finally (notably in Brucker's major study the *Critical History of Philosophy*) the Chinese and Japanese. The story was taken down to the Middle Ages and even later. Some of these histories were written for their own sake, others with polemical intent, to encourage scepticism by emphasising the contradictions between one philosopher and another. They do not abandon a biographical framework altogether, but they do modify it by discussing the development of philosophical schools or 'sects'.[34]

THE HISTORY OF DISCIPLINES

Out of the history-of-philosophy tradition branched the studies of specific disciplines.[35] Histories of astronomy, for example, were written by Johann Kepler and Adam Smith.[36] Baldi's lives of mathematicians (on the model of Vasari or Diogenes Laertius) was followed in the eighteenth century by Montucla's study of the development of the discipline.[37] At the end of the eighteenth century, a history of chemistry, which made a considerable effort to place the development of the subject in its social and cultural context, was offered by its author, a Göttingen man, as a contribution to a series of histories of arts and sciences on which 'a society of learned men' were currently at work.[38]

In a brief general survey like the present chapter there is obviously no space to discuss the history of these disciplines one by one, any more than to give details on the history of inventions, which goes back to Polydore Vergil at the beginning of the sixteenth century; the history of history, from La Popelinière onwards, and the history of writing, the subject of two important monographs in the seventeenth century.[39]

As a case study of developments within disciplines, it may be useful, however, to devote a paragraph or two to the history of the history of medicine. Some sixteenth-century physicians (notably Vesalius and Fernel), took sufficient interest in history to place their own work in the context of the intellectual revival or Renaissance through which they were living. The first substantial study, of medical history however, was published considerably later, at the end of the seventeenth century.

The history of medicine by Daniel Le Clerc (the brother of the critic Jean Leclerc) begins by surveying earlier studies and dismisses them for concentrating on biography. 'There is a big difference between writing the history of biographies of physicians . . . and writing the history of medicine, studying the origin of that art, and looking at its progress from century to century and the changes in its sytems and methods . . . which is what I have undertaken.[40] Leclerc's title page also notes his concern with medical 'sects' along the lines of the history of philosophy, which he seems to have taken as his model.

Unfortunately Le Clerc's account (like Martini's history of music) never got beyond classical antiquity. For the modern part of the story it was necessary to wait until 1725 and the second volume of Freind's *History of Physick*, which took the story from the Arabs to Linacre (deliberately stopping short of Paracelsus). As his title-page boasted, Freind differed from Leclerc in concentrating on 'practice'. His second volume is as much a history of illness (notably the sweating sickness, venereal disease, and scurvy) as it is a history of medicine. It is almost a history of the body.[41]

THE HISTORY OF MODES OF THOUGHT

Another development from the history of philosophy in this period bears a striking and not altogether illusory resemblance to some of the 'new directions' preached and practised today. It is necessary to walk an intellectual tightrope at this point, to give the eighteenth-century historians of mentalities the credit that is due to them without turning them into clones of ourselves or of the *Annales*.

In the seventeenth century, John Selden had already recommended the study of 'what was generally believed in all ages', adding that in order to discover this, 'the way is to consult the liturgies, not any private man's writings'.[42] In other words, rituals reveal mentalities. John Locke was acutely aware of differences between modes of thought in different parts of the world: 'Had you or I been born at the Bay of Saldanha, possibly our thoughts and notions had not exceeded those brutish ones of the Hottentots that inhabit there.'[43] This relativist argument, nourished by recent accounts of Africa, gives obvious support to Locke's polemic against innate ideas. However it is not such a long step from a concern with variations in thinking in different places to a concern with different periods. It may well have been the revolution in thought associated with the rise of the 'mechanical philosophy' which made some Europeans aware of the intellectual 'world they had lost'. Curiously enough, the eighteenth-century scholar Richard Hurd employs a similar phrase when discussing the rise of reason since Spenser's day: "What we have gotten by this revolution, you will say, is a great deal of good sense. What we have lost is a world of fine fabling.[44] At all events, one finds this awareness in Fontenelle, in Vico, in Montesquieu and elsewhere in the eighteenth century, in the context of attempts to understand alien features of early literature and law.

Fontenelle's essay on the origin of *'fables'* (or as we would say, 'myths') argued that in less polished ages (*ces siècles grossiers*), systems of philosophy were necessarily anthropomorphic and magical.[45] Vico arrived independently at similar conclusions, expressed with rather more sympathy for what he called the 'poetic logic' of early man.[46] A Danish scholar called Jens Kraft published in 1760 a general description of the 'savage mind', or more exactly of savage peoples (*de Vilde Folk*) and their 'mode of thought' (*Taenke-Maade*).[47] A similar phrase had been used by Montesquieu when he was trying to reconstruct the logic of the medieval ordeal, explaining it by what he called 'the mode of thought of our ancestors [*la manière de penser de nos pères*].[48] The same kind of concern with an exotic mentality underlay the increasing interest in the history of chivalry, studied by La Curne de Sainte-Palaye.[49] Voltaire drew heavily on Sainte-Palaye's work in his essay on manners. So did German writers, notably Herder and Eichhorn. British men of letters did the same. William Robertson argued in his famous 'view of the progress of society' that 'chivalry . . . though considered commonly as a wild institution, the effect of caprice, and the source of extravagance, arose naturally from the state of society at that period, and had a very serious influence in refining the manners of the European nations'.[50] Richard Hurd of Emmanuel College had already discussed the romances of chivalry (and even the *Faerie Queene*) as expressions of what he called the 'Gothic system' of 'heroic manners'.[51]

Hurd's friend Thomas Warton had similar interests. His essay on the rise of 'romantic fiction' argued that it originated 'at a time when a new and unnatural mode of thinking took place in Europe, introduced by our communication with the East', in other words the Crusades. His essay on Spenser showed rather more sympathy for alien mentalities, indeed empathy with them, and his observations on method have lost none of their relevance today:

> In reading the works of an author, who lived in a remote age, it is necessary that . . . we should place ourselves in his situation and circumstances; that we may be the better enabled to judge and discern how his turn of thinking, and manner of composing, was biass'd, influenc'd and as it were tinctur'd, by very familiar and reigning appearances, which were utterly different from those with which we are at present surrounded.[52]

The history of unspoken assumptions and of representations remains central to the enterprise of cultural history.

THE HISTORY OF CULTURE

Given the increasing number of histories of arts and sciences in the early modern period, it is scarcely surprising to find that some people were concerned to fit them together and see them as a whole, as a 'General History of Culture'.[53] Before that phrase came into use, some writers discussed connexions between the histories of the various 'arts' (liberal, mechanical, or both) as the Spanish humanist Juan Luis Vives did, for example, in his polemical treatise *On the Causes of the Corruption of the Arts* (1531), in which the history of learning, conceived more or less along the lines of Valla's history of language, was pressed into the service of a campaign for the reform of universities. Among the causes listed by Vives were 'arrogance' and 'wars'.

The principal model of general cultural history in the early modern period might be described as the model of the *translatio studii*, in other words the successive dominance either of different regions of the world or of different disciplines. For example, the French humanist Le Roy argued in his remarkable essay in comparative history, the *Vicissitudes*, that 'all liberal and mechanical arts have flourished and declined together [*tous arts libéraux et mécaniques ont fleuri ensemble, puis décheu*', so that different civilisations, Greek, Arab, Chinese and so on, have their different peaks and troughs.[54] Francis Bacon was acquainted with the work of Le Roy, as he was with the treatise by Vives, and this acquaintance underlies Bacon's famous call for 'a just story of learning, containing the antiquities and original of knowledge and their sects, their inventions, their traditions, their diverse administrations and managings, their flourishings, their oppositions, decays, depressions, oblivions, removes, with the causes and occasions of them.'[55] The reference, unusual for its time, to the 'administrations and managings' betrays the man of affairs.

Bacon never found time to write such a history of learning, but his programme inspired some eighteenth-century writers, notably Voltaire and D'Alembert. Voltaire's *Essay on Manners* and *Age of Louis XIV* have a good deal to say on the revival of letters and 'the progress of the human mind [*les progrès de l'esprit humain*]', contrasting ignorance, credulity and barbarism with learning, enlightenment and civilisation. Voltaire also noted, like Le Roy, that the fine arts 'generally perish and are reborn together [*d'ordinaire périssent et renaissent ensemble*'. D'Alembert gave a similar account of intellectual progress in his preliminary discourse to the *Encyclopédie*.[56]

Decline attracted attention as well as progress and there was considerable debate about the reasons for cultural peaks and troughs. Some scholars suggested that despotism leads to cultural decline – this was the opinion of the humanist Leonardo Bruni, as it was the view of Shaftesbury and had been that of Tacitus.[57] Others searched for physical rather than moral causes, notably the climate, which Vasari had invoked as an explanation for Florentine artistic achievements, and which was discussed in a more systematic manner in the theoretical writings of the abbé Dubos, together with patronage, wealth, manners and other factors.[58]

A concern for the relation between what we call 'culture' (*le cose d'ingegno*, creative matters) and what we call 'society' (*umani costumi*, 'human customs') can be found in a remarkable essay published in 1775 by the Italian Jesuit Saverio Bettinelli and dealing with the *risorgimento* or 'revival' of Italy after the year 1000.[59] Bettinelli ranges from art, literature and music to chivalry, commerce, luxury and festivals. A systematic comparison of his essay in synthesis (which draws heavily on Vasari and Tiraboschi) with that of Jacob Burckhardt would do a great deal to clarify the relation between what might be called the 'classical model' of cultural history and its predecessors.

The idea that a culture is a totality, or at least that the connexions between different arts and disciplines are extremely important, underlies one of the major achievements of early modern scholars: their development of techniques for detecting forgeries. These techniques of detection depended on an increasingly sharp awareness of anachronism. From Lorenzo Valla's exposure of the so-called 'Donation of Constantine' in the middle of the fifteenth century to the rejection of the poems of 'Ossian' at the end of the eighteenth century, there is a long series of debates on the authenticity of particular texts or, more rarely, artefacts such as medals.[60] In these debates the protagonists are forced to formulate their criteria more and more precisely. Valla, for example, noted anachronisms in the Donation's style or mode of expression (*stilus, modus loquendi*). Richard Bentley, in his *Dissertation upon the Epistles of Phalaris*, that famous exposure of a forged classical text, went into rather more detail on the history of Greek, noting that the 'idiom and style' of the letters 'by the whole thread and colour of it betrays itself to be a thousand years younger' than the ruler to whom they had been attributed.[61]

Thomas Warton discusses his criteria still more fully in his exposure of the 'medieval' poems Chatterton sent to Horace Walpole. Warton used his knowledge of what he called 'the progression of poetical composition' to show up the forgery and noted anachronisms both in the language ('optics', for example), and in the style (full of abstractions and 'sophistications' impossible in the fifteenth century).[62]

A view of culture as a whole, implicit in demonstrations such as these, gradually became more and more explicit in the use of such terms as 'the spirit [or genius] of the age'. In seventeenth-century English texts it is possible to find phrases such as the following: 'the temper and geniuses of times alter' (Stillingfleet); 'the genius of every age is different' (Dryden); 'the general vein and humour of ages' (Temple). In the age of Montesquieu and Voltaire (more especially the Voltaire of the *Essai sur les moeurs*), references to changes in the *esprit général*, or *esprit humain*, or *génie*, become relatively frequent. The same goes for the Scots in the age of Hume and Robertson: 'the spirit of the nation', 'the spirit of enquiry', 'the humour of the nation', 'the reigning genius', 'the genius of government', and so on.

When the term *Kultur* came into general use in Germany in the 1780s, it may, like the term *Geist*, have marked a sharper awareness of the links between changes in language, law, religion, the arts and sciences on the part of Herder and other writers (such as Adelung and Eichhorn) who used these expressions. All the same this awareness was not something completely new. It should be added that Herder made considerable use of the work of such earlier historians of ideas and of the arts as Saint-Palaye and Goguet.[63]

In other words, it is not quite accurate to assert that cultural history was built on 'Hegelian foundations', however influential Hegel's concept of the *Zeitgeist* was to be in the nineteenth and twentieth centuries.[64] Hegel built his structure on the foundations of work of the previous generation of German intellectuals, notably Herder; they built on that of the French, and so on, back to Aristotle, who discussed the internal development of literary genres such as tragedy in his *Poetics*, while his teleological views might entitle him to be called the first recorded Whig historian.

It is appropriate for several reasons to end this essay on the origins of cultural history at the end of the eighteenth century. In the first place, because the idea of the history of culture was establishing itself in Germany, at least in the circles of Herder and Eichhorn. In the second place, because it was at this time that Condorcet was writing a history of the world organised around the idea of intellectual progress and divided into periods, some of which were based on cultural criteria such as the invention of writing and printing and the coming of Descartes.[65] In the third place, the years around 1800 make an appropriate point at which to conclude because the rise of Ranke and the document-based narrative political history associated with him and, still more narrowly, with his school, had the effect of marginalising, if not eliminating, the sociocultural history which had flourished in late eighteenth-century Europe from Edinburgh to Florence, from Paris to Göttingen. This is not to say that no distinguished contributions to the genre were made in the nineteenth century. Michelet's conception of history was broad enough to include culture (notably in his volume on the French Renaissance). Guizot's lectures on the *History of Civilisation in France* and the *History of Civilisation in Europe* went through many editions in French and other languages. Jacob Burckhardt's classic study of *The Civilisation of the Renaissance in Italy* was published in 1860, and was much appreciated in the later nineteenth century, although it attracted relatively little notice at the time of publication. The history of eighteenth-century art by the brothers Goncourt received considerable acclaim, as did Sainte-Beuve's study of the world of Port-Royal. The list could be extended almost indefinitely. All the same, the gap had widened between professional history, concerned with politics, documents and hard facts, and cultural history, which was abandoned to the amateur. The return of cultural history to academic respectability is a theme best left for another time.

Notes

1. R. Wagner, *The Invention of Culture*, Englewood Cliffs, 1975, p. 21.
2. For an important contribution to the 'cutting of the culture concept down to size', as he puts it, see C. Geertz, *The Interpretation of Cultures*, New York, 1973.
3. Compare and contrast H. Butterfield, *The Whig Interpretation of History*, London, 1931, with M. Foucault, *Les mots et les choses*, 1966, English trans. as *The Order of Things*, London, 1970.
4. On the rise of the term *'Kultur'* in Germany in the 1780s, W. H. Bruford, *Culture and Society in Classical Weimar*, Cambridge, 1962, ch. 4.
5. J. G. Eichhorn, *Allgemeine Geschichte der Kultur*, Göttingen, 1796.
6. L. Edelstein, *The Idea of Progress in Classical Antiquity*, Baltimore, 1967
7. On the 'dark ages', L. Varga, *Das Schlagwort vom 'finsteren Mittelalter'* Vienna, 1932 A useful brief survey of humanist views of the rebirth of literature and learning in W. K. Ferguson, *The Renaissance in Historical Thought*, Cambridge, Mass., 1948 pp. 20f.
8. On Bruni and Biondo. C. Grayson, *A Renaissance controversy, Latin or Italian?*, Oxford, 1959. On the four periods, A Castellesi, *De sermone latino*, 1516. P. Bembo, *Prose della volgar lingua*, Venice, 1525, Book 1, ch. 17. Important early accounts of the development of Italian can be found in V. Borghini, *Scritti sulla lingua*, ed. J. R. Woodhouse, Bologna, 1971 and C. Cittadini, *Le origini della volgar toscana favella*, Siena, 1604.
9. G. Puttenham, *The Arte of English Poesie*, London, 1589. On him, R. Wellek, *The Rise of English Literary History*, Chapel Hill, 1941.

10. E. Pasquier, *Recherches de la France*, Paris 1566, discussed in G. Huppert, *The Idea of Perfect History*, (Urbana, 1970; C. Fauchet, *Origine de la langue et poésie françoises*, Paris, 1581.

11. B. Aldrete, *Del origen y principio de la lengua castellana*, Rome, 1606.

12. D. Morhof, *Unterricht von der Teutschen Sprache und Poesie*, Kiel, 1682.

13. A Rivet de La Grange, *Histoire littéraire de la France*; on him, J.-M. Goulemot, 'Histoire littéraire et mémoire nationale', *History and Anthropology* 2, part 2, 1986, pp. 225–35. G. Tiraboschi, *Storia della letteratura italiana*, 11 vols, Modena 1772–95.

14. T. Warton, *The History of English Poetry*, 4 vols, London, 1774–8 on which see Wellek, *Rise*; L. Lipking, *The Ordering of the Arts*, Princeton, 1970, pp. 352f; J. H. Pittock, *The Ascendancy of Taste*, London, 1973, ch. 5.

15. J. Dryden, *Discourse concerning the Origin and Progress of Satire* London, 1693, cf. I. Casaubon, *De satyrica Graecorum poesi*, Paris, 1605.

16. P.-D. Huet, *Lettre sur l'origine des romans* (1669: second ed., Paris, 1678); T. Warton, digression 'On the Origin of Romantic Fiction in Europe' in *History*.

17. L. Ghiberti, *I commentari*, ed. O. Morisani, Naples, 1947. On this text, E. van der Grinten, *Enquiries into the History of Art–Historical Writing*. Venlo, Holland, 1953.

18. On Vasari's own life, see T.S.R. Boase, *Giorgio Vasari, the Man and the Book*, Princeton, 1979.

19. On Vasari as propagandist, A. Chastel, *Art et humanisme à Florence au temps de Laurent le Magnifique* Paris, 1961 pp. 21f.

20. Z. Wazbinski, 'L'idée de l'histoire dans la première et la seconde édition des *Vies* de Vasari', in *il Vasari storiografo e artista*, Florence, 1976, 1–21, noting similar themes in Vasari's correspondence with Borghini.

21. E. H. Gombrich, 'Vasari's *Lives* and Cicero's *Brutus*', *Journal of the Warburg and Courtauld Institutes* 23, 1960 pp. 309–21.

22. G. Baglione, *Vite*, Rome, 1642; C. Ridolfi, *Meraviglie*, c. 1646; ed. D. von Hadeln, Berlin, 1914; R. Soprani, *Vite de'vittori genovesi*, Genoa, 1674; C. C. Malvasia, *Felsina Pittrice*, Bologna, 1678.

23. K. van Mander, *Het Schilderboek*, Haarlem, 1604; the Amsterdam, 1936, edition is translated into modern Dutch; J. von Sandrart, *Deutsche Akademie*, 1675–9; I used the Munich, 1925 edn; H. Walpole, *Anecdotes of Painting in England* 1761; London, 1879. On Walpole, Lipking, *Ordering*, pp. 127f. The fact that the studies by Daniel Morhof on German literature and Joachim von Sandrart on German painting were published at more or less the same time is worth noting. On Walpole, Lipking, 1970 pp. 127f.

24. G. B. Adriani, 'Lettera a Giorgio Vasari', 1567, in *Raccolta Artistica* 1, Florence, 1846, 3–69; F. Junius, *De pictura veterum*, Amsterdam, 1637; on Junius, Lipking, *Ordering*, pp. 23f; A. Félibien, 1660, *Origine de la peinture*. Félibien was *historiographe des bâtiments* to Louis XIV. On him, van der Grinten, *Enquiries into the History of Art–Historical Writing* (Delft, 1952).

25. J. J. Winckelmann, *Geschichte der Kunst des Altertums*, Dresden, 1764; on him, van der Grinten.

26. V. Galilei, *Dialogo della musica antica e moderna*, Florence, 1581; G. Mei, *Discorso sopra la musica antica e moderna*, Venice, 1602.

27. W. C. Printz, *Historische Beschreibung der edelen Sing- und Kling-Kunst*, 1690.

28. G. B. Martini, 1757, *Storia della musica*; Bonnet-Bourdelot ed., *Histoire de la musique* Paris, 1715; P. J. Caffiaux, 'Histoire de la musique' (written 1754–6), on which see *Grove's Dictionary of Music and Musicians*, ed. S. Sadie (20 vols, London, 1980), under 'Caffiaux'. M. Gerbert (1774) *De cantu et musica sacra*; C. Burney, 1776–89 *A General History of Music*; J. Hawkins, 1766, *General History of the Science and Practice of Music*. On the last three scholars, E. Hegar, *Die Anfänge der neueren Musikgeschichtschreibung um 1770 bei Gerbert, Burney und Hawkins*, 1933, repr. Baden-Baden, 1974. On the last two, Lipking, *Ordering*, pp. 229f, 269f. J. N. Forkel, *Allgemeine Geschichte der Musik*, 2 vol, Göttingen, 1788–1801.

29. The equivalent for the Reformation of Ferguson's study of the Renaissance (cited above, note 7) is A. G. Dickens and J. Tonkin, *The Reformation in Historical Thought*, Cambridge, Mass., 1985.

30. F. de Raemond, *Histoire de la naissance, progrès et décadence de l'hérésie de ce siècle*, 1523; L. Maimbourg, *Histoire du Calvinisme*, Paris, 1682; J. B. Bossuet, *Histoire des variations des églises protestantes*, Paris, 1688.

31. On the idea of doctrinal development, see W. O. Chadwick, *From Bossuet to Newman*, 1957, revised ed Cambridge, 1987.

32. G. Arnold, *Unpartheyische Kirche- und Ketzer-Histoirie*, 4 vols, Frankfurt, 1699–1700. On Arnold, E. Seeberg, *Gottfried Arnold*, Meerane, 1923. On the history of church history, P. Meinhold, *Geschichte der kirchlichen Historiographie*, Freiburg and Munich, 1967.

33. G. B. Vico, *Scienza Nuova*, 1725; revised and enlarged, 1744: ed. F. Nicolini, Bari; 1942, called for 'a history of human ideas [una storia dell'umane idee]'; paragraphs 347, 391. Vico borrowed the phrase from J. Brucker who called the first edition of his history of philosophy (cited below, note 34) *Historia de ideis*.

34. These works include O. Heurn, *Barbarica Philosophia*, Leiden, 1600; G. Horn, *Historia philosophiae*, Leiden, 1655; T. Stanley, 1655, *History of Philosophy*; J. F. Reimann, *Historia philosophiae sinensis*, Braunschweig, 1727; A. F. Boureau-Deslande, *Histoire critique de la philosophie*, Amsterdam, 1735; J. Brucker, *Historia critica philosophiae*, 6 vols, Leipzig, 1767. On these histories there has been a crop of recent studies, such as M. Rak, *La parte historica*, Naples, 1971, Braun, 1973, Del Torre, 1976.

35. L. Graham, W. Lepenies and P. Weingart, *Functions and Uses of Disciplinary Histories*, Dordrecht, 1983.

36. On Kepler, N. Jardine, *The Birth of History and Philosophy of Science*, Cambridge, 1984. A. Smith, 'History of Astronomy' in his *Essays on Philosophical Subjects*, London, 1795, 1–93.

37. B. Baldi, *Vite dei matematici*, written 1586–87; J. E. Montucla, *Histoire des mathématiques*, 2 vols, Paris 1758.

38. J. F. Gmelin, *Geschichte der Chemie*, 3 vols, Göttingen, 1797–9.

39. P. Vergil, *De inventoribus*, 1500. On him, D. Hay, *Polydore Vergil*, Oxford, 1952 and B. Copenhaver, 1978. The seigneur de La Popelinière, *Histoire des histoires* (Paris, 1599) on whom see H. Butterfield, *Man on his Past*, Cambridge, 1955 and George Huppert, *The Idea of Perfect History*, Urbana, 1970. On writing, H. Hugo, *De prima scribendi origine*, Antwerp, 1617; B. von Malinckoff, 1638 *De natura et usu litterarum*. The last two studies were used by Vico for the discussions of orality and literacy in his *New Science*.

40. D. Leclerc, *Histoire de la médicine*, 1696; I used the Amsterdam, 1702 ed, preface: 'Il y a bien de la différence entre faire l'histoire des médecins ou écrire leurs vies . . . et faire histoire de la médicine, ou rechercher l'origine de cet art, et voir quels ont été ses progrès de siècle en siècle, quels changements il y a eu dans les systèmes et dans les méthodes . . . qui est ce que j'ai entrepris.' Incidentally, his otherwise full survey of the historiography of medicine omits Jessenius (1600), an account which (though brief), comes close to meeting his criteria.

41. J. Freind (1725) *The History of Physick from the Time of Galen to the Beginning of the Sixteenth Century*.

42. J. Selden, *Table-Talk*, posthumous, 1689.

43. J. Locke, *Concerning Human Understanding*.

44. Quoted in Pittock, *Ascendancy*, p. 85.

45. B. de Fontenelle, *De l'origine des fables*, 1724; ed. J.-R. Carré, Paris, 1932.

46. Vico, *Scienza nuova*, especially Book 2.

47. J. Kraft, *Kort Fortaelning af de Vilde Folk*, Sorø, 1760.

48. Montesquieu, *De l'Esprit des Lois*, Paris, 1744, Book 28, ch. 17.

49. La Curne de Sainte Palaye, *Mémoires sur l'ancienne chevalerie*, Paris, 1746–50. On him, L. Gossman, *Medievalism and the Ideologies of the Enlightenment*, Baltimore, 1968

50. W. Robertson, *History of Charles V*, London, 1769.

51. R. Hurd, *Letters on Chivalry*, London, 1762

52. T. Warton, *Observations on the Faerie Queene*, London, 1754, p. 217.

53. The phrase is Eichhorn's (above, note 5) and his general history is presented as an introduction to the 'special histories [*Specialgeschichte*]' of the different arts and sciences.

54. J. L. Vives, 1531, *De causis corruptarum artium*; L. Le Roy, *De la Vicissitude des choses*, 1575; (I used the Paris, 1584 edn). On him, W. Gundersheimer, *Louis Le Roy*, Geneva, 1966.

55. F. Bacon, *Advancement of Learning*, London, 1605.

56. Voltaire, *Essai sur les mœurs* 1744–56; ed. R. Pomeau, 2 vols, Paris, 1963; *Le siècle de Louis XIV*, D'Alembert, 1751, *Discours préliminaire*.

57. L. Bruni, *Historiarum florentini populi libri xii*, c. 1415; ed. E. Santini, Città di Castello, 1926, pp. 14f; Earl of Shaftesbury, *Characteristicks*, London, 1733, p. 238.

58.   The distinction between 'causes morales' and 'causes physiques' is to be found in J. B. Dubos, 1719, *Réflexions critiques*, vol. 2, chs 12–13.

59.   S. Bettinelli, *Risorgimento d'Italia negli studi, nelle arti, e ne'costumi dopo il Mille*, 1775, ed. S. Rossi, Ravenna, 1976. There is, oddly enough, no reference to this study in Ferguson, *Renaissance* (above, note 7).

60.   E. Vico, *Discorsi sopra le medaglie*, Venice, 1555, deals with the art of detecting fakes, as do later treatises such as those by Spon and Evelyn. J. Levine, *Dr Woodward's Shield*, Berkeley, 1977, is a fascinating case study of eighteenth century discussions of the authenticity of an artefact.

61.   R. Bentley, *A Dissertation upon the Epistles of Phalaris*, London, 1697, p. 51.

62.   T. Warton, *An Enquiry into the Authenticity of the Poems attributed to Thomas Rowley*, London, 1782.

63.   J. G. Herder, *Ideen zur Philosophie der Geschichte der Menschheit*, 1784–91, 2 vols, Berlin, 1965. In vol. 2 he discusses the 'Rittergeist' (pp. 449f) and the 'Kultur der Vernunft' (pp. 469f). On Herder's conception of culture, W. H. Bruford, *Culture and Society in Classical Weimar*, Cambridge, 1962, ch. 4. On C. Adelung and his *Versuch einer Geschichte der Kultur des Menschlichen Geschlechts*, 1782, J. Garber, 'Von der Menschheitsgeschichte zur Kulturgeschichte', in *Kultur zwischen Bürgertum und Volk*, ed. J. Held, Berlin, 1983 pp., 76–97.

64.   E. H. Gombrich, *In Search of Cultural History*, Oxford, 1969.

65.   Marquis de Condorcet, *Esquisse d'un tableau historique des progrès de l'esprit humain*, written c. 1793; ed. Y. Belaval, Paris, 1970. His use of Voltaire's phrase in his title is worth noting.

3

Cultural History in a New Key: Towards a Semiotics of the Nerve

George Rousseau

George Rousseau locates his text – the discourse of nerves in the eighteenth century – in a long perspective, that of man escaping 'the prison of his solipsistic self' in order to communicate with the outside world. Man has developed his memory to a stage infinitely more complex than that of any computer, in that in the brain's interlocking cell system it is capable of experiencing not only the nervous event, but also the recollection of the nature of that event. This kind of distinction between experiences relates to divisions of memory and learning, but, antecedent to these, the experience of a chemical reaction consequential on the nervous event which produced an unconditioned responsiveness. Rousseau refers in his analysis to the evolutionary processes of mankind, focusing on a specific period within his slow growth. He proceeds to relate it to a dominant discourse in medical, literary and social texts.

Rousseau offers a 'New Key' to cultural history by reminding us of the openness of its perspectives: 'Everything we think and do is ultimately nervous' and in remembering this we cut away 'all national and epochal categories'. The declaration of a metonymic status for nerves as an exercise in eighteenth-century semiotics – even to a new mythology of the nervous system – is Rousseau's theme. It relates to a new type of awareness, distinctive to the eighteenth century, and one, as Rousseau demonstrates, involving differentials in class, medicine and sex. He describes this chronological event as a kind of 'tidal wave'.

Rousseau explains sociological repercussions of the nervous system, its fashionable cultivation, its implications for fantasising, its connections with economic shock and its obvious identification with sex. In his concluding account of the 'Formation of the Nervous Personality in

Cultural History', Rousseau presents a diversity of perspectives in relation to that swollen term 'Romanticism', as well as throwing light on some
basic preconceptions about our own twentieth-century academic crisis.
The exhilaration of interdisciplinary perspectives, in research and teaching, which Rousseau explores is inseparable from our attribution of
significance to the past, a sense of relevance and totality which is in
danger of being lost in so many areas of the humanities and elsewhere.

CULTURE VIEWED IN GEOLOGICAL TIME

It may appear odd to begin a chapter in *European* cultural history
with a poetically sweeping statement culled from the work of a
contemporary physicist whose research has earned him a place in
the pantheon of science. All the odder when our discussions
today centre so pre-eminently on local versus global knowledge,
relativism rather than absolute reason, and regional ideologies –
especially now in the sciences – rather than on immutable laws of
nature derived from cold reason and logic; but I trust my drift will
soon become clear in relation to this seemingly remote opening. In
Knowledge and Wonder: The Natural World as Man Knows It, Victor
Weisskopf explains how organisms developed in history and what
the accretion of a particular function meant for the differentiation
between the bacterial world and man:

> The nervous system is perhaps the most important innovation
> in the progression from the bacterium to the higher species.
> Nerves are long strands of special cells that, like telephone
> wires, transmit messages from one place to another . . . The
> brain itself is a complicated tangle of an enormous number of
> nerve cells, as many as ten billion, which are interconnected
> and arranged in a way we do not yet understand. But this
> tremendous unit of nerve cells is able to react to the stimuli
> coming from the outside. It can think and feel.[1]

Having established that man's nervous capability is what diffe-
rentiates him from all other living forms and creatures on the
earth, Weisskopf describes what this nervous apparatus has meant
for human destiny viewed over geological time:

> The greatest step forward in this trend for better coping with
> environment was the development of the nervous system. This

is a special combination of interlocking cells capable of tran-
smitting stimuli from one part of the unit to the other. Thus,
coordination became possible between the functions of different parts. The most important innovations made possible by
the development of the nervous system were the sense organs.
They are special cell accumulations that are sensitive to messages from the external environment such as light, sound,
pressure, smell, etc. The messages received are transmitted
through connecting nerve cells to other parts of the unit so that
the unit is able to coordinate locomotion and other reactions to
the outside conditions.[2]

Then Weisskopf demonstrates the utility of this co-ordination
capability in prehistoric times:

As a result, the units could react on changes in the environment
in many ways that were most useful for the protection of the
individual and for the acquisition of food. The structure could
move toward light; it could recognize food by its smell or its
shape; it could avoid danger by moving away or by protecting
itself when a large object approached. Our unit acquired what
we call a 'behavior'[3].

But if nervous co-ordination permitted man to communicate with
the outside world and escape the prison of his solipsistic self, as
well as acquire the first versions of a behaviour, the further
organisation of this unit allowed for a brain of a particular type
with retrieval capabilities previously unknown in geochemical
history. The transition was so consequential that it is worth
quoting Weisskopf's lucid description of it at length, especially for
a non-scientific readership possibly unfamiliar with this segment
of the primitive history of our race:

The development of a nervous system was so useful and
effective that any mutation or sexual combination leading to a
larger or more intricate nervous system gave rise to increasingly
successful units. Thus a continuous evolution toward an
increase in nerve cells began, and led to the formation of a
brain. This organ is an accumulation of a large number [i.e. over
ten billion] of interconnected nerve cells capable of storing the
effects of the stimuli that the unit has received. The storage was

the beginning of what we call memory. An action that previously has had good results with respect to food intake or avoidance of pain is kept in memory and repeated readily if similar circumstances recur. Obviously the ability to 'remember' such situations was an enormous asset for our units and helped their struggle for survival under difficult conditions. It supplied the ability to learn from experience.[4]

Here then is early man – the first experiential organism who learns by remembering:

> At the beginning, such memory and learning mechanisms were not very complicated. With modern electronic equipment one can easily construct a device with a 'nervous system' that remembers past situations and determines its actions on that basis. A machine controlled by a modern computer may serve as an example.[5]

Yet Weisskopf's example now captures the essence of the unit's organisation, as it soars to its main point:

> A system of interlocking nerve cells is in many ways equivalent to a system of interconnected electronic vacuum tubes or transistors. A device with a few thousand transistors can perform most impressive acts of remembering situations and avoiding them later on. But, in fact, the brain of even an insect is a more complicated device. It contains ten to a hundred thousand nerve cells. The human brain has as many as ten billion; it is infinitely more complex than any man-made computer.[6]

Weisskopf's summary of the development of life hangs on this event of brain formation, as we ourselves stand reeling over the implication that a mere insect has a more highly developed brain than Weisskopf's system of interconnected electronic vacuum tubes, and that man's brain is infinitely more complex than any man-made computer. One of these implications is the boundary – the almost ineffable demarcation – before and after the nervous event. To think, analogously and in the context of another boundary (this one linguistic), as the poet W. H. Auden wrote in 'Venus Will Now Say a Few Words':

Think – Romans had a language in their day.
And ordered roads with it, but it had to die.

So let us imagine there was a time when all reactions to the external stimuli were *completely* and *entirely* determined by chemical structure without the advantages of memory and learning. Chronologically, more contemporaneously to think that when Vladimir Horowitz moves us to tears he achieves all this solely – or almost solely – by the use of nerves and brain; that he is not feeling or interpreting Scarlatti or Schumann in some unique way, not achieving his successes at an intellectual level occasioned by greater understanding, but better co-ordinating, better summoning the synapses of his own nervous apparatus. This disparity is the one so consequential, it seems to me, for the cultural history of the Enlightenment, remote as nerves and synapses may appear at first glance to readers expecting a cultural history based on sociopolitical institutions and the ideas that surrounded them.

THE NERVES IN EARLY MODERN EUROPEAN CULTURE

This analysis of life over millions of years will instil wonder in any observer, but tells us virtually nothing about recent history: the last few thousand years, the last few centuries. Weisskopf demonstrates to what degree this nervous organisation rested entirely on combinations. His very language explains that: connections, interlocking communications, transmission, co-ordination, function, efficiency. It is clear from his metaphors that the more nervously complex the organism became, the better 'combined' and therefore more efficient, its processes of organisation. And it is evident from his language that everything modern man celebrates is in some way the direct consequence of this nervous capabiliity. Nervous capability, to echo Keats, was therefore meta-regional and meta-national: it transcended parts of the earth and countries, affecting the whole species rather than a part. Anything indigenous to the nations – the English, French, Dutch or Germans – would be insignificant in comparison to it; and the fact that England has recently been an island, France more peninsular, and Germany more landlocked, all these pale in comparison to this unassailable point about the development of nervous organisation. The bewildering matter is not merely that *everything* cognitive and functional is neurophysiological, but that literally everything we think and do is ultimately nervous. And then, to think that the entire analysis of inchoate subjects, like high and low culture in the Enlightenment, is necessarily neurophysiological. This is a recognition that does not dawn easily on those (like most of us writing in this volume) who are used to thinking of national and epochal categories. And yet, if we are to garner the point about nervous development, or what might more dramatically be called nervous determinism, we must begin with the far gaze – the distant view – rather than, more immediately, the middle of the Enlightenment. The scientists among us always want to pause, of course, on the plateaus of nervous development and ponder life at the next altitude, so to speak; the historians on its peaks of cultural history. But what is the cultural dimension of nervous development? From Mesopotamia to Munich, Babylonia to Berlin, from Latium to London, nerves and brains have barely been interpreted in their sociocultural contexts. Here Weisskopf and his fellow physicists can offer only limited inspiration. The Greeks had a sophisticated theory of nerves and brain based on invisible spirits no one had seen but which all were certain existed.[7] But, and it is a crucial adversative, they never connected brain with soul, nor soul with brain, the brain then not lodging in the head at all. This view endured more or less unchanged throughout the ancient and medieval world. Every philosopher commented on the subject. Few topics could compete with it, it being the primary proof of God's existence in an anthropocentric universe in which God had to prove to man why he had created him different from other living creatures. Thus motion and matter, soul and body, existed in particular relationships which mechanical philosophy changed, as it created a dualistic order of mind and body, brain and soul, and then, through its mechanistic anatomists, removed the brain to the head. In 1766, the *Annual Register* devoted columns to the nervous theories of an obscure French physiologist, Monsieur Bertin, offering him as much journalistic space as news of war and peace. The *Register* wanted its readers to know that Galen had understood nerves as well as any modern:

This great man, says M. Bertin, saw very well, upwards of 1600 years ago, that a fluid ought to produce all the wonderful effects

which we observe in the exercise of our motions and sensations; and he derived its source from the brain, from whence it
diffused itself thro' the rest of the body. If he [Galen] could not
see what modern anatomy has discovered, he could still less see
those spirits, that subtil fluid.[8]

Notwithstanding his limitation, Galen was credited with the
discovery. The philosophical analogy was thus continuous: from
the acclaimed Galen and the forgotten Bertin to our twentieth-
century Ramon y Cajals and other neurophysiologists, all certain
of the vital 'subtle fluid', whether it be mystical substance or
electrophysical wave particles. Yet with this difference: among the
historical periods, the first to cling to nervous physiology with a
vengeance was the eighteenth century, and in some qualified
senses it is historically valid to claim that much of the eighteenth-
century Enlightenment was one magisterial footnote on nervous
physiology, a remarkable attempt to secularise cognition
and perception through the brain and its vassal nerves. Other
eras demonstrated interest of course, but nothing remotely
approaching the eighteenth century's, which, among other activities, naturalised, theologised, demonised, mechanised, climatised,
medicalised, internalised, metaphorised and analogised the
nerves.

The century's energy in this activity was extraordinary. It, so to
speak, naturalised them as it made the brain and nerves the basis
of a vast number of research programmes in secular natural
philosophy.[9] Philosophised them into a dualism of mind and
body from which Western Civilisation has yet to recover, always
attributing this mind–body split to Descartes, it being, more
accurately, the proof of a late Renaissance nerve craze that set
everyone looking for the key to these vital spirits.[10] (See Plate 1.)
Theologised them in both the conservative and radical theology of
the day, as nerves were said (by the conservatives) to be a beneficent
God's physiological gift to a wicked people who needed them for
reformation, as well as (in radical versions such as the Boyle
Lectures) revelation of God's goodness in endowing his creatures
with the unit of organisation they most needed.[11] Demonised
them as empiricists and spiritualists continued to endow them
with magical and alchemical powers no one had ever seen.[12]
Mechanised and vitalised them in countless anatomical and physiological debates then raging all over Europe.[13] Taxonomised

them as well, into stronger and weaker nerves, greater and lesser, major and minor, pigmented and non-pigmented, white and black, red and yellow, as Linnaeus and Cullen and many others purported in their nosological schemes.[14] Darwinised them too, as Erasmus Darwin suggested when claiming that the nervous system had been evolving all along – in creatures that swarm as well as in higher intelligent animals – and would eventually evolve into something much grander than it was at the end of the eighteenth century.[15] Pathologised them into normal and abnormal states – the state of affairs, so to speak, of the nerves that coloured all human health and determined longevity.[16] And biologised the nerves in the embryological discussions about reproduction, preformation and epigenesis.[17] In all these activities it was conceded, with remarkably little opposition, and as Hume and other Scots philosophers scrupulously argued, that, whatever memory was, the brain and its vassals the nerves could never be far away. If learning and attention require memory more than anything else, we instantly see what an extraordinary homage to the nerves this is. So crucial were these nerves to the complex machine called man (a beast machine of a much more complex type), that the eighteenth century – if one may be metonymic about its diverse efforts in this area – almost worshipped in its temple. The *temple of nerves* is not an inappropriate name for this intellectual house.

This vast theoretical labyrinth had its counterpart in the socialisation of the nerves, as it were, in the ordinary daily life of the time. The nerves were medicalised, academised, globalised, climatised, electrified, genderised and sexualised. Concommitantly, the nerves are engraved in the social history of the day: at spas and resorts, among doctors and patients, among the flourishing cults of sensibility that served first and foremost, to separate the social classes in an era when aristocratic title in itself was insufficient, and when antagonisms between the social classes took more hostile forms than mutual derogation. The nerves were academised as virtually every European medical school, regardless of its reigning beliefs, assigned its students to write dissertations on this subject: at Leiden, Harderwyk, Reims, Paris, Montpellier, Marburg, Halle, Wurzberg, Giessen, Göttingen, Leipzig, Erfurt, Jena, Helmstedt, Dresden, Basel, Padua, Rome.[18] I have found no medical schools where dissertations on the nerves were not written. The nerves were literally electrified as Wesley, Franklin, and Mesmer, each in his own way, set to regenerate one social class or another, high and low, by this nervous use of electricity. The nerves were globalised, nationalised, regionalised and internationalised, as different countries, climates and regions were held accountable for particular states of the nerves and their diseases. For the first time, one could talk of French nerves, Dutch nerves or Italian nerves, while paradoxically being cautioned that, whatever local, indigenous conditions prevailed, the nerves themselves were universal, common to all people on the face of the earth. And the nerves were genderised and sexualised as crucial differences of male and female (such as hypochondriasis and hysteria), caucasian and black, oriental and mohammedan, heterosexual and hermaphroditical, were attributed to this or that nervous strength or defect, or (as Spallanzani and LeCat maintained) to the nerve tips in the dermis of the skin, which extended to the cerebrum and cerebellum of the brain. For the first time in medical history, conditions as different as jaundice and low intelligence were attributed to nervous causes. This stage represented a vast change from the explanations of previous generations and shows us how cultural history can retrieve discourses and cross boundary lines left undiscovered by more traditional disciplines.

The nerves were also internalised and mentalised into the most imaginative processes of which language and art were then capable. In psychology and art criticism throughout Europe, the nerves occupied centre stage, whether in discussions, such as Edmund Burke's of aesthetic sublimity (*Enquiry into the Sublime*, 1757) or more technical debates about the painter's hand as he holds the brush and strokes the palette, and the pianist's fingers. The nerves were also visually represented in a broad repertoire ranging from anatomy textbooks to satirical cartoons, some of which are reproduced in this chapter. The nerves had been versified as a major *topos* in all countries, perhaps nowhere more extensively than in England, allegedly the home of the mad, the insane, in, for example Dr Malcolm Flemyng's long epic poem in six cantos called *Neuropathia*, published in 1747;[19] hundreds of lines of Latin hexameter verse celebrating – as Victor Weisskopf has more recently celebrated in a very different context, as discussed at the opening of this chapter – the utility of the nervous pathways. Most intriguingly for students of language and literature, the nerves were also metaphorised and analogised, as a whole new vocabulary developed consisting of words we hardly recognise today. This was based on flaccidity and tension, acridity and tone, fermentation and putridity, and, in words that are no longer in any modern dictionaries, 'hippohiatrical' functions and 'levigations' of the nerves; on biliousness, chyle, spasmodic colics and unnatural ferments, affections and cachexies, censoriums and climacterics, contextures and exquisite particles, ferments and fibres of the brain, fluxes and effluvia, tubes and performations. It produced a maze of neologisms such as 'black humour' (whose first use is not in a playwright such as Beckett but in a *medical* text of the 1720s),[20] deobstruents, dimoculations, empyrheumatics, and a repertoire of slang terms and abbreviations whose meanings have long been lost: hypp, hyppos, hyppocons, markambles, moonpalls, strong fiacs, hockogrogles.[21] And – most intriguing to me – it generated an entire vocabulary of neurospasts, as John Evelyn called these puppets on strings, a concept that fascinated the period, especially in the form of electrified neurospasts.[22] Even literary criticism and social commentary were culture-bound by this degree of specificity, as critics Thomas Warton and Samuel Johnson, among many others, sought to define the gradually evolving 'nervous style', which they construed as a particularly masculine type of muscular and sinewy English prose best described as 'nervous'. The developing style was viewed as superior to all others; it partook of the optimism and progress which was the tenor of the day. Within this linguistic activity, generated in an era when language theory was rapidly changing, the *nerve* itself became the sign of a semiotics of analogy.

To invoke the nerves then, whether in medical, philsophical or any other type of discourse, as, for example, Mandeville or Cheyne had, was usually to indulge in radical analogising, as both *A Treatise of the Hypochondriack and Hysterick Passions* and *The English Malady* demonstrate, and no linguistic trope was then so important for philosophical and scientific analysis as analogy. (See Plate 2.) Hedonistically speaking, the nerves also presided over the seats of pleasure and pain. To claim, as Dubois instructs the Marquis de Sade's Juliet, that all pain is in the nerve, was then to utter a paradigm too well-known for further amplification. As for insanity and madness, even Dr William Battie, who is sometimes called the father of modern psychiatry, long before Pinel and Esquirol held that lunacy lay entirely in the nerves, without recourse to gender. Diseased spirits, diseased nerves, diseased imagination: this was the sequence of the mind's malady – the surest sign in recognizing lunatics. As for the erotic lunacy that springs from love-sickness (states of mind Breuer and Freud were later simply to call hysteria), even this variety was neutralised, as the English poet Anthony Selden wittily wrote in 1749:

> While Grief and Shame her Face o'erspread,
> Upon her Knee she lean'd his Head.
> Then points the Dart, and with her Hands
> The crystal-rooted Film expands.
> But, O! the rack was so immense,
> So twing'd the *Nerve*, and shock'd the Sense,
> He begg'd her, yelling with Despair,
> The fruitless Torture to forbear,
> Confounded with the horrid Pain,
> He storm'd, and rav'd, and rag'd in vain.

RANK AND CLASS: THE FASHIONABILITY OF NERVES

It was predictable, if not inevitable, that nerves would become fashionable, given this intensity of mythologisation, but not democratic – in the sense that nerves had been created equally in all persons – within this neuralising of culture high and low. That the nerves became fashionable even when viewed from the perspective of political and ideological tropes in written texts and spoken interchanges testifies to their vigour and degree of infiltration. For centuries, and certainly since the discussions of Guicciardini and Machiavelli, the body politic had been a commonplace to describe the mysteries of government, yoking together politics with the body – or corpus – of civic polity.[23] In the eighteenth century these tropes alter to 'nervous government', as James Lowde, an early follower of Malebranche and Locke, noted in his tract on man viewed in his anatomic and political dimensions.[24] But, as the political state was nervous, so too was the individual, and the analogies between the nervous one and the nervous many, the small and the large, the private and public, increased proportionally to this new nervous mythology. Nor were social distinctions omitted; if anything, nervous mythology segregated the social rank and file anew and provided all the classes with an important new model of aristocratic life. Nerves also permitted behaviour to be predictab.e, and enabled an acceptable code of social behaviour at a time when it seemed there might soon be none. The new social and geographical mobility of the eighteenth century obscured worth and station, which now had to be asserted. The easiest ways were external: especially fashion (through clothes) and illness (by disease). These exterior signs, anew, became the tropes of rank and class. If the lower classes emulate the upper in all centuries and live vicariously through them, they did so in the eighteenth, as seamstresses and charwomen, pickpockets and prostitutes like Moll Flanders and Fanny Hill, fantasised that they too could be as 'nervous' as their gentlewomen mistresses. 'My nerves are all unstrung,' a corpulent and robust servant exclaims, emulating her mistress in a minor novel of 1748.[25] But it would be wrong to think this mythology of nervous culture required an *antecedent* scientific theory. Just the reverse is true: Haller's theories of nervous sensibility do not validate the principles of nervous government or nervous aristocratic life, but the reverse. His hypotheses profoundly manifest his *own* nervous culture – in Switzerland, Germany, Europe, the world: no less than Freud's in *fin-de-siècle* Vienna, for science is culture-bound, partaking of the varying degrees of positivism and ideology that permeate every age.[26] So too for imaginative literature so far as this osmosis is concerned, as *Tristram Shandy* is permeated with the same animal spirits and fibres that will become analogised in Scottish treatises on the law and other branches of government. For writers of discourses as diverse as those by Haller and Sterne one assumption is held in common: that the nervous myth is already widely disseminated. Yet, as the nerves produced no mortal disease like consumption or cancer, they were not morbidly feared and no reason existed to demystify or demythologise them to the same degree. The more mysterious the vital fluid (the unseen spirit within the hollow tube) – so the inner voice of the upper classes might have spoken could they have been conscious of these complex processes – the better for all those now reasserting their class station in a society when doubt about this hierarchy was pervasive. It was a curious collusion of sorts between those who generated (formulated and articulated) physiological theory and those (political figures, business people, professionals) who led the masses.

Gentility and delicacy were thus reinvigorated and rearmed with new tropes. For snobs, parvenus and social climbers, the way to rise was simple: be hyppish, be nervous, be bilious, be rich (See Plate 6). The sequence was plain. If consumption was then the disease of poverty and deprivation, nerves was the condition of class and standing. How odd that this cultural shift should occur just when the sign of upper-class authority in England and France was perceived image rather than power, and when the genders were growing theoretically further apart than they had been in many centuries, as the historians of sex and the family have shown us. If it was fashionable to blush and weep and faint, it was even more glamorous to present with nerovus symptoms. It was smart to associate with those who were also nervous; better still to be in a constant correspondence, as so many fine ladies then were, with others equally nervous. To be nervous was to be romantic; to be romantic was divinely wished among those middle-class new-comers who until recently never thought they could be. Even suicide was considered a viable alternative, and suicide then was widely held to be an act, as Hume and others claimed, leading directly from diseased nerves – the *sine qua non*, the precondition – of deranged imagination and certifiable lunacy.[27] In all this tumble of social differentiation was a sense that the upper classes were writing themselves out, as it were, of chronic nerves; but the very opposite is true. The reader's penetration *into* the book *Clarissa* coincides – literally as well as conceptually – with penetration into her own body; the more Clarissa writes, the more nervous she becomes.[28] This is why Adam Smith could believe that sympathy cemented civil societies as well as trade imbalances among na-tions, and what is sympathy if not a predisposition of the nerves associated into higher states of feeling and ideation?[29]

The social ramifications of this newly nervous culture were not to be minimised, as whole professions, if not entire genders (women), realigned and reasserted themselves under the weight, in part, of nervous mythology. If the rich felt themselves obliged to prove their difference, what better way to assert difference than by looking different and frequenting different places? Bath and Tunbridge, Harrogate and Scarborough, Llandrindod and Llan-wryst, not to speak of the Belgian spas (especially Spa) and the Aix-les-Bains, and the various 'Maria-bads' (Maria baths) of Central Europe that then came into their own, as did the profes-sions of doctors, physicians, apothecaries, nurses, midwives, quacks, mountebanks, empirics who now catered to the whims and whimsies, the caprices of the neurasthenic rich. 'He was the greatest of the nerve doctors,' Dr John Makittrick Adair was to concede about his conspicuous rival of the previous generation, Dr George Cheyne[30] – a bewildering claim in view of the universal jealousy of doctors and when Cheyne's exorbitant fees are rehearsed. For all these reasons it makes sense to invoke a newly constituted category called 'nervous discourse', without worrying excessively about charges of engaging in unitary label-making, and especially if we define this term ('nervous discourse') as a network of contradictory narratives and explain what is meant by the semiotics of the nerve.[31]

We are searching, then, for an understanding of this pervasive sign – the nerve – rather than its disciplinary diachronic history. We want to fathom how it is that a particular sign arises within a particular culture and under what specific conditions. But we will not be satisfied by its logocentric legacy only: those traces left in words alone. We want a more holistic picture that conjoins words and things; that separates discourses rather than disciplines (history, language, science, medicine); and that will explain the nerve in the light of the whole picture of civilisation then, not merely one of its manifold components. Given the structures of authority that obtained in the eighteenth century and the fluidity of the social classes, it was predictable that the upper class should have contrived these mechanisms of separation with virtually no opposition from the medical profession, which considered itself an intrinsic part of the newly defined rich. Medicine and ideology – the only ideology most doctors knew was the ideology of the pound; they were the last collective group to oppose the new nervousness on philosophically rational or inductively empirical grounds. Of course they battled among themselves, just as other professionals do today, especially when ideologies come into conflict; some had their scruples, their principles, their philosophy. But viewed from without, from this distance of time after the lapse of two centuries, they appear to have been somewhat in league with the rich, as mi' lady this had her private doctor that, who – so common in the diaries of the time – 'was called to her side for nerves every day this week'.[32] This dynamic *sorting-out*, this renewed separation of the rich, precipitated a reinvigorated emulation by the lower classes; these social processes lie at the heart of the cults of nervous sensibility and the mythology they engendered.

If the demarcations between the social classes were then fragile and requiring of these disparate kinds of reaffirmation, so too (although of a different parity) were the body's anatomic nerves, as doctor after doctor pleaded for a 'tonic strengthening' of them, a phrase that means little to cultural historians today unless it is decoded and glossed.[33] The principles and methods of tonic strengthening baffle us even when anatomic and physiological equivalencies are taken into account. To strengthen the nerves would seem, linguistically, to be a metonymy for toughening the character or (as North Americans might say in the vernacular) getting one's act together. In our quasi-macho western-world twentieth-century culture, the nerves remain genderised and imbued with the sense of femininity. In the eighteenth century, nerves were palpably real, although often metaphorised for ex-cessive effects. To be sure, there were some who condemned this fragility and its attendant nervous physiology, who claimed that nerves were not so all-important, but their voices were somehow muted and their numbers waned as the most fashionable persons hastened to the great nerve doctors of the day.[34] There was no actual conspiracy or collusion in this nervous tidal wave: it swept through the culture as so many other waves have. To distance it and see it for what it was: this is the hard task for the cultural historian. To think that it would *not* take its toll on the imaginative literature of the day remains the foible of our internalist literary historians who read at the level of individual texts only.[35] No wonder, then, that Henry Mackenzie, for example, who under-stood men and women of feeling as well as anyone, and who fictionalised his beliefs about the new creatures of sentiment he saw as heroic, wrote to a friend plainly: 'this is an Age of Sensibility'. And it is little surprise that Jane Austen believed she was responding to the aesthetic of an era when endorsing it under her own imprint as a generation of 'Sense and Sensibility'. (See Plate 3.)

Town development and urban planning were affected as much as anything else. One can imagine the Baths and Tunbridges, the Harrogates and Scarboroughs under these ruthless circumstances of gain and profit. Here, lurking everywhere, were not merely doctors and diseases, rich patients and their undiagnosed condi-tions, but pump rooms and assembly halls, booksellers and musicians, architects and landscape gardeners, charities, drums and routs: all commanding vast amounts of money and wealth. (See Plate No. ??) Not to have weak nerves and a delicate constitution was to be out of place here. Lady Luxborough (an addict of Bath who was also Bolingbroke's sister) assured her

constant correspondent, the poet William Shenstone: 'My disorder . . . turned to a fever of a slow kind, chiefly nervous,
attended with pains in my bowels, which, added to want of rest,
have weakened me so much, that I have not yet crossed my
room."[36] Shenstone replies: 'As your Complaints are *entirely
nervous*, [you] must have an undoubted tendency to further it!'
The exchanges of Mrs Ralph Allen and Mrs Beau Nash – not to
mention their lesser female epigoni – were similar, written in what
seems a kind of code language to us now.[37] Selina, the wealthy
Countess of Huntingdon and another exclusive Cheyne patient,
was not much better off, sunk, as she almost always was, in
nervous depressions of religious origin, even after the completion
of her methodist chapel.[38] (See Plate 4.) Little was different in
fiction: in *Evelina*, Lady Louisa Larpent despairs when her lover
leaves her; Lovel comforts her: 'Your Ladyship's constitution is
infinitely delicate,' only to evoke Louisa's retort, " 'Indeed it is,'
cried she in a low voice, 'I am nerve all over!' "[39] The sign is even
evident in the most ephemeral gibberish of the time. The silly
farrago that called itself a *Register of Folly . . . written by an Invalid*,
while Smollett and Christopher Anstey were still at Bath in the
1760s, trivialised these ailments by personifying them in absurd
couplets:

> Tho' I own I am sorry such trifles still flurry
> My Ogilby-nerves, to produce such a hurry.[40]

Other 'valetudinarian guides' provided their own versions of
nervous mythology then cranking out a million-pound industry.
One finds criticism of the developing system in certain quarters –
the objection that nervous mythology is merely a hoax to induce
consumption of pills and potions, doctors and diets, resorts and
retreats in a culture that was already consuming extraordinary
amounts of commercial produce – but no substantial objections
that changed anything. An anecdote, whose veracity has never
been corroborated, makes the point: near the end of his life,
Samuel Johnson described the sense of diseased or weak nerves as
'medical cant',[41] but the objection was a drop in the bucket, as
those learned who inveighed against the trade in nervous drugs.
Actually the repertoire of nervous therapies has yet to be compiled: not merely quack nostrums but the dozens of panaceas
ranging from what we would call health food diets (Cheyne's

regimen of 'lettuce, seed, milk, and wine') and balneological treatments (whether of cold water or hot, mineralised or sulphuric) to James Graham's celestial beds and aphrodisiac cures for the nervously sterile and barren (one wonders why Sterne never took his Tristram to Bath as Austen does Lydia), but also Mesmer's electric shocks and animal magnetisms which flourished in the salons of the rich, and which were calculated to stimulate even the most withered nerves of any person.[42] These nervous nostrums themselves would fill pharmacopoeias, extending from analeptic and assa foetida pills; from Anderson's drops and William Tickell's aetherial spirit and Ward's aether pills, to Raleigh's confection, Bishop Berkeley's tar water, Dover's drops, Pierre Pomme's recipes (See Plate 5), John Hill's wild valerian roots, Mrs Stephens's juleps, Backer's cure of dropsy, to the more generic class of pearl and closet cordials, plain Nantz, quicksilver, calyx of zinc, acid of lemon rind, rhubarb and magnesia, not to mention hyppish medicines like extract of saturn (whatever that was pharmaceutically), prescribed in John Goulard's 1777 *Treatise on the Effects of . . . Lead* and Malcolm Flemyng's (the physician–writer already mentioned as the author of *Neuropathia*) tartars of mercury a few decades earlier, and without considering the effect of all these preparations on the royal patent office and their implications for profit and gain.[43]

THE SOCIAL MILIEU OF NERVES

It was in this atmosphere and social ambiance that the literature of 'sensibility' (as its writers *themselves* called it) flowered, and it seems to me essential to be alert to *their* nomenclature. For the decoding of the sign is as much an analysis of the word as anything else. Semiological interpretation requires close linguistic interpretation viewed within the contexts of the culture: anthropological, sociological, historical, etc. What then was this literature of sensibility? Whether viewed in its Smollettian version in *Humphry Clinker* (1771), a version tied geographically to a spa locale as this geographically vivid novel opens, or its many other prose and poetic forms during the second half of the eighteenth century, the literature of sensibility itself broke off from its earlier versions of a hundred years before (in England as written by Milton and Dryden, in France by Marivaux and Crebillon), and became highly medicalised. Smollett's irritable hero Matt Bramble attributes his misanthropy to 'the nerves of an invalid, surprised by premature old age, and shattered with long suffering', only to have his nephew Jery Melford pooh-pooh Matt's nervous explanation and substitute another nervous one: 'tender as a man without skin, who cannot bear the slightest touch without flinching.'[44] Bared nerves indeed, but if the nerves, as our contemporary physicist has shown us while taking a very different gaze, endowed humankind with the most sophisticated communication system imaginable, they nevertheless mandated these reasserted social stratifications when the upper classes came under pressure to prove who they were. It was predictable that novelists like Smollett (a practising physician, medically trained and thoroughly conversant with the scientific debates about nerves) would directly respond to these transformations.[45]

Their economic dimension has received less attention than one thinks, for the cost of sensibility, in whatever version, was significant. The hordes of quacks who hung on and about the spas were many, yet even the tribe of certified doctors and apothecaries in Bath (not to mention the fashionable Continental watering holes) was large and continually proliferating. These were no ordinary doctors but the shamans of the rich. When the Duchess of Northumberland returned to Sion House, having visited her cousin, the Duchess of Newcastle, at Bath, she exclaimed surprise at 'the wigs and golden canes everywhere about the parades and crescents'.[46] For centuries there had been rich patients for doctors to treat; what differed now was the way the doctors went about diagnosing. The point is not – as some medical historians have shown – that medical practice suddenly altered under the weight of new evidence or theory, but that a cultural myth engulfed medical theory *itself*, privileging the nerves and exalting them as never before. The physicians' status was as important as the patients'. Bath was, of course, a unique type of resort, but even there in 1740 – for example – all but three of the physicians had Oxbridge degrees, the exceptions being two from Leiden, and one, actually Dr Cheyne himself, from Edinburgh.[47] The Bath Corporation and the hospital it regulated placed some controls on this medical undergrowth, but fees and therapies, and what we would call the quality of the care given, remained almost exclusively in the physicians' hands. The doctors quarrelled among themselves, and entered into paper wars calculated to raise their socioprofessional status and increase their number of patients, allegedly because 'nervous diseases' were on the rise. Even the Prime Minister, Robert Walpole, had come to Bath to be treated 'for nerves' by the famous doctor and President of the Royal Society, Richard Mead.[48] But the development of nerves was not exclusively British, emphasised as it was in this island culture. S. A. Tissot, the Swiss Protestant physician whose claim to fame was, in part, his anti-masturbatory campaign, had been as explicit about the role of nerves in human life and human culture as any Bath doctor. His *Essai sur les maladies des gens du monde* and his *Traité des nerfs et de leurs maladies* spoke loudly and plainly about the nervous culprits.[49] Tissot's approach to nerves was anthropological: to classify medical conditions by nations and regions. But its symptomology was culturally identical with his British colleagues', and, while Tissot was being translated into English in the 1760s (works such as his *Essay on Diseases Incident to Literary and Sedentary Persons*), Robert Whytt, the Scottish physician and professor of medicine in Edinburgh, was lecturing to medical students in Britain's now most forward-looking university about the crucial significance of nerves, as well as training a generation of physicians who would invade Bath after Cheyne. By the time the American colonies revolted in 1776, Tissot's works in English had been widely disseminated and Whytt had become a household name, especially known as the 'nerve doctor'. Tissot's account appeared to be the authoritative medical explanation: how people grew ill and under what conditions. Its subtext was otherwise: be nervous, be fashionable, be sought-after; the paradigm was a prescription, an equation of social truth that could as easily be reversed. *Au fond* Tissot's rhetoric had its intended effect of hurling any aspiring social climber, or one who had already arrived there, into 'nerves'.

Early anthropologist though he was, Tissot had not explained the sociology of the phenomenon: how nerves considered as an ethic, or even ideology, caught on. This was left to James Makittrick Adair, a Scottish doctor, educated under Whytt at the University of Edinburgh, who became Cheyne's successor in Bath at the end of the century and the wealthy eccentric Philip Thicknesse's adversary.[50] Adair churned out book after book on nervous conditions and their treatment, especially under his own regimens for recovery; but in actuality these were self-advertisements calculated to make him appear the discoverer –

and healer – of a new province of medicine. Whether true or not (and there is some validity to his claim that he had genuine expertise in the field) he stood to profit. He justified his literary productions on the semi-original grounds that medicine itself was a *social* institution:

> Should any of my fashionable readers express their surprise at meeting with a dissertation on fashion in a medical essay, my reply is ready; that as medicine, as well as some other arts, is become subject to the empire of fashion, there can be no impropriety in considering by what means this has been effected.[51]

Impropriety there was not, but plenty of distortion. Claiming modestly that he hoped to chronicle the rise of fashionable disease in the eighteenth century, Adair's descriptions are as revelatory for our semiotic purposes in decoding the sign of the nerve as anything Cheyne wrote (see Plate 7). Always acknowledging his teacher's famous essay on nervous diseases of 1764, Adair, like Cheyne, served up to his readers the explanations they wanted to hear:

> Upwards of thirty years ago, a treatise on nervous diseases was published by my quondam learned and ingenious preceptor DR. WHYTT, professor of physick, at Edinburgh. Before the publication of this book, people of fashion had not the least idea that they had nerves; but a fashionable apothecary of my acquaintance, having cast his eye over the book, and having been often puzzled by the enquiries of his patients concerning the nature and causes of their complaints, derived from thence a hint, by which he readily cut the gordian knot – '*Madam, you are nervous*'; the solution was quite satisfactory, the term [nervous] became quite fashionable, and spleen, vapours, and hyp, were forgotten.[52]

It is as if a single word, magically, had such transformative power. Although forgotten among the denizens of Lady Luxborough's circle low spirits and nervous ailments extended further back than to the time of their mothers and aunts. The cultural historian has a longer gaze and sees how similar are Sydenham's hysteria, Mandeville's hypochondriasis, Robinson's 'spleen', Cheyne's 'English malady', Haller's 'sensibility', Whytt's 'nervous diseases', and now – in the 1780s – Thomas Coe's 'bilious conditions' – the maladies of the bile – on which Adair claims to build his own theory.[53] But neither medical symptomology nor a glossary of linguistic transformations (from the language of the hyp to the byzantine neologisms of 'bilious concretions' and 'bilious solids') makes the crucial point as much as *fashionable disease*. Cheyne had justified the spread of nerves on grounds of the progress of expanding civilisations: 'We have more nervous diseases,' he wrote in the *English Malady*, 'since the present Age has made Efforts to go beyond former Times, in all the Arts of Ingenuity, Invention, Study, Learning, and all the Contemplative and Sedentary Professions.'[54] By the 1780s, though, Adair abandoned progress for fashion; for him in the 1770s, disease was romantic, glamorous, idealised: proof of difference. Yet it must not remain static, because tides of taste change, as does geography in an era of unprecedented social mobility. What Adair recounts about its taxonomic transformations from melancholy and spleen and hysteria to biliousness and now nerves, Dr Thomas Dover had described in 1732 – a half-century earlier – of its *geographical* spread:

> At first, the *Spleen* was said to be the entire Property of the Court Ladies; here and there indeed a fine Gentleman was pleas'd to catch it, purely in Complaisance to them. Soon after, Dr. *Ratcliffe* [sic] out of his well-known Picque to the Court Physicians, persuaded an Ironmonger's Wife of the City into it, and prescribed to her the Crying Remedy of carrying Brick-dust; the City Physicians took the Hint; and the Country Doctors remov'd it into the Hundreds of *Essex*, whence a learned Academick brought it with him to *Cambridge:* Soon after it was heard of in the Fenns of *Lincolnshire*, and it crossed the *Humber* in 1720. The Contagion [of spleen] has at last extended itself into *Northumberland*.[55]

On one level Dover's delightful bagatelle amounts to little more than an eighteenth-century version of modern communication theory, i.e. how information spreads, even through the shires and backroads of eighteenth-century England; on another, its infectious wit is too silly to be discredited: the same fictive play of mind apparent in Pope's *Dunciad*, as the goddess's roll-calls echo round the town. Yet this social genealogy of spleen appears in a purportedly serious medical work, Dr Dover's *Treatise on Hypochondriacal and Hysterical Diseases* (1732), aiming to explain why disease is so fundamentally genderised; the specific reasons

why men develop hypochondria and women hysteria; a book
every bit as didactic as Cheyne's *English Malady* or Adair's
Fashionable Diseases. But, like theirs, Dover's also assumes the
force of the unwritten assumption: the notion that, although both
men and women have nerves, females' nerves are the more
delicate, the more sensitive. We see what this unwritten paradigm
was if we look later to the nineteenth century, even to Charcot and
Breuer and Freud. In the nineteenth, women will be said to be
more prone to hysteria than men, not so much out of any innate
anatomic difference that translates into unavoidable physiological
process, but rather because they labour to conceal their feelings.
This suppression, usually of sexual desire – it is said – hurls them
into unavoidable hysteria; in the eighteenth century, the patholo-
gically normal body does the work of the feelings. Cheyne's and
Adair's patients are not nervous because they have *suppressed their
emotions*; quite to the contrary, all their hysteria arises from bodily
conditions, especially loosening and tightening (flaccidity and
tautness of the solids and fluids) in the nervous system.[56] So the
point is not so much that male nerves are less sensitive and fragile
than those of the female, as that states of mind such as hypochondria and hysteria are entirely predetermined by the body. It is
small wonder, then, that the most elusive states of mind –
imagination, creativity, genius, even memory – would be medicalised under the weight of such emphasis on the body.

Furthermore, when almost everyone in the late eighteenth
century was, it seems, aping the fashions of the wealthy and great
under the need to assert class distinction, why should *disease* be
omitted from the variety of methods? The phenomenon of emulating aristocracy *to this extreme degree* is itself unparalleled before
the eighteenth century; why then should the splenetic fits of
Queen Anne or the Duchess of Marlborough go unnoticed, when,
as we have seen in virtually every middle-class novel of the period
from Defoe to Fanny Burney, most lower-class females expend
extraordinary amounts of energy observing the mannerisms of
'gentlewomen' and then emulating them (or pretentiously copying
them, as the case may be)?

What needs decoding and dismantling, then, is not the tone of
Dr Dover's astonishing and exorbitant passage about nerves
invading England's fens and marshes, as Dover had recounted,
but the embedded, unwritten assumptions that inform it. This is
the genuine work of a semiology that hopes to retrieve the

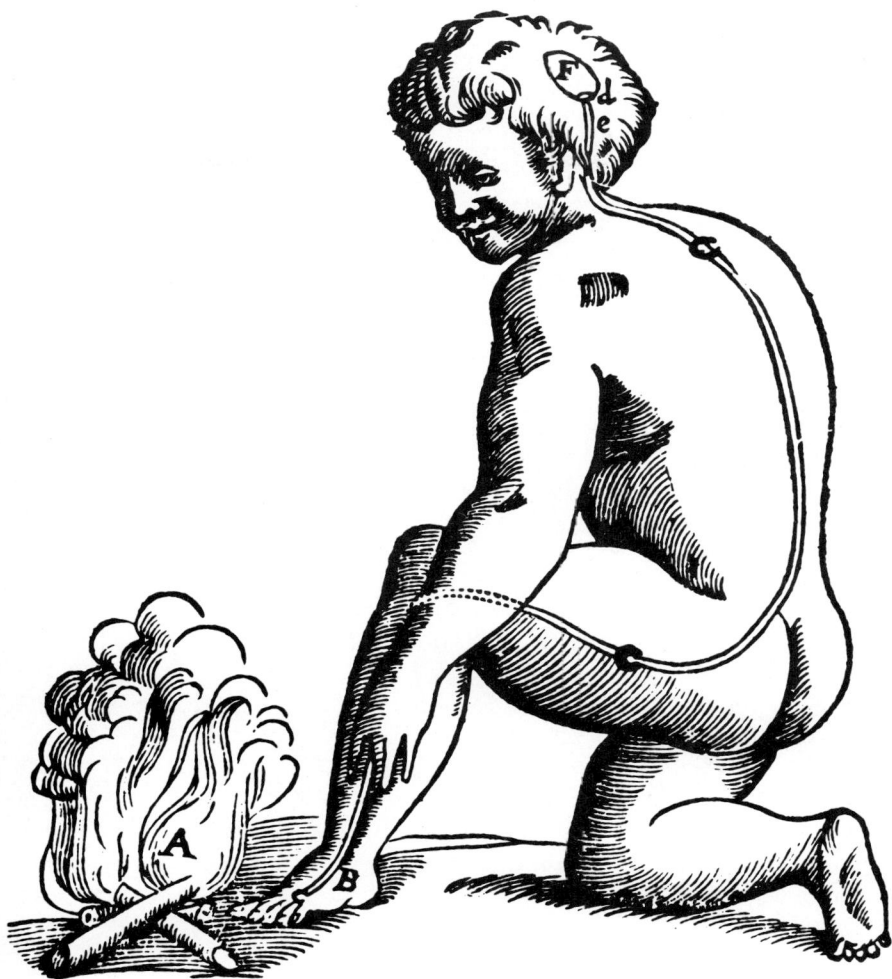

1. *Descartes' Nervous Man.* French edition, facing title-page.

2. *The Third Vision of Christoph Haizmann which Occurred while He was Most Seriously Ill.* Source: Oesterreichische Nationalbibliothek, MSS 14,084. Date: 1677. The Bavarian man Christoph Haizmann was seized in August 1677 with nervous convulsions and acute mental illness. The record of his derangement survives in a diary, nine paintings showing his visions while afflicted, and in dozens of statements made by priests and holy men, medics and lay people who observed his derangement. This is the third of the nine paintings and contains these words (translated from the German): 'The third time he [the Devil] appeared after one and a half years in this loathsome guise, with a book in his hand, which was full of sorcery and black magic. I was able to amuse myself with it, and drive away melancholy.' Haizmann's case was studied by Richard Hunter and Ida Macalpine in *Schizophrenia 1677* (London, 1956).

3. Thomas Rowlandson, engraving of *Justice, Philanthropy and Sensibility.* ca. 1780. Notice *'Sensibility'* on the right, personified with a haggard look and wracked by nervous illness. Tearful and sullen and possessed of straggly hair, she has mounted a candle on a muff on her left hand and holds a copy of a book by Jean-Jacques Rousseau in her right. Her left foot is wrapped up for the gout.

4. *(left) Thomas Rowlandson's Anatomy of Melancholy.* 1808. Caption: 'Tis a Misery to be born, a pain to live, a trouble to die.' The old melancholic is seated in his chair before his fire on the right. Above are his pills and potions and three important signs adorn the walls: the skeleton portending imminent death; the portrait of Democritus referring to Burton (whose title-page of *The Anatomy of Melancholy* reads 'by Democritus Junior'); and a painting or drawing above the fireplace with snakes at the top containing an inscription reading 'Sorrow and grief,' and a dagger held by disembodied hands with another inscription reading 'in suffering is all.' A sheet titled 'Remedies against Discontents — Cure of jealousy' is pinned to the wall. At the table behind him are a man and woman enjoying wine and song, suggesting that lechery is the cure-all and the poor man's antidote to melancholy.

PIERRE POMME, MED . CONSULT. DU ROI,
ET DE LA GRANDE FAUCONERIE DE FRANCE

L'Natoire pinx   Aliis Vitam, Immortalitatem Sibi.   *Sharp sculp*

5. Portrait of Pierre Pomme. Frontispiece of the English translation of *A Treatise on Hysterical and Hypochondriacal Diseases* (London: Elmsly), 1777.

6. James Gillray's *Following the Fashion, 9 December 1794*. Two women of very dissimilar proportions, the thin one fashionable, the other obese and clearly unfashionable, yet each defining the extremity of fashion. Under the fashionable thin lady is written: 'St James's giving the TON. a Soul without a Body'; under the fat one, 'CHEAPSIDE aping the MODE. a Body without a Soul.'

MEDICAL CAUTIONS,

FOR THE CONSIDERATION OF

I N V A L I D S;

THOSE ESPECIALLY WHO RESORT TO

B A T H:

CONTAINING

E S S A Y S

O N

FASHIONABLE DISEASES;

DANGEROUS EFFECTS OF HOT AND CROWDED ROOMS;

REGIMEN OF DIET, &c.

AN ENQUIRY INTO THE USE OF MEDICINE DURING A COURSE OF MINERAL WATERS;

AN ESSAY ON QUACKS, QUACK MEDICINES, AND LADY DOCTORS;

AND AN APPENDIX, CONTAINING A TABLE OF THE RELATIVE DIGESTIBILITY OF FOODS, WITH EXPLANATORY OBSERVATIONS.

PUBLISHED FOR THE BENEFIT OF

The GENERAL HOSPITAL at BATH.

By JAMES MAKITTRICK ADAIR, M. D.

Member of the Royal Medical Society,
And Fellow of the College of Phyſicians, Edinburgh.

——— Idoneſ dicere vitæ.
Nullius addictus ̣urate in verba magiſtri.
Hor. Lib. I. Epiſt. I.

BATH, PRINTED BY R. CRUTTWELL;

AND SOLD BY

J. DODSLEY, AND C. DILLY, LONDON; AND BY ALL THE BOOKSELLERS IN BATH.

M DCC LXXXVI.

---

7. Title-page of James Makittrick Acair's *Treatise on Fashionable Diseases*, Edinburgh, 1786.

8. *Thomas Rowlandson's The Hypochondriac*. 1788. Here, again, the hypochondriac is male, seated in illness and daydreaming: His visions in sequence from left to right: 1. A pagan male satyr with a goblet holding out the cup of libation and lust. 2. Another pagan Hercules/St George-like figure with his knife killing the serpent who is behind him. 3. A mad driver in a carriage filled with women, who seems to be abducting them, why or wither is not at all clear. 4. A huge hand holding out a gigantic knife — but with no body, so perhaps a paranoid vision and fear. 5. The upper half of a torso whose gender is unclear and who seems to be plunging or falling, perhaps even drowning. 6. The heads of two males in states of extreme fear, especially if read according to the principles of physiognomy and the temperaments. 7. An elderly hag holding out a rope and pistol for him to commit suicide. 8. Death in the form of a skeleton with an arrow about to pierce through his heart. 9. A dagger above his head also for him to end himself. His table is littered with pills and potions and uneaten food, and his servant and the physician (identified by his wig and cane) mourn his sorry state in the right hand corner. The tetrameter verse attached underneath reads:

> The Mind distemper'd — say what potent charm,
> Can Fancy's Spectre — breeding rage disarm?
> Physics prescription, art assails in vain,
> The dreadful phantoms fleating cross the brain!
>
> Until with Esculapian skill, the sage M.D.
> Finds out at length by self taught palmistry
> The hopeless case — in the reluctant fee:
> Then, not in torture such a wretch to keep.
> One pitying bolus lays him sound asleep.

The box next to his chair may be filled with his important belongings and papers.

9. *The Hypochondriac* by John Atkinson (1775–1831), drawn at the end of the eighteenth century. Atkinson, like Rowlandson and Gillray, was one of the best-known caricaturists of the day. Here the male hypochondriac is viewed sitting in his parlor, having converted it into a sick man's ward, his bed near by and dressed as a hospital invalid. His hands clasped, he is cold and sick and praying, his eyes shut and his mouth chewing on a pill whose identity is not clear in the engraving. A sheet of paper hangs over the table; he has been writing something and let it go. His dog's bone is on the floor but there is no dog; perhaps in his anxiety over his ailments he has let the dog die.

10. *Lunatic in a Cell*. ca. 1770. Engraving in the Huntington Library. The eyes suggest that he is a madman, the mouth, lips and teeth anguish and delusion. The position of his hands is significant, with his left hand holding his chest/intercostal diaphragm area and the right clutching his genital area. He has removed his breeches or undergarment, which now lies on the rack.

11. *Madwoman in Terror,* ca. 1775, Mezzotint by W. Dickinson after a painting by Robert Edge Pine. Engraving in the Wellcome Institute in London. The portrait illuminates the female iconography of madness, in this instance a young woman of perhaps twenty or so whose wild hair is strung with straw, and whose eyeballs flash with terror and fear. A bandana is wrapped around her head; in fury she has torn the garment from her breast which now lies bare. A feathery or animal garment clings loosely around her, and she is chained and roped, evidence that she poses a threat to others and is dangerous to herself. Window high up in the left corner makes clear that this is a cell where she has been incarcerated.

12. *Lavater's Physiognomy*. An iconography of the male from the Holcroft 1793 translation, plate 4, n.p. No nervous figure here but notice the melancholic male at the bottom, especially when he is aligned with the madman and lunatic. His eyes and lips are crucially expressive, as in the iconography of the humours or temperaments.

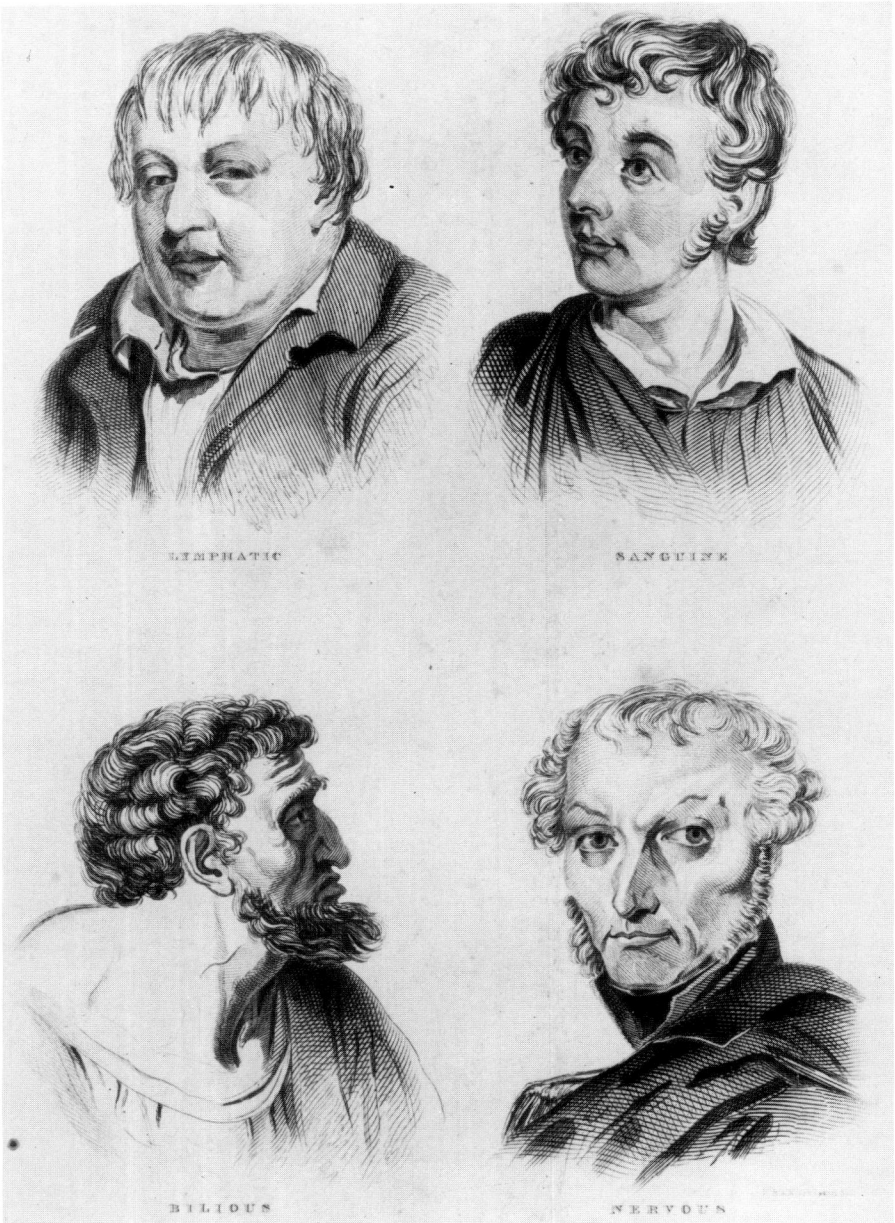

LYMPHATIC　　　　　SANGUINE

BILIOUS　　　　　NERVOUS

13. Early nineteenth-century engraving of the temperaments, derived in part from LeBrun: *lymphatic; sanguine; bilious; nervous*. The expression of the eyes and lips provide the clue and the cheeks reflect the degree of passion. All are male because the temperaments generally were iconographically understood as masculine. The nervous male resembles a minister of state: driven, engrossed, professional, perhaps a statesman or aristocrat who has been idolised and romanticised.

significance of a particular sign within lost cultures. Yet the systems of all these fashionable 'nerve doctors' – from Willis to Cheyne, from Sydenham to Mandeville, from Garth to Mead, from Haller to Tissot, from Hartley to Cullen – can never be dismantled until we can isolate and identify why these thinkers could uniformly claim, as Adair does here, that 'no part of the physiology has engaged the attention more, or reaped greater consequences in our time, than the nerves.'[57] No one today wants to revert to those odious Hazlittian 'spirits of the age' that characterised epochs often by the most simplistic of labels, or regress to Basil Wiley's loathsome world views and world pictures. Certainly no one should claim that this was an Age of Nerves (see Plate 8), as if upper-case 'Ages' were discreet things whose boundaries could be charted, as previous cultural historians have argued for Ages of Reason and Ages of Passion. But for the upper classes, much social differentiation *did* lie in the nerves, just as nervous philosophy and sympathetic reasoning resonated with meaning as a separating out mechanism for the Adam Smiths, the Humes and the Scottish moralists: the same resonance that causes imagination theory to become so highly medicalised in the eighteenth century,[58] and, alternatively, that prompts an anonymous writer in 1744 – a dunce perhaps? – to think that there could be a readership for a prose work he hazards to call *The Anatomy of a Nervous Woman's Tongue: A Medicine, A Poison, A Serpent, A Fire and Thunder.*[59] We will soon see who this developing readership was.

The fantasies inspired by this nervous mythology also require decoding and dismantling. They are as intriguing as the projects of Fellows in the Royal Society trying to ascertain what the vital nervous fluid was and attempting to dissect and reproduce the nerves. Yet if the constellation of illnesses passing under the rubric of consumption was then the *fatal* English malady – the disease from which people actually died – nervous sensibility was the *life force*: the vital *je ne sais quoi* of the upper class; the spring of vitality and creativity that set it apart from the *hoi polloi* but which could also bring it misery in the form of depression, accidie, indolence, as in Thomson's castle, or lassitude in the shape of the noonday demon, the waste of sloth.[60]

The remarkable fillip of the semiological version of analysis is that it brings passages to life that would otherwise remain dead. Entire hulks of writing that were formerly consigned to the closets of obscurity or the shades of hermeticism suddenly gather meaning. One such place is the correspondence of Richardson the novelist and his female confidante. Mrs Donnellan consoled her friend, the novelist, in words that could be the epigraph of this chapter:

> Misfortune is, those who are fit to write delicately, must think so; those who can form a distress must be able to feel it; and as the mind and body are so united as to influence one another, the delicacy is communicated, and one too often finds softness and tenderness of mind in a body equally remarkable for those qualities. Tom Jones could get drunk, and do all sorts of bad things, in the height of his joy for his uncle's recovery. I dare say Fielding is a robust, strong man.[61]

Robust, that is, unlike Richardson! This is no mere 'attempt to console Richardson for his perpetual ill-health', as Ian Watt long ago suggested,[62] or, if such consolation, certainly not merely a mindless female comfort, but the clearest indication – the very semiotic I have been attempting to identify and isolate for scrutiny – of a veritable revolution in social thinking. Mrs Donnellan's unstated premises are the mythologies of the age which can be schematised and epitomised as follows:

1. the soul is limited to the brain;
2. the brain performs all its work through the nerves;
3. the more exquisite and delicate one's nerves – morphologically speaking – the greater the ensuing degree of sensibility and imagination;
4. upper-class people are born with more exquisite nervous anatomies; the tone and texture of their nervous systems are more delicate than those of the lower classes;
5. greater nervous sensibility makes for greater writing, greater art, greater genius.

It is a rather odd sequence, alien from the pluralistic habits of mind so firmly ingrained in late twentieth-century culture. Difference, indeed, is the chief signpost of cultural semiotics: not to read these differences often entails vast loss. Even when the poet Pope, whose self-delusive but nevertheless ironic, dying words were 'I was never hyppish in my whole life,'[63] lamented 'this long disease, my life', and complained in his letters about 'this crazy constitution', his complaint indicated difference. Chronic nerves were living emblems of gentility and delicacy. There was no reason to avoid them, no virtue in doctors concealing them from their patients, as in the cases of cancer and consumption. Philander Misaurus, an alias for a Grub Street hack writing for 'females of parts' in 1720, advised them: 'When sharp, fermenting Juices (not easily miscible) shall meet, and by their furious Contest, cause cruel Twitchings of your nervous Fibres; comfort your Heart, and be extreamly pleas'd.'[64] Though technical and couched in hard words, the advice was heeded, particularly among those anxious about their status. John Midriff, another fashionable nerve doctor like Dover and Adair, wrote a long book in 1720 for those 'who have been miserably afflicted with these Melancholy Disorders since the Fall of the South-Sea, and other public stocks.'[65] Forty-eight years later, long after the emotional turbulence caused by personal economic loss in the bubble had subsided, Daniel Smith, a deist well-read in Newtonian philosophy, was found expounding the same ideas in a medico-theological idiom: *A Dissertation upon the Nervous System to show its influence upon the Soul*.[66] Nervous mythology was not a credo for one generation, but a type of discovery whose positivistic energy was so great that it has carried down through the late twentieth century, as our neurophysiological activities make evident.

To return to our Enlightenment, the physicians of the fashionable and smart sets were swift to isolate 'nerves' as the cause of all disturbance in their patients, almost as if they had identified the crucial gene of ailment and distress. Indeed, the discovery of nerves, unlike the diagnosis of cancer or consumption, was cause for celebration, as in Boswell's case, who touted his melancholy far and wide.[67] Nerves were neither the signs nor the symptoms of ephemeral illness but an inherited condition that, if undetected, could lie dormant only for so long. Inherited like wealth or milk-white skin, nerves and their fibres were unique among the organic structures: ingrained, they could neither be bought nor stolen, copied nor caught. This is why Elizabeth Carter, the brilliant letter-writer, ministered to her ailing correspondent Catherine Talbot with the evangelism of a prophetess. 'The low spiritedness . . . of which you complain, assures me you cannot be well, nor ever will be, while you have the strange imagination that a weak system of nerves is a moral defect, and to be cured by reason and argument.'[68] As we saw in the communication of Mrs

Donnellan and Richardson, the sequence here is also crystalline: weak nerves are not the signs of moral defect, as Elizabeth Carter stresses, but the proof of discrimination and delicacy. The patient should therefore never reason herself out of them, as Talbot seems eager to do. Miss Carter even psychologises the nerves here with a corollary about attention 'I must enjoin you for two months to amuse yourself, and wile away the time, and be as trifling and insignificant . . . and never during that time to apply to anything that requires close attention.'[69] *Far niente*, an Italianate do nothing: this was the best cure for a condition whose mortal consequence was inconsequential. But it focused attention and concentration: it was the villain, the perfidious culprit; the same steady close attention that invaded the nerves of literary and sedentary persons, as Tissot had shown, and caused them to become neurasthenically depressed. For those prone to the dictates of the imagination, such as scholars, writers and religious types, a life of focused attention was as dangerous as the worst fistula or cancer. So the mythology went; the reality was otherwise: Richardson did not die of focused attention any more than Carter or Talbot (or Horace Walpole for that matter) expired from the fatigue of letter writing.

Ponder it though one may, the nerves would never consume the body, as in other medical conditions. Exempt from contagion, no pollution could be caught from them. 'I am genuinely relieved,' exclaimed Lady Mary Wortley Montagu's sister, Lady Mar, 'to learn that the *worst* is delicate nerves; this I can manage; the excrescences of a diseased liver, stomach, or bowels would be so much worse.'[70] Nervous sensibility was thus a dissemination rather than a disease; an outreach whose extension was the *sine qua non* of fashion. Nerves could be painful, but the pain was said to be mentally lodged and never posed the threat of death to the body. Even the poets were amazed at the proximity of pain and pleasure in the nerves. Hence Samuel Garth, the poet of *The Dispensary* and a leading physician at the turn of the eighteenth century, remarked: 'How the same Nerves are fashion'd to sustain the greatest Pleasure, and the greatest Pain!'[71] Within this context of pain the nerves were an anti-gout, often accompanying the real gout, but much more discriminating in its victims. And the proof – in the collective fantasy – that nerves were the supreme life force of the fashionable was that nerves would never lead to death, only to the *fear* of death: *timor mortis*.

An apocryphal story about Samuel Johnson's last days survives from the early nineteenth century, white-washed over the pages of the *European Magazine*.[72] It recounts that, just a few months before his death, Johnson consulted Nan Kivel, the fashionable London physician. Johnson provided his full case history, only omitting *timor mortis*, the fear of death. Kivel seized upon the omission; to this Johnson replied: 'Alas, it is so, it is so . . .' To which Dr. Kivel rejoined: 'I only wanted that symptom [the fear of death] to make yours a complete case of hypochondriasis, which will only require a little exertion on my part, and rather more on yours, to *entirely cure*.' Johnson soon died, but not because of spastic intercostal involvement, then thought to lie in the seat of hypochondria. The noteworthy aspect is Kivel's confidence in an 'entire cure' despite the diagnosis of male hypochondriasis, and the fact that Regency readers wanted to hear this story mythologised in this way. Other onlookers who could pierce through the flapdoodle of these (often crude) discourses of the nerve often screamed catcalls: sometimes in an altogether different mode, as in Austen's assault in *Sense and Sensibility*, where the hypocrises of the ethic of sensibility are exposed through the characters of the circle hanging on the Dashwood women; sometimes trivially, as for the 1732 caricaturist who claimed, facetiously, in an engraving 'Of the Hypp: The pleasures of melancholy and madness', that 'there are Pleasures in Madness, which the Splenetick, of all sufferers of the nerve, are least acquainted with'.[73] (See Plate 9.) To those who were neither parvenus nor social climbers, nor anxious about their niche in polite society, the vast cultural octopus of nerves seemed a remote social phenomenon, let alone a valid or invalid scientific hypothesis: a cluster of concepts or ideas which never could or would impinge on them. They never grasped what the debate about nerves entailed. For the others, especially the social climbers, and those who were already located in places of high station, nerves had become a way of life, touching on everything important: sex, love, sanity, insanity, and, most crucially, one's social standing.

As the eighteenth century wore on, the myth intensified. Accreted to it eventually was a sense that the reckless and the lecherous, more politely the sensuous and the erotic, behaved as they did out of an innate propensity lodged in the nerves rather than because the nerves had grown diseased in any way. Historically, the fact is that they were eating themselves into the grave, indulging in lechery, and generally wrecking their health with late nights. The discourses of the nerve that constituted the fabric of the mythologies I have been discussing coped with that reality. They especially did so by emphasising that nerves signified no disease of passion, as nineteenth-century tuberculosis would, but were the sign of *passion itself*. Nerves and sex were thus intimately connected, as they would be in the oeuvre of the Marquis de Sade:[74] direct concrete proof that one had been capable all along of understanding passion's kingdom. Those who were not nervous could never respond adequately to sexual desire, let alone at the level of 'toujours la chose génitale'. This concretion of the body is what unites all the discourses of the nerve: Mandeville, Robinson, Tissot, Bienville – the entire company. The doctors' explanations reveal why: nervous persons could contract diseases with devastating somatic effects; in the myth, though, *all* their troubles were nervous, whether they were diagnosed as hypish, splenetic, or as hysterical women in the older nomenclature, or nervous in the newer, or whether diagnosed as hypochondriacal men. Again and again, gender, class and race determined the shape of the sign: nerves *in relation to these aspects*.

More than anything, then, I have been attempting to demonstrate that, as the middle classes at mid-century continued to demand liberty and the rabble the franchise in suburban Middlesex and other boroughs, the upper classes increasingly aimed to set themselves apart. Nerves provided them with a myth about their origins: an aristocratic model of life they could follow.

THE FORMATION OF THE NERVOUS PERSONALITY IN CULTURAL HISTORY

By these diverse cultural means, entailing different social practices formed in diverse social institutions, the nervous personality of the nineteenth and twentieth centuries jelled into a type we continue to recognise today: the idealised consumptive type; the romantic poet or artist wasting away and eventually decaying; the neurotic genius who comes almost directly from William Cullen's lecture notes; in women, the creative Crazy Janes (as in Blake's poem) and compulsive anorexics (as in the notorious fasting woman in Tutbury, Staffordshire) who will haunt the nineteenth-century imagination. (See Plate 10.)

The difficult aspect of the coagulation and the stereotype, so to speak, is not its various strands or internal contradictions, but the process of organic formation itself. It was a slow, dynamic growth extending over many decades, eventually lending credence to the belief that those who were nervous partook of a type of vitality nowhere else to be seen, even if the vitality – the Shavian Life Force – itself could only be anatomically pinpointed. This principle of vitality had been not merely medically but culturally grounded; eventually it was imperialistic, extending its vast sway from Dr William Battie (who held that madness itself actually resided in the nerves–see Plate 11) and the already mentioned Dr Cullen (whose 'neuroses' of 1768 were the first set of classifications of nervous types),[75] to early nineteenth-century accounts claiming that genius mandated sensitive nerves. Seen whole, it was a cultural wave extending from the nebulous borderlines of sanity and insanity in the Restoration (as Dryden had said in 1682, 'Great Wits are sure to madness near ally'd)[76] to the medicalising of the creative act under the strain of genius, and eventually to the nervous agony of creative writers like Richardson, Cowper and Chatterton, who in their very different ways were inmates of its all-too-familiar prison. 'When I was young,' Theophile Gautier wrote, 'I could not have accepted as a lyrical poet anyone weighing more than ninety-nine pounds.'[77] More than a hundred years earlier, Mrs Donnellan, as we have seen, ventured to apply a version of this angle of vision to hypochondriacal novelists like Samuel Richardson. In brief, what had been reserved for the parades and crescents of Bath and England's newly developing seaside resorts became the way of the world in her towns and cities by the early nineteenth century. But it would be wrong to think of the nervous type itself as a *nineteenth* century development. It developed much earlier. The neurasthenic woman suffering from a myriad of female maladies – from anorexia and hysteria and dementia among other types – certainly flowered in the nineteenth century; but she was not, so to speak, born then. If Crazy Jane and her cohorts infuse the iconography of Byron's and Walter Scott's society, they nevertheless appear throughout the annals of late eighteenth-century discursive (literary as well as medical) literature.

As the nineteenth century evolved, nervous mythology altered, was not eradicated but transformed, as it gradually became apparent that a newly constituted English aristocracy need not distance itself in these same ways any longer. Disease remained the reward, however ironically, for sin – as it was to be for Emma

Bovary – but not for mere neurosis or self-indulgence, as it has become in our twentieth century. Yet nervous disease became more localised and specialised than it had been in the eighteenth century. Upper-class male hypochondria practically vanished as a topic of investigation – this under the new nineteenth-century obsession with sexuality as a regulating force and in the belief that females, not males, were incarnations of the senses (see Plate 12). The new idea was that males were subject to stress in the workplace that made them prone to a type of melancholy unknown to women, as in Charles Lamb's bizarre 'tailor's melancholy.'[78] Coupled to this male ailment were a whole series of female nervous maladies predicated on a developing science of female hysteria that would culminate in the discourses of Gilles de la Turette and Breuer and Freud. As tuberculosis and cholera competed with nervous ailments for attention and government subsidy, there was less spotlight on exclusively nervous conditions and hence on the older competing discourses of the nerve. Lunacy itself came to be seen as the higher sensitivity, especially after the reforms of Pinel, Esquirol and Charcot; and it too was partly unhinged from its former, monolithic, neurologic base. The intimate bond that had existed between the upper classes and their inherited nervous apparatus was severed but not gone, replaced by a new moralising and psychologising of illness that made disease the symbol of human character, as it remains in our time with AIDS. In the case of fatal disease, which *nervous* diseases had never been, it was a *hamartia* over which no one could triumph, high-born or low. Not even in the neurasthenic versions associated with French decadence was our nervous condition said to be morbid.[79] Proust, like Wilde and other decadents in their Franco-English milieu, linked his neurasthenia to creativity; not to be nervous and ill, he came to believe, was not to write. His long seance in bed was not so different from Wilde's retreats to the seaside, where Wilde wrote in what he perceived to be exquisite solitude, almost always ill, or at least reputedly suffering. And Schumann's reputation, we must not forget, rose after he threw himself into the Rhine. None of these versions was so very far removed from Richardson's neurasthenic creativity, although we have constructed a mental notion that somehow the eighteenth century was immune from these developments; but Richardson's creative condition also flourished under the distress of a nervous ailment which his physician, Dr Cheyne, could never precisely define to his inquisitive patient.

The remainder of my story in the nineteenth and twentieth centuries has yet to be pulled together. The sheer bulk of extant material entails an *embarras de richesse* for the cultural historian; I can only suggest the shadows of its discourses here. The literally hundreds of scientific and parascientific books written about the nerves in relation to man and woman generically viewed, ranging from Thomas Trotter's *Nervous Temperaments* (1807) and John Cooke's *Treatise on Nervous Diseases* (1822) in England, to Broussais' books in France in the 1820s, especially his *Traité de la nervosité et de la folie*, a type of early nineteenth-century Foucaldian approach that stresses the discourses of nervous physiology and links the clinical nerve to its social manifestation.[80] The nineteenth-century development of a theory of character, already evident in Jane Austen, also flowers in De Quincey's *English Opium Eater*, the Brontes, Melville's *Ambiguities* and Carlyle, and will show moral fibre to be lodged in the nerves. Thus in *Mansfield Park*, when extraordinary revelation is about to be made, Austen shrewdly narrates: 'It was not in Miss Crawford's power to talk Fanny into any real forgetfulness of what had passed – when the evening was over, she [Fanny] went to bed full of it, her nerves still agitated by the shock of such an attack by her cousin Tom, so public and so persevered in.'[81] To the end of *Mansfield Park*, nerves hold a key to character, as they do in others of Jane Austen's novels, especially when Sir Thomas is about to pass judgment on Fanny; 'he knew her to be very timid, and exceedingly nervous'. These are no metaphoric representations of anatomy but the thing itself – the literal nerves which will hurl Austen's heroines into some of their most poignant moods.

The culture of Europe ca. 1800 is infused with this unspoken paradigm: from the literary representations of nerves in Blake's 'Auricular Nerves of Human Life' in *The Four Zoas*, to D. H. Lawrence's dichotomy between 'a nervous attachment rather than a sexual love' in *St. Mawr*. The aesthetics of sympathy and empathy, from Burke in his *Sublime*, through various transformations in Novalis, Keats ('negative capability'), Jean Paul, and eventually the *Einfühlung* (i.e. empathy) that will form the basis of *fin-de-siècle* psychological aesthetics. The nineteenth-century cults of blushing and tears, not merely the old sorrows of Werther, but now the new sorrows of Charlotte too (as in Charlotte Smith),[82] and the pervasive malaise and ennui such moral tears inevitably induce, a malaise and decay extending at least to the French

existentialists of our century. The nineteenth-century theories of
the optic nerve in relation to the painter's gaze, evident not only in
Turner and the English School but in other painters as well; and
the nineteenth-century aesthetics of the imagination, follow so
predictably from the eighteenth's and which has claimed that
Mozart's music was greater than all other because 'it assaulted the
nerves more'. Then there is Coleridge's paean to the nerves as the
true sources of growth and organic form: 'They [the nerves] and
they alone can acquire the philosophic imagination, the sacred
power of self-intuition, who within themselves can interpret and
understand the symbol, that the wings of the air-stylop are
forming within the skin of the caterpillar . . .'[83]

   All these are discourses requiring retrieval. Among the types of
materials that need to be culled and interpreted are nineteenth-
century medical 'theories' of the affluent classes, as in Thomas
Beddoes' *Hygeia; or . . . The Personal State of our Affluent Classes*
(1802–3), which continues to promote the significance of the
nerves, as well as Moritz Heinrich Romberg's famous *Nervous
Diseases of Man* (1853, English translation–see Plate 13) composed at
the peak of Victorian civilisation, George Miller Beard's description
of neurasthenia in his now famous 1880 *Practical Treatise on Nervous
Exhaustion* as the new disease of American civilization, Abraham
Myerson's *The Nervous Housewife* (1920), to the more eccentric
Daniel Schreber's – Freud's patient – *Memoirs of my Nervous Illness*.
This development reaches a peak during the time when Virgina
Woolf claims in her diaries of the 1920s that 'writing calls upon
every nerve in my body to hold itself taut',[84] and Sylvia Plath
reveals to Anthony Alvarez just before her death that her suicide
will be no swoon, no attempt 'to cease upon the midnight with no
pain', but something to be felt in the nerve ends and fought
against 'at the level of the nerve tips'.[85] A second wave, so to
speak, developed when Charles Darwin and other zoologists of
the nineteenth century elevated these same nerves in their phylo-
genetic studies of the emotions of animals, thereby returning us,
as it were, to our physicist, Victor Weisskopf, who views the
nervous system with a geochemical gaze and who sees its aesthetic impulse and influence spread over geological time.

   There is, of course, an opposition to each of these cultural
movements – a counter-culture, as it were, which has not been
explored here for reasons of space, extending from Mary Wollsto-
necraft, who denounces nervous women in *The Rights of Woman* as

useless creatures who accomplish nothing, to all sorts of moralists who see in these nervous mythologies and nervous discourses running wild in the nineteenth century no hope for the progress of culture. But the movement is there none the less: pervasive, writ large, indelible. Eventually it will have to be studied, if for no other reason than that neurophysiology, now in such a positivistic and imperialistic phase, continues to claim to have made such strides in our own time.[86]

CONCLUSION

Let me conclude on a note about significance: the significance of this story, the significance of these different discourses of the nerve, and the crucial matter of privileging these discourses over others. The contradictions of the nerve story are obvious: no inner logics, no agreement among themselves, only obeisance to the mythologies of social class, a type of social determinism of cultural practices and arrangements. Equally significant are the discursive practices of these narratives. Previously, we have viewed these discursivities in isolation: as the narratives of literature, the narratives of science, the narratives of history, and so forth, without viewing them comparatively.[87] And however distinct these discursive narratives, we have usually viewed them from *within* rather than without: that is, as insiders rather than out-siders; as practitioners or critics of the distinct narratives of literature, of science, of history, and so forth, with the conse-quence that we have lost the gaze of the outsider, whose perspect-ive can be the more acute by reason of distance, balance, objectiv-ity and sturdiness. So that those who are most familiar with the discursive practices of literature – for example – might actually see deeply into the narratives we have called science, and historians into the narratives commonly reserved for the literary critic's eye. Nor have we comparatively studied allusions and tropes common to all these narratives, to establish, as it were, a grammar of allusions, common to all the various discursive narratives.

But it would require another essay to interpret the social processes I have been discussing, especially the dynamics of class formation, and the antagonisms of the upper and lower classes, just as another chapter would be needed to evaluate the theoretical models best suited to this material. But most of all, the discourses of the nerve are significant for embedding the deepest so-called scientific and metaphysical questions of the last hundred years: what is the universe, what is human life, what are mental processes? Can mental processes operate without a body? What is a computer? What is the body of a computer? Can a computer think for itself, feel, make love, use its imagination, grieve? What is artificial intelligence? What is sexual desire, sexual attraction, sexual orientation? All these questions have been asked in our century within the context of biology. But more recently, and as the new biology, psychology and sociobiology have shown themselves to rely on an even more fundamental neurophysiology, the deepest of these questions would all seem to have neurophysiological underpinnings. These developments demonstrate why the action, so to speak, and heat in science today (especially the trends in funding) lies at the juncture of neurophysiology and computer science, the points of reference where one can explore questions about mental processes operating without a body. And perhaps this is why the human body itself, and its various discourses, have been so predominantly privileged in the last few decades. Indeed, no set of discourses has been more emphasised than those of the body, isolating their tropes and metaphors as well as their cultural referents and comparative allusions.

But neurophysiology did not spring full-blown, as if from Athena's head, in the twentieth century. It has an older legacy, especially in the seventeenth and eighteenth centuries. In the face of these ancient but nevertheless somewhat contradictory discourses of the nerve I leave them with much wonder and awe, bewildered at the idea of our contemporary neurophysiologists that for us humans there is only nerve and brain, and nothing *but* nerve and brain, a notion the eighteenth century would not have believed itself all that uncomfortable with. To think that in the most abstract and non-referential discourse of all – classical music – that even there, and especially in its performance and interpretation, there should be brain and nerve primarily. Some would say only. Horowitz performing classical music – Scarlatti, Schumann, Chopin, Rachmaninoff – as nothing but an extraordinary nerve machine! Perhaps in the end the new positivistic neurophysiologists are right: nerves have perhaps been the greatest gift of all. It may be so, but it nevertheless remains an odd position when viewed *outside* Weisskopf's geological time and *inside* the parochial approach usually taken to cultural history.

Notes

This essay was originally delivered in a much shorter version in Aberdeen, Scotland in July 1987 under ordinary constraints of time, and the reader will soon see that my style abounds in ellipticisms (wherever possible two words instead of ten). I have allowed this version to stand rather than reconstruct the essay along somewhat artificial lines. Each style – the oral and the written – obviously has its advantages, and I trust that readers expecting a more formal and discursive version from this somewhat oral one will forgive whatever infelicities have crept into this version. Of course, the relation of orality (especially oral theory) to the nervous physiology developed here is interesting in itself. Unless noted otherwise, the place of publication is London.

1. Victor Weisskopf, *Knowledge and Wonder: The Natural World as Man Knows It,* Cambridge, 1979, p. 223 *et passim.*
2. Ibid., p. 264.
3. Ibid.
4. Ibid., p. 265.
5. Ibid.
6. Ibid.
7. For nerves and the ancients see: Friedrich Solmsen, 'Greek Philosophy and the Discovery of the Nerves', *Museum Helveticum* 18, 1961, pp. 150–67.
8. *Annual Register,* III, 1766, p. 234.
9. An extended note on the historiography of nerves provides some perspective here. As the seventeenth and eighteenth centuries progressed, nerves played an increasingly prominent role in all sorts of research agendas, including those of the laboratory as well as in more logocentric projects, as I tried to demonstrate over a decade ago in 'Nerves, Spirits and Fibres: Toward the Origins of Sensibility, *Studies in the Eighteenth Century,* ed. R. F. Brissenden, Canberra, 1975, pp. 137–57. My point, then and now, has been that there was a progression from nerves to the cults of sentiment and sensibility, and that European Romanticism could not have occurred without this sequence. It is, to be sure, a diachronic theory, and nowhere have I ever maintained that nerves and sensibility were *the* (superlative) cause of Romanticism. In this essay, I attempt to show more fully than previously the roles of the nerves in cultural history. But see also, for a medical historian's view of the subject, George Rosen, 'Emotion and Sensibility in Ages of Anxiety: A Comparative Historical Review,' *American Journal of Psychiatry* 6.124, 1967, pp. 771–83.

   Sensibility has had, of course, its own historiography, although it has been a ragged one, carved up by specialist disciplines, never gazed at sturdily or synoptically; see, for example, L. I. Brevold, *The Natural History of Sensibility,* Detroit, 1962; Caroline Thompson, 'Sensibility', *Psyche* XV, 1935, pp. 46–161; and for an astute lexical critique of the word that nevertheless limits its range to the narrow field, Raymond Williams, *Keywords: a vocabulary of culture and society,* 1976, pp. 235–8. There has not even been a bibliographical survey of *primary* works, such as Joanna Heywood's *Excessive*

Sensibility, a tradition including such famous novels as Austen's *Sense and Sensibility*.

These traditions would require a book to adumbrate properly, especially in relation to the scientific movement, more specifically the rise and dissemination of mechanism then, but some important primary foci include: the works of Thomas Willis during the Restoration; later on, ca. 1705–20, the Boyle Lectures; in the 1750s, see Richard Barton, *Lectures in Natural Philosophy, Designed to be a Foundation*, 1751; Albrecht von Haller, 'Elementa Physiologiae Corporis Humanae', in *The Natural Philosophy of Albrecht von Haller*, ed. Shirley A. Roe, New York, 1981. Important secondary work includes: Edwin Clarke, 'The Doctrine of the Hollow Nerve in the Seventeenth and Eighteenth Centuries', *Medicine, Science, and Culture: Historical Essays in Honor of Owsei Temkin*, eds. Lloyd G. Stevenson and Robert P. Multhauf, Baltimore, 1968 pp. 123–41; Theodore M. Brown, 'From Mechanism to Vitalism in Eighteenth-Century English Physiology', *Journal of the History of Biology*, 7, 1974 pp. 179–216; Jacob Bronowski, 'A Sense of the Future: Essays in Natural Philosophy', in Rita Bronowski and Piero E. Ariotti (eds), *The Visionary Eye; essays in the arts, literature and science*, Cambridge, Mass, 1978; and, in relation to the sciences of man, S. Moravia, 'From Homme Machine to Homme Sensible: Changing Eighteenth-Century Models of Man's Image', *Journal of the History of Ideas* 39, 1978 pp. 45–60, and *Filosofia e scienze umane nell 'eta dei lumi*, Florence, 1982. Even the Swiss professor of philosophy and philology at the University of Basel during this period, Samuel Werenfels, whose writings were influential for rhetoric and style in England, develops a programme that includes 'nervous science' in discussions of the rhetoric of sublimity; see, for example, his *Discourse   of   Logomachys,   or   Contraversys   [sic]   about Words . . .* (1711).

But the agenda was not limited to natural science; it was also evident in the arts (as in Daniel Webb's *An Inquiry into the Beauties of Painting*, London, 1760, where the nervous system is discussed in relation to art), and in music (as in Richard Browne's *Medicina musica: Or a Mechanica. Essay on the Effects of Singing, Musick, and Dancing, on Human Bodies*, 1729). Guichard Duverney, a late seventeenth-century French anatomist who made the ear his organ of expertise, believed the sense of hearing among humans to be the most divine of all; the nerves in the ear constructed more subtly by the Deity and prompting 'Men and Birds to excite one another to sing'; see *A Treatise of the Organ of Hearing*, 1737; originally pub. 1683, p. 88. This agenda was also evident in theories of acting and dancing (as in John Hill's, *The Actor*, 1750), as well as theories about the branches of government and political economy (as evident in Adam Smith's discourses). For nerves and theories of acting, see George Taylor, '"The Just Delineation of the Passions": Theories of Acting in the Age of Garrick,' *Essays on the Eighteenth-Century English Stage*, 1972. This widely disseminated agenda was a cultural development of the Enlightenment of whose ideology and influence we have yet to take stock. A sense of its breadth is discussed, most perceptively and intuitively, in Christopher Lawrence, 'The Nervous System and Society in the Scottish Enlightenment', *Natural Order: Historical Studies of Scientific Enlightenment*, ed. Barry Barnes and Steven Shapin, Beverly Hills, 1979 pp. 19–40; even so, Lawrence merely scratches the surface; much more remains to be done outside the local confines of eighteenth-century Edinburgh.

But even the novice reading through these diverse discourses of the nerve soon realises that the nerves were genderised throughout this period, especially as discourses about the nature of women's bodies developed; see, for example, Edward Shorter, *A History of Women's Bodies*, Harmondsworth, 1983. The means by which nerves became genderised – male nerves taking one set of attributes, female ones another, more delicate, if hysterical version – would also require another essay, if not a book in itself. Suffice it to comment here that, as theories developed separating the genders further and further than they had been, and accounted for all types of hermaphrodites and monsters, as well as sexual deviants (in our anachronistic language homosexuals and lesbians), the nerves were thoroughly implicated, and it is equally inconceivable to imagine Enlightenment discourses of these anatomical types without discussion of the nerves. By mid-century a physician such as J. Raulin could maintain in his *Traité des affections vaporeuses du sexe*, Paris, 1758, that nervous disorders were limited entirely to the *female* sex; over a century later, Albert Moll, a German doctor, claimed in his treatise, *Berühmte Homosexuelle: Grenzfragen des Nerven-und Seelenlebens* Wiesbaden: 1910, 11, no. 75 that the etiology of homosexuality in both genders was caused entirely by defective, degenerating nerves. The nerves, then, were anything but delimited in their perceived ability to account for the generation of physiological and psychological types.

The recent neurophysiological critique of nerves is at once much more idealistic and positivistic; i.e., claiming that neurophysiology explains everything, thoroughly confident in the view that no other set of explanations, either mental or physical, can compete with it. See, for example: John Eccles, *The Neurophysiological Basis of Mind*, Oxford, 1953; E. Graham Howe, *Invisible Anatomy: A Study of Nerves, Hysteria and Sex*, 1955; Walther Riese, *A History of Neurology*, New York, 1959; I. H. Burn, *The Automatic Nervous System*, Oxford, 1963; J. Spillane, *The Doctrine of the Nerves*, 1981; *Historical Aspects of the Neurosciences: A Festschrift for Macdonald Critchley*, New York, 1982; E. Clarke and L. S. Jacyna (eds), *Nineteenth-Century Origins of Neuroscientific Concepts*, Los Angeles, 1987.

10.   Mind–body dualism was still in its post-Cartesian flowering: being massively attacked on all sides, but still far from overthrown. The most bewildering physical and metaphysical question debated then was whether the nerves were inherently a part of mind (soul) or body, or some substance in between, and there was no agreement about the proper method of asking and answering this question. There was also (ca. 1700–80) a vast developing discourse of the

nerves in relation to mental faculties, passions and insanity, and to
the specific role of the nerves played in pathological states. For the
dualism of mind and body, see L. J. Rather, *Mind and Body in
Eighteenth-Century Medicine*, 1965 and M. D. Wilson, 'Body and
Mind from the Cartesian Point of View', *Body and Mind: Past,
Present and Future*, ed. R. W. Rieber, New York, 1980. The most
thorough treatment is found in G. S. Rousseau (ed.), *The Languages
of Psyche: Mind and Body in Enlightenment Thought*, Berkeley and
Los Angeles, 1990, whose bibliography of primary and secondary
works should be consulted for nerves as well. For 'vital spirits' and
vitalism, see particularly: Jacques Roger, *Les Sciences de la Vie*, Paris,
1963; A. A. Cournot, *Materialisme, Vitalisme, Rationalisme*, ed. Claire
Salomon-Bayet, Paris, 1979; Richmond Wheeler, *Vitalism – Its History and Validity*, 1939; John W. Yolton, *Thinking Matter: Materialism in Eighteenth-Century Britain*, Minneapolis; 1983.

11.   The argument from nature, more locally from anatomy and physiology, was made many times, with reference to both genders and
under virtually every type of ideological banner, conservative and
radical, and in practically every political shade then available. A
conventional example is found in William Derham's *Creation of the
World*, 1712, one of the Boyle Lectures, and in the next generation in
the physician–philosopher David Hartley's influential *Observations
on Man, his frame . . .* , 1749, containing 'pt. 1: Observations on the
frame of the human body and mind, and on their mutual connexions and influences,' but there were others. In general, the clergy
were especially quick to claim that defective nerves, often arising
from a diseased religious melancholy, would lead to morbid
hypochondria and hysteria, about which more will be said later. As
late as the 1760s, R. J. Boscovich, the philospher of science, was
inquiring about the role played by nerves within the human
organism's functioning (see his *Theory of Natural Philosophy*,
Venice, 1763) and in the 1780s the Catholic apologist Laurent
François Boursier was still explaining how those who had fallen
from grace through sin also fell into convulsions through the
explicit deterioration of their nerves; see his *Mémoire théologique sur
ce qu'on appelle les secours violens dans les convulsions* (Paris, 1788).

12.   For the generalised view, see Herbert Thursten, *The Physical
Phenomenon of Mysticism*, 1950. There remains no study of what I
label *the tradition of counter-nerve*, embodied in the critiques –
especially through the trope of analogy (*analogia*) – of the mechanistic approaches to the nerves developed by Paracelsus and van
Helmont through Swedenberg, Blake, Ebenezer Sibley (in *A Key to
Physic, and the Occult Sciences: opening to mental view, the system and
order of the interior and exterior heavens; the analogy betwixt angels,
and spirits of men*, 1794) and eventually Carlyle; a post-Rabelaisian
world of jumbled discourses rather than social structures, culled
from competing disciplines, some anti-scientific, others not, which
Bakhtin would have well understood if he had stumbled upon
counter-nerve. For some sense of this tradition of counter-nerve
before the seventeenth century, see Brian Vickers, *Scientific and

Occult Mentalities in the Renaissance, Cambridge, 1984. It is a tradition that flowered throughout Europe, as rich and diverse (if not empirically predictive) as that of the nerves. For example, de Valmont, a French speculator, produced a long *Dissertation sur les Maléfices et les Sorciers selon les principes de la théologie et de la physique, ou l'on examine en particulier l'état de la fille de Tourcoing,* Tourcoing, 1752, dealing with witchcraft in relation to nervous physiology, and there were others throughout the period who continued to believe that the nerves could be manipulated in supernatural ways: alchemically, zodiacally, nutritionally, demonically. Throughout the nineteenth century, there were attempts to retrieve this critique, as in Richard Robert Madden's (he was the author of a best-selling Victorian book about nightmares, gothic illusions, dreamlike monsters, male *couvade* – the entire spectral nightime world) 'Nervous States-Inspired Religious Vision', in *Phantasmata or Illusions and Fanaticisms of Protean Forms,* 2 vols, 1857, 2. 517, and in Walter Cooper Dendy's (he was the Sussex surgeon who also wrote poetry and travel literature) 'Fantasy from Sympathy with the Brain', in *Psyche: A Discourse on the Birth and Pilgrimage of Thought,* 1845, pp. 115–16. The most serious attempt to retrieve counter-nerve was made at the turn of this century by a French physician, Lucien Nass, who ransacked the closet of history to discover what extreme convulsive states had done to figures of the past; see his *Les Névroses de l'histoire,* Paris, 1908, a book as mystical as it is envious of the scientific.

13.   Looking at its empirical dimensions we can now see, in hindsight, that this was nothing less than the history of the anatomy and physiology of the eighteenth century, as Jacques Roger showed long ago in *Les Sciences de la Vie,* Paris, 1963.

14.   Cullen *Vitalism,* 1750; see also n. 75. The role played by the nerves in the Enlightment debates over racism was considerable and should not be minimised by scholars interested in the eighteenth-century discourses of sex, race and gender. For one development, see G. S. Rousseau, 'Le Cat and the Physiology of Negroes', *Racism in the Eighteenth Century,* ed. Harold Pagliaro, Cleveland, 1973 pp. 369–87. The nerves were especially crucial in these debates; for example, R. C. Dallas, writing in a *History of the Maroons,* 2 vols, 1803, adjudged that negroes could never be integrated into 'cold climes' because their nerves and fibres could not withstand 'the pinching of frost' (I, pp. 200–1).

15.   See Maureen McNeil, *Under the Banner of Science: Erasmus Darwin and his Age,* Manchester, 1986, and Peter Morton, *The Vital Science: Biology and The Literary Imagination,* 1984, for discussion of the nerves in Darwin's works.

16.   Such prolific commentators on nerves in relation to health as Nicholas Robinson, George Cheyne and Robert Whytt had much to say on this subject. For Robinson, see: *A new system of the spleen, vapours, and hypochondriack melancholy; wherein all the decays of the nerves, and lownesses of the spirits are mechanically accounted for. To which is subjoined, a discourse upon the nature, cause, and cure of*

melancholy, madness, and lunacy, 1729 and *A new theory of physick and diseases, founded on the principles of the Newtonian philosophy*, 1729.

17. Some idea of the range of this application in biology is found in Brian Easlea, *Witch hunting, Magic and the New Philosophy*, Brighton, Sussex, 1980, esp. ch. 4; Shirley A. Roe, *Matter, Life and Generation: Eighteenth-Century Embryology and the Haller-Wolff Debate*, Cambridge, 1981, and 'John Turberville Needham and the Generation of Living Organisms', *Isis* 74, 1983, pp. 159–84; C. U. M. Smith, *The Problem of Life: An Essay in the Origins of Biological Thought*, London 1976.

18. England and Scotland did not practise a tradition requiring medical students to produce a Latin medical dissertation as did the Continental universities, but many medical treatises dealing with the nerves were written in English, as, for example, David Bayne's *New Essay On the Nerves*, 1738, or, a generation later, John Hill's (the notorious Renaissance man of mid-Georgian England sometimes publicly known as the 'Inspector' or the quack Dr Hill) *Construction of the Nerves*, 1768. In Germany, a spectacular medical treatise about the nerves not originally written as a university medical dissertation was J. F. Isenflamm's *Versuch einiger praktischen Anmerkungen über die Nerven zur Erläuterung verschiedener Krankheiten derselben, vornehmlich hypochondrischer und hysterischer*, Autälle, 1774. The Dutch, who produced the largest number of medical dissertations after the Germans, poured forth thesis upon thesis dealing with the bile in relation to nervous disorders, as in T. W. Gartzwyler's *De bile atra, ejusque effectibus*, Leyden, 1742. In Italy, many medical works on the nerves also appeared, such as Giovanni Giacinto Vogli's *Fluidi nervi in istoria*, Padua, 1720.

19. See Malcolm Flemyng, *Neuropathia: sive de morbis hypochondriacis et hystericis*, 1740. Flemyng, who was obsessed with mechanistic and vitalistic questions about the nerves, had also written 'A New Critical Exam of an Important Passage in Locke's "Essay On Human Understanding" to which is added an extract from the fifth book of anti-Lucretius, concerning the same subject . . .', 1751. John Armstrong, another physician who (like Flemyng) also wrote poetry, produced *The Art of Preserving Health*, 1744, a long didactic poem teaming with images of nerves, spirits and fibres.

20. Beckett's nervous laughter in his plays.

21. In James Makittrick Adair's *Medical Cautions for the Consideration of Invalids . . . Containing Essays on Fashionable Diseases*, Bath, 1786. Adair, MD, was a member of the Royal Medical Society, as well as Fellow of the College of Physicians in Edinburgh. The *Medical Cautions* was also perpetually sold by Dodsley in London, as it was a bestseller.

22. See John Evelyn, *The History of the Rebellionn*, 2 vols., 1850, 2. 281. The 'nervous style' in English prose is discussed below, in n. 41. Suffice it to say here that it had roots in Port Royal Grammar and in Ben Jonson's 'full-blooded style', whose rhetorical components

were correlated to the anatomical organs; but in Jonson style is skittish and fickle and can meander any sexual way, male or female, whereas the aesthetics of nervous prose during the Enlightenment always mandated its masculinity.

23. For the body politic as a phrase and concept in English, see David Armstrong, *Political Anatomy of the Body*, Cambridge, 1983; Martha Banta, 'Medical Therapies and the Body Politic', *Prospects, An Annual of American Cultural Studies*, ed. Jack Salzman, Cambridge, 1985; John O'Neill, *Five Bodies: The Human Shape of Modern Society*, Ithaca, 1985; and John Blacking, 'The Anthropology of the Body, *ASA Monographs*, ed. John Blacking, 1977, Monograph 15, pp. 19–21.

24. See John Lowde, *A Discourse concerning the nature of man . . . both in his natural and political capacity*, London, 1694.

25. An entire vocabulary of words originating as technical terms in anatomy that later lost their technical usage and became common household phrases begs for study. These include: tension, corruption, delicacy, irritation, sensibility. Indeed, much of the vocabulary of the School of Taste in the period from Reynolds to Wordsworth appropriated this technical anatomical language for its own aesthetic purposes; for discussion of this specific appropriation see G. S. Rousseau, 'The Language of the Nerves: A Chapter in Social and Linguistic History', *The Social History of Language*, eds. Peter Burke and Roy Porter, Oxford, 1991, in press.

26. This idea has been much discussed in our time in the works of Roland Barthes, Pierre Bourdieu, Nancy Cartwright, Paul Feyerabend, Michel Foucault, Ronald Giere, Jürgen Habermas, Ian Hacking, Mary Hesse, Karin Knorr-Cetina, T. S. Kuhn, Larry Laudan, Bruno Latour, Jean-François Lyotard, Michael Mulkav, Steven Shapin. Sharon Traweek.

27. The close tie between suicide and nerves was constantly noticed at that time, especially as applicable to the situation of persons in high rank and class. Later on, in the 1770s, as sentimental cults were more dispersed, and as increasingly more persons aped the habits of the great, suicide grew more common, its etiology and dynamic changing as well. In France, J. P. Falret called suicide a class malaise in *De l'hypochondrie et du suicide. Considérations sur les causes, sur le siège et le traitement de ces maladies, sur les moyens d'en arreter les progrès et d'en prévenir le développement*, Paris, 1822. The social history of suicide in the Enlightenment remains to be written.

28. For whatever complex reasons, the feminists have not explored this aspect of Richardson's masterpiece, although they have understood so much else about it. A broad approach is found in Catherine Gallagher and Thomas Lacqueur, eds, *The Making of the Modern Body*, Berkeley and Los Angeles, 1986; see also Ann van Sant's forthcoming study of sensibility and the novel (Cambridge, 1991).

29. See Adam Smith, *Theory of Moral Sentiments*, Edinburgh: 1759.

30. James Makittrick Adair, *Essays on Fashionable Diseases*, 1786.

31. That is, in the theoretical sense that semiotics provides the deepest clue to the concept of the 'fibre' (here one wants to say nerve-centre,

except for the obvious ineptitude) of a culture; see Tzvetan Todorov, *The Conquest of America*, New York, 1985. Good work in this semiotic vein that is also particularly germane to the cultural history of the Enlightenment is found in Sylvain Auroux, *La Sémiotique des encyclopédistes: Essai d'épistémologie historique des sciences du language*, Paris, Payot, 1979.

32.   Henrietta Knight [Lady Luxborough], *Letters of Lady Luxborough . . . to the poet William Shenstone*, London, 1775.

33.   Tonic strength then denoted the degree of essential health of the nerves, its opposite being a state of morbid weakness, but there were many synonyms, common usages, and metaphoric abbreviations (that is, exquisite delicacy) applied linguistically as well. By the 1730s a dense metaphoric jungle of words describing this constellation, both healthy and diseased, had arisen. In his dialogical *Treatise of the hypochondriack and hysterick diseases*, 1711, Mandeville often enquires about the meaning of the 'tonic strength' of the nerves; see pp. 160, 172; later on John Armstrong versified some of the same ideas of tonic strength in his long didactic poem, *The Art of Preserving Health*, 1744. More recently, the late Raymond Williams has teased out some of the extended metaphors of sensibility in *Keywords: a vocabulary of culture and society*, 1976, pp. 235–8, but without referring to the great nervous underbelly – anatomically and metaphorically – of the development. If he had, he would have discovered a rich untapped vocabulary of phrases such as 'tonic strength', 'essential tension', 'exquisite tautness', and 'irritable', which were originally medical, but which by mid-century had passed into common parlance as part of the diverse cults of sensibility, about which more is said below. Moreover, tonic strength of the nerves was believed by many of the so-called 'nerve doctors' to be seasonal, producing the most 'tonic period' in the spring and summer, when nerves could enjoy the benefits of the six non-naturals (exercise, diet, good air, sleep, regular evacuation, passions); their worst as the leaves were falling under cold, grey, dark skies; see the medical exposition of this theory in Andrew Wilson, MD, *Short Remarks on Autumnal Disorders of the Bowels*, Newcastle upon Tyne, 1765.

34.   The great nerve doctors of the day included, in England, such well-known authors as Thomas Willis, perhaps the first physician to elevate the nerves; Thomas Sydenham, important for his theory of hysteria, as well as his generally empirical approach to nervous disorders; Bernard Mandeville; George Cheyne, whose *English Malady*, 1733, was one of the century's best-selling books; Robert Whytt, the so-called philosophical doctor, whose *Observations on the nature, causes, and cure of those disorders which have been commonly called nervous, hypochondriac, or hysteric*, Edinburgh, 1765, became the classic statement of his generation; Thomas Coe, Francis Adair, and many others. Their lives and practices beg for a proper narrative. Even John Fothergill, Johnson's friend, whose medical practice did not specialise in the nerves, wrote *An Account*

of a Painful Affection of the Nerves of the Face, Commonly Called Tic Douloureux, 1804.

35. New Historicism has further shown us why these doctors were bound to exert terrific power and sway in a society as stratified and hierarchical as that between 1660 and 1820 in England, the so-called long eighteenth century; see D. Veeser, The New Historicism, New York, 1989.

36. Henrietta Knight [Lady Luxborough], Letters of Lady Luxborough . . . to the poet William Shenstone, London, 1775.

37. Mrs Ralph Allen, an educated woman whose great parlour and reception rooms in Bath could be considered the English equivalent of a salon, would have known more than most mothers of the period about the intimacy between the fevers of their children and the inflammation of the nerves; it had been spelled out by many of the nerve doctors she herself had heard pronounce on these matters in the privacy of her own home; see Thomas Kirkland, MD, A Treatise on Child-Bed Fevers . . . to which are prefixed two dissertations, the one on the Brain and Nerves; the Other on the Sympathy of the Nerves, and on Different Kinds of Irritability, 1774, esp. pp. 168–172.

38. See C. F. Mullett, ed., The Letters of Dr George Cheyne to the Countess of Huntingdon, San Marino, Calif, 1940. Richardson's prose is permeated with the language of the nerves which forms an intrinsic part of his version of sensibility; for his personal commentary about nerves, see Anna L. Barbauld ed., The Correspondence of Samuel Richardson, 1804, 4, pp. 30, 283–4, and Raymond Stephanson, 'Richardson's "Nerves": The Physiology of Sensibility in Clarissa,' Journal of the History of Ideas 49, 1988, pp. 267–85. At this time nervous mythology was intrinsically tied to myths about the English nation and their developing nationalism as the most melancholic people on earth: depressed by their perpetually foul weather, dispirited by new stresses of high living, even unusually suicidal; as the poet Thomas Gray would say in a letter dated 27 May 1742, a nation epidemically stricken by 'White Melancholy' and 'Leucocholy'.

39. Frances Burney, Evelina, ed. Edward A. Bloom, 1968, p. 286 (vol. 3, letter III), where Mr. Lovel tells Lady Louisa Larpent that 'Your Ladyship's constitution is infinitely delicate', to which Louisa replies: 'Indeed it is,' cried she, in a low voice, 'I am nerve all over!'

40. Register of Folly, 1773. See also Peter Wagner, ed., Christopher Anstey: The New Bath Guide, Hildesheim, 1989.

41. Johnson's 'nervous prose' has received some attention as 'masculine' and 'energetic'; see Cecil S. Emden, 'Rythmical Features in Dr Johnson's Prose', RES 25, 1949, pp. 38–54; John Arthos, The Language of Natural Description in Eighteenth-Century Poetry, Ann Arbor, 1949; W. V. Reynolds, 'Johnson's Opinions on Prose Style', RES 9, 1933, p. 433–46; and the classic study by W. K. Wimsatt, Philosophic Words, New Haven, 1948. But the development of an Enlightenment nervous style at large, crossing national boundaries and different

cultures, has not been viewed within the contexts of the semiotic of the nerves. Considered synoptically, nervous style was an ellision for all things masculine in language, tough, strong, assertive, taut, concise – anything but feminine and soft, loose and spacious, weak and flaccid. It was a much admired, if also phallocratic, style in the mid-eighteenth century, whose cultural production and dynamic has not yet been explored. Fielding, Johnson, Smollett, Goldsmith – all were decorated, so to speak, at one time or another, by some *male* critic or commentator, as their critical heritages show, for displaying this nervous *je ne sais quoi* in their prose, no one more so than the second of these, the literary lion of the age; and when Charles Churchill, the decadent satirist of the 1760s, commented in *The Apology* (line 164) on Smollett's 'nervous weakness', his ironic inversion merely underscored the opposite, that is, that an irritable temperament in real life had produced such a 'nervous style' in art. Elsewhere, Dr James Drake, a medical doctor whose tropes are ridiculed and whose metaphors are satirised in the pages of Sterne's *Tristram Shandy*, and a man who had written the most popular textbook of anatomy in a generation until Cheselden's replaced it in the 1730s, summed up 'nervous style' succinctly when he wrote of a colleague's that 'it [his prose style], both *Latin*, and *English*, was Manly yet Easie; Concise, yet Clear and Expressive'; see James Drake, *Anthropologia Novum*, 1707, p. ix. A much fuller discusion of nervous style is found in Rousseau in *The Social History of Language*, (see note 25).

42.   Much has been written about Mesmer, of course, in many languages and countries, but often without clear sight of the direct role he played in nerve therapy. But what was animal magnetism if not the strongest stimulus the nerves could receive from an artificial, external source?

43.   The late eighteenth-century was the era *par excellence* of developmental patent medicine, the first patent medicines having been brought out in the 1770s after the Patent Office had opened in England; it is not surprising that a flurry of these quack therapies and remedies would be rushed to the public before they could be scrutinised by the officers of the Patent Office. See J. H. Young, *The Toadstool Millionaires*, Princeton, 1961.

44.   Lewis Knapp, ed., *The Adventures of Humphry Clinker*, Oxford, 1966, 34.

45.   Matthew Bramble, Smollett's last hero, serves as a perfect example of his maker's (Smollett's) intuition. Bramble has spent much of his life trying to understand his 'nerves', only to discover that they continue to elude him.

46.   Sion House MSS.

47.   Dr William Derry has compiled a still unpublished mss archive of the eighteenth-century Bath doctors. As early as 1699 the soothing effects of these spa waters specifically on the *nerves* had been commented upon (Benjamin Allen, *The Natural History of the Chalybeat and Purging Waters of England*, 1699). A generation later,

Dr Thomas Guidott claimed that the restoration of the nerves to health was the principal value of a visit to the pump rooms (Thomas Guidott, *An Apology for the Bath*, 1724), indicating how well-understood stress already was in developing urban sprawl. But British Enlightenment theory did not merely generate abstract discussion of societal stress; it explicitly located that stress in a particular part of the anatomy in an attempt to discover how the nerves could be repaired and strengthened after depletion through wear and tear. For nerves in relation to social rank and class in Bath society, see Georges Lamoine, '*La vie littéraire de Bath et de Bristol 1750–1800*' (University of Paris III doctoral dissertation, 1978). Comments on Bath doctors and their patients, sorted out by class and wealth, are mentioned in an anonymous tract in the British Library: *Two Letters from a Physician in London, to A Gentleman at Bath . . . with some Observations on the Present . . .*, 1744. Useful work on Dr George Cheyne at Bath is also being conducted at present by Dr Anita Guerrini. Most of all, though, it is necessary to demonstrate how this semiotics and mythology of nerves reflected views then held regarding gender, class and race.

48. Dr Richard Mead, thought by some to be the nation's leading physician and a former President of the Royal Society, also wrote about the nerves, especially within the terms of Newtonian aether; see his *Mechanical Account of Poisons*, 1702, pp. 9–21, reprinted in his *Collected Works* 1762, pp. 455–61 for nervous juices and fluids.

49. A useful study of Tissot's theory of nerves in relation to his medical practice and therapy is found in Heinrich Walther Bucher, 'Tissot und sein Traité des Nerfs,' *Zürcher Medizingeschichtlicher Abhandlungen*, ed. E. H. Ackerknecht, Zurich, 1958.

50. If cultural history crosses the lines of traditional disciplines and teaches us how to view these boundaries and borders with scepticism, it also allows us to retrieve lost discourses such as those of the crucial nerve, as Weisskopf in our opening section would say; and within this specific domain it demonstrates that Adair merits a full-length biography, as do Dr George Cheyne and the Bath eccentric and proflic commentator Phillip Thicknesse. Useful information about Cheyne's career as the doyen of 'nerve doctors' is found in William Falconer, *Remarks on Dr. Cheyne's Essay on Health and Long Life*, Bath: Leake, 1745.

51. James Makittrick Adair, 'Medical Cautions for the Consideration of Invalids', 1786, in *Essays on Fashionable Diseases*, 1786.

52. Ibid., 4–9.

53. Thomas Coe, *A Treatise on Biliary Concretions*, 1757. Coe, like other leading physicians (Cadogan, Hill, Robinson) claimed that the gout could be an entirely 'nervous affliction' whose first sign was the debilitation of the nerves and fibres.

54. George Cheyne, *The English Malady: Or a Treatise of Nervous Diseases of All Kinds*, Bath and London, 1733.

55. See Thomas Dover, *The Ancient Physician's Legacy*, 1733, which went through several editions in only a few years and was trans-

lated into French within twelve months as *Leys d'un ancien médicin àa sa Patrie*, The Hague, 1734.

56.   This direct link between nerves and hysteria requires full treatment, and is being discussed in a book by G. S. Rousseau and Roy Porter called *Hysteria in Western Civilization*, now in preparation at the University of California Press. Briefly, the theory of the eighteenth-century (in so far as one can reduce its diversity and generalise about it) was that all mental and emotional states depend on this elasticity or tightness of the nerves. Mechanists and vitalists alike, indeed most others too, shared in the belief, especially in the notion of tension as the key element. Through this doctrine the looser cultural concept of 'tension' between persons, and even more internally between one part of the psyche and another, arose, and was eventually metaphorised into popular culture at large as a psychological state. The precise mechanisms by which the nerves interacted with fluids in different degrees of tension, often causing melancholy and even the more extreme hypochondriasis (in men) and hysteria (in women), was the subject of many medical dissertations in Europe; see, the material presented in the Appendix below.

57.   Adair, *Essays on Fashionable Diseases*, 1786, p. 12. As a medical theorist Adair had been much influenced by the Montpellier medical writer François Boissier de Sauvages, a Stahlian vitalist who believed that the soul (brain too?) activated the nervous mechanisms of the body, whose *Nosologia methodica*, 1768, represents an extreme Linnanean application to taxonomise all disease.

58.   The imagination was becoming medicalised under the influence of the seventeenth-century mechanists, and became increasingly so in the eighteenth century; for this development, see G. S. Rousseau, 'Science and the Discovery of the Imagination in Enlightened England', *Eighteenth-Century Studies* III, 1969, pp. 108–5; for the Aristotelian tradition, see Michael V. Wedlin, *Mind and the Imagination in Aristotle*, New Haven, 1989. Some of this work, as found in C. G. Gross, *De morbis imaginariis hypochondriacorum*, 1755, specifically addressed the imagination in relation to somatic diseases generated in the locale of the hypochondrium. In 1691, Timothy Rogers, a sedentary MA from Oxford, published a confessional treatise, *A Discourse concerning Trouble of Mind, and the Disease of Melancholy, linking mind and melancholy through the medium of the Nerves.* Others, such as the German physician J. F. Mossdorff, writing *De valetudinariis imaginariis, von Menschen, die aus Einbildung kranck werden*, 1721, were more concerned with illnesses that had no detectable somatic manifestations (that is, what we would call psychological conditions). In Italy, Lodovico Antonio Muratori, the empirical philosopher–poet whose book on imagination and dreams (1747) was widely discussed, suggested that the imagination played a central role in the formation of illness. In England, J. Richardson (of Newent) wrote *Thoughts upon thinking, or, a new theory of the human mind; wherein a physical rationale of the formation of our ideas, the passions, dreaming, and every faculty of the soul is*

attempted upon principles entirely new, 1755, and suggested that the nerves mediate between ideas and illness. In all these discussions, and others, the nerves played a central role.

59. I have found only one copy of this obscure work, in the BL.

60. Richard Kuhn has surveyed the long tradition in *The Demon of Noontide: Ennui in Western Literature*, Princeton, 1976, but is rather inadequate on the Enlightment, leaving out such obvious candidates as melancholic Boswell – perhaps the greatest sufferer of the century, as his Dutch journals show – who even titled his most sustained work of periodical journalism *The Hypochondriack;* see the edition by Marjorie Bailey called *Boswell's Column*, 1951.

61. See Anna L. Barbauld, ed., *The Correspondence of Samuel Richardson*, 1804, 4, p. 30.

62. Ian Watt, *The Rise of the Novel*, Berkeley and Los Angeles, 1957, p. 184.

63. George Sherburn, ed., *The Correspondence of Alexander Pope*, Oxford, 1956, IV, p. 526. In his *Essay on the Genius and Writings of Pope*, 1762, Joseph Warton attempts to show that much of Pope's genius was tied to a delicate sensibility founded on a nervous personality. Warton also considered 'nervous' composition as one of 'three different species,' which he adumbrates in the *Essay*, I, p. 170. Adam Smith commented in his *Theory of Moral Sentiments*, Edinburgh, 1759, on the stylistic (i.e. couplet) 'nervous precision of Mr. Pope'.

64. Misaurus Philander, *The Honour of the Gout*, 1720, p. 18–19.

65. The full title deserves a place in the history of stress-related illnesses associated with global economic depression, such as the worldwide crash of 1929; see John Midriff, *Observations on the Spleen and Vapours; Containing Remarkable Cases of Persons of both Sexes, and all Ranks, from the aspiring Directors to the Humble Bubbler, who have been miserably afflicted with these Melancholy Disorders since the Fall of the South-sea, and other publick Stocks; with the proper Method for their Recovery, according to the new and uncommon Circumstances of each Case*, 1721.

66. William Smith, *A Dissertation upon the Nervous System*, 1768, whose purpose was to show its influence upon the soul. In France, Le Camus, a physician, also constructed a *Médecine de l'Esprit*, 1769, showing the link between the nerves and the soul.

67. Boswell's melancholy has been studied by Alan Ingram in *Boswell's Gloom*, London, 1984, but without attention to the scientific, medical, or cultural semiotics of the matter.

68. See Elizabeth Carter, *The Correspondence of Elizabeth Carter and Catherine Talbot*, 4 vols, 1809, 2, p. 156. More generally the passions, reason, morality and insanity were linked together specifically by the nervous apparatus, as suggested here and in dozens of other similar passages in different kinds of writing by both sexes. Two generations after Elizabeth Carter wrote, the prolific (if also prolix) Reverend Trusler, the moraliser of Hogarth who made his fortune by combining alleged medical expertise with clerical eccentricity,

claimed to have penetrated to the truth about *cowardice* – in his view the most *feminine* of all moral defects, implying just the kind of *genderised nerves* we have seen gradually developing throughout the century. Trusler wrote in his *Memoirs,* Bath, 1806, p. 46:

> What then is cowardice? – It is the effect of weak nerves – Who would not be brave if he could? *Acquired* courage may be the result of strong reasoning, refined courage, and a sense of duty, as in the simple case of the officer: *mechanical* courage, is often the effect of example, as in the soldier: – one man keeps the line, because another does, they consider themselves merely as parts of a great machine; but *natural* courage is the effect of strong nerves, which every man is not blessed with [compare Mrs Donnellan's advice to Samuel Richardson and my synoptic paradigm in note 61 above]. I might pity a coward, but I would not condemn him for want of resolution, more than I would condemn a weak man for want of strength. They are, like *nerves,* gifts of Providence bestowed on particular men.

69.   Ibid, 2, p. 156.

70.   Robert Halsband, ed , *The Complete Letters of Lady Mary Wortley Montagu,* Oxford, 1965, II, 63.

71.   See Frank H. Ellis, ed., *Poems on Affairs of State: Augustan Satirical Verse, 1660–1714, Volume VI: 1697–1704,* New Haven, 1970, 64, lines 35–36.

72.   *European Magazine,* 1812. William Cowper, the poet, almost blindly subscribed to a genderised version of nerves, but the myth was so broadly disseminated throughout his culture that one can hardly fault him for being less vigilant than he was to its sexual resonances. See his letter to the Reverend Unwin in *Collected Letters,* ed. Thomas Wright, 1780. for 2 July, 1780:

> . . . I like your epitaph, except that I doubt the propriety of the word immaturus; which I think, is rather applicable to fruits than flowers; and except the last pentameter, the assertion it contains being rather too obvious a thought to finish with: not that I think an epitaph should be pointed like an epigram. But still there is a closeness of thought and expression necessary in the conclusion of all these little things, that they may leave an agreeable flavour upon the plate. What ever is short should be nervous, masculine, and compact. Little men are so; and little poems should be so; because, where the work is short the author has no right to the plea of weariness; and laziness is never admitted as an available excuse in anything.

73.   'Of the Hypp', is to be found in the *Universal Spectator,* November 18, no. 214; *Gentleman's Magazine,* 2, 1732, 1062–63.

74.   See Pierre Fedida, 'Les Exercises de l'imagination et la commotion sur la masse des nerfs: un érotisme de tête,' in *Oeuvres complètes du Marquis de Sade,* 16 vols, Paris, 1967, 9, p. 613–25. Perceptive discussion of the nerves in Sade's prose is found in David Morris, 'The Discourses of Pain in Revolutionary France,' in G. S. Rousseau (ed.) *The Languages of Psyche: Mind and Body in Enlightenment*

Thought, Berkeley and Los Angeles, 1990, pp. 291–300. While Sade was generating his fictional version of moral and revolutionary hedonism, Cabanis, among the most philosophical of physicians of the post-revolutionary period, correlated the nerves to specific stages of human perfection in an almost Lamarckean and pre-Darwinian sense; see Pierre-Jean-Georges Cabanis, *On the Relations Between the Physical and Moral Aspects of Man*, ed. George Mora, 2 vols, Baltimore, 1981.

75.   See William Cullen, *Nosologia;* translated as *Nosology; or, a Systematic arrangement of diseases*, Edinburgh, 1768; 2nd edn, 1800, p. 238. J. M. Lopez Pinero has traced the tradition from Willis and Cullen down to current time in his *Historical Origins of the Concept of Neurosis*, Cambridge, 1983.

76.   *The Works of John Dryden, The California Dryden*, ed. H. T. Swedenberg *et al.* 18 vols, Berkeley and Los Angeles, 1961–2, p. 10.

77.   In the same Paris milieu in which Gautier and his fellow decadents flourished, Pierre Jules Descot, a physician, published *Dissertation sur les affections locales des nerfs*, Paris, 1882, showing how all pleasure and pain was situated in the nerves at the tip of the genitals and why these erotogeneous zones were consequently the most crucial part of human anatomy, for pleasure as well as reproduction.

78.   *The Works of Charles Lamb*, 7 vols, 1903–5. Across the English Channel, the literary-medical milieu in England was also interwoven with figures having an impact in each realm. In Lamb's world, the physician-poet Thomas Trotter could publish a significant study of *A View of the Nervous Temperament*, 1807, which correlated personality types according to their anatomical –physiological constitutions, as well as a volume called *Sea Weeds: Poems written on various occasions, [written] chiefly during a naval life*, Newcastle and London, 1829.

79.   Taking her cue from Cheyne's *English Malady* of 1733 (see note 34 above), Professor Elaine Showalter has studied the conditions under which the nerves were invoked in analyses of female somatic and psychogenic disorders in the nineteenth century; see *The Female Malady: Women, Madness and English Culture, 1830–1980*, 1987. During the peak of high Victorianism, countless doctors wrote about the nerves; in Germany, discourses of the nerve were as important as they were in England, and treatises such as the German physician M. H. Romberg's (*Nervous Diseases of Man*, 1853) were quickly translated into English.

80.   This link remains the one to be explored among various discourses, and it is a glaring shortcoming of this essay that I do not undertake it here. My excuse (such as it is) that I have not had the space will perhaps not stand up, but I nevertheless wish to acknowledge how crucial it seems to me to establish these networks of connection.

81.   The extraordinary matter to be grasped here is not that Austen should allow common parlance about nerves to invade her highly eclectic prose vocabulary, but rather that she permits it without

more irony, as any systematic lexical study of her use of nervous language would show. (I have collected over two dozen of these passages but do not include them here for reasons of space). Whole ranges of scientific vocabularies and their metaphors are denied entry to her fictive discourse; but the nerves enter with little if any resistance; the question is why. Perhaps Austen knew more about neural medicine than has been credited to her. As she was composing her novels of sentiment and delicacy, her *Emma* and *Mansfield Park* (which has the largest number of uses of nervous vocabulary and which is drenched in the female sensibility of Richardson and Frances Burney), English doctors in her geographical locale, such as Dr M. Hall, were writing *On the mimoses: or, A descriptive, diagnostic and practical essay on the affections usually denominated dyspeptic, hypochondriac, bilious, nervous, chlorotic, hysteric*, 1818.

82.   For this tradition, see note 9 above and Robert Brissenden, *Virtue in Distress: Studies in the Novel of Sentiment from Richardson to Sade* London 1974.

83.   Coleridge's anatomy and medicine have not received the attention they deserve, despite Trevor H. Levere's excellent study of his science, *Poetry Realized in Nature: Samuel Tayor Coleridge and Early Nineteenth-Century Science*, New York, 1981; without understanding these two realms one cannot comprehend Coleridge's contribution to the discourse of the nerves. One would have thought that his philosophical lineage as a Hartleyan and his aesthetics of immediacy would automatically privilege the nerves; see Wallace Jackson, *Immediacy: the Development of a Critical Concept from Addison to Coleridge*, Amsterdam, 1973; but although Coleridge writes abundantly about immediacy there is less material about nerves in his prose than one would have imagined; nevertheless see his pronouncements 'On Sensibility,' in *Complete Works*, Princeton: Bollingen, 1962–. At the same time Coleridge was pronouncing, such scientific associates of his as Drs Thomas Young (the prolific naturalist who wrote about colour theory) and John Cooke (the president of the Medico-Chirurgical Society) were also writing about the nerves: Young especially in a *Treatise on Phthisis*, 1822, and Cooke in a two-volume *Treatise on Nervous Diseases*, 1823; Boston edn 1824.

84.   Virginia Woolf's relation to this tradition merits some attention, not least because she herself was among the most 'nervous' of writers and connected the creative act to the state of the nerves during creation. Like Mary Shelley's mad scientist, whose 'nervous agony' was renewed at the mere sight of a 'chemical instrument' ever since the appearance of his vision, she often composed under nervous duress and extreme agitation. The passage in *To the Lighthouse* in which Lily is struggling with her painting captures this essential belief about the relation of physiology, desire and artistic creation: 'Phrases came. Visions came. Beautiful pictures. Beautiful phrases. But what she wished to get hold of was that very jar on the nerves –

the thing itself before it has been made anything.' Sterne was Woolf's favourite prose writer of the eighteenth century, though she also read and delighted in the witty prose of Addison and Steele (as one would know from reading *Orlando*); yet it is inconceivable that in her constant reading of Sterne she had overlooked his own fascination with nervous prose (note 41 above) and the various ways in which Sterne and his contemporaries had transformed the discourse of animal spirits, nerves and fibres – literally from the first paragraph of *Tristram Shandy* – turning it upside-down and metaphorising and satirising medical dissertations about nerves of just the type discussed in this essay. For further discussion of Sterne in this sense, see G. S. Rousseau, 'Smollett and Sterne: A Revaluation', *Archiv für das Studium der neuren sprachen und Litteraturen*, CCVII, 1972, pp. 286–97. Yet Woolf should be viewed in a wider, and more medical, context than this. She was growing up in a late Victorian England that had heard (for example) medically trained lecturers like Andrew Wilson speaking on *The Origin of Nerves. A Lecture Delivered Before the Sunday Lecture Society on 24 December 1878*, London, 1879. And she herself was profoundly interested in theories of nervous disorders and neurosis, in part as a result of her own mental states when she composed, but also in view of her oblique sexuality. Her diaries continually exude wrenching remarks about the effort her writing wrung from her: 'it calls upon every nerve to hold itself taut'. Later on, in her mature years during the 1920s, there was talk everywhere – Havelock Ellis, Edward Carpenter, D. H. Lawrence, Walt Whitman, Otto Weininger, even within the Bloomsbury circle – about the relation of nervous mechanism and physiology in sex and love. In passing, one suspects that Woolf might have sympathised with Schreber's analysis of his own nervous condition; see *Daniel Paul Schreber: Memoirs of My Nervous Illness*, 1955.

85.   A. Alvarez, *The Savage God: A Study of Suicide*, New York, 1970, p. 19. J. Babinski and J. Froment, *Hysteria or Pithiatism and Reflex Nervous Disorders in the Neurology of War*, 1918 p. 311.

86.   By the turn of this century a whole school of thought had developed in the belief that nervous ailments could be treated successfully by moral therapies; see Arnold Stocker, *Le traitement moral des nerveux*, Geneva, 1945. Most have been discredited by now.

87.   But now, in our post-disciplinary age, the discourse of postmodernism, as Habermas has suggested, brings them together.

APPENDIX

These dissertations were written largely by medical students and their professors, although some (indeed the first work, by Albert, and the cultural historical work by Dubois d'Amiens) were composed by non-medical writers. The reader will soon see that their number dramatically increased in the nineteenth century, although the practice was already institutionally fixed by the eighteenth century, where hardly a year goes by without several such tracts appearing. The list below is highly selective. An exhaustive bibliography would be many times larger, and might even be impossible to compile, given the large number of such works that have disappeared and the poor handwritten catalogues of most Continental libraries during the eighteenth century.

J. Albert, *Essai sur l'hypochondrie* (Paris, 1813).
M. Albertus, *De hypochondriaco-hysterico malo* (Halle, 1703).
T. H. Arens, *De mali hypochondriaci symptomatis et causis* (Berlin, 1844).
F. Arnisaeus, *De malo hypochondriaco* (Copenhagen, 1654).
G. J. A. Baltz, *De malo hypochondriaco* (Berlin, 1845).
J. F. Becker, *De morbo hypochondriaco* (Berlin, 1820).
J. C. Below, *Dissertatio casum matronae hypochondriacae exhibens* (Erfurt, 1685).
J. Ben, *De suffocatione hypochondriaca* (Leiden, 1683).
C. A. Berthelen, *De hypochondriasis origine* (Leipzig, 1846).
A. L. Birotheau, *Sur l'hypochondrie* (Paris, 1830).
Sir Richard Blackmore. *A treatise of the Spleen and Vapours: or hypochondriacal and hysterical affections, with three discourses in the nature and cure of the cholick, melancholy, and palsies. Never before published* (London, 1725).
E. Blum, *De dolore hypochondriaco, vulgo sed falso putato splenetico* (Leipzig, 1671).
J. G. Boemer, *De hypochondria* (Berlin, 1817).
E. J. F. Bourrelly, *Sur l'hypochondrie* (Paris, 1819).
F. Bouteiller, *Essai sur l'hypochondrie* (Paris, 1820).
J. Bouwer, *De affectione hypochondriaca* (Utrecht, 1688).
J. L. Brachet, *Recherches sur la nature et le siège de l'hystérie et de l'hypochondrie* (Paris, 1832).
P. Brand, *De malo hypochondriaco* (Copenhagen, 1676).
J. C. C. Brandt, *De malo hypochondriaco rite cognoscendo* (Wittenberg, 1811).
J. H. Brechtfeld, *De morbo hypochondriaco* (Helmstedt, 1662).
H. L. J. Brequin, *Sur l'hypochondrie* (Paris, 1831).
P. A. Brunereau, *Du siège, de la nature, des causes de l'hypochondrie* (Paris, 1857).
C. G. Burghart, *De malo sic dicto hypochondriaco* (Wittenberg, 1703).
J. Cahen, *De natura atque causis hypochondriae* (Berlin, 1843).
J. H. Calestroupat, *Sur l'hypochondrie* (Paris, 1823).
A. F. V. Carilian, *Sur l'hystérie et l'hypochondrie* (Paris, 1818).
J. B. L. P. Castagnon, *Essai sur l'hypochondrie* (Paris, 1858).
H. Cellarius, *De affectu hypochondriaco* (Jena, 1671).

M. Chabert, *De hypochondria* (Paris, 1805).

J. P. Champagne, *Sur l'hypochondrie* (Paris, 1827).

A. E. C. A. Chauvin, *Parallèle de l'hypochondrie avec la mélancholie* (Strasbourg, 1824).

L. H. Chevalier, *Sur l'hypochondrie* (Paris, 1820).

G. Clasius, *De therapia passionis hypochondriacae* (Halle, 1713).

C. C. Colnot, *Etude sur le délire hypochondriaque* (Paris, 1878).

M. A. Colohri, *De passione hypochondriaca* (Frankfurt, 1751).

D. Corbet, *De hypochondriasi* (Edinburgh, 1821).

G. S. Cotta, *Dissertatio aegrum chylificatione laesa hypochondriaca laborantem exhibens* (Jena, 1689).

J. Cowling, *De hypochondriasi* (Edinburgh, 1768).

T. Cupples, *De hypochondriasis causis* (Edinburgh, 1777).

A. L. Dejoye, *Essai sur l'hypochondrie* (Paris, 1866).

H. G. Delagrye, *De l'hypochondrie* (Paris, 1817).

Nicholas François Dellehe, *Tentamen medicum de affectione hypochondriaca seu hysterica* (Avignon, 1788).

J. B. Derivaux, *Essai sur l'hypochondrie* (Strasbourg, 1836).

E. F. Dubois, *Ueber das Wesen und die gründliche Heilung der Hypochondrie und Hysterie. Herausgegeben und mit einer Einleitung versehen von Dr. K. W. Ideler* (Berlin, 1840).

E. F. Dubois d'Amiens, *Histoire philosophique de l'hypochondrie et de l'hystérie* (Paris, 1837).

J. M. D. Duc, *Sur l'hypochondrie* (Paris, 1827).

G. Duché, *De la nature essentielle de hypochondrie* (Paris, 1833).

A. Dufour, *Etude sur l'hypochondrie et de délire hypochondriaque* (Paris, 1860).

J. C. Dupont, *Recherches sur l'affection hypochondriaque* (Montpellier, 1798).

G. G. Dynnebier, *De morbo hypochondriaco* (Berlin, 1820).

J. F. Entlicher, *De hypochondriasi* (Prague, 1813).

G. Erdmann, *De hypochondriasi* (1847).

J. B. Ernoul-Provoté, *Essai sur l'hypochondrie* (Paris, 1816).

F. F. Ettling, *De hypochondriasi* (Berlin, 1850).

A. A. Etzel, *De morbo hypochondriaco* (Vienna, 1789).

G. B. Faber, *Ulterior expositio novae methodi Kaempfianae curandi morbos chronicos inveteratos, praecipue malum hypochondriacum* (Tübingen, 1755).

J. P. Falret, *De l'hypochondrie et du suicide. Considérations sur les causes, sur le siège et la traitement de ces maladies, sur les moyens d'en arrêter les progrès . . . le développement* (Paris, 1822).

J. Faure, *Sur l'hypochondrie* (Paris, 1823).

J. Feist, *Morbi hypochondriaci cum hysterico comparatio* (Berlin, 1819).

J. Fellner, *De hysteria et hypochondria* (Würzburg, 1837).

J. C. Fischer, *De malo hypochondriaco* (Erfurt, 1713).

Malcolm Flemyng, *Neuropathia; sive de morbis hypochondriacis et hystericis, etc.* (1740).

A. Fracassini, *Naturae morbi hypochondriaci ejusque curationis mechanica investigatio* (Verona, 1754).

L. Fraser, *De morbo hysterico sive hypochondriaco* (Edinburgh, 1750).

G. Fruth, *De hypochondria* (Munich, 1842).

M. Fuker, *Disquisitiones nonnullae circa hypochondriam* (1833).

S. V. Gadebusch, *De affectione hypochondriaca* (1685).

P. S. Garboe, *Experimenta quaedam circa malum hypochondriacum* (Halle, 1762).

G. M. Gattenhof and F. Zuccarinus, *Hypochondriasis* (Heidelberg, 1769).

F. P. Gauné, *Sur l'hypochondrie* (Paris, 1826).

M. Geiger, *Microcosmus hypochondriacus, sive de melancholia hypochondriaca tractatus* (Munich, 1652).

A. B. de La Geneste, *De morbo hypochondriaco* (Leiden, 1763).

J. A. Genser, *Dissertatio pathologiam mali hypochondriaci inquirens,* (Wittenburg 1797)

Oscar Giacchi, *L'isterismo e 'ipochondria avvero il malo nervosa . . . Giudizii fisio-clinici-sociali* (Milan, 1875).

W. Gibbons, *On hypochondrrasis* (Philadelphia, 1805).

M. Giraldus, *De singulari sensibilitate hypochondriacorum ejusque causis* (1749).

P. M. B. Goullin, *Sur l'hypochondrie* (Paris, 1821).

A. A. Grenet, *Sur l'hypochondrie* (Paris, 1840).

C. G. Gross, *De morbis imaginariis hypochondriacorum* (1755).

J. F. Haack, *De affectione hypochondriaca* (1678).

A. Hafner, *De hypochondriasi ut morbo coenaesthesis* (1808).

M.Hall, *On the mimoses: or A descriptive, diagnostic and practical essay on the affections usually denominated dyspeptic, hypochondriac, bilious, nervous, chlorotic, hysteric, etc.* (London, 1818).

A. Haro, *Considérations générales sur l'hypochondrie* (Strasbourg, 1834).

C. V. Hareaux, *Essai sur une variété d'hypocondrie particulière aux femmes de l'âge critique* (Paris, 1837).

A. Hay, *De affectionibus hystericis et hypochondriacis* (Leiden, 1765).

F. L. Hedenaberg, *De differentia et similiandinibus hypochondriae et hysteriae* (1815).

G. Heideman, *De hypochondriae caussis* (Berlin, 1838).

H. G. Herfelt, *De affectione hypochondriaca* (Duisberg, 1678).

J. G. Heyman, *De praecipuo literatorum morbo affectione hypochondriaco* (Leiden, 1732).

Nathaniel Highmore, *Exercitationes duae, quarum prior de passione hysterica, altera de affectione hypochondriaca.* 2d ed. (Amsterdam, 1660).

Nathaniel Highmore, *De hysterica et hypochondriaca passione. Responsio epistolaris ad Doctorem Willis* (London, 1670).

J. Hill, *Hypochondriasis. A practical treatise on the nature and cure of that disorder; commonly called the hyp and hypo* (London, 1766).

J. F. Isenflamm, *Versuch einiger praktischen Anmerkungen Ueber die Nerven zur Erläuterung verschiedener Krankheiten derselben, vornehmlich hypochondrisch und hysterischer* (Autälle, 1774).

J. M. Israel, *De hypochondriaco malo monita quaedam* (1798).

J. N. Jessenwanger, *Dissertatio sistens morbum hypochondriacum et hystericum* (1778).

D. A. Koch, *De infarctibus vasorum in infimo ventre ceu caussa plurium pathematum chronicorum, speciatim eorum, quae sub mali hypochondriaci nomine veniunt* (Strasbourg, 1752).

L. I. Kohen, *De morbo hypochondriaco* (1729).

V. Lebas, *Observation de mélancholie, et quelques propositions sur cette maladie* (Paris, 1820).

J. Le Blanc, *Sur l'hypochondrie* (Paris, 1826).

A. A. Lecadre, *Sur le siège et la nature de l'hypochondrie* (Paris, 1827).

J. G. Lehmann, *De duumviratu hypochondriorum* (Leipzig, 1689).

P. G. Léhu, *Sur la pathidie, vulgairement nommée hypochondrie, considérée en général, et particulièrement sous le rapport de son siège* (Paris, 1831).

J. G. Leidenfrost, *De mali hypochondriaci ad minimum sextuplici specie* (Duisberg, 1797).

J. G. Leisner, *De malo hypochondriaco-hysterico* (1749).

L. M. Le Siner, *De l'hypochondrie* (Paris, 1841).

Louyer-Villemary, *Sur l'hypochondrie* (Paris, 1802).

L. Löwenberg, *De hypochondria* (Berlin, 1841).

B. Mandeville, *A treatise of the hypochondriack and hysterick diseases* (London, 1730).

C. T. Matschke, *De stabilienda hypochondriae et hysteriae notione* (1806).

C. H. Matthiae, *Morbi hypochondriaci cum hysterico comparatio* (Würzburg, 1845).

A. Mecklenburg, *De hypochondria* (Berlin, 1851).

A. C. Meineke, *De vera morbi hypochondriaci sede indole, ac curatione* (1719).

J. Meyer, *De natura morbi hypochondriaci* (Berlin, 1867).

C. F. Michéa, *Traité pratique, dogmatique et critique de l'hypochondrie* (1845).

A. F. F. Mohring, *Dissertatio sistens cogitata quaedam de malo hypochondriaco atque hysterico* (1798).

C. Mongin-Montrol, *Sur l'hypochondrie* (Paris, 1823).

De Montallegry, *Hypochondrie-spleen ou névroses trisplanchniques. Observations relative à ces maladies, et leur traitement radical* (1841).

G. H. Morin, *De hypochondrie* (Paris, 1831).

L. Müller, *Dissertation sur le spasme et l'affection vaporeuse* (Strasbourg, 1813).

F. W. Nolte, *Die Hypochondrie* (Utrecht, 1840).

S. Ochlitius, *De passione hypochondriaca* (Jena, 1666).

J. J. Otto, *De malo hypochondriaco* (1722).

M. Pallier-Lapeyrière, *Coup d'œil philosophique sur l'hypochondrie* (Paris, 1837).

A. F. Pelgrom, *De morbo hypochondriaco* (Leiden, 1759).

William Perfect, *Cases of Insanity . . . Hypochondriacal Affection . . .* (London, 1781).

Joannes Fridericus de Pre, *Dissertatio inauguralis medica de melancholia hysterica . . .* (Erfunt, 1728).

F. Private, *Coup d'œil sur l'hypochondrie* (Paris, 1827).

J. T.Rauch, *De affectu hypochondriaco* (Jena, 1755).

E.H. Reichel, *De hypochondria et hysteria* (Jena, 1803).

J. Reid, *Essays on hypochondriacal and other nervous affections* (Philadelphia, 1817).

T. Remmets, *Ueber die Hypochondrie* (Bonn, 1872).

C. Retenbacher, *De mali hypochondriaci causa proxima* (1838).

J. E. Riemer, *De affectu hypochondriaco* (1728).

H. Rigius, *De affectione hypochondriaca* (1649).

C. Ringelmann, *Ueber die Natur, das Wesen und die Behandlung der Hypochondrie und Hysterie* (1824).

Nicholas Robinson, *A new system of the spleen, vapours, and hypochondriack melancholy; wherein all the decays of the nerves, and lownesses of the spirits are mechanically accounted for. To which is subjoined, a discourse upon the nature, cause, and cure of melancholy, madness and lunacy* (London, 1729).

A. Rossi, *De hypochondriasi* (1842).

G. Roth, *De hypochondriasi* (1833).

William Rowley, *A treatise on female, nervous, hysterical, hypochondriacial, bilious, convulsive disease; apoplexy & palsy with thoughts on madness & suicide, etc.* (London, 1788).

J. L. Rudiger, *De variabili hypochondriacorum mente* (1746).

H. O. Schacht, *De melancholia hypochondriaca* (1693).

E. Schiller, *De hypochondria* (Prague, 1841).

J. B. Schlosser, *Ueber die Hypochondrie* (Munich, 1838).

F. G. Schroeerus, *De morbo ex hypochondriis* (1760).

G. Schultz, *Dissertatione sistens aegrum laborantem malo hypochondriaco scorbutico* (1670).

W. G. Schuyt, *De differentia inter hypochondriacum et hysteriam* (Amsterdam, 1847).

S. Schwartz, *Nonnulla ad malum hypochondriacum spectantia* (1757).

C. D. Seboldt, *Mali hypochondriaci, veri ac nervose, seu morbi sine materie aucta, notio et natura* (1796).

J. F. Seyffert, *De hypochondriasi* (Leipzig, 1824).

J. Siess, *Dissertatio sistens ideam pathematum hypochondriaco-hystericorum cum singulari huc faciente historia morbi* (1780).

J. C. Sommer, *De melancholia imprimis hypochondriaca* (1706).

J. G. Sonnenmayer, *De vero ortu mali hypochondriaci et hysterici* (1769).

J. P. Spring, *De malo hypochondriaco* (Munich, 1758).

J. M. Starckloff, *De sputatione hypochondriacorum* (Halle, 1730).

J. Stark, *De malo hypochondriaco* (Edinburgh, 1783).

A. Staub, *Allgemeiner Leitfaden zur Bearbeitung der Hypochondrie und Hysterie* (Würzburg, 1826).

J. A. Steininger, *Centuria positionum medicarum de melancholia hypochondriaca* (Wittenberg, 1625).

J. C. Storck, *De malo hypochondriaco* (Altdorf, 1685).

L. Storr, *Untersuchungen über den Begriff, die Natur und die Heilbedingungen der Hypochondrie* (Stuttgart, 1805).

J. T. Strassburg, *De affectu hypochondriaco* (1696).

J. D. Strauss, *Dissertatio aegrum affectu hypochondriaco, capitisque steatomate laborantem exhibens* (Giessen, 1683).

J. L. Sustermann, *De valetudine ex hypochondriis* (Göttingen, 1752).

Thomas Sydenham, 'Processes Integri: Chap. 1: On the Affection called Hysteria in Women; and Hypochondriasis in Men.', *The Works of Thomas Sydenham*, trans. R. G. Latham, 2 vols, (London, 1848).

F. P. A. Tartivel, *De l'hypochondrie* (Paris, 1852).

L. Theill, *De malo hypochondriaco* (Jena, 1668).

P. Thewalt, *Ueber die Ursachen der Hypochondrie nebst einigen begleitenden Bemerkungen* (Würzburg, 1846).

J. C. Tode, *Nödig underwisning für hypochondrister som wilja rätt lära känna sitt tillstränd och förbättra det. Ofversättning fränstränd och förbättra det.* (Stockholm, 1809).

J. C. Troppinniger, *De malo hypochondriaco* (Leipzig, 1676).

W. Turner, *De morbo hypochondriaco* (Edinburgh, 1756).

D. van Buren, *De affectione hypochondriaco* (Leiden, 1711).

C. van der Haghen, *De melancholia hypochondriaca* (1715).

D. J. van der Meersch, *De hypochondria* (1817).

P. van Suchtelen, *De melancholia hypochondriaca* (1718).

P. Venables, *De hypochondriasi* (Edinburgh, 1803).

E. Vielloehner, *De hypochondriae et hysteriae differentiis* (Berlin, 1841).

J. C. I. Voigt, *Tractatus medicus Galeno-chymicus, de passione seu affectione hypochondriaca, authoritatibus Galeni et Hippocratis suffulsus* (Prague, 1678).

L. de Wahl, *De causa hypochondriae proxima* (Berlin, 1832).

G. Walther, *De mali hypochondriaci natura et causis* (Berlin, 1845).

G. Wehrmeister, *De hypochondriasi* (1846).

B. N. Weigelius, *De malo hypochondriaco* (1745).

Robert Whytt, *Observations on the nature, causes, and cure of those disorders which have been commonly called nervous, hypochondriac, or hysteric, to which are prefixed some remarks on the sympathy of the nerves.*, 2 edn. 8 vols (Edinburgh, 1765).

Thomas Willis, *Affectionum quae dicuntur hystericae et hypochondriacae, pathologia spasmodica vindicata, contra responsionem epistolarem Nathanael Highmori* (Leiden 1671).

C. F. Winneke, *De morbo hypochondriaco e plethora oriundo* (1792).

J. M. Wirtz, *De sede et causa proxima hypochondriae* (Bonn, 1830).

C. L. Wischke, *Mali hypochondriaci veri ac nervosi signa et diagnosis* (1795).

C. Witter, *De hypochondria* (Berlin, 1837).

T. Wittmaack, *Die Hypochondrie (Hyperaesthesia physica, Romberg) in pathologischer und therapeutischer Beziehung, nebst einigen vorgängigen Bemerkungen iiber die Bedeutung der psychischen Heilmittel* (Leipzig, 1857).

P. Zacchia, *De' mali hipochondriaci Libri tre* (Rome, 1644).

P. Zacchia, *De affectionibus hypochondriacis libri tres. Nunc in Latinum sermonem translati ab Alphonso Khonn* (1671).

G. V. Zeviani, *Del flato a favore degli ipocondriaci* (Verona, 1794).

K. J. Zimmermann, *Versuch über Hypochondrie und Hysterie* (Bamberg, 1816).

J. C. Zopef, *De malo hypochondriaco* (Jena, 1676).

C. Zurborn, *De hypochondriasi* (Berlin, 1845).

G. Zwingenberg, *De malo hypochondriaco* (Berlin, 1856).

4

Bodies of Thought: Thoughts about the Body in Eighteenth-Century England

Roy Porter

Roy Porter uses the polarity of mind and body to show how the praise of the former at the expense of the latter has been a recurring theme in Western culture, whether in medieval religion or twentieth-century Freudian theory.

The eighteenth century saw both the disciplining of the body and its 'aetherialisation' into invisibility. Porter discusses how recent historiographical trends depict an emerging capitalism taking advantage of the body's sensibility to pain to impose itself upon the mass of the population; other approaches see the disciplining of the body by the imposition of cleanliness as a sign of a civilising (mind-related) process, or perhaps an attempt to keep at bay social threats associated with dirt and danger. The control of the 'wildness' of the body is paralleled in the later Enlightenment by the attempt to be humane. Rather than being beaten or chained, the body was to be ignored, and, as in the case of madness, the mind was to be reformed. Both tendencies emphasise the mind over the body. At the same time the images of the body as secular and lacking vitalistic powers, as machine-like or animal-like, that originated from philosophical and scientific developments, served further to reduce the status of the body.

Porter's chapter tells us how one of the most basic components of culture – the body – (for without it where would we find our representations, images, metaphors, identities and stigmas?) has been systematically downgraded so that the eighteenth century, for instance, could become the age of sensibility. The study of the body, in other words, holds the key to the understanding of a culture which wishes to erect a set of dominant mind-centred values.

However the body did not cease to exist in the eighteenth century or in any other period, and Porter in a more positive vein argues that a cultural history of the body is possible. He points to the work of feminist historians who have shown how concepts of 'woman' and 'femininity' are created and reproduced within culture, and how in the eighteenth century new knowledge and ideas about the female body helped to shape cultural attitudes. Porter's other example of a mediation between the history of the body and the history of culture is the history of health and illness. Cultural determinants clearly played a major role in the way pain, for instance, was expressed, and conversely the existence of illness and health may shape culture. Given the pressures exerted by our intellectual traditions the attempt to integrate the history of the body with that of the mind may not come to be accepted, but it can bear valuable fruit.

HISTORIOGRAPHICAL ORIENTATIONS

While writing his *Essay on the Principle of Population*, Malthus developed toothache. The mental concentration of composition, he observed, could blot out the excruciating physical pain. But only temporarily. The good Anglican parson was no saint, no ascetic, no fakir, and the imperatives of the flesh, as befitted his own theory, soon reasserted themselves.[1]

Malthus used this personal anecdote to undermine the claims of contemporary perfectibilist radicals such as Condorcet and Godwin who pinned their faith in progress in the age of the French Revolution upon the inexorable march of mind. Rather as, in Utopian Marxism, the state would eventually wither away, so for Godwin, once the nobler faculties became perfected, the body would itself in effect evaporate and so turn incorruptible. Thereby improvements in environment, life-styles and medicine would finally realise, in secularised mode, the message of John Donne's 'Death, Thou shalt die'. Secular immortality would in turn render procreation obsolete, and so man's primitive and irrational sexual urges would mercifully subside. Freed from the corporeal prison, from the cycle of birth, copulation and death, the future lay wide open for pure intellect.

Godwin's aspirations epitomise, in extreme form, that main-stream ideological denigration of the body which has comprised the backbone of the Western intellectual tradition.[2] Its elements and arguments are far too well known to require any extensive rehearsal here. Particularly through the Platonic notion of *homo duplex*, man treated as a hierarchical grafting of mind upon body, Greek thought left a cultural legacy which placed supreme value upon intellect and reason, logic and philosophy, encouraging a distrust for the body in so far as it was the breeding ground for vulgar and anarchic sensual appetites.[3] Classic exemplars (the suicides of Socrates, Cato, Seneca, etc) celebrated the noble freedom of the disembodied will and the triumph of reason over sordid dunghill flesh. The Judaeo-Christian heritage for its part then systematically contrasted the lapsarian carnal lusts endemic to this vale of tears to all that was spiritual, immaterial and transcendental, and, through monasticism in particular, instituted practical regimes of chastity and the mortification of the flesh.[4]

The value-world of Renaissance culture in turn paid homage in its own, frequently neo–platonic, terms to the notion of Cosmic Mind, and a reformulated insistence upon mind–body hierarchical dualism provided the foundation for the Cartesian affirmation of rational consciousness as the uniquely human faculty, the divine in man, the ghost in the machine.[5] Romantic Idealism was later to champion the primacy of consciousness (soul, imagination and poetic genius) over crass, philistine materialism, while 'Victorianism' proclaimed the empire of 'high mindedness' over the native stirrings of the flesh.[6]

Sociologies of knowledge routinely, of course, predict that ruling class ideologies would set reason in the saddle, governing the flesh; what is more noteworthy is that radical movements – even ones which, like Marxism, have espoused a basically materialist ontology – have themselves aimed to distance themselves from what they see as 'vulgar materialism' or 'vulgar reductionism' (e.g. as embodied in such dicta as Moleschott's 'man is what he eats'). It is no accident that several recently fashionable recensions of Marxism (the humanist Marx, the structuralist Marx) are ones which stress the irreducible role of consciousness or theory in the enterprise. 'Materialist', 'reductionist', 'biologistic' (and, today, 'socio-biologistic') remain stock terms of abuse, not least in 'progressive' circles.[7]

We must not exaggerate such ancestral contempt for this mortal coil. Powerful counter-currents have been at work from time to time seeking to demystify mysticism, spiritualism and intellectualism, and to reinstate the body as the *fons et origo* of all things human. For instance, drawing heavily upon the 'corpuscular' natural philosophy of the Scientific Revolution, such leading Enlightenment thinkers as Diderot and d'Holbach made corporeality – embodied existence experienced through the senses and the nervous system – the core of their sciences of man,[8] as did Laurence Sterne more teasingly in *Tristram Shandy* – despite the notorious curse proclaimed by Dr Slop upon Obadiah's body![9] And of course pragmatic medical materialism has always proceeded on the working hypothesis that man is coterminous with the structures and functions of his organic constitution.[10]

Nor must we oversimplify the character of the traditional hegemony of the spirit and distrust of the body. After all, Christianity – its horror of gross carnality notwithstanding – was uniquely a religion of the incarnate Deity, the eucharist, and the resurrection of the body. Orthodox Latin Christendom recoiled at gnosticism and Manicheism. Bodily asceticism was a means, not an end, and the Church always insisted that such disciplines of denial themselves required to be strictly disciplined. In a similar way, Greek philosophy typically privileged mind over matter, yet it also demanded that the healthy mind should inhabit a healthy body: the doctrine that it was essential to undergo the sufferings of rotting flesh to experience artistic creativity was an aberrant *fin de siècle* heresy.[11]

It is important to insist upon such qualifications. Even so, it remains true that our intellectual heritage has been one which programmatically polarises mind and body, and prizes the former. One final instance will indicate how this bias still operates upon our historiographical sensibilities in ways which remain highly persuasive. In his early psychiatric practice Freud concluded that many of his neurotic female patients suffered from hysteria as a result of having been sexually assaulted as children (as indeed they told him). For reasons which are complex and contested, Freud abandoned this interpretation, embracing the view that the women's stories were not memories of real physical assault but fantasies, rooted in the unconscious, about traumatic events which had only ever taken place in their imaginations; through adumbrating this theory of repressed desires, Freud gave birth to psychoanalysis. Thus Freud switched from an essentially somatic, physicalist explanation (real assault) to one located merely 'in the mind'; and proposed an equally psychiatric treatment (the 'talking cure'). The vast majority of commentators have praised Freud for his supposedly profound insight in directing attention away from the mundane life of the body to the apparently much more fascinating one of the consciousness.[12] One might of course counter-argue that what we see is a gigantic and ghastly instance of mystification. Whereas in former centuries the disparagement of the body was most commonly upheld by religion or prudery, today it is buoyed up by intellectual elitism.

Thus, as Vico and other Enlightenment philosophical anthropologists claimed, the European intellectual tradition seems to have followed a course of 'deanthropomorphisation' over the centuries.[13] Time was, they suggested, in the early history of the race, when the human body was of paramount importance as an exemplar, because the body was all that primitive people knew, experienced and controlled. Everything else – society, the environment, the cosmos – was explained by analogy with the workings of the human body: the body was good to think with.[14] In time the extensions of man (civilisations, technology, the exploration of Nature) came to dwarf the body, which lost its privileged role as universal yardstick, and man ceased to be the measure of all things. Classically, for example, during the Scientific Revolution, the traditional macrocosm/microcosm analogy was relegated from the status of cosmological truth to being a mere poetic conceit.[15]

Indeed, the tables were turned. The extensions of man came to dominate the body: for instance, as Otto Mayr has shown, when society ceased to be seen as an organism, the human body itself came to be analogised as a machine (mechanomorphism), above all in the century between Hobbes's *Leviathan* (1650) and LaMettrie's *L'Homme Machine* (1747).[16] With industrialisation, man's overlordship over Nature – and indeed over his own species – increasingly depended upon mind-management, not mere muscle-power. Indeed, in late industrial society, the body as a source of power and labour (and hence value) has been upstaged, a development allegedly encouraging the secondary emergence of narcissism (the exploitation of the beautiful, sexy, healthy body), in ways crucial to the economy of consumer capitalism.[17]

Our intellectual tradition is thus one which has programmatically disparaged – even defiled and reviled – the body. It is telling that the most substantial attempt hitherto to create a sociology of the body, Bryan S. Turner's *The Body and Society*, is dedicated 'To Karen's Mind', an ironic reminder of the unthinkability of breaking the mental mould.[18] And it is thus no accident that the history of the body has been seriously neglected. The journal *Mind* was founded a century ago; the *Journal of the History of Ideas* has now been flourishing for half a century. We have profound studies ranging from *The Savage Mind* to *The Victorian Frame of Mind*; *l'histoire des mentalités* blossoms for popular culture alongside the history of ideas for philosophical thought.[19] On the Enlightenment itself, the framework for modern scholarship was set out by Ernst Cassirer in his utterly idealist *The Philosophy of the Enlightenment*, a work which, by implication at least, saw the key struggle of the *Aufklärung* as the attempt to establish a secular, critical epistemology: even theories about the nature and role of the body lay beyond Cassirer's philosophical horizons (significantly, medicine is hardly ever mentioned in his book).[20] Even today, despite all the shafts of light obliquely thrown onto the subject through the researches of demographers, family historians, art historians and the like we lack as yet a solid corpus of analysis on the history of bodies.[21]

I have thus been arguing that scholars have largely ignored the history of the body, precisely because the body itself has been devalued within our intellectual tradition. In the central part of this essay I shall focus on three main areas in which this imbalance might be redressed. First I shall examine certain domains in which, during the eighteenth century itself, the nature of the body, in respect both to individual consciousness and to society at large, was particularly problematic. By concentrating on what disturbed and divided contemporaries the aim is to avoid anachronism, the assumption that there are certain priorities in respect of the body – such as cleanliness – which are inherent and timeless and have simply been better or worse grasped and realised in different ages. Cultural historians and anthropologists such as Françoise Loux have effectively demolished such a view.[22]

Second, I shall briefly examine certain trends in scholarship which have sought to bring the question of the history of the body into focus. I shall examine their apparent strengths and weaknesses. It is noteworthy that such writings have not, on the whole, emerged from the classic matrices of Enlightenment scholarship, but from newer, more 'marginal' initiatives, not least from academic feminism. And lastly, I shall try to sketch in some areas in which research appears particularly needed and is likely to prove fruitful.

THE PROBLEM OF THE BODY

In this, the central section of this paper, I shall primarily discuss the status of the body in the eighteenth century, as conceptualised in recent, influential historical interpretations. These have largely concentrated upon endeavours to discipline the body as part of a wider attempt to assert sociocultural control, especially over the masses. I shall introduce arguments and evidence both for and against this powerful body of interpretation, before discussing alternative viewpoints through which the body as an object of discourse should also be regarded.

Because, as indicated above, the flesh was seen as ontologically inferior, it served as the traditional target of blame in systems of values and in practical sociomoral control. Modern scholarship has accustomed us to see groups such as women, blacks, homosexuals, witches, etc, as 'scapegoats' in earlier societies.[23] In many respects, the value-systems of such societies treated the body itself as the basic scapegoat of all, in that it was made to bear responsibility for the ills and shortcomings of fallen man, of which mind, spirit or soul was typically exonerated.

This process is most strikingly visible in the ways in which the eighteenth century, continuing age-old traditions, still routinely inflicted physical punishment upon the flesh. Everywhere beatings remained the informal medium of interpersonal discipline, while the law continued to exact its vengeance through penalties ranging from the lash to the gibbet, not to mention judicial torture. It is true, of course, as I shall explore below, that what may be called 'mindless' physical brutality was increasingly condemned by Enlightenment spokesmen. Yet their typical strategy was not to anathematise corporeal punishment altogether but to aim to render it more effective, enduring or painful – for example by substituting hard labour for the traditional whipping.[24]

One of the key maxims of the Enlightenment was that prevention was better than cure. And it is thus hardly surprising that programmes flourished for forestalling the mayhem of the culpable body through its prior disciplining. In part these were aimed at the goal of better *self-control*, and thus they were associated with household education and disciplining. The manuals for good behaviour – both religious and civil – pouring off the printing presses ever since the sixteenth century had set great store by the submission of the body and on the cultivation of manners,

decency and decorum. This goal of bodily submission was continued through the Enlightenment, above all thanks to the immensely influential handbook by John Locke, *Some Thoughts Concerning Education* (1693), which, alongside parallel instruction
manuals, as Fenella Childs has demonstrated, inculcated new
ideas of physical restraint – the capacity to bear pain, a physical
hardihood, and an emotional reticence.[25] Foucault argued in a
rather comparable way that the growing concern with good health
and long life arising during the Enlightenment affords a further
sign of a new priority to discipline the body.[26] Norbert Elias drew
attention to 'the civilising process' visible in the development of
body controls and hygiene (clean bodies, clean habits, clean talk).
And Schama's investigation of cleanliness and bodily control
amongst Dutch Calvinists during their Golden Age illuminates the
effectiveness (both social and psychological) of such strategies in
creating a *cordon sanitaire* against social threats seen to be dirty,
dangerous and contaminating.[27]

Such trends obviously need much interpreting, for 'cleanliness'
has not been seen, time out of mind, as a virtue and, in some
peasant cultures, excessively scrupulous cleanliness may be
viewed as a threat to health, removing protective layers around the
skin. So we must probe the cultural possibilities of cleansing. For
certain groups, cleanliness could provide a pretext for assertiveness, and decency carried overtones of moral superiority. This is
evident in British 'clean-up' movements, which of course emerged
long before the age of Victoria. After all, Thomas Bowdler was a
Georgian; but, before Bowdler, it had been John Wesley who
placed cleanliness next to Godliness, and the proper comportment
of the body in a polite society had never been so much bruited as
in the age of Addison, Steele and Mandeville. In works such as *The
Virgin Unmasked*, Mandeville teasingly discussed the ambivalence
of body morality (concealing the body could be more titillating
than revealing it.[28]

Physical self-control of this kind, as lauded *per excellence* by
Wesley with his goal of the self-policing of the body, typically
accompanied the desire to police the bodies of others to secure
better social and moral–religious order. French historians of early
modern cultural transformations, Muchembled, Flandrin and
Delumeau in particular, have paid great attention to the attempts
of ecclesiastical and civil authorities to regulate the bodies of the
common people through persuasion, prescription and, ultimately,

physical coercion.[29] Muchembled above all has argued that, within traditional quasi-pagan peasant culture, the body was revered as a potent instrument, endowed with organs with magical powers – blood, faeces, the penis and the womb. If vulnerable to famine, disease and death, the body was also the dionysian life-force behind riot and orgiastic excess. This carnival counter-culture of the body was, however, subjected to systematic surveillance and effective repression, not least by the ecclesiastical apparatus of the Counter Reformation, through witch trials, church courts, confession, and the instilling of a new sexual morality underlining marriage and legitimacy.

Contemporary England witnessed parallel attempts, led by Puritans, for the religious reformation of morals and manners.[30] They may have met with some success. Historical demographers have demonstrated that bastardy figures were notably lower in Stuart times than they later became in the more secular environment of the first industrial nation, suggesting that moral discipline – external and internal – exerted some real influence.[31] Georgian England witnessed further assaults upon an explosive body-culture with the suppression of bloodsports and fairs, and the attempts of capitalist employers to drum regular work- and time-discipline into their workforce (significantly newly styled as 'hands').[32]

Plebeian bodies were thus assailed by ideological social control, as from the pulpit. The physical sanctions of the law also threatened them – the whip, the pillory, the gallows. But, as Foucault particularly stressed, the people's bodies also became subjected to, and coerced by, a new political technology of the body emerging especially strikingly during the eighteenth century – the routines of the factory floor, the drills of the school, the fatigues of the parade ground, the punishments of the reformatory. From baby training in the domestic family, through schooling, to the army or the factory floor, the state and the logic of capitalism laboured to turn out docile subjects and an obedient workforce, via the systematic disciplining of people's bodies. Only recently, so the argument runs, has the logic of capitalism somewhat relaxed this relentless, 'Protestant' emphasis on the disciplined body, on a 'this worldly asceticism'; today the imperative has switched from the iron-disciplined machine-like productive 'hand' to the consumer, brimful of wants and needs, whose desires are now to be inflamed and encouraged.[33]

It remains unclear, however, how accurate a picture is given by historians such as Muchembled who have seen popular cultures of the body being successfully suppressed in the name of the panoptic, therapeutic state and the dictates of capitalism. Aspirations may well have vastly outstripped achievements. It is arguable, as Burke amongst others has claimed, that elite culture was less concerned with crushing popular culture than with distancing itself from and elevating itself above it, and developing its own distinct dematerialising body language, rituals and refinements. Folklore, popular sexual mores (e.g. the tradition of pre-marital intercourse followed by marriage on pregnancy) and grassroots medical magic proved immensely resilient against indoctrination and infiltration from above.[34]

It is also important to emphasise that, regardless of the putative advance of the social policing of the body, as depicted by Muchembled, Foucault and others, in other important respects the eighteenth century was an epoch notable for its respect, both theoretical and practical, for the individual autonomy and proprietorship of the body. One need not accept at face value the accounts of the indefeasible ownership of one's own labour as advanced in liberal political economy, but it is no accident that the philosophical critique of slavery, based upon self-proprietorship of one's body, was generated by the Enlightenment. And my own recent researches into the sociocultural relations between sick people and their doctors during this period give abundant testimony of the degree to which, in case of illness, the ultimate authority in respect of choice of treatment was commonly accepted as residing not in the physician but in the patient. It was the advent of state medicine in the nineteenth century – for instance, the introduction by legislation of compulsory smallpox vaccination – which significantly subordinated the private to the public health.[35]

One further aspect of the strategy of elite culture for 'reforming' the body should be mentioned. Alongside the disciplining of the body, indeed, one might almost say, the fulfilment of that disciplining, was the desire to render the body effectively aetherialised and invisible, and thereby to throw the emphasis upon the mind. It is a tendency prominent, for example, in the second half of the eighteenth century in discussions of sex, which increasingly rejected the corporeality associated with traditional libertinism (the grossness of the Restoration) in favour of the delicate sensations of the age of sensibility.[36] A parallel can be seen in Enlightenment discussions of policy in penology, in which the goal of punishing the mind rather than the body becomes paramount. Especially from the late eighteenth century, penal reformers argued that it was 'nobler' or more 'humane' not to scourge the flesh but to reform the mind (in Mably's terms, 'punishment should strike the soul rather than the body'). The therapeutism underpinning modern penology marks yet another instance of the shifting status of the body, one which by sparing the flesh strongly reiterates its inferiority. It would thus be a mistake to regard the trends of eighteenth-century thinking as unidirectional; cross-currents and counter-movements were powerful, re-establishing the hegemony of mind, even while granting greater indulgence in some respects to the desires of the body.[37]

As I have argued, social historians have concentrated their attention of late upon practical techniques devised during the Enlightenment for the education, control and disciplining of the anarchic body. But the status of the body was also undergoing change at this time through its revaluation within thought-systems and value-systems. The Scientific Revolution of the seventeenth century destroyed conventional belief in the traditional elements and qualities as the basic components of the physical universe, and opened up a vast debate about the constitution of things, not least the human body and its concomitant consciousness.[38] In their very distinct ways the Cartesian movement in France and the Lockeian in England both encouraged the explanation of the human frame in mechanistic terms. Consciousness was, of course, exempted, though this was formulated in ways which left it relatively easy for their successors, such as D'Holbach in France and Hartley and Priestley in England, to subsume mind itself within the laws of mechanism and materialistic explanations.[39]

Enlightenment materialism has been fully evaluated elsewhere, and it is not my aim to re-examine it here, beyond insisting that the debates it engendered demonstrate very clearly how completely the very categories of mind and matter, body and soul, were all in the conceptual melting-pot. One strategy emphasised the attractions of the 'materialisation' of everything, for if man was ultimately matter, then man was fully open to scientific inquiry, thus precluding inevitable ignorance. Yet there were great attractions too in retaining thought as an independent, autonomous realm. For the men of the Enlightenment were, *par excellence*, independent thinkers. Championing the non-reducibility of ideas was congruent with promoting their own status. This was a dilemma satirised by Swift and debated by Diderot: if consciousness were just a secretion, even a morbid secretion, of organised matter, why should the thoughts of the intelligentsia possess any claims to authority?[40] Key contributors to this debate as to the dependence of mind upon matter were profoundly uncertain of their ground. Thus David Hartley, simultaneously a medical doctor and a sincere Christian, expressed his own deep uncertainty as to where body stopped and mind began.[41]

My aim here is not to explore Enlightenment philosophies of mind and matter at the theoretical level, but rather to touch upon the fine texture of the practical dilemmas constantly raised as to the interplay of mind and body. Doctrines about rationality and responsibility afford a good point of entry. Traditional theologico-moral systems presupposed that a man's duty lay in governing his relatively anarchic, animalistic body by means of the noble faculty of his mind, reason or will. (Precisely because they lacked reason, mere beasts were not typically held blameworthy for their own destructive actions.) If a man failed to exert that self-control, he was held guilty of vice, sin or crime. But what if this framework of responsibility lapsed? That is, if a person demonstrably lacked the capacity to control – and thus take responsibility for – his own thoughts or physical actions.In that case, such a person was traditionally termed insane, or *non compos mentis*. What needs to be emphasised, however, is that in particular during the eighteenth century, the source of such a failure of control was seen as arising from some defect of the body. In other words, lunacy and other irrational states were construed essentially as somatic disorders.[42]

There were good enough medical reasons for such organic aetiologies of insanity: some physicians still clung to the theory of bodily humours: within this, yellow bile or choler could be seen as causing mania, black bile or 'melancholy' could be regarded as the source of depressive conditions.[43] Others newly stressed the role of the nervous system, or lesions of the skull or brain, in triggering insanity.[44] My point is that there were additionally extremely powerful *sociocultural* reasons for blaming insanity on the body. On the one hand, and most importantly within the explanatory priorities of the Enlightenment, somatic aetiologies eliminated the dangerous possibility of infernal or diabolical possession as the cause, a theory previously popular, but one which Enlightenment minds found perilous, scandalous and (they hoped) exploded.[45] On the other hand, pinpointing organic aetiologies also exonerated the personality itself: it could be a strategy of generating more sympathetic attitudes – typical of Enlightenment humanitarianism in general – towards the insane, through stressing that insanity had roots in bodily defects no less beyond the control of the sufferer than, say, being stricken with smallpox.[46] In the light of this disposition to somatize what we now call 'mental disorder', it is crucial to remember that, when seventeenth- and eighteenth-century writers spoke of 'hysteria' or 'hypochondria' or 'neurosis', they were typically referring to what they construed as *bona fide* organic complaints.[47]

Given room, it would be possible to follow up this particular way of mapping behaviour and thoughts upon the mind/body continuum in detail in other specific areas. Thus, merely to mention a few, habitual drunkenness was very commonly regarded as a physical disease in the eighteenth century, analogous to 'pica', or the longings of pregnant women to gorge themselves on strange foods.[48] Similarly, abnormal sexual dispositions or appetites, such as nymphomania, were rarely viewed as primary 'psychiatric' disorders but were commonly attributed to physical malformations of the genitalia or lesions of the reproductive system (traditionally the womb itself had been held responsible for 'hysteria').[49]

It must be emphasised, however, that counter-currents were also flowing during the eighteenth century, stimulated by Enlightenment values. A gradually developing revulsion from the harshness of traditional physical remedies for insanity – the use of whips and chains – encouraged gentler means, including attempts to tame and retrain the mad by charismatic personality, soothing words, kindness and example. Such 'moral means', often called 'moral management' or 'moral therapy', itself squared well with the Enlightenment conviction that knowledge conferred power, that morality was itself a force, and that progress lay in the triumph of the refined over the rude. The capacity of civilised means to rescue unfortunate lunatics paralleled the Enlightenment belief in its mission towards children, savages, slaves and the masses. Thus the reconstrual of insanity as essentially a mental condition, indeed as a product of mental ignorance or misorientation, clearly had its own ideological appeal in the eighteenth century, before emerging as a key doctrine in the new nineteenth-century science specifically called 'psychiatry'.[50]

SOME HISTORIOGRAPHICAL LEADS

I have argued that, both in theory and practice, the redetermination of the status of the body became especially important during th eighteenth century, not least because of its this-worldliness, indeed secularisation: man, asserted Erasmus Darwin, physician, evolutionist but no Christian, is 'an eating animal, a drinking animal, and a sleeping animal' (one assumes that this third term was not the one he used in front of men, but this maxim was recorded by the prim Quaker, Mary Anne Schimmelpenninck).[51] The existing historiography of the Enlightenment hardly does justice to these debates, although good discussions are available of the materialist philosophies of such figures as LaMettrie.[52]

Where historians of ideas have feared to tread, literary historians and critics have moved in. In certain instances, their work has been extremely illuminating. Numerous students of *Tristram Shandy*, for instance, have rightly insisted on how carefully Sterne traces – part seriously, part satirically – the organic causes of the particular temper of his hero, not least that almost fatal loss of 'animal spirits' (superfine fluids) which attended his very conception when Mrs Shandy inquired of her husband whether he had remembered to wind up the clock.[53]

'Post-structuralism' and its successors have generated other attempts on the part of literary scholars to expose the (possibly unconscious) history of the body through the deployment of hermeneutic techniques of close reading, trading upon the metaphorical equivalence between the body of the writer and the body of his fictive text. The most ambitious work in this genre, one endebted both to French deconstructionism and to Left Bank psychoanalysis, has been Francis Barker's *The Tremulous Private Body*. By way of semantic analysis of what appears to be an arbitrary sample of key 'texts' (*Hamlet*, Rembrandt's 'Anatomy Lesson', Pepys's *Diary*, etc) Barker comes to the conclusion that the body, which traditionally had been a public object, became privatised, as an object of narcissistic shame, within bourgeois culture. Indeed he suggests that the 'body' disappeared altogether as an instrument of eroticism, being displaced by the 'book'.

These are, however, grandiose, and, indeed, stupid, conclusions to derive from a paucity of evidence. Barker's interpretation is rendered all the more shaky because he ignores existing scholarship on many of his texts, and is uninterested in the contexts afforded by social history.[34]

Attempts to winkle out the subtle meaning of what texts such as novels are saying about bodies could carry authority only if supported by a sure grasp of the wider realities of the times: the status of the body within the context of the law (ownership, property), within social and gender structures, relations of production, moral codes, notions of decency, etc. The strength of feminist studies over the last fifteen years lies precisely in the fact that they have indeed advanced on many different fronts at once. For that reason, what we now know, for example, about the standing of women's bodies under the law[55] can readily be juxtaposed against what novels tell us of the rights and wrongs of eighteenth-century women,[56] and what medical studies have to say about the precariousness of their lives – their diseases and risks of dying in childbirth.[57]

One particular strength of recent feminist scholarship lies in its denial that the notion of 'woman' is in some sense natural and timeless, and its counter-insistence that such gender concepts are constantly being produced and reproduced within culture and discourse.[58] Indeed it can confidently be asserted that the eighteenth century, with its cults of politeness, the family and motherhood, increased the cultural perception of the differentness of men and women (men were to work within the public sphere, women were to be ornamental and domestic, within the private, at home), and generated appropriate new notions of 'femininity': the idealisation of woman as mother, as agency of moral regeneration and cultural refinement, and at the same time as sexual ornament (the belle).[59] These developments arguably both liberated and repressed. Enlightenment images of women abandoned the crass misogyny of the Aristotelian tradition (woman as monstrous form of male), so powerful still in Renaissance writings which emphasised the sexual insatiability of women and the sinful pollution of childbirth.[60] On the other hand, the new stress on the refined nature of the female seen as the missionary of refinement was equally incapacitating, and encouraged new notions of helplessness and intellectual delicacy.[61]

What must be stressed here is that feminist scholarship has rightly drawn attention to a new sensitivity present in eighteenth-

century texts when faced with the very question of what constituted gender *per se*; and has contended that discourse about the
physical body played a large part in constituting such knowledge.
The absolute nature of the divide between the masculine and the
feminine was underlined, for instance, by a striking new tendency
to deny the reality of hermaphrodites.[62] It was also signalled by
what seem to have been the first ever complete anatomical
drawings of the female skeleton, ones which seem to emphasise
bone structures fit for female social functions: the ample pelvis,
suitable for childbirth, and the correspondingly diminutive
head.[63]

On the basis of such studies, it has been argued by Tom
Laqueur that the eighteenth century witnessed a radical reformu-
lation of the very idea of gender difference. New physiological and
gynaecological theories were emerging of female sexual anatomy
and the female reproductive cycle. Above all, the old Greek notion
that conception occurred through the intermingling of fluids
jointly ejaculated at mutual orgasm by both men and women was
exploded. Once it became understood that female orgasm was not
necessary for conception, a view of the biological (and by implication social) sexual passivity of women readily gained currency,
particularly amongst men, but, it seems, amongst women as
well.[64] Thereby the traditional doctrine that woman was essentially an inferior version of man increasingly yielded to one which
viewed woman not as inferior but as essentially different.
Whether or not that view was truly novel is open to dispute. One
of the values, for example, of Edward Shorter's work on the history
of women's bodies has been to emphasise that the difference of
female biology had long been recognised in Western culture (by
men who, for example, shunned the pollutions of menstruation
and childbed, and by women who developed women-only rituals
based around such functions).[65] In a rather parallel way, Barbara
Duden has recently drawn attention to the power of traditional
notions, lay and medical, concerning the uniqueness of the female
body, with its special capacity to generate the ferment of life, in
her study of the views about health and sickness held by German
women in the eighteenth century.[66]

All such studies, playing on the mutual fruitfulness of feminist
history and new histories of sexuality, appear highly promising.
Their message seems to be that we are in danger of being misled
by abstractions unless we emphasise the complex historical interplay of high-level discourse (e.g. moral systems as they at-

tempted to regulate decency or sexuality), the changing physical realities of the body itself and its changing cultural representations.

FUTURE DIRECTIONS

I have argued that the history of the body has been traditionally neglected, and have drawn attention to certain attempts to redress this imbalance. There are furthermore, certain major projects in progress which will additionally increase our understanding, not least a study of the heights of English people over the ages, through which it should be possible to gain a clear picture of changing patterns of physique, of healthiness and, inferentially, of standards of living.[67] Nevertheless much remains to be done. I shall not attempt to set out here a general agenda, for it smacks of presumption to tell other scholars what they ought to be doing.

I wish, however, to draw attention to one particular area, commonly neglected, which I believe is central in mediating between the history of the physical body and many dimensions of the history of culture and society: that is, the history of health and disease. Historians of medicine have typically lavished their attention upon the theories and practice of the medical profession itself; this form of 'great docs' history can be only of marginal interest here. But medical historians are increasingly occupying themselves with questions of health and sickness and treatments seen from the sufferers' point of view, and are examining the significance of forms of discourse about the body healthy and the body sick shared between sick people and their medical advisors.[68] This new-style medical history, which pays prime attention to individual people's intimate personal experience of their own embodied existence, promises to throw light upon many questions, beyond the admittedly interesting question of what people actually did when they fell sick.

For one thing, people's reflections upon their own states of health and sickness form an excellent index of perceptions, individual and collective, of the status of the flesh. Various signs indicate, for instance, that sufferers recorded pain in greater detail and with more attention in the passage from the seventeenth to the eighteenth century.[69] This would confirm suggestions made by scholars of the 'age of sensibility' that such feelings actually came to be experienced, and even luxuriated over, more acutely during the Enlightenment.[70] This in turn means, not that eighteenth-century people had 'superior' feelings in any objective sense, but, rather, that there was a growing preoccupation with monitoring bodily states, probably commensurate with a comparable decline in gauging the state of the soul, as those traditions of religious introspection so common in the aftermath of the Reformation waned or became confined to pockets of Protestant dissent.[71]

One noteworthy cultural embodiment of this tendency towards organic introspection is the preoccupation during the eighteenth century with 'hypochondria' and its shift of meaning. As noted earlier, 'hypochondria' traditionally connoted a physical disorder of the abdomen, associated with bad digestion. During the eighteenth century it was increasingly also used in a rather more metaphorical sense – that with which we are familiar nowadays – to depict pains lacking defined somatic cause; it thereby became a tag for the sickness of being morbidly preoccupied with one's own health (thereby, in turn, suggestively spawning imaginary pains). The boom in 'hypochondria' thus signals new concerns, by implication, above all, the desire for, even the expectation of, physical *health*, countering which pain was an unwelcome intrusion, and possibly a new preparedness to resort to medication to achieve it. In the secularised world of the Enlightenment, physical existence became the site for those aspirations of life traditionally assigned to Heaven.[72]

This instance of hypochondria suggests that, in a multitude of ways, people's bodily processes and dysfunctions triggered patterns of experience which had profound implications for wider ideological construals of the self and its relations to society. It is clear, for example, that the highly fashionable language of 'nerves' and nervous disorders, spurred by Enlightenment physiological investigations into the nervous system, gave educated people an idiom through which they could relate their organic condition to their emotional state: blushing, trembling, weeping, the pounding heart, the tingling sensation overtly related feelings and behaviour. Such manifestations achieved public cultural kudos in the figure of the man or woman of sensibility.[73] There is a highly complex continuum stretching from the physical sensations verbalised by the individual to the public language of morality and aesthetics; and it is best pictured not as a one-way process but as a feedback system mediating corpus and culture: the body is determined no less than it determines. Various scholarly traditions, not least ethnomethodology, cultural anthropology and perhaps psychohistory, may prove of help in this investigation.[74]

For too long the history of Enlightenment thought has been treated as if it were a current leading from Descartes and Locke to Kant, bent on elucidating the philosophical relations between epistemology and ontology. Yet in *je pense, donc je suis*, the *je* includes a *moi* which feels, falls sick, experiences pain and so forth – in short, has a body not less than a mind of its own, indeed has a body *with* a mind of its own. Medical history might prove one aid to that reintegration of the body with the mind which will enable us better to understand the real project of the Enlightenment.

Notes

1. Malthus's toothache is illuminatingly discussed in Catherine Gallagher, 'The Body Versus the Social Body in the Works of Thomas Malthus and Henry Mayhew', in C. Gallagher and T. Laqueur, eds, *The Making of the Modern Body*, Berkeley and Los Angeles, 1987, pp. 83–106.

2. For evidence see J. Passmore, *The Perfectibility of Man*, London, 1970; for critical comment see T. Polhemus, ed., *Social Aspects of the Human Body*, Harmondsworth, 1978.

3. See Bennett Simon, *Mind and Madness in Ancient Greece*, Ithaca, 1978; E. R. Dodds, *The Greeks and the Irrational*, Berkeley and London, 1951; H. North, *Sophrosyne: Self-knowledge and Self-Restraint in Greek Literature*, Ithaca, 1966.

4. See. F. Bottomley, *Attitudes to the Body in Western Christendom*, London, 1979; B. S. Turner, 'The Body and Religion: Towards an Alliance of Medical Sociology and Sociology of Religion', *Annual Review of the Social Sciences*, iv, 1980, pp. 247–86.

5. Though this is often misinterpreted. See for correctives S. Tomaselli, 'The First Person: Descartes, Locke and Mind-Body Dualism', *History of Science*, xxii, 1984, pp. 185–205; T. Brown, 'Descartes, Dualism and Psychosomatic Medicine', in W. F. Bynum, Roy Porter and Michael Shepherd, eds, *The Anatomy of Madness*, 2 vols, London, 1985, ii, pp. 40–62; R. B. Carter, *Descartes' Medical Philosophy*, Baltimore, 1983.

6. P. Fryer, *Mrs Grundy: Studies in English Prudery*, London, 1963; M. Jaeger, *Before Victoria*, London, 1956; E. J. Bristow, *Vice and Vigilance*, Dublin, 1977; M. Quinlan, *Victorian Prelude*, New York, 1941; E. Trudgill, *Madonnas and Magdalens*, London, 1966.

7. For instance, see L. Althusser, *For Marx*, London, 1969; L. Althusser and E. Balibar, *Reading Capital*, London, 1970; S. Avineri, *The Social and Political Thought of Karl Marx*, Cambridge, 1970; M. Cherno, 'Feuerbach's "Man is What He Eats": a Rectification', *Journal of the History of Ideas*, xxiii, 1962–3, pp. 397–406. There are onslaughts against materialism in M. Berman, *The Re-enchantment of the World*, London, 1982, and F. Capra, *The Turning Point: Science, Society and the Rising Culture*, New York, 1982.

8. For the Enlightenment, the science of man and the body, see F. Duchesneau, *La Physiologie des Lumières*, The Hague, 1982; J. Roger, *Les Sciences de la Vie dans la Pensé Française du XVIIIe Siècle*, Paris, 1971; J. Roger, 'The Living World', in G. S. Rousseau and Roy Porter, eds, *The Ferment of Knowledge*, Cambridge, 1980, pp. 253–83; C. Kiernan, *Science and Enlightenment in Eighteenth-Century France*, Geneva, 1968; R. French, *Robert Whytt, The Soul and Medicine*, London, 1969; L. Crocker, 'Diderot and Eighteenth-Century Transformism', in B. Glass, O. Temkin and W. Straus, eds, *Forerunners of Darwin*, Baltimore, 1959, pp. 114–43.

9. On Sterne, See Roy Porter, 'Against the Spleen' in Valerie Grosvenor-Myer, ed., *Laurence Sterne: Riddles and Mysteries*, London, 1984, pp. 84–9; M. New, 'At the Backside of the Door of Purgatory', in *ibid.*, pp. 15–23; J. Berthoud, 'Shandeism and Sexuality', in *ibid.*, pp. 24–38; E. A. Bloom and L. D. Bloom, ' "This Fragment of Life": From Process to Mortality', in *ibid.*, pp. 57–74; D. Furst, 'Sterne and Physick: Images of Health and Disease in *Tristram Shandy*, PhD thesis, Columbia University, 1974; J. Rogers, 'Ideas of Life in *Tristram Shandy*', PhD. thesis, University of East Anglia, 1978; A. G. Fredman, *Diderot and Sterne*, New York, 1973; F. Doherty, 'Sterne and Hume: A Bicentenary Essay', *Essays and Studies*, xxii, 1969, pp. 71–87.

10. W. I. Watson, 'Why Isn't the Mind–Body Problem Ancient?', in Paul K. Feyerabend and Grover Maxwell, eds, *Mind, Matter and Method*, Minneapolis, 1966, pp. 92–102; L. J. Rather, *Mind and Body in Eighteenth-Century Medicine*, London, 1965.

11. For Christian theology see John A. T. Robinson, *The Body: A Study in Pauline Theology*, London, 1952. For 'degenerationist' psychiatry and art see Max Nordau, *Degeneration*, New York, 1895; W. R. Bett, *The Infirmities of Genius*, London, 1952; T. B. Hyslop, *the Great Abnormals*, London, 1925; Roger L. Williams, *The Horror of Life*, London, 1980; Jean Pierot, *The Decadent Imagination*, Chicago, 1981.

12. On Freud, see William J. McGrath, *Freud's Discovery of Psychoanalysis*, Ithaca, 1986. See also H. F. Ellenberger, *The Discovery of the Unconscious: The History and Evolution of Dynamic Psychiatry*, New York, 1971; R. W. Clark, *Freud: The Man and the Cause*, London, 1982, F. Sulloway, *Freud: Biologist of the Mind*, New York, 1979 and J. M. Masson, *The Assault on Truth: Freud's Suppression of the Seduction Theory*, New York, 1983. Some psychoanalysts have denied the somatic roots of all illness. See G.

Groddeck, *The Book of the It*, London, 1950; G. Groddeck; *The Meaning of Illness*, London, 1977. The history of Mesmerism offers a parallel; what began as a physical cure turned into a purely psychic phenomenon. See R. Darnton, *Mesmerism and the End of the Enlightenment in France*. Cambridge, Mass., 1968; G. Sutton, 'Electric Medicine and Mesmersm', *Isis*, lxxii, 1981, pp. 375–92; V. Buranelli, *The Wizard from Vienna: Franz Mesmer and the Origins of Hypnotism*, London, 1976; F. A. Mesmer, *Mesmerism: a Translation of the Original Medical and Scientific Meeting of F. A. Mesmer, M. D.*, trans. G. L. Bloch, Los Altos, Cal., 1980; F. Rausky, *Mesmer, ou la révolution thérapeutique*, Paris, 1977; Jonathan Miller, 'Mesmerism', *Listener*, 22 Nov. 1973, pp. 685–90.

13. For perspectives on this see I. Couliano, *Eros et Magie à la Renaissance*, Paris, 1984; Max Weber, *The Sociology of Religion*, London, 1966; E. B. Tylor, *Primitive Culture*, London, 1871; H. Jennings, *Pandaemonium*, London, 1985.

14. Leonard Barkan, *Nature's Work of Art: The Human Body as Image of the World*, New Haven, 1975: E. M. W. Tillyard, *The Elizabethan World Picture*, Harmondsworth, 1972; J. B. Bamborough, *The Little World of Man*, London, 1952; Donald G. MacRae, 'The Body and Social Metaphor', in J. Benthall and T. Polhemus, eds, *The Body as a Medium of Expression: An Anthology*, New York, 1975, pp. 59–73.

15. L. Mumford, *The Condition of Man*, London, 1944, L. Mumford, *Technics and Civilization*, London, 1934.

16. O. Mayr, *Authority, Liberty and Automatic Machines in Early Modern Europe*, Baltimore, 1986.

17. C. Lasch, *The Culture of Narcissism*, New York, 1979.

18. B. S. Turner, *The Body and Society. Explorations in Social Theory*, Oxford, 1984. Turner's book is the boldest attempt yet to create a sociology of the body. There is a stimulating discussion of the neglect of the body in literature in Virginia Woolf's essay, 'On Being Ill', in *Collected Essays*, vol. iv, London, 1967, pp. 193–203. For Woolf's own problems with 'embodiment', see S. Trombley, *'All That Summer She Was Mad'. Virginia Woolf and Her Doctors*, London, 1981. And more generally see the discussion in G. S. Rousseau, 'Science and Literature, the State of the Art', *Isis*, lxix, 1978, pp. 583–91; G. S. Rousseau, 'Literature and Medicine: the State of the Field', *Isis*, lxii, 1981 pp. 406–24.

19. For a sample see J. Yolton, *Thinking Matter. Materialism in Eighteenth-Century Britain*, Minneapolis, 1983; J. Yolton, *Perceptual Acquaintance from Descartes to Reid*, Minneapolis, 1984; C. Levi Straus, *La Pensée Sauvage*, 1962, *The Savage Mind*, London, 1966; W. E. Houghton, Jr., *The Victorian Frame of Mind 1830–1870*, New Haven, 1957.

20. Ernst Cassirer, *The Philosophy of the Enlightenment*, trans. by F. C. A. Koelln and J. P. Pettegrove, Boston, 1955. For attempts to demystify Cassirer's neo-Kantan idealism see R. Darnton, 'In Search of the Enlightenment: Recent Attempts to Create a Social History of Ideas', *Journal of Modern History*, xliii, 1971, pp. 113–32.

21. Some further discussion of these issues and further bibliography can be found in Roy Porter, 'Body Politics: Approaches to the Cultural History of the Body', in Peter Burke, ed., *New Perspectives on Historical Writing*, Cambridge, forthcoming.

22. See Françoise Loux, 'Popular Culture and Knowledge of the Body: Infancy and the Medical Anthropologist', in Roy Porter and Andrew Wear, eds, *Problems and Methods in the History of Medicine*, London, 1987, pp. 81–98, and her many other works there cited.

23. S. Gilman, *Seeing the Insane*, New York, 1982; S. Gilman, *Difference and Pathology*, Ithaca and London, 1985; H. Mayer, *Outsiders. A Study in Life and Letters*, Cambridge Mass., 1984.

24. M. Foucault, *Discipline and Punish*, trans, A. Sheridan, London, 1977; M. Ignatieff, *A Just Measure of Pain: The Penitentiary in the Industrial Revolution, 1750–1850*, New York, 1978.

25. Fenella Childs, 'Prescriptions for Manners in Eighteenth-Century Courtesy Literature', PhD thesis, Oxford, 1984; L. A. Curtis, 'A Case Study of Defoe's Domestic Conduct Manuals Suggested by *The Family, Sex and Marriage in England 1500–1800*', *Studies in Eighteenth Century Culture*, x, 1981, pp. 409–28; James L. Axtell, *The Educational Writings of John Locke*, Cambridge, 1968; M. J. M. Ezell, 'John Locke's Images of Childhood: Early Eighteenth-Century Responses to *Some Thoughts Concerning Education*', *Eighteenth-Century Studies*, xvii, 1983/4, pp. 139–55.

26. See M. Foucault, *A History of Sexuality*, vol. i, *Introduction*, London, 1978; J.-L. Flandrin, *Un Temps Pour Embrasser*, Paris, 1983.

27. See generally N. Elias, *The Civilizing Process*, Oxford, 1983, and more specifically S. Schama, 'The Unruly Realm: Appetite and Restraint in Seventeenth-Century Holland', *Daedalus*, cviii, 1979, pp. 103–23; S. Schama, *The Embarrassment of Riches. An Interpretation of Dutch Culture in the Golden Age*, London, 1987; G. Smith, 'Prescribing the Rules of Health: Self-Help and Advice in the Late Eighteenth Century', in Roy Porter, ed., *Patients and Practitioners. Lay Attitudes to Medicine in Pre-Industrial Society*, Cambridge, 1985, pp. 249–82.

28. For Mandeville's provocations see B. Mandeville, *The Virgin Unmask'd*, London, 1709, esp. pp. 1–4, 'A Discourse Upon Nakedness and Dress', and the general discussion in Roy Porter, 'A Touch of Danger. The Man Midwife as Sexual Predator', in G. S. Rousseau and Roy Porter, eds, *Sexual Underworlds of the Enlightenment*, Manchester, 1988, pp. 214–40.

29. Jacques Donzelot, *The Policing of Families*, trans. Robert Hurley, New York, 1979; Jean-Louis Flandrin, 'Amour et mariage', *Dix-huitième Siècle*, xii, 1980, pp. 163–76; Jean-Louis Flandrin, *Le Sexe et l'Occident*, Paris, 1981; Philippe Ariès, 'L'Amour dans le mariage', *Communications Sexualités Occidentales*', xxxv, 1980, pp. 116–22; Robert Muchembled, *Popular Culture and Elite culture in France, 1400–1750*, trans. L. Cochrane, Baton Rouge, 1978.

30. K. Wrightson, *English Society 1580–1680*, London, 1982; E. J. Bristow, *Vice and Vigilance: Purity Movements in Britain Since 1700*, Dublin, 1977.

31. P. Laslett, ed., *Bastardy and its Comparative History* London, 1980.

32. These issues are discussed in R. Malcolmson, *Popular Recreations in English Society 1700–1850*, Cambridge, 1973.

33. Foucault's main relevant works are *Madness and Civilization: A History of Insanity in the Age of Reason*, London, 1967; *The Order of Things: An Archaeology of the Human Sciences*, London, 1970; *The Archaeology of Knowledge*, London, 1972; *The Birth of the Clinic: An Archaeology of Medical Perception*, London, 1973; *Discipline and Punish*; *The History of Sexuality*, vol. i, *Introduction*, London, 1978. See also C. Gordon, ed., *M. Foucault: Power/Knowledge*, Brighton, 1980, especially the essay 'Body/Power', pp. 55–62; M. Featherstone, 'The Body in Consumer Culture', *Theory, Culture & Society*, I, 1982, pp. 18–33; R. Jacoby, 'Narcissism and the Crisis of Capitalism', *Telos*, xliv, 1980, pp. 58–65; S. Brownmiller, *Femininity*, London, 1984; J. B. Hess and L. Nochlin, *women as Sex Objects*, London, 1973.

34. E. P. Thompson, 'Time, Work-Discipline and Industrial Capitalism', *Past and Present*, xxxvii, 1967.

35. For analysis of the status of the body within eighteenth century popular medicine, see Dorothy Porter and Roy Porter, *Patients' Progress*, Cambridge 1989, esp. chs 5–8. For some valuable seventeenth-century parallels see Lucinda McCray Beier, *Sufferers and Healers. The Experience of Illness in Seventeenth-Century England*, London, 1987.

36. See above all Jean Hagstrum, *Sex and Sensibility, Erotic Ideal and Erotic Love from Milton to Mozart*, London, 1980; see also the discussion in the Introduction to Rousseau and Porter, eds, *Sexual Underworlds*; and Roy Porter, 'Mixed Feelings. The Enlightenment and Sexuality in Eighteenth-Century Britain, Manchester, 1982, pp. 1–27.

37. See the works cited in reference 24.

38. For mid-eighteenth century rejection of mechanism in the life and human sciences, and the quest for a unifying science which would be more satisfactorily materialistic and monistic, yet also do justice to the categories of life, vitality, process, energy and sensitivity, see A. O. Lovejoy, *The Great Chain of Being*, Cambridge, Mass., 1936, ch. 8; T. S. Hall, *A History of General Physiology*, Chicago, 1969); F. Duchesneau, *La Physiologie des Lumières*, The Hague, 1982; J. Roger, *Les Sciences de la Vie dans la Pensée Française du xviiie Siècle*, Paris, 1971; J. Roger, 'The Living World', in G. S. Rousseau and Roy Porter, eds, *The Ferment of Knowledge*, Cambridge, 1980, pp. 253–83; T. Brown, 'From Mechanism to Vitalism in Eighteenth-Century English Physiology'. *Journal of the History of Biology*, vii, 1974, pp. 179–216; H. W. Piper, *The Active Universe*, London, 1962; E. Sewell, *The Orphic Voice*, London, 1961; L. Crocker, 'Diderot and Eighteenth-Century Transformism', in B. Glass, O. Temkin and W. Straus, eds, *Forerunners of Darwin*, Baltimore, 1959, pp. 114–43.

39. See Yolton, *Thinking Matter*; E. Halévy, *The Growth of Philosophic Radicalism*, London, 1928; A. Vartanian, *Diderot and Descartes. A Study of Scientific Naturalism in the Enlightenment*, Princeton, 1953.

40. See, for example, A. Wilson, *Diderot. The Testing Years*, New York, 1957; J. Doolittle, *Rameau's Nephew*, Geneva, 1960; H. Dieckmann, *Cinq Leçons sur Diderot*, Geneva, 1959.

41. See the discussion in Roy Porter, *Mind Forg'd Manacles. A History of Madness in England from the Restoration to the Regency*, London, 1987, esp. pp. 195–6.

42. See Porter, *Mind Forg'd Manacles, passim*, but esp. pp. 55–61 and 176–84.

43. See Stanley W. Jackson, 'Galen: On Mental Disorder', *Journal of the History of the Behavioural Sciences*, v, 1969 pp.365–84; Stanley W. Jackson, 'Melancholia and the Waning of the Humoral Theory', *Journal of the History of Medicine and Allied Sciences*, xxxiii, 1978 pp. 367–76; Stanley W. Jackson, *Melancholia and Depression From Hippocratic Times to Modern Times*, New Haven, 1986.

44. See G. S. Rousseau, 'Nerves, Spirits and Fibres: Towards Defining the Origins of Sensibility; with a Postscript', *The Blue Guitar*, ii, 1976, pp. 125–53.

45. M. MacDonald, *Mystical Bedlam: Madness, Anxiety and Healing in Seventeenth-Century England*, Cambridge, 1981.

46. W. F. Bynum, 'Rationales for Therapy in British Psychiatry: 1780–1835', *Medical History*, xvii, 1974. pp. 317–34; M. Fears, 'Therapeutic Optimism and the Treatment of the Insane', in R. Dingwall, ed., *Health Care and Health Knowledge*, London, 1977, pp. 66–81; M. Fears, 'The "Moral Treatment" of Insanity: A Study in the Social Construction of Human Nature', PhD thesis, University of Edinburgh, 1978; A. Digby, *Madness, Morality and Medicine*, Cambridge, 1985.

47. Porter, *Mind Forg'd Manacles*, pp. 44–50.

48. Roy Porter, 'The Drinking Man's Disease: The Prehistory of Alcoholism in Georgian Britain', *British Journal of Addiction*, lxxx, 1985, pp. 385–96; J. Hirsh, 'Enlightened 18th-Century Views of the Alcohol Problem', *Journal of the History of Medicine*, iv, 1949, pp. 230–6; W. F. Bynum, 'Chronic Alcoholism in the First Half of the Nineteenth Century', *Bulletin of the History of Medicine*, xlii, 1968 pp. 160–85.

49. Porter, *Mind Forg'd Manacles*, pp. 195–8; Roy Porter, 'Love, Sex and Madness in Eighteenth-Century England', *Social Research*, liii, 1986, pp. 211–42.

50. Foucault, *Madness and Civilization*; Joan Busfield, *Managing Madness. Changing Ideas and Practice*, London, 1986; Peter Sedgwick, *Psycho Politics*, London, 1982; M. Donnelly, *Managing the Mind*, London, 1983; G. S. Rousseau, 'Psychology', in G. S. Rousseau and Roy Porter, eds, *The Ferment of Knowledge*, Cambridge, 1980, pp. 143–210.

51. Quoted in Desmond King-Hele, *Doctor of Revolution. The Life and Genius of Erasmus Darwin*, London, 1977, pp. 187.

52. Ann Thomson, *Materialism and Society in the Mid-Eighteenth Century. La Mettrie's Discours Préliminaire*, Geneva and Paris, 1981.

53. See the items cited in note 9.

54. See R. Barthes, *Le Plaisir du Texte*, Paris, 1973; T. Eagleton, *Literary Theory*, Oxford, 1983; J. Culler, *On Deconstruction*, London, 1983; J. Derrida, *Writing and Difference*, London 1978. For a broader approach to the subject see V. B. Leitch, *Deconstructive Criticism: an Advanced Introduction*, London, 1975.

55. See Susan Staves, *'Our Fortunes are in Your Possession'. Married Women's Separate Property 1660–1830*, Cambridge, Mass., forthcoming.

56. The best introduction is in P. M. Spacks, *The Female Imagination*, London, 1976; see also her *Imagining a Self. Autobiography and Novel in 18th-Century England*, London, 1976, and Jane Spencer, *The Rise of the Woman Novelist from Aphra Behn to Jane Austen*, Oxford, 1986.

57. A good starting-point is Edward Shorter, *A History of Women's Bodies*, New York, 1982.

58. This is the central theme of L. Friedli, 'Crossing Gender Boundaries in Eighteenth-Century England', PhD thesis, University of Essex, 1987.

59. See L. Jordanova, ed., *Languages of Nature*, London, 1986; L. Jordanova, 'Naturalising the Family: Literature and the Bio-Medical Sciences in the Late 18th Century', in ibid., pp. 86–116; L. Jordanova, 'Gender, Generation and Science: William Hunter's Obstetrical Atlas', in W. F. Bynum and Roy Porter, eds, *William Hunter and the Eighteenth-Century Medical World*, London, 1985, pp. 385–412; L. Jordanova, 'Conceptualising Power over Women', *Radical Science Journal*, xii, 1982, pp. 124–8; L. Jordanova, 'Natural Facts: a Historical Perspective on Science and Sexuality', in C. MacCormack and M. Strathern, eds, *Nature, Culture and Gender*, Cambridge, 1980, pp. 42–69; L. Jordanova, 'The Popularisation of Medicine: Tissot on Onanism', *Textual Practice*, 1, 1987, pp. 68–80; see also C. Duncan, 'Happy Mothers and Other Ideas in 18th-Century Art', *Art Bulletin*, lx, 1973, pp. 570–83.

60. See, for instance, Ian McLean, *The Renaissance Idea of Woman*, Cambridge, 1980.

61. See Paul Hoffman, *La Femme dans la pensée des Lumières*, Paris, 1977.

62. Lynne Friedli, ' "Passing Woman" – A Study of Gender boundaries in the Eighteenth Century', in Rousseau and Porter, eds, *Sexual Underworlds*, pp. 242–68. Also relevant are many of the contributions to R. P. Maccubbin, ed., *Unauthorized Sexual Behavior during the Enlightenment*, special issue of *Eighteenth-Century Life*, 1985.

63. Londa Schiebinger, 'Skeletons in the Closet: The First Illustrations of the Female Skeleton in Eighteenth-Century Anatomy', in C. Gallagher and T. Laqueur, eds, *The Making of the Modern Body. Sexuality and Society in the Nineteenth Century*, Berkeley, 1987, pp. 42–82.

64. See Tom Laqueur, 'Orgasm, Generation and the Politics of Reproductive Biology', in Gallagher and Laqueur, *The Making of the Modern Body*, pp. 1–41. On the social development of separate spheres see Leonore Davidoff and Catherine Hall, *Family Fortunes*.

Men and Women of the English Middle class, 1780–1850, London, 1987; and more generally P. Gay, *The Bourgeois Experience, Victoria to Freud,* vol. 1, *A Sentimental Education,* vol. 2, *The Tender Passion,* New York, 1984 and 1986; and J. B. Elshtain, *Public Man, Private Woman. Women in Social and Political Thought,* Oxford, 1981.

65. See Shorter, *Women's Bodies;* Shorter, *The Making of the Modern Family,* London, 1976; Shorter, 'Illegitimacy, Sexual Revolution and Social Change in Europe, 1750–1900', *Journal of Interdisciplinary History,* ii, 1971, 237–72; Shorter, 'Capitalism, Culture and Sexuality: Some Competing Models', *American Historical Review,* lxxviii, 1975, pp. 604–40.

66. Barbara Duden, *Geschichte unter der Haut. Ein Eisenacher Arzt und seine Patientinnen um 1730,* Stuttgart, 1987.

67. This is a project led by Professor Roderick Floud of Birkbeck College, University of London, currently in progress.

68. See the 'Introduction' to Roy Porter, ed., *Patients and Practitioners,* Cambridge, 1985, pp. 1–22; and in the same volume Jonathan Barry, 'Piety and the Patient: Medicine and Religion in Eighteenth-Century Bristol', pp. 147–76 and Joan Lane, ' "The Doctor Scolds Me": The Diaries and Correspondence of Patients in Eighteenth-Century England', pp. 205–48;' see also the 'Introduction' to Porter and Wear, *Problems and Methods;* W. F. Bynum, 'Health, Disease and Medical Care', in G. S. Rousseau and Roy Porter, eds, *The Ferment of Knowledge,* Cambridge, 1980, pp. 211–15. For a detailed example of this new approach see Lucinda McCray Beier, *Sufferers and Healers. The Experience of Illness in Seventeenth Century England,* London, 1987.

69. See in particular Andrew Wear, 'Interfaces. Perceptions of Health and Illness in Early Modern England', in Porter and Wear, *Problems and Methods,* pp. 230–56; and K. Keele, *Anatomies of Pain,* Oxford, 1957.

70. See, for example, J. Todd, Sensibility, London, 1986.

71. See A. Wear, 'Puritan Perceptions of Illness in Seventeenth Century England', in Roy Porter, ed., *Patients and Practitioners,* Cambridge, 1985, pp. 55–99.

72. See Roy Porter, 'The Patient in the Eighteenth Century', in Andrew Wear, ed., *The Social History of Medicine,* Cambridge, forthcoming; for hysteria, see I. Veith, *Hysteria: The History of a Disease,* Chicago, 1965; J. Boss, 'The Seventeenth-Century Transformation of the Hysteric Affection', *Psychological Medicine,* ix, 1979, pp. 221–34; J. Wright, 'Hysteria and Mechanical Man', *Journal of the History of Ideas,* xli, 1980, pp. 223–47. For hypochondria see E. Fischer-Homberger, 'Hypochondriasis of the Eighteenth Century – Neurosis of the Present Century', *Bulletin of the History of Medicine,* xlvi, 1972, pp. 391–401.

73. Such psychosomatic dimensions are sensitively explored in Johanna Geyer-Kordesch, 'Cultural Habits of Illness: The Enlightened and the Pious in Eighteenth-Century Germany', in Roy Porter, ed., *Patients and Practitioners,* Cambridge, 1985, pp.

177–204. For the wider notions of selfhoods involved here see J. N. Morris, *Versions of the Self*, New York, 1966; S. D. Cox, *'The Stranger Within Thee': The Concept of Self in Late Eighteenth-Century Literature*, Pittsburgh, 1980; J. O. Lyons, *The Invention of the Self*, Carbondale, 1978.

74. See, for example, E. Goffman, *Stigma: Notes on the Management of Spoiled Identity*, Harmondsworth, 1968; E. Goffman, *The Presentation of Self in Everyday Life*, Harmondsworth, 1971.

5

The Representation of the Family in the Eighteenth Century: A Challenge for Cultural History

Ludmilla Jordanova

Jordanova argues that cultural history must go beyond the stage of description and be more critical and analytic. Using the example of the family, she points out that some historians have tended to take the family as a 'social given', an unproblematic natural entity to be integrated into the general economic and social history of a period. Other historians have seen the family in affective terms, indicating feelings and mentalities between relatives. Yet, argues Jordanova, the work of Phillipe Ariès, and, to a lesser extent, Lawrence Stone is flawed in that the sources they use, especially pictures, are seen to be unproblematic. Pictorial images are viewed by historians as faithful representations of a reality that existed in the past. Instead of this approach pictures have to be understood as constructed representations behind which may lie social power relations, powerful idealising forces, all moving styles and genres in particular directions. Detailed study, for instance, of the way people are grouped, may indicate how mothers and daughters were perceived, or the placing of servants in a picture can give a clue as to whether they were felt to be part of the family or lying outside it. Jordanova argues for sophistication: different viewers, an apprentice or a merchant, would have given different meanings to the same picture.

At the heart of Jordanova's approach is a view shared by the other contributors, even if expressed in different ways. This is that cultural history can encompass all of history. The claim is perhaps easier to argue for from a critical tradition where highly persuasive and subtle views of the relations between cultural processes and the political, economic and social nature of a society have been evolving away from the mechanistic approaches of earlier Marxist writers. Jordanova writes that we must refuse to accept the family or indeed society as 'natural givens', but must see them as constructs, constitutive of social relationships.

'The basic ties of the family . . . are at the heart of our society and are the very nursery of civic virtue.'

(Margaret Thatcher)[1]

When Margaret Thatcher speaks thus about 'the family' she draws on several centuries of debate, concern and emotion surrounding an institution that is deemed central to individual and collective experience. Her words eloquently convey the aura that surrounds this abstraction – they are knowingly emotive, and hence they inadvertently reveal the cultural potency of the family as an idea. The fact that these very sentiments were frequently articulated in eighteenth-century Europe must be a matter of some interest to historians of culture, not least because they found their way into an impressive variety of verbal and visual forms. Explaining this historical phenomenon presents a challenge to cultural history and, through an understanding of the nature of this challenge, we can come to a better appreciation of the enterprise of cultural history and of the significance of the history of the family within it. In order to gain such insights we must first consider the history of the family as it is currently practised.

Historians of the family have so far shown little interest in its representation.[2] They treat the family as a social given, the contours of which are to be traced in specific historical setting. The result is usually a history of the family at a given time and place, with primacy given to description rather than analysis. Although there are historians who have focused on what the family is thought to be at various times and for different social groups, it is generally taken to be an unproblematic category, largely by virtue of its supposed biological status, which links it with nature, reproduction and the channelling of instinct. It is further assumed that, for the purposes of historical scholarship, the family is to be connected primarily with social and economic phenomena, especially in so far as they can be considered the manifestations of biological imperatives. Furthermore many historians who study the family do so because they believe it constitutes a fundamental aspect of everyday life for the majority of the population. The development of a new historical sub-discipline devoted to the subject is thus closely connected with the recent emergence into prominence of social history as a field that, however it is defined, stands in opposition to the conventional foregrounding of the world of politics.

There are, of course, influential scholars for whom the family is less an economic or social unit than an 'affective' one, at least for certain historical periods. Accordingly, it is the quality of the relationships between kin that assumes prominence. One might imagine that pioneering scholars of this persuasion, like Philippe Ariès and Lawrence Stone, who concern themselves with *mentalités*, feelings, and sentiments, would be engaged in writing a cultural history of the family, but this is not in fact the case.[3] In order to discuss how the cultural history of the family can be undertaken most effectively, it is therefore necessary to offer both a critique of existing approaches and alternative strategies.

The historiographical issues that arise in relation to the history of the family are complex; they will be explored in more detail shortly, particularly in relation to the question of evidence. Here it may be helpful to introduce the notion of representation. A cultural history of the family will perforce give a central position to the concept of representation. As a theoretical issue, representation occupies a prominent position in current debates in the humanities; it is not the exclusive property of any single discipline, being as applicable to words as to visual images, to history as to art and literature.[4] When scholars use the term they commit themselves to shunning simplistic approaches to the past that claim to capture it as it really was, and to embracing the challenge of working out how ideas are constructed, how languages are constantly both constituting and transforming experience. Although this approach has found favour among many literary critics and art historians, historians are much more reluctant to take it seriously. This is particularly true of those working on the family, many of whom seek to recapture parts of the past that deserve a voice but that have hitherto been relegated to secondary status because they pertain principally to the private domain. Recent generations of social, economic and demographic historians were certainly justified in wanting to open up a field to which little attention had previously been paid. What cannot be applauded is their treatment of sources as direct descriptions of the past, their neglect of visual materials and their refusal to treat the family as a cultural phenomenon.

There are a number of respects in which the family is best seen in cultural terms; it is not exclusively *determined* by material conditions but formed through habit, custom and convention according to prevailing beliefs; it touches on ideas of many different kinds and is present in a wide variety of cultural forms, including art, drama, poetry, fiction and so on. As well as being an element of social organisation, and a primary component of experience, the family is, in addition, an abstract idea. While it would therefore be possible to treat its past as a subject for the history of ideas, this would be unsatisfactory if we failed to show how the idea of the family was culturally embodied, and how these embodiments not only served the interests of specific groups but were also sites of conflict over what 'the family' was to mean and how it was to be represented. To neglect the cultural dimensions of the family is thus to neglect many of its most important historical properties.

In order to clarify what a cultural history of the family entails, we can best return to the pioneering work of Stone and Ariès. The English title of the latter's book, *Centuries of Childhood* is misleading, since it was the relationship between the concept of childhood and the concept of the family that concerned him. Taking a long chronological sweep from the middle ages to the eighteenth century, Ariès examined the evolution of these two ideas. Yet his is not purely an intellectual history, because it deals with changing feelings by tracing their expression in institutions and cultural forms such as painting and architecture. Iconography, for Ariès, is an index of large changes: it 'enables us to follow the rise of a new concept: the concept of the family'. In turn, this concept had 'become a value, a theme of expression, an occasion of emotion'.[5] His chapter devoted to images takes highly selected examples to make generalisations about shifts in attitudes.[6] This is an intuitive approach: one that assigns emblematic status to what appear as arbitrary cases. It would be wrong to condemn such an orientation outright, since, in the hands of a perceptive observer, it can yield striking insights. But it must be admitted that it is unsystematic. This manifests itself in two ways that are of particular relevance to the present chapter.

First, the conditions under which evidence has been produced are never examined; all evidence, be it visual or verbal, is treated as indicative, symptomatic, without any demonstration of this being offered. Such justification can be provided either by claiming that the evidence is 'representative' or by contextualising it, so that readers, by placing it, can assess its usefulness for themselves. Ariès does neither of these. Second, he is fond of global generalisations from which definitions of key terms are notable by their absence. For example, throughout the book he is at pains to connect the development of the child-centred, private family with social developments such as the dominance of the middle class. He concludes 'there is therefore a connection between the concept of the family and the concept of class'.[7] Such an approach is suggestive, yet over-reliant on Ariès's historical instincts – he never defines class, nor does he discuss chronological and geographical variations in class formation.

Ariès works on a large canvas, and paints with abstractions. The result is a picture of a whole society in the process of transformation. Indeed, he claims: 'these questions take us to the very heart of the great problems of civilization'.[8] It is a sentiment with which Stone is perfectly in tune, since his book, *The Family, Sex and Marriage in England, 1500–1800*, charts 'massive shifts in world views and value systems' and examines the rise of what he calls 'affective individualism'; 'perhaps the most important change in *mentalité* to have occurred in the Early Modern period, indeed possibly in the last thousand years of Western history.'[9] If the sweep of these two volumes is broadly comparable, the historical approaches underpinning them are quite distinct. Stone proclaims himself as a cultural historian concerned with *mentalités*, hence with large-scale transformation, but he also wishes to stress the empirical rigour of his methods. The strength and representative character of his 'data-base' are stressed. It is not just that he has examined many examples of a wide variety of sources, but he is also at pains to point out the interpretative difficulties they raise. None the less, these are not presented as serious, and they extend only to written materials – there is no recognition that visual sources pose their own interpretative challenges. Written sources indicate general trends, and in this respect Ariès and Stone are at one – sources offer relatively unproblematic access to the past.

Stone is careful to define key terms like family, household and lineage, and to address directly the question of social difference – the cultural stratification of family types, as he terms it. He stresses fragmentation and divisions between groups, assigning to the gentry and the professional classes the role of leading in value changes. Although Stone attacks a number of theoretical positions associated with the study of the family, especially those derived from functionalist sociology and psychoanalysis, he himself embraces the language of functions and holds, even if they are never fully articulated, psychological theories. But where Ariès seems to find shifts in ideas and emotions as integral to social and cultural change in general, Stone by contrast speaks of 'changes in culture *emerg[ing] from* changes in religion, social structure, political organization, economics, literacy and so on.'[10] In this formulation culture derives from and is thereby secondary to other historical phenomena.

I conclude from this brief discussion of Ariès and Stone first, that neither has undertaken to write cultural history in the fullest sense of the term, and, second, that they both see visual materials as simply and unproblematically illustrative of larger trends; by implication they are therefore either transparent or amenable to the same interpretation as written sources. A cultural history of the family requires that the historian consciously develop ways of interpreting diverse categories of sources in order that their special characteristics be recognised, that all these categories are read against each other to allow tensions as well as consistencies to emerge, that social difference be properly theorised. The acid test of how Stone and Ariès handle such matters in relation to pictures is the use of illustrations in their own books. Stone's 43 illustrations are largely drawn from caricatures and satirical prints (26 fall clearly into this category) without there being any discussion of the status of caricature as evidence. Furthermore the list of plates provides only very minimal information about each picture. The English edition of Ariès's book has no illustrations at all, despite the fact that the argument refers to numerous images. The French edition contains 24 illustrations, about which a certain amount of information is provided. The text none the less treats this category of evidence as perfectly straightforward. It seems, then, that, while Stone and Ariès are interested in pictures of the family, neither of them is truly interested in representation. The result is a series of problems that dog the use of visual materials by historians – the linked issues of 'realism', 'projection' and 'idealisation'.

Historians generally assume pictures to be more or less faithful depictions of scenes that enjoyed an existence independent of the image in question. Indeed, without such an assumption the way illustrations are generally used in history books would not make sense. But, as Michael Fried has so cogently argued, pictures are not evidence of anything outside themselves: 'the only evidence we have of that original situation and determining point of view is the painting itself, which obviously can't be taken to establish the existence of either'.[11] We can call this package of ideas and practices 'realism'. It implies that visual materials offer a form of access to the past that is fairly direct. The difficulties of these easy, settled assumptions are well illustrated by the case of portraiture. Among paintings, and particularly in relation to the family, portraits offer an accessible fund of images. It is possible to use them in three distinct ways. First, they can be treated as documents about those they depict; here the task of identifying sitters with as much exactitude as possible assumes overriding importance. Second, we can use portraits to trace patronage networks and to show the social and economic linkages between artists, patrons, sitters, their families and associates. For this approach exact attribution is also helpful, but it is not the sole object of the exercise. Third, portraits can become the occasion for posing generic questions about the nature of portraiture itself in a given historical context. Here we might ask about artistic conventions, especially as they relate to class, status, age and gender groupings, and, in consequence, the particular identity of the sitter becomes less important.[12] These conventions are of interest precisely because we can use them as indicators of those cultural processes through which roles and self-images are fashioned.

If we employ the first approach, it is easy to see how a commitment to 'realism' goes along with an unself conscious reaction to pictures that is highly projective. There is a powerful tendency to see what we want and expect to find. When we look at a portrait in this mode, we seek the character written in the face because we assume the picture captures, more or less well to be sure, the independent personality of the sitter. To a degree these projective processes inevitably occur, but this does not mean that we should be unaware of them. The point is especially important in relation to images of the family, because this idea continues to grip our imaginations so forcefully that we are bound to search especially urgently for the nature of the relationships between husband and wife and between parents and children, but in terms that are our own. Representations of the family and of intimate relationships seem to particularly invite fantasies about the nature of familial closeness because we invest this area with so much significance.

I advocate the third approach, which is in no way confined to portraiture, because it gives us access to the processes of cultural history – representation as process, not static description. Having seen that a belief in 'realism' is deceptive, we still have to come to terms with 'idealisation', however. It is perfectly possible for an image to be 'realistic' and 'idealising' at the same time. It can proclaim itself to be a depiction of something real (a claim we are not, of course, obliged to take at face value), while it also exaggerates certain features in order to draw a particular emotional response that lifts the viewer beyond their immediate experience and into some more abstract, generalised reaction. Again, pictures of the family raise this issue with special force, since many mother and child images are idealised in just the way I have been describing – they draw you on to imagine the mother–child dyad in general, perhaps especially in relation to the Holy Family. To see a portrait, or indeed any representation, as simply a faithful rendering of a particular individual or group of individuals admits no space between an original scene and the image within which the historian can operate. By contrast, once we recognise that simple notions of realism are untenable, that processes of idealisation need to be unpacked, that there are complex mediating processes between images and both their makers and their audiences, the way has been opened for a cultural history of representations of the family. Furthermore we also have the tools at our disposal to show how these processes differ from one historical situation to another. It so happens that the collective investment in the family took on particular, and especially intense, forms in the eighteenth century.

We have already noted that historians prefer to see their sources as having a straightforward relationship to a range of persons and events that enjoy the status of reality. Although they may be willing to admit that some interpretative work needs to be done on these materials, they none the less want to think in terms of description rather than representation. I do not wish to draw an overly stark contrast between description and representation, but it is convenient here to consider the differences between them in order to clarify the particular problems raised by studying the cultural history of the family. A marriage between social and cultural history will force attention upon this issue because the fields that have largely given rise to cultural history, such as art history and literature, are not so much concerned with evidence and description as with imagination and creativity. To join two areas, one of which is concerned with the 'real' (social history), the other with the imaginary (cultural history) is bound to give rise to problems. I have put this crudely in order to make clear why, in an area like the history of the family, traditionally the domain of deterministic *social* and *economic* approaches, examining culture is particularly difficult.

We can all agree that culture has some material component. Yet we cannot agree on either its extent or the precise ways in which ideas and experience interact. Thus, for example, Jane Austen's fictitious families bear some relationship to historical experiences, otherwise she could not have written about them, nor could readers have understood her books. The 'realist' genre that they inhabit leads us to expect such a relationship.[13] Despite the fact that many people still refer to her novels as *evidence* of how families conducted themselves, treating such writings as 'evidence' cannot be successfully defended as a rational position. At the same time, however, it would be unwise to sever all the links between literature and life. Here, then is the dilemma – how is it possible to understand the relationship between society and cultural constructs without crudely collapsing them together as two forms of the same historical phenomenon, thereby making culture society in another guise – the implication of treating an Austen novel as historical information? The alternative approach, which posits complex, interactive relationships between social and cultural phenomena, demands a consideration of representation as that which stands between these two levels.

Possibly these difficulties of linking social and cultural history are particularly acute when we take a theme like the family. Everyone thinks they know what 'the family' is. Everyone has strong views as to what it ought and ought not to be. Everyone experiences 'the family' in one form or another, even if only as a social/cultural ideal, and these experiences are embedded in the psyche at such a profound level that it is difficult to bring them up for conscious inspection. Furthermore, as noted above, it is customary to treat the family as natural, as the unquestioned basic social unit, and in societies that endow nature with authority this has a disabling effect on independent thinking.[14] So, whatever the approach taken, those who work on the family face peculiar difficulties; those who want to do the cultural history of the family even greater ones, because whereas 'culture' implies conscious construction, 'family' is deemed a natural given. Such a tension appears to vitiate the whole enterprise – a tension that can only be resolved by treating society itself as a construct, by refusing to accept *anything* as a natural given.

It immediately follows from this that we can focus on culture as the amalgam of processes whereby *all* aspects of society are constructed, sometimes specifically in order to *appear* as natural. It also follows that *all* history is cultural history, since there can be no processes, whether economic, social or political, which are not mediated through ideas, concepts, theories, images or languages. Art and literature cease then to be extras, focused on after the 'real' history has been done; they become constitutive of social relations. These ideas have been commonplace among literary and art historians for some time, but not among general historians. Two reasons for their lack of interest in culture and in the cultural history of the family in particular are pertinent here. First, the commitment to various forms of economic determinism is profound, if rarely made explicit. Second, the political, as conventionally conceived (public male power), continues to dominate and, in the current ideological climate, appears to be gaining ground, as the revival of conventional political and diplomatic history suggests. Accordingly, culture, however this unusually dense term is interpreted, becomes secondary, both in terms of its importance to society as a whole and of its capacity to explain historical phenomena. And, construed as a primarily *private* institution, the family can appear fascinating in a voyeuristic way, as a subject for mere social description.'[15]

Certainly, all this is in the process of change. Take, for example, the recent book by Leonore Davidoff and Catherine Hall, *Family Fortunes: Men and Women of the English Middle Class, 1780–1850*, which deals with the formation of the middle class through a detailed examination of religion, ideology and family/household organisation in two regions.[16] They are as much concerned with what people read and wrote, saw and depicted as with how much money they earned or how many children they had. They argue that class formation is mediated by gender, and that in turn gender is socially-cum-culturally constructed in a number of ways, so that ideology and economics both play a part but neither is given absolute priority. The *culture* of evangelicalism, like languages of gender, becomes as potent a historical force as changes in the organisation of production and the market. Davidoff and Hall's work is quite unusual in attempting to bring together different levels of analysis and in eschewing economic determinism and it points out some of the roads cultural historians of the family may wish to travel along.

In particular, how the diverse forms of evidence we deploy were produced is clearly a central consideration. Historians of the family have usually treated written and visual materials as direct, unmediated evidence, but, more importantly, they have mostly failed to consider how either their sources or the attitudes they supposedly express were *formed*. Without this the status of the sources cannot be assessed, nor can they be read at more than one level. It is not just *what* they say (for example, that they mourn a spouse or child) but *how* they say it (for example, the metaphors used to express grief) and under what conditions. The misguided, but long-running, debate about whether parents in the past loved their children exemplifies these points.[17] To assert that they either did or did not is not the goal of historical scholarship, partly because it implies a crude, over-drawn polarity about which we can only offer our prejudices. Rather, the cultural historian is concerned with the quality of parent–child relationships, with what these mean, and with what they represented. And, just as culture is integral to social relations, so images and metaphors are integral to culture. Historians, whatever their focus, ignore them at their peril. There is a double mediation here. Societies cannot function without concepts that affect, control and express their constituent processes. These concepts are put into play through languages, which thus also stand in a mediating relationship to fundamental ideas. No society can work without myriads of images (in the most extended sense) because, like languages – I include visual as well as verbal forms here – they are the very medium of thought and experience.

Images/representations are all-pervasive. What we dignify by the name of 'art' is just the organised, validated and self-conscious aspect of image making. The high-mindedness we like to associate with that field (art with a capital A) can be misleading. Pictures partake of the same processes of formation and consumption as other cultural artefacts; they embody the same strains and tensions. To a fully historical treatment of 'Art' we will eventually want to add a treatment of other kinds of artefacts that takes full account of their visual dimensions, as well as of their social location. To suggest that material culture should play a larger role in cultural history is to claim that no artefacts are excluded *a priori* from the historical enterprise. This means that drawings, prints, caricatures, inn signs, chap books, ballad sheets, playing cards, book illustrations, newspapers and posters, as well as painting with its diversity of genres, are relevant to the representation of the family in the eighteenth century. Yet we cannot treat these diverse types of evidence as equivalent, since the means, the settings and the occasions of their production differ dramatically.

We look at visual representation in the past through an exceptionally distorting lens. The contemporary art market, as well as evaluations of aesthetic merit, inform our judgements about 'important' or 'good' artists and about the contents of the major canon. Categories like 'important', 'major' or 'good' are hard to pin down, but creativity, capacity for innovation and the subject chosen all play a part. Relatively few portraitists or genre scene painters enjoy high status, and where they do it is often for quite special reasons. Chardin is a good example of this, since he contributed to 'low-status' genres, yet he currently enjoys a high status, largely because of admiration for the technical side of his work. By itself, family portraiture has never enjoyed high prestige within art, and such pictures are generally seen as having primarily historical/antiquarian value, especially in relation to the preservation of the stately homes in which they are mostly hung. Their merit is construed in *documentary* terms. The Reynolds exhibition, held at the Royal Academy in London during 1986, is a case in point.[18] The first items of information about the exhibits given in the catalogue were generally about who the people depicted were, placing them in kinship and patronage networks.

All these judgements inform the selection of pictures for public display. In one sense the elaborate processes through which 'Art' is constructed should not affect the enterprise of cultural history. However it inevitably does so because these processes define our visual repertoire, they establish cultural norms and standards, determined not by past societies but by present ones. 'Taste' has changed dramatically, so that not only did the range of visual materials in the past differ from those that are currently on display, but the importance accorded to particular categories has markedly altered.[19] Although there is a vocabulary that assists us in explaining changing artistic norms and preferences, associated with the terms 'style' and 'taste', such terms fail to capture the social and regional differences present in the historical record. It is clear that provincial taste in eighteenth-century England was in marked contrast to that of metropolitan art patrons. The stiff, formal, posed portraits of families and children persisted there long after they had ceased to be fashionable in London circles.[20] In other words, the standards of high art for that period, as they are fixed by art history, are historically misleading, and discourage us from asking questions about coexisting, but contrasting, visions of the family. If we accept that pictures of named families and individuals reveal something of the role models and self-images of that society, then the simultaneous existence of such discrepant pictures raises important historical issues.

A more genuinely historical assessment of representations of the family faces certain difficulties, which are not unlike those faced by historians of science not so long ago when they sought permission to study 'lesser' figures. However, it is relatively easy to examine the written work of such individuals in major libraries, much less easy to go through the store rooms of art galleries and stately homes. Nevertheless major artists *can* yield peculiarly valuable insights; not because of their 'genius', but because of their capacity to capture dominant, contemporary moods and preoccupations, and to experiment in historically significant ways. In the eighteenth century Reynolds, Gainsborough and Greuze, for example, each managed to grasp and give expression to contemporary experiences in relation to kinship in unusually apt ways. By any standards they were exceptional; at the same time, their work continues to yield insights into the period.

The demand, frequently articulated by historians, for representative sources, is misguided. Indeed the very term 'representative' implies that a series of documents could somehow *reflect* accurately its parent society. This is an illusion, since sources are always mediated in some form or other. Patently atypical sources can be extraordinarily revealing. Highmore's illustrations to *Pamela*, like the novel itself, are not 'typical' in any respect, nor are they obvious examples of 'high culture'[21] They are, however, enormously rich as historical sources, in, for example, articulating commonplaces, presenting anxieties about class, gender and status, and giving concrete form to deep-seated moral concerns. It is certainly not inconsistent to demand both that we consider a wider range of original materials – provincial as well as metropolitan, low as well as high art, images currently considered of poor artistic quality as well as those deemed masterpieces – and that we continue to study 'major' figures.

A new approach to the representation of the family will need to be built on a firm foundation. These foundations in their turn require an organising plan, one central component of which is a chronological framework. Far from being a matter of using available information to establish clear shifts, the question of chronology in relation to representations of the family is exceptionally tricky. It has become customary to follow the pioneering work of Philippe Ariès and assert that, some time during the seventeenth and eighteenth centuries, children ceased to be treated as miniature adults and that childhood was recognised for what it really was, a special state with its own characteristics and needs.[22] With this recognition of childhood as a special phenomenon, went, according to this historical thesis, a distinctive image of the family as isolated, emotional, child-centred and bourgeois. Despite a number of searing attacks on this thesis, it continues to be reiterated by historians of both art and the family, who point to phenomena such as the prolongation of childhood by more extended education, greater intimacy in domestic ties and less sociability with the world at large. These shifts were, it has been suggested, reflected in changing depictions of the family and its members, which become less formal, more intense emotionally, and often depict playful children delighting their parents. How far can these historical processes be traced in pictures themselves? Looked at in very broad terms, we can discern motifs and changes of convention that are consistent with this thesis. The way in which family members touch each other more, are even sometimes entwined, and the increasingly elaborate visual links between different parts of the canvas in eighteenth-century painting could all be used to support the thesis. *But*, alternative examples could be given that would hardly present such a neat historical account. We could point to the persistence of the stiff formality and stylised poses in the work of some painters, when others had already adopted the looser approach, or to the continued isolation of the father from other family members that is a perennial feature of the composition of portraits, as instances where the Ariès approach requires considerable modification.[23]

It may be worth noting in passing that there is a serious methodological difficulty here over the kinds of pictures that can reasonably be compared with one another. The Ariès thesis demands that we compare medieval and late eighteenth-century pictures of children and families. There is a difficulty in comparing pictures from different periods in this way; are we comparing like with like? Historical change itself makes such comparisons difficult, since shifts in genre, class and audience are all involved, as are profound alterations in the role pictures played in people's lives. The comparison drawn between Hogarth's *The Graham Children* (the offspring of a London apothecary) of 1742 and van Dyck's *The Five Eldest Children of Charles I*, painted in 1637, exemplifies the point. It has been suggested that Hogarth's work 'deliberately invited comparison with Van Dyck's famous [painting]'[24] but in what sense are two pictures, painted in such different circumstances and settings, and by artists working a century apart and with such divergent relationships to their subjects, comparable?

It is also worth noting that those who have criticised Ariès are no better off when it comes to explaining representations of the family and offering a coherent chronological account. For example, a recent critic, Linda Pollock, assumes that diaries, autobiographies and so on reflect a relatively unchanging reality; from her perspective it is equally hard to explain shifts in and the co-existence of different modes of representation, and the alleged continuity in parent–child relations simply enables her to sidestep the important interpretative issues.[25]

There are, broadly speaking, two main candidates for explaining the absence of linear change here; class and style. It would be possible to argue that changing conceptions of childhood arise in specific class fractions and then percolate, or are by various means disseminated, to other classes – this is what Stone argues, and it would be possible to test this out in relation to family portraiture, by analysing the class affiliations and aspirations of both sitters and artists over a wide range of paintings for a specific period.[26] It would also be possible to explain the complexity of representations of the family in formal terms by invoking such notions as style. This would be a difficult undertaking, partly because it begs the central question of how styles themselves arise and change and how this is to be explained historically. There is, however, some evidence suggesting that this would be a fruitful line of attack, and indeed it seems likely that contemporaneous differences in style are themselves linked with the class/status images both artists and sitters are striving to project.

In his major study *Les Peintres de la Vie Familiale. Evolution d'un Thème*, Louis Hautecour addressed the question of chronological change.[27] He associated pictures of the family *above all* with the eighteenth century, and posited as possible reasons for this the popularity of Dutch genre scenes, Anglomania (in France), the impact of Rousseau and the preoccupation with sentiment, among other phenomena. Unfortunately his approach never encourages him to ask about the definition of 'the family' in the first place. It may be helpful then to ask, what is this thing 'the family' that is being represented? There cannot be any direct answer to this because 'the family' is an abstraction, albeit a changing one, which is readily understood, then as now, but which cannot be simply defined. That indeed is its appeal. It is fruitless to talk of histories of the representation of the family without attempting to specify more closely what is being represented. To do this some consideration of genre and content is essential.

'The family', in different forms, was represented in genre scenes, in portraiture, in conversation pieces, in frontispieces and book illustrations, in history painting and in prints, to name only the most obvious categories relevant to the period. Each of these has its own history, a history which includes class dynamics and range of subject matter. In each case something distinct is being represented. In genre scenes it could be domesticity, the life of the household or domestic (dis)order, especially in relation to 'the people', while portraits tend to depict blood relations, property and lineage. There is significant diversity among portraits; some stress father–son relationships, others the mother–child bond, and whereas some depict the entire family – nuclear or extended – others focus on children. Book illustrations and history paintings, by contrast, proclaim the fictional/mythical nature of their subject matter, and there 'the family' is pre-eminently an element in a larger narrative and may lack the signifiers of class so fundamental to other traditions. In this connection it would be useful to compare portraits with genre scenes. We have a chance to do this with Reynolds, who painted many child portraits, with the sitters either in their own clothes or dressed up, and who also produced 'fancy pictures', which are more akin to genre scenes. They show children too: 'they were almost invariably pictures . . . of beggar or cottage children in other words of very poor children'.[28] These two classes of images differ markedly; the former are generally bright and light in tone, the latter sombre, and where portraits announce the secure social position of the child to the viewer, fancy pictures evoke the poor, those who are déclassé, outside polite society. Different genres speak to different facets of the family in a given historical situation. That they do so is also in part because of the intricate matching between genre and appropriate subject matter.

There are a number of ways of categorising the content of images of the family. It can be done simply in terms of what they depict, such as courtship, christening, daily life within the household, adultery, illicit love, mothers and children, work, leisure and the family members included. Equally significant are the ways in which the relationships between members are visually conveyed, and the setting in which families are represented. Pictures may evoke other abstractions in addition to 'the family', such as love, sexuality, intimacy, pleasure, crisis, conflict, moral purity and so on. And it is just as important to note the absences, the subjects thought *unfit* to be represented. Furthermore the content may be arranged in such a way as to elicit a specific response in the viewer, allowing pictures to act as morality lessons, *memento mori*, idealisations to be emulated and so on.

The *setting* is a crucial part of the subject matter; it is immediately apparent that locating the family in an actual home, an imaginary home, real property, imaginary property, generalised nature, generalised past, an identifiable time and/or place determines to a large degree the range of meaning the image can hold and the status viewers will give to it. At the same time, it is important to stress that what I have called 'content' is never self-evident. What may at first sight appear to be a simple portrait can be seen at another level as a painting about property and lineage. What looks like a quaint celebration of popular life may also be a moral discourse. Such ambiguity is not to be explained simply by saying that each picture can be decoded in a number of different ways, for this presumes, mechanistically, a fixed range of meanings in discrete signifiers. Rather, a multiplicity of meanings is to be understood in terms of the social processes of the culture that responds to the image, as Ronald Paulson has shown in relation to Hogarth's series about the industrious and idle apprentices.[29] It is because of their different experiences, their distinct social relationships that two groups, say masters and apprentices, can read the same series differently. Furthermore, just as social processes are an integral part of the reception of pictures, so they are of their construction.

In the processes involved in making a picture, the relationship generated between artists and their subject matter are of particular importance. For example the difference between the artist depicting real people and fictional ones is crucial, because in the former we have to consider the actual negotiations and social relationships between patron and painter, since these may constrain the artist's choice of pose, setting and general artistic conventions. Hautecoeur and Duncan imply that women *chose* to be painted as, say, sentimental mothers.[30] Eighteenth-century portraits of mothers are thus the result of elaborate transactions between sitters and artists, with each side carrying an equally elaborate cultural baggage. While it is possible that wealthy sitters in particular were in a position to exert pressure upon artists, it is also plausible that sought-after painters, like Reynolds, had strong ideas not only about poses, background, decor and so on, but also about the prior artistic models they wanted to draw on, emulate and hence evoke in viewers' minds. None the less the control exercised by the artist in genre painting, even where models were used for the figures, was potentially far more extensive.

Although economic transactions between artists and sitters are significant, it would surely be a mistake to suppose that the relationship between them can be understood mainly in terms of *overt* forms of power. Hard as it may be to analyse, these relationships also had a psychic dimension, and it is likely that this assumes special importance when issues, like the family, are raised, about which all human beings have intense feelings at different levels of awareness.[31] We can see this with particular clarity in the special case of the artist depicting his or her own family, particularly when self-portraits are included. Elizabeth Vigée-Lebrun's pictures of herself and her daughter are a well-known example, but equally intriguing are two works by Nollekens depicting his own children, Gainsborough's pictures of his daughters, Largillièrre's portrait of himself with wife and daughter and Vestier's portrait of his wife and child that includes his own likeness as a partially veiled canvas.[32] These cannot be seen as just like other forms of portraiture, since the relationships that gave rise to them were so particular. Perhaps another special case is the depiction of the Holy Family, not especially common in the eighteenth century, where the relationship between artist and that which he or she is portraying may have a determining influence on the outcome because painting is also an act of devotion. There is ample evidence during the eighteenth century of the family being treated as a sacred entity, and it is now appropriate to draw out some of those attributes that characterise representations of the family in the period.[33]

It is important not to reify 'the family'. What the term means and denotes is amazingly labile, hence there is no *thing* that representations of the family depict, only sets of ideas. It is therefore to be expected that each epoch has its own distinctive range of images, the very distinctiveness of which offers the major clues to the specific issues the family was currently being used to explore. We need then to be aware of some of the broader themes that characterise thinking about the family in this period, partly in order to avoid a simplistic use of style as an explanation for change.

There can be no doubt about the general importance of the family as a theme in eighteenth-century thought and culture. It is evident in legal debates, in actual legislation, in the extensive concern about the functioning of inheritance provisions, and in the equally intense medical concern about the health of family members.[34] It is just as clear in the philanthropy of the period, where it was precisely an abstract notion of the family that organised responses to foundlings, poverty and prostitution.[35] Political theorists remained concerned with the relationships between the family and the state or body politic – as much in England where formal patriarchalism was hardly taken seriously, as in France where it was.[36] Even if we turn to debates about production and consumption, in their more theoretical form in political economy or in their more pragmatic one in the provision of poor relief, the family remains a central term.[37]

In writings about the family many subjects were discussed which found visual expression; these included wet-nursing, the special status of children, the bond between mothers and children, the link between women as mothers and as sexual creatures. Other common themes, such as courtship, adultery and prostitution bear on the family indirectly, although none the less centrally. Yet another set of themes, no less central to debates about the family, was little explored in *visual* terms. These themes include the work of women and children, abandonment and infanticide, illegitimacy, the act of marriage, death of family members and widowhood. Such silences are indeed eloquent. Some never were the subject of sustained artistic endeavour, but others, such as female and child labour, offered considerable visual potential to later generations. There also seems to have been a particular problem with depicting the family in an *urban* setting during the eighteenth century. Family portraits are often set, either partly or completely, out of doors, while a high proportion of relevant genre scenes are interiors. Where family-related themes are shown in an urban setting, as, for example, in Hogarth's Gin Lane, the personal relationships are shown to be seriously defective. Naturally, shifts in the facets of the family chosen for representation partly reflect changes in the theory and practice of art, but it would be mistaken either to reduce these to a succession of styles or to assume that they are *internal* to art.

An obvious example of this issue is the influence of Dutch genre painting on eighteenth-century artists, and on those concerned with the family in particular. Hautecoeur attributes exceptional importance to this guiding tradition for those depicting 'family life', because he has in mind a somewhat naive notion of realism. For example, of Chardin he wants to claim that he painted petty-bourgeois life 'as it really was' because that was the milieu he himself inhabited. This hardly explains the nature of Chardin's success, nor why his pictures possess such distinctive qualities. Presumably a fair number of painters came from not dissimilar backgrounds without producing similar pictures. Furthermore, to identify the persons and objects contained in the paintings as really part of Chardin's household does not explain their significance on the canvas. When eighteenth-century artists and audiences responded with special enthusiasm to Dutch art, they were reacting to its social, political and economic resonances. They may indeed have been seduced by its claims to realism and

naturalism, but we should not take the claims, either of the
original painters or of their eighteenth-century devotees, at their
face value. In fact, Dutch art, and that derived from it, is enmeshed
with questions of class, because its subject matter privileges
middle-class groupings broadly defined, and eschews the overtly
mythological subject matter that was so important to patrons of
high art in both the seventeenth and eighteenth centuries. Indeed,
if we are searching for themes that characterise eighteenth-century
approaches to the representation of the family, class must undoubtedly be considered as of outstanding importance.

There were a number of ways in which class functioned in
representations of the family in the eighteenth century. Of course,
to formulate the question in such stark terms begs a lot of
questions about the nature and pace of class formation in European society at this time. We must begin with the term 'class' itself
– like family, it must not be reified; it is, as E. P. Thompson has
said, not a thing but a relationship and, as many historians of the
period have now shown, class was as much bound up with culture
as it was with economics.[38] I apply it where commentators/artists
explicitly draw the reader/viewer's attention to social rather than
to fixed legal differences (of status, wealth, rank) *and* indicate
conflict of some form between the resulting groups. For example,
the antagonism towards aristocratic life-styles is such a prevalent
theme in literature written by or aimed at professional, philan-
thropic, 'middle-class' people that it can hardly be ignored, and it
must have the term 'class conflict' applied to it. This endows the
portrayal of decadent personal behaviour by identifiable upper-
class protagonists as well as of worthy, sentimental family bond-
ings with a sharp relevance and vibrancy. At the same time,
idealisations of family relationships often convey a form of class-
lessness quite consistent with the use of nature/the natural as
emotive guiding terms in relation to the family. The 'good' mother
is the natural mother who, turning away from social artificiality,
rears her children by instinct. Such a mother does not need to be
grounded in the specificity of her social location because the
quality of her mothering can transcend her actual position. We can
see a similar situation developing in relation to children, who,
being increasingly if problematically associated with nature, can
be depicted *outside* society, that is as beyond divisiveness and
beyond the decadence of the *ancien régime*. Of course, many
portraits still did locate both mothers and children socially, but

they did not have to. Where nature is used to elide class, it does not mean that it is absent. For instance, the way in which putatively natural family relationships are presented in fact *covertly* conveys the ideas of a particular class. The dynamics between that and other classes are therefore inevitably built in. A sense of class thus manifests itself in many different forms; with the natural often veiling the social.

From the written literature we learn that relations between employers and servants were perceived as a growing problem that was linked to social antagonisms during the eighteenth century, presumably because servants were still perceived as integral in *some* way to 'the family'.[39] We know that the term 'family' was generally used inclusively in English to embrace all household members. Raymond Williams states in his definition of 'family' in *Keywords:* 'In none of the pre-mC17 senses, therefore, can we find the distinctive modern sense of a small group confined to immediate blood relations.'[40] However, he is unsure *when* the restricted meaning came to dominate, although he finds it well established in the nineteenth century.

I have not been able to find any traditions of *portraiture* which included servants routinely; rather, portraits in the eighteenth century seem designed to reinforce property, lineage and a certain quality of intimate relationships. A striking exception to the point about servants, Reynolds' portrait of Clive, his wife, daughter and Indian female servant, is unusual in a number of respects and thereby acts as confirmation of the point.[41] Often, when eighteenth-century commentators expressed anxiety about the role of servants in households, they had sexual matters in mind. Greuze's *The Launderess* of 1761 is an interesting example of this. It must be admitted that a launderess is not a typical domestic servant; none the less they did serve the needs of households. Greuze's young woman is seated in a slightly chaotic kitchen, and looks up from her work to gaze at the viewer directly, with a pert expression. The erotic suggestions are clear, and they were picked up by Diderot: 'this little launderess is charming, but she's a rascal I wouldn't trust an inch'.[41] In his picture Greuze has therefore blended together female sexuality, the domestic sphere and service. Sexual misdemeanours are often shown as being a problem of servants or of those who are somehow déclassé. It would be possible to recast this and say that there is considerable interest in exactly how the employing family should manage their relationships with their servants, who are coming to be seen as 'not-family' and as of a distinct class background. We therefore need an account of eighteenth-century images of the family which takes account both of the potent associations established between *nature* and the family, which leads to an effacement of signs of class, *and* of the intense preoccupation with class, that is *social* differences as they manifest themselves through the family and household.

The idealisation of mothers and children – the centrepiece of the natural family – is an obvious feature of the period. But what about fathers? Carol Duncan and Norman Bryson both suggest that later eighteenth-century France experienced a peculiar crisis in relation to fatherhood, a political crisis as much as anything, which is clearly evident in pictures.[43] There were certainly a number of ways in which, even in relatively conventional family portraiture, fathers were rendered peripheral, largely through a mode of composition that set them apart, behind chairs or not linked to the main grouping. Yet we certainly could *not* argue that the male line, as the medium through which rights, property and status were transmitted, declined in importance over the eighteenth century. This neatly demonstrates a point made earlier: that to expect representations to *reflect* social processes is wrongheaded. At the same time it also indicates how very intricate a job it is to tease out all the mediations between society and culture.

Such jobs are not just the domain of cultural history in particular, but of history in general. If the practice of cultural history can show historians ways in which to analyse the *construction* of societies, economies and political systems, it will perform an exceptionally valuable service. If ideas of reflection can give way to those of representation, so much the better. An area like the history of the family is exceptionally ripe for such an approach, because the family encompasses so many distinct, yet related, dimensions of human existence.

Notes

1. Margaret Thatcher, 'Address to the General Assembly of the Church of Scotland', *Observer*, no. 10259, 22 May 1988.
2. Most of what has appeared on the subject will be cited in subsequent notes. For a general survey of the history of the family as a field see M. Anderson, *Approaches to the History of the Western Family 1500–1914*, London, 1980.

3.   P. Ariès, *L'Enfant et La Vie Familiale sous L'Ancien Régime*. Paris, 1960, 2nd ed 1973, translated as *Centuries of Childhood*, London, 1962; Harmondsworth, 1973; L. Stone, *The Family, Sex and Marriage in England 1500–1800*. London, 1977; Harmondsworth, 1979, abridged, unillustrated edition.

4.   See particularly the journal *Representations*, Berkeley, 1983 on.

5.   Quotations from Ariès, *Centuries of Childhood*, pp. 351 and 8 respectively.

6.   Ibid., ch. 14.

7.   Ibid., p. 398.

8.   Ibid., p. 9.

9.   Quotations from Stone, *The Family, Sex and Marriage*, 1977, pp. 3 and 4 respectively.

10. Ibid., p. 4, my emphasis.

11. M. Fried, 'Reading, Writing and Disfiguration in Thomas Eakins' Gross Clinic', *Representations*, no. 9, 1985, pp. 33–104, quotation from p. 72.

12. An outstanding example of this approach is David Solkin, 'Great Pictures or Great Men? Reynolds, Male Portraiture, and the Power of Art', *Oxford Art Journal*, 9, 1986, pp. 42–9.

13. I. Watt, *The Rise of the Novel: Studies in Defoe, Richardson and Fielding*, Harmondsworth, 1963, remains a useful account of the philosophical and fictional issues that I am here referring to as 'realism'.

14. I have attempted to explore this issue in an eighteenth-century context in 'Naturalizing the Family: Literature and the Bio-Medical Science in the Late Eighteenth Century', in L. Jordanova, ed., *Languages of Nature, Critical Essays on Science and Literature*, London, 1986, pp. 86–116.

15. The public–private distinction is therefore central to any discussion of the family and its representation; see J. B. Elshtain, *Public Man, Private Woman*, Oxford, 1981, J. B. Elshtain, ed., *The Family in Political Thought*, Brighton, 1982; S. Benn and G. Gaus, eds, *Public and Private in Social Life*, London, 1983.

16. L. Davidoff and Catherine Hall, *Family Fortunes, Men and Women of the English Middle Class, 1780–1850*, London, 1987.

17. L. Pollock, *Forgotten Children: Parent–Child Relations from 1500–1900*, Cambridge, 1983, chs 1 and 2; S. Wilson, 'The myth of motherhood a myth', *Social History* ix, 1984, pp. 181–98.

18. N. Penny, ed, *Reynolds*, London, 1986.

19. R. G. Saisselin, 'Neo-classicism: Images of Public Virtue and Realities of Private Luxury', *Art History*, 4, 1981, pp. 14–36.

20. See, for example, the cover illustration on Davidoff and Hall's *Family Fortunes* (a detail from W. Williams, *Conversation Piece, Monument Lane, Edgbaston*) and items 202 and 203 in *Manners and Morals. Hogarth and British Painting 1700–1760*, London, 1987, p. 218, portraits of children by Christopher Steele and George Romney, both of which are described as 'provincial'. The work of Arthur Devis is another case in point.

21. *Manner and Morals*, pp. 156–9.
22. P. Crown, 'Portraits and fancy pictures by Gainsborough and Reynolds: contrasting images of childhood', *British Journal for Eighteenth-Century Studies*, vii, 1984 pp. 159–67 (& 11 plates); *Manners and Morals*, e.g. pp. 15, 35, 113, 129, 135 and 141.
23. In addition to the examples given in note 20, *Manners and Morals*, which is full of paintings related to the family, offers numerous examples of the coexistence of radically different approaches to portraiture in the same period. Even moving into the later period, for example, the heydays of both Reynolds and Gainsborough, the father of the family is frequently placed either behind a chair (for example, Gainsborough's *the Baillie Family* c. 1784 in The Tate Gallery) or to one side of the painting, sometimes with other males (for example, Reynolds' *The Marlborough Family*, 1778).
24. *Manners and Morals*, p. 141
25. Pollock, *Forgotten Children*.
26. The 'percolation' approach was brilliantly dissected by Keith Thomas in his review of Stone, 'The Changing Family', *Times Literary Supplement*, 21 October 1977, pp. 1226–7.
27. L. Hautecœur, *Les Peintres de la Vie Familiale: Evolution d'un Thème*, Paris, 1945, esp. ch. 3.
28. P. Crown, 'Portraits and fancy pictures', p. 159; see also Penny, *Reynolds*, pp. 32–4, 264–5, 269–70.
29. R. Paulson, *Popular and Polite Art in the Age of Hogarth and Fielding*, Notre Dame, 1979, ch. 2, The Apprentice; see also S. Shesgreen, 'Hogarth's "Industry and Idleness": a reading', *Eighteenth-Century Studies*, ix, 1975–6, pp. 45–68.
30. Hautecœur, *Les Peintres de la Vie Familiale*, C. Duncan, 'Happy mothers and other ideas in 18th-century Art', *Art Bulletin*, lx, 1973, pp. 570–83.
31. R. Wollheim, *Painting as an Art*, London, 1988, esp. ch. 5, attempts to tackle this question.
32. Hautecœur, *Les Peintres de la Vie Familiale*, reproduces examples from Vigée-Lebrun, Largillièrre and Nestier; examples from Nollekens and Gainsborough are to be found in *Manners and morals*, in which see also p. 153 for a picture by Highmore that is probably of his own family.
33. Although it deals only with France, D. G. Charlton sketches in these themes in the context of eighteenth-century culture in *New Images of the Natural in France*, Cambridge, 1984; see especially ch. 7.
34. In relation to law, see, for example, Stone, *The Family, Sex and Marriage*, 1979, p. 32 and chs 5, 7 and 8, S. M. Okin, 'Patriarchy and Married Women's Property in England: questions on some current views', *Eighteenth-Century Studies*, xvii, 1983–4, pp. 121–38; J. F. Traer, *Marriage and the Family in Eighteenth-Century France*, Ithaca, 1980; and on health see, C. Lawrence, 'William Buchan: Medicine laid open', *Medical history*, xix, 1975 pp. 20–35, L. Jordanova, 'The popularisation of medicine: Tissot on Onanism', *Textual Practice*, 1, 1987, pp. 68–79 and R. Porter, ed, *Patients and Practitioners: Lay*

Perceptions of Medicine in Pre-industrial Society, Cambridge, 1985; chs 6–10 deal with the eighteenth century; see especially ch. 9.

35. R. K. McClure, *Coram's Children: The London Foundling Hospital in the Eighteenth Century*, New Haven, 1981, J. S. Taylor, 'Philanthropy and Empire; Jonas Hanway and the infant poor of London', *Eighteenth-Century Studies*, xii, 1979, pp. 285–305.

36. In addition to the items cited in note 15 above, see E. Kennedy and S.Mendus, eds, *Women in Western Political Philosophy*, Brighton, 1987, and G. Schochet, *Patriarchalism in Political Thought*, Oxford, 1975.

37. P. Buck, 'People who counted: political arithmetic in the eighteenth century', *Isis*, lxxiii, 1982, pp. 28–45, J. McManners, *Death and the Enlightenment*, Oxford, 1981, ch. 4, K. Smith, *The Malthusian Controversy*, London, 1951.

38. E. P. Thompson, *The Making of the English Working Class*, Harmondsworth, 1963, especially the Preface, and his important article, 'Eighteenth-century English society; class struggle without class?', *Social History*, iii, 1978, pp. 133–65, Davidoff and Hall, *Family Fortunes*, esp. Prologue.

39. Indirectly this is a major theme in Richardson's *Pamela* (first published in 1740) – see note 21 above; also relevant is C. Fairchilds, *Domestic Enemies: Servants and their Masters in Old Regime France*, Baltimore, 1984, esp. part 2.

40. R. Williams, *Keywords. A Vocabulary of Culture and Society*, rev. edn, London, 1983, p. 132.

41. Penny, *Reynolds*, pp. 216–17; another outstanding exception, although from a later period, is William Mulready's *Interior with a Portrait of John Sheepshanks*, 1832–4, in which the servant is as prominent a figure on the canvas as the named sitter; see M. Pointon, *Mulready*, London, 1986, p. 94 and plate xii.

42. This painting is in the Getty Museum at Malibu; *Handbook of the Collections*, Malibu, 1986, p. 111 where Diderot's remark is also quoted.

43. N. Bryson, *Word and Image: French Painting of the Ancien Régime*, Cambridge, 1981, esp, ch. 5; C. Duncan, 'Fallen Fathers; Images of Authority in pre-Revolutionary French Art', *Art History*, iv, 1981, pp. 186–202.

6

'Intellectual Ornaments': Style, Function and Society in Some Instruments of Art

Martin Kemp

Martin Kemp's chapter serves as a contrast and also partial confirmation of Jordanova's approach. Kemp writes that the existence of rigidly demarcated intellectual disciplines means that cultural artefacts are often put into interpretative categories which do not reflect their real nature. The plea for cross-disciplinary study (which Kemp realises will be difficult to fulfil) goes together with a rejection of the fashionable semiotic readings of texts which are intrinsically reductive of the variety and vitality of cultural artefacts. Clearly, Kemp from his particular background in art history, wants to keep the individual and the untidiness of history in the foreground and is suspicious of any historical determinism, whatever the amount of mediation that may lie between cause and effect. Yet, although from a very different theoretical position, he, like Jordanova, sees the value of cultural history. Kemp's vision of the new history, especially as regards the history of style, is that of a loose, intuitive, associationist technique so that the true nature of similar objects and their social contexts can emerge uninfluenced by the categories of pre-existing taxonomies.

Kemp uses as his example optical devices 'for the achieving of miracles of art' in the early modern period and in the late eighteenth and early nineteenth century, and he uses them to illustrate how a new, 'style history' can be applied to artefacts that do not fit into the standard categories of the history of art. The questions he sees posed for cultural historians are those of survival, patronage, value and collectability – all requiring re-examination and cutting across our conventional taxonomies. His illustrations suggest a shared discourse and mythology but, more important, a shared knowledge and belief demonstrating a less easily recoverable identity.

As one reads Kemp's analysis it becomes clear that for him boundaries disappear, the horizon enlarges and changes, allusions and associations multiply and cultural history becomes the means to achieve an integration of the individual object and its artists with the social and mental nexus that surrounds them, which is not deterministic but gives full play to the individualism of the historian and the artist.

However much we may pay lip-service to the breaking of boundaries between intellectual disciplines as currently defined – and however much as historians we may recognise that our categories fail to mesh in significant ways with those of the periods with which we are concerned – compelling forces are working to ensure that the current classifications are reinforced rather than weakened. The forces are both institutional and intellectual, in complexly associated ways. The professional institutionalisation of branches of historical endeavour seems to have an inexorable force of its own. The various disciplines, corresponding in large measure to the taxonomies of current endeavour in society, have been reinforced by structures within each of our organisations of higher education and by the proliferation of professional societies of increasing size and self-importance. At the same time, the internalised histories of the disciplines, as represented in specialised journals, conferences and so on, have developed to a point of elaboration – technically and bibliographically – that tends to exclude 'outsiders'. Indeed, specialised exclusivity is a requisite for the foundation, growth and survival of the discrete, subject-based departments in Universities and Polytechnics in Britain and abroad.

The gains in professionalism and dangers of compartmentalisation are obvious to the historian, but I do not think it is always recognised how profoundly the internalised history of each individual discipline may in itself be weakened and at worst vitiated by the current system.

Although there have been encouraging recent signs that historians in a number of disciplines are willing to court the professional perils of operating beyond the conventional boundaries of their ostensible subject, the main bases for historical endeavour

continue to be located firmly within the conventional classifications. I think that the problems are illustrated in a particularly
vivid way by the history of man-made objects or artefacts. This
'branch' of history does not exist as such – it is not wholly identical
with the history of 'material culture' – but needs to be synthesised
from various bodies of objects which are generally handled
separately within various artistic and technical disciplines. I am
thinking of a kind of history in which a print, a candlestick, a
porcelain figure, a kettle, a kaleidoscope, a thermometer and an
agricultural implement are invited to speak of their shared cultural
ambiance, not in terms of a cosmetic recreation of a past culture, as
a series of tableaux in a historical Disneyland, but by respecting
the subtle visual language spoken by each object individually and
within different groupings.

Existing atempts to read the 'signs' of artefacts, particularly in
the recently-fashionable semiotic, structuralist, post-structuralist
and deconstructionist modes, seem to me to categorise visual
qualities far too crudely in the service of a dogmatic set of
socioeconomic prescriptions. In such systems, visual material only
seems to become of value when it can be categorised according to
certain common denominators and made to correspond to some
gross assumptions about historical causation. The gross assumptions seem at first sight to exhibit real explanatory power and to
present a basis upon which cultural history can proceed. However,
faced with the sheer variety and vitality of artefacts originating
within even a single culture, the explanatory systems appear to me
to be profoundly unsatisfying. I should like to suggest in this
chapter that a new kind of style history may have a role to play
both in breaking down the existing classifications of objects
within historical disciplines and in showing that the interplay
between institutional forces and the cerebral life of the individual
needs to be understood in a far more subtle manner than any of us
has yet achieved. The breaking-down of taxonomies is the more
clearly achievable of these aspirations, and will provide a more
convenient initial goal.

The way an object is tackled by the historian is utterly dependent upon the *kind of thing* it is taken to be, according to our
categories of knowledge. The parameters of the questions to be
asked and, therefore, the relevant evidence, are conditioned by its
assumed classification. Thus the questions asked about a 'work of
art' have a particular nature – and the answers are given in a

vocabulary of a specific kind – while those concerning, for example, a 'scientific instrument' are essentially different. It would of course be absurd to claim that an altarpiece and an astrolabe do not require different questions to be asked of them – differences relating fundamentally to function (in the broadest sense). But the way we have come to view the ontology of the objects, as reflected for example in the divisions between and within different types of museum, may create serious distortions with respect to the original functional context and may even result in their being seen as the wrong kind of object altogether.

This problem becomes most transparently obvious when we study a set of objects which appears to fall outside or between existing categories in such a way as to have been subject to no sustained internal history of its own. The devices or instruments that are to be the subject of this study comprise such a set. It is a symptom of the problem that they do not have a clear collective name. 'Artists' devices', 'artists' instruments', 'drawing machines', or some such term does not bring readily to mind a generally recognisable category of object with a clear set of examples within acceptable parameters. The majority of the objects at which I will be looking lurk uneasily in the hands of keepers of scientific instruments, particularly those in charge of collections devoted to optics. The result in this context is that they tend to be regarded as peripheral or curious, since they do not function as scientific instruments should, while the need is generally removed for art historians to look at them at all.

However I believe that they have a good deal to tell us, in the histories both of science and of art. And, as objects that fall into a 'non-category', they can provide a convenient means of questioning the validity of existing taxonomies. If we look at the intellectual and social nexus from which the devices originated we will find that they cast light on questions of patronage, collection, the statuses of arts and sciences, attitudes to nature in relation to human endeavour and so on. They can also shed light upon the important but neglected question of historical survival. Objects only survive in significant numbers if there has been a reason or a series of reasons for preserving them over the ages. The survival may well relate to the original nature of the object from the outset as something valuable or collectable. Thus a 'scientific instrument' made as a luxury object for a *wunderkammer* – as an 'intellectual ornament' – is more likely to survive than a larger-scale device built to serve a specific observational need at a particular moment.

In fact, even looking within what appears to be the reasonably secure functional category of 'scientific instrument' we may begin to see that our modern categories provide a less than appropriate tool for their understanding. The collections of instruments in museums are invariably seen as bearing witness to a vision of scientific progress through a landscape punctuated by monuments of observational achievement and peopled by the conventional heroes and villains in the story of science.[1] The telescopic lenses of Galileo (Plate 1) become totems of instrumental progress and precious relics of a scientific saint.[2] We tend to assume in the case of other astronomical instruments in museums, such as astrolabes, that the functional context for their interpretation is clear. They are observational devices which are to be valued for their degree of precision and for what they tell us of science of that age. Yet much of the astronomical paraphernalia that survives from the Renaissance, including astrolabes and, even more obviously, armillary spheres (Plate 2), has little observational value in terms of advanced astronomy. Many of the devices are simply too small to be of much service in detailed observations of the stars.[3] Rather, they appear to be delightful crystallisations of astronomical concepts; they are, to use the phrase in my title, 'intellectual ornaments', luxury objects fabricated and adorned at considerable expense within the context of Renaissance patronage. It is because of the very fact that they were, from the first, collectable objects that they have survived, while some of the larger-scale, less obviously 'artistic' instruments used for observational purposes have perished.

Questions of style have a vital role to play in making such judgements. Style history has become unfashionable in the history of art, and in its earlier incarnations tended to become an internalised, jargon-ridden exercise of the most inward-looking kind. However I think there is a form of style history that can establish cultural nexuses spanning conventional taxonomies of function in a rewarding way. According to criteria of style, sixteenth-century armillary spheres and related instruments belong more comfortably with a connoisseur's *bronze* (Plate 3) than they do with a nineteenth-century sextant.

The sense of style I am using here does not primarily concern issues of dating and attribution, but rather a language of visual 'qualities' that conveys meaning in a social context. My way of proceeding will be associational and quite deliberately exhibits a kind of looseness, yet I believe this rather intuitive approach can lead us back to some precise questions about the intellectual and material circumstances which have given rise to particular families of artefacts.

In talking about such 'families' of stylistic qualities, I am not trying to forge a new series of categories that can be explained causally according to certain crude principles in terms of 'product', 'consumption' and so on. Rather, I believe that the 'families' are almost infinitely open and flexible. The same object may speak a different visual language within one of its families than in another. Thus the visual qualities of the Giovanni Bologna bronze become eloquent in different ways in different contexts – in, for instance, a hypothetical museum display of bronze statuettes from the Renaissance to the nineteenth century, or in an exhibition of cultural and scientific artefacts from the Medicean court. Neither of these contexts is the 'right' one. They are both 'right' and 'wrong' in different ways, and each has its validity in terms of the different strands in the infinitely complex web of historical causation.

With these qualifications in mind, I will be broaching considerations of style, function and society through a series of devices associated with the art-historical contexts with which I am most familiar. These devices are optical machines for the achieving of 'miracles of art' (to use the phrase of Leon Battista Alberti, the author of the first book on art theory).[4] I will concentrate on two contrasting but strongly related phases in the design of such machines: firstly during a period of about 80 years on either side of 1600; and secondly during a period of popularisation during the social revolutions of the late eighteenth and early nineteenth centuries. I will try to suggest how the styles of the devices can be read as if they are objects of applied or even fine art in a variety of intellectual and social contexts.

The ambition to invent a machine for the imitation of nature appears to have been peculiar to the Western tradition of naturalism in arts from the Renaissance onwards. It is predicated upon the belief that the direct imitation of 'what we see' is both desirable and possible. But the imitation of nature was accompanied by a series of concepts such as beauty, imagination and style which emphasised the role of individual talent. The reservations about mechanical imitation were apparent from the earliest mentions of such devices. When Alberti was discussing the use of the 'veil' – a loosely woven cloth stretched across a pictorial window frame – he recorded the opinion of 'those who say it is no good for the painter to get into the habit of using these things, because, although they offer him the greatest help in painting, they render the artist unable to do anything without them'.[5]

Leonardo, in spite of his insistence on the foundation of art in nature, was even more explicit:

> There are some who look at the things produced by nature through glass or other surfaces or transparent veils. They trace outlines on the surface of the transparent medium [Plate 4] . . . But such an invention is to be condemned in those who do not know how to portray things without it, nor how to reason about nature with their minds . . . They are always poor and mean in every invention.[6]

Such reservations did not, however, discourage increasingly elaborate attempts to devise such machines for the imitation of nature. Their first golden age occurred in the sixteenth century. This happened at a time when the painter's science of perspective was subject to increasing attention from leading practitioners of practical mathematics, such as Federigo Commandino, Ignazio Danti, Giovanni Battista Benedetti and Guidobaldo del Monte.[7] It is not surprising that the devices originating from the orbit of such scientists should show strong allegiances with the increasingly fashionable instruments in the fields of terrestrial and celestial mensuration. Let me show you what I mean by looking at the kind of devices discussed by Danti in his 1584 commentary on the perspective treatise, *Le due regole*, by Jacopo Barozzi da Vignola.[8] One device is a relatively abstract demonstration piece which provides basic instruction in perspective diminution (Plate 5). It was credited to Tommaso Laureti, to whom we will return. The other is a perspective machine of a practical if eccentric kind, invented by Baldassare Lanci. The woodcut illustration (Plate 6) gives only a rudimentary idea of Lanci's device for the recording of a panoramic scene on paper mounted within a hemi-cylinder. Fortunately, Lanci's device has survived in Florence (Plate 7), and is signed and dated 1557.[9] It is recognisable as one of an entirely characteristic group of devices for mensuration originating from the Medici court of the mid-sixteenth century. Indeed, its engraved decoration shows it in use as a surveying device, when the central pivot of the drawing machine is unscrewed.

Viewed as a cultural artefact rather than simply as a scientific instrument, its style, coupled with the name of its author, brings a series of associations in its train. Baldassare Lanci was one of Cosimo de Medici's engineers, specialising in military architecture.[10] His skills as a perspectivist are fully manifested in a surviving design for a Florentine stage scene (Plate 8), in which a number of key buildings have been subjected to some judicious relocation for the sake of visual coherence.[11] Lanci's device breathes the world of this courtly context. It is a luxury object manufactured under a princely patron to whom artist, engineers and scientists alike looked for support – including, as we know, Ignazio Danti, until the death of grand Duke Cosimo I. To describe Lanci's device as an 'executive toy' would be unfair to both patron and designer, since both men were genuinely concerned with its intellectual-cum-technical merits, but its appeal to the patron did undoubtedly include its entertainment or 'curiosity' value, together with its ability to enhance the aura of enlightened magnificence through which Cosimo signalled his qualities to the world at large. It belongs to the world of the Renaissance *studiolo*, in which astrolabes and armillary spheres rub shoulders with lutes, classical cameos and unicorn horns. The *studioli* of the sixteenth century, most notably Francesco de Medici's room in the Palazzo Vecchio, had become increasingly concerned with elaborate cosmologies of scientific and arcane knowledge.[12] Similar themes of courtly intellectualism are demonstrated on a grander and more public scale in the great room in the Palazzo Vecchio, decorated with Dantiesque maps and filled with a gorgeous display of celestial instruments, including the astrolabe associated with Danti and Antonio Santucci's stupendous sphere (Plate 9). Santucci's career followed an interesting progression in this context. He began as a specialist fabricator of devices and became progressively involved as an observational astronomer, a career that stresses that such instruments bear a far from simple relationship to observational work.[13]

When Danti moved to Gregory XIII's Papal court at Rome, he settled into an environment whose intellectual and visual style was much in tune with that to which he was accustomed. His work in the Torre dei Venti of the Vatican, newly constructed by Gregory in connection with the reform of the calendar, transforms a whole room into a kind of gigantic scientific instrument (Plate 10), in which precise mensuration mingles with extreme decorat-

1. *Galileo's Objective Lens with Ivory Mount of 1677 by Vittorio Croster*, Florence, Museo di Storia della Scienza.

2. Girolamo della Volpaia, *Armillary Sphere*, 1564, Florence, Museo di Storia della Scienza.

3. Giovanni Bologna, *Astronomy*, 1573, Vienna, Kunsthistorisches Museum.

4. Leonardo da Vinci, *Draftsman drawing an Armillary Sphere on a Glass 'Window'*, Milan, Biblioteca Ambrosiana, Codice At antico, f.1ra.

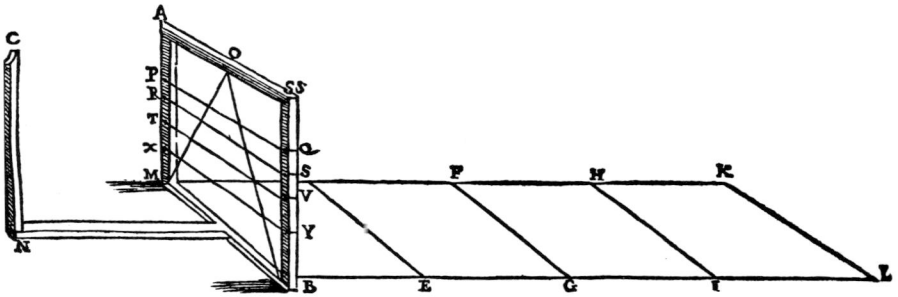

5. *Perspective Device by Tommaso Laureti*, from I. Danti, *Le due regole della prospettiva pratica*, Rome, 1583.

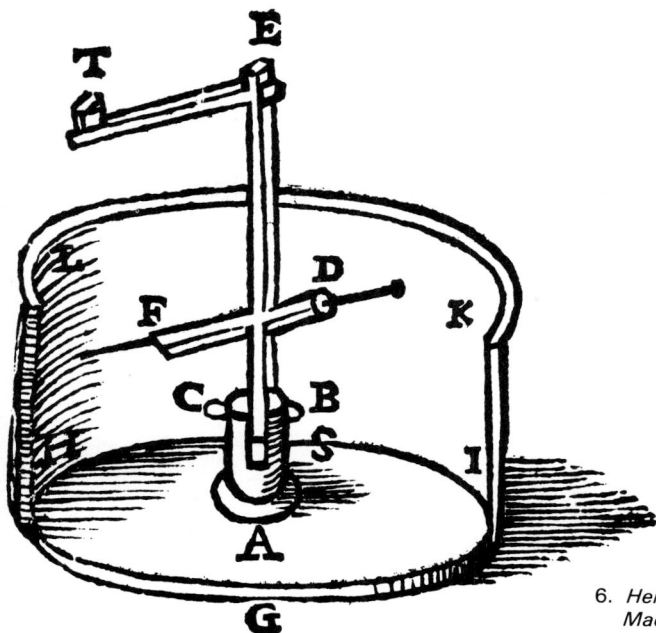

6. *Hemicylindrical Perspective Machine by Baldassare Lanci,* from Danti, *Le due regole.*

7. Baldassare Lanci, *Universal Surveying and Hemicylindrical Perspective Machine,* 1557, Florence, Museo di Storia della Scienza.

8. Baldassare Lanci, *Florentine Scene Design for 'La Vedova'*, 1569, Florence, Uffizi, Gabinetto Disegni e Stampe.

9. Antonio Santucci dalle Pomerance, *Large Armillary Sphere*, 1588–93, Florence, Museo di Storia della Scienza.

10. Ignazio Danti, with paintings by Pomarancio (Cristoforo Roncalli), *Ceiling of the Torre dei Venti*, c. 1581, Rome, Vatican.

11. Ottaviano Mascherino, Lorenzo Sabbatini and Giovanni Antonio Vanosino da Varese, *Ceiling of the Sala Bologna*, 1575, Rome, Vatican.

12. Joost Aman, *Portrait of Wenzel Jamnitzer*, engraving.

13. Wenzel Jamnitzer, *Compositior. of Geometrical Solids*, from *Perspectiva corporum regularium*, Nuremberg, 1568.

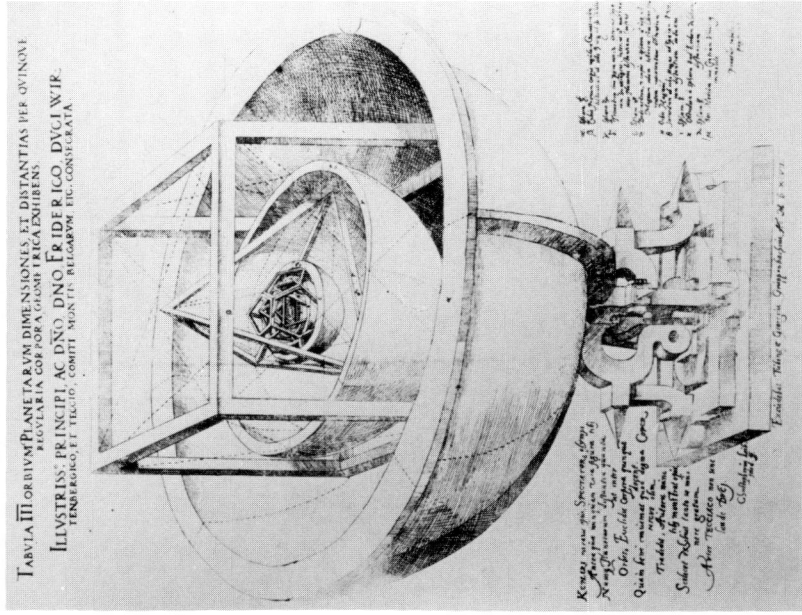

TABVLA III ORBIVM PLANETARVM DIMENSIONES, ET DISTANTIAS PER QVINQVE REGVLARIA CORPORA GEOMETRICA EXHIBENS.

ILLVSTRISS. PRINCIPI, AC DÑO. DNO. FRIDERICO. DVCI WIR. TENBERGICO, ET TECCIO, COMITI MONTIS BELGARVM ETC. CONSECRATA.

14. Johannes Kepler, *Geometrical Scheme for the Planetary Orbits,* from *Mysterium cosmographicum demonstratum per cinque copora geometrica,* Tubingen, 1596.

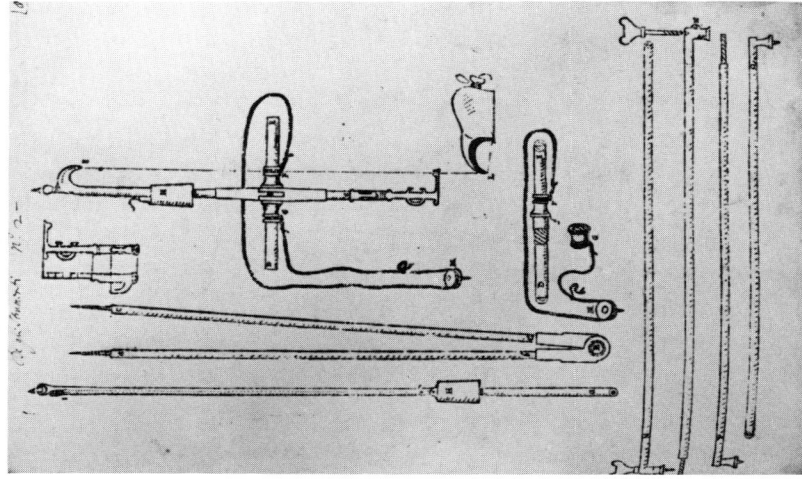

15. Ludovico Cigoli, *Components of the Universal Perspective Machine* from *Prospettiva pratica,* Florence, Uffizi, Gabinetto Disegni e Stampe.

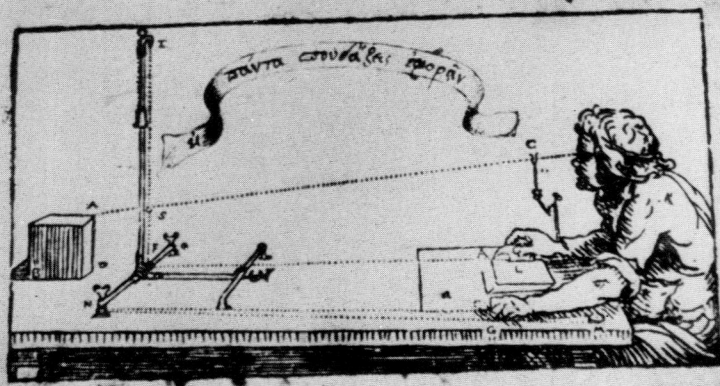

16. Ludovico Cigoli, *Universal Perspective Machine in Use*, detail of title-page from *Prospettiva Pratica*.

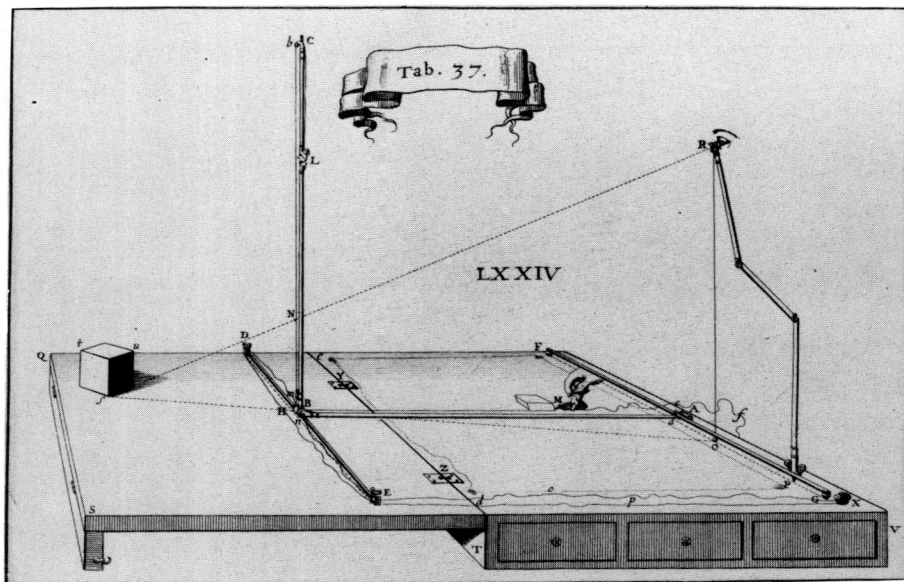

17. *Cigoli's Universal Perspective Machine*, from Jean François Niceron, *La Perspective curieuse ou magie artificielle,* Paris, 1638.

18. Christoph Schiener, *Uses of the Pantograph,* title-page from *Pantographice, seu ars delineandi*, Rome, 1631.

19. *Sir Christopher Wren's Perspective Machine,* from *Philosophical Transactions of the Royal Society,* IV, 1669.

20. *Drawing of a Physionotrace*, Paris, Bibliothèque Nationale.

21. *Physionotrace Portrait of P. H. Cochois by Bouchardy of Paris*, Chalon-sur-Saone, Musée Nicéphore Niépce.

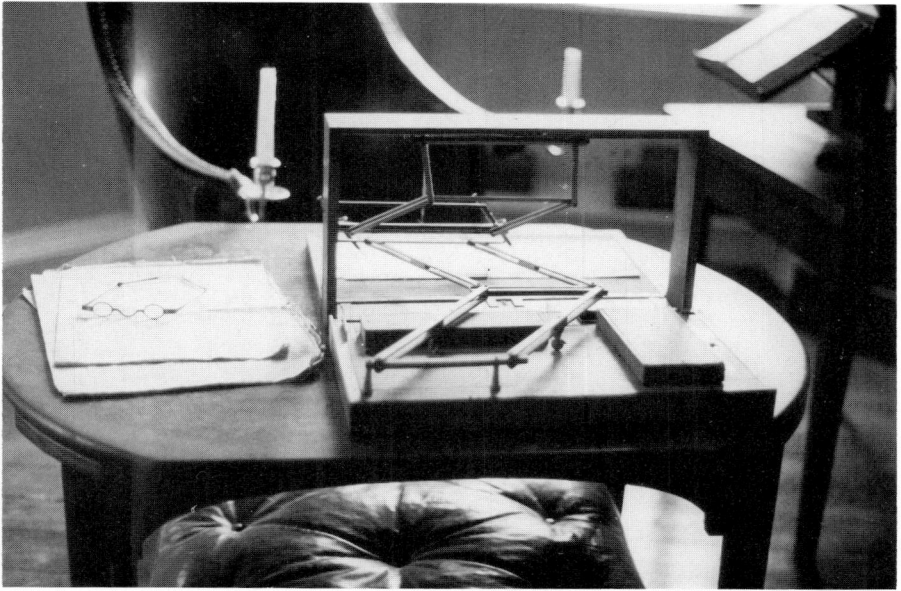

22. *Thomas Jefferson's Writing Machine*, Monticello, Jefferson's Study.

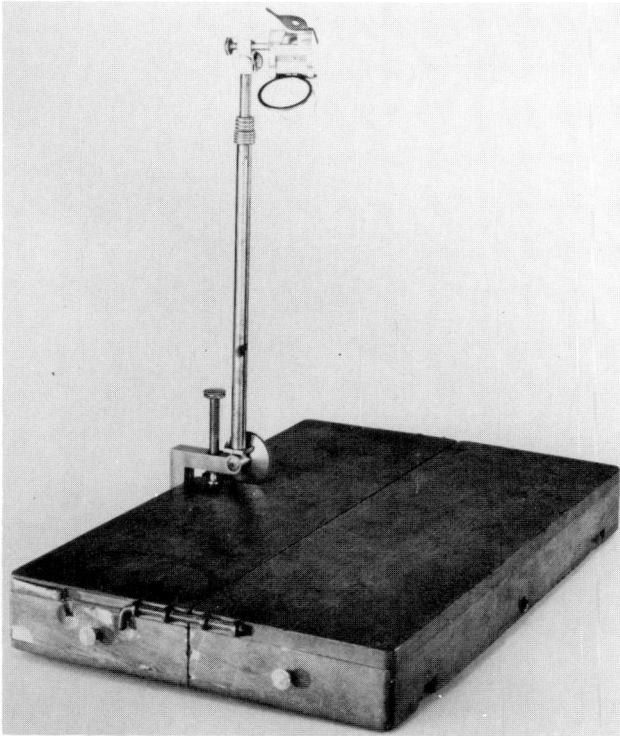

23. *Camera Lucida with Box*, London, Science Museum.

24. Basil Hall, *Camera Lucida Sketch of Sir Walter Scott and Abbotsford,* Edinburgh, National Portrait Gallery.

25. Sir John Herschel, *Camera Lucida Drawing of Tintern Abbey*, 1829, Nash Collection.

26. Paul Sandby, *A Sketching Party at Rosslyn Castle*, New Haven, Yale Center for British Art.

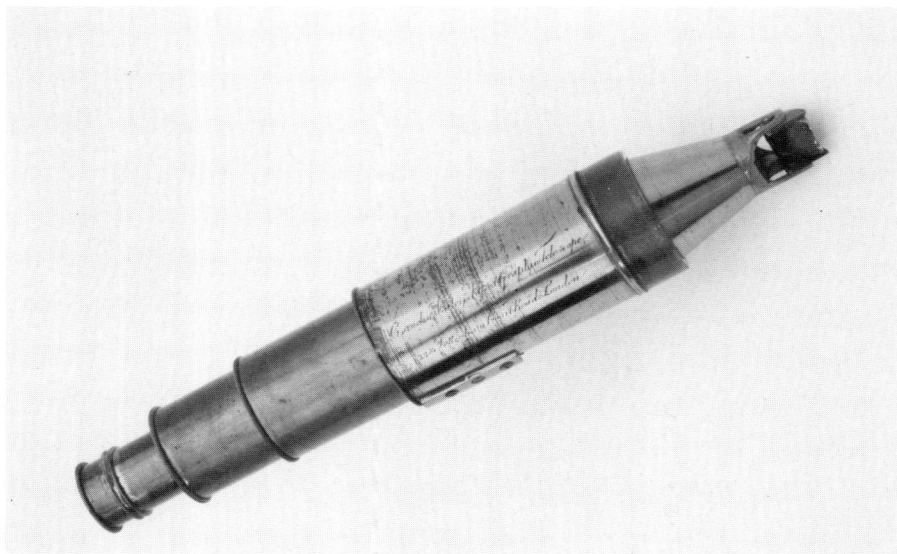

27. *Cornelius Varley's Graphic Telescope*, London, Science Museum.

28. John Sell Cotman, *Palais de Justice, Rouen*, 1818, Art Market, 1978.

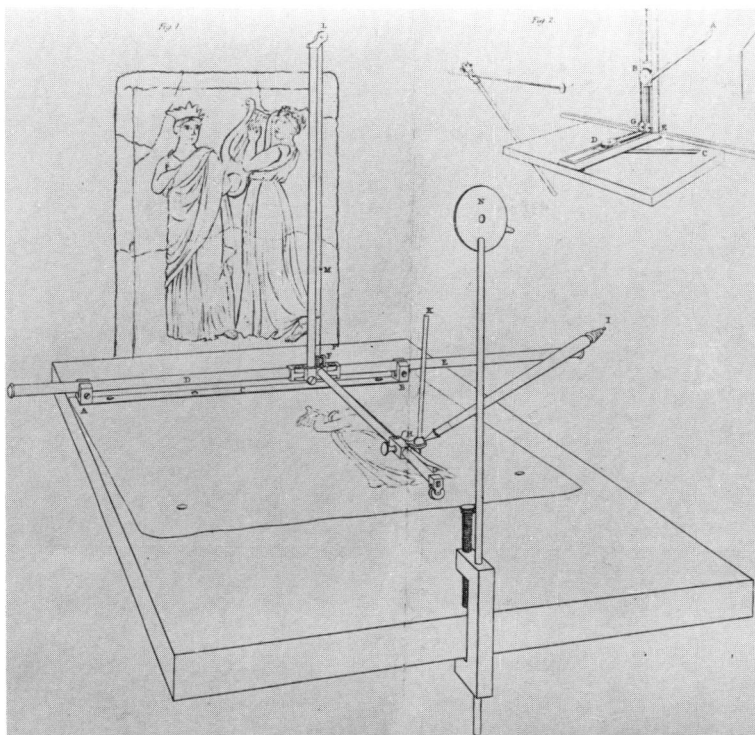

29. Sir Francis Ronalds, *Perspective Machine in Operation*, from *Mechanical Perspective
. . .*, London 1838.

30. *Lenticular Stereoscope of the Brewster Type*, London, Science Museum.

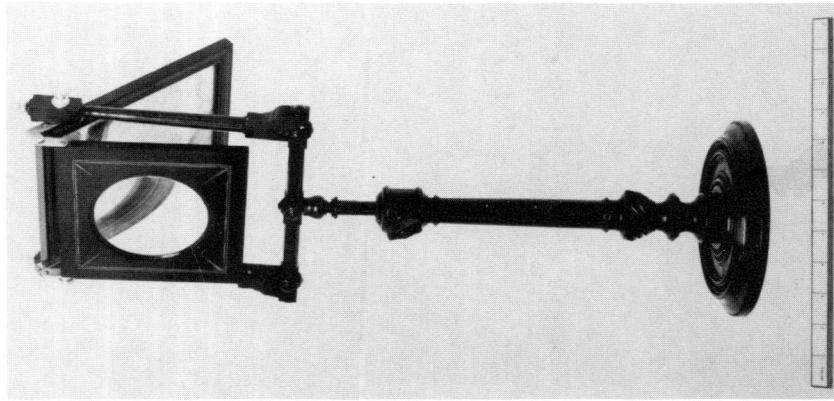

31. Zograscope or Optical Diagonal Machine, London, Science Museum.

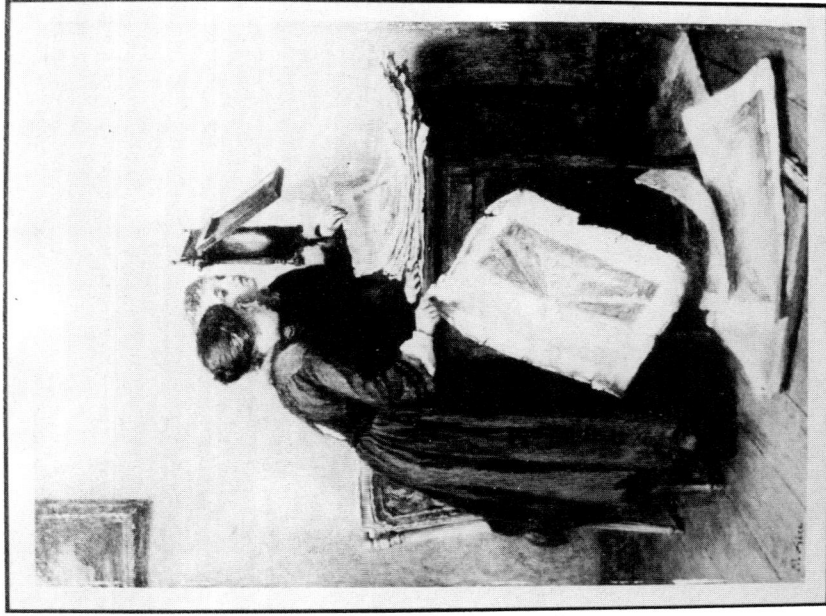

32. Pierre Edmond Frère, The Zograscope, New York, Brooklyn Museum.

ive artifice.[14] The illusionistic decoration is not irrelevant to the functions of Danti's anenometer and meridian line. The *all'antica* optical sophistication of the foreshortened figures and perspective architecture relies on the same philosophy of optics, applied mathematics and cosmology that provided the intellectual context for the Gregorian reform of the calendar. Danti's own writings leave no doubt that this was the case, and he admired the skilled illusionistic decorations by his Bolognese friend Tommaso Laureti (whose perspective device we have already seen) with no less enthusiasm than an astrolabe. The room adjoining the Torre dei Venti, the Sala Bologna (Plate 11), pulls these and other themes together – illusionism, celestial and terrestrial mapping – under the aegis of a Bolognese Pope who was patronising those Bolognese artists who specialised in illusionism and supporting Danti as a mathematicising scientist who had developed important Bolognese contacts on his own account during his years in that city.[15]

If we wanted to begin to build a comparable nexus in Northern Europe during the same period, we might begin with the great silversmith Wenzel Jamnitzer, whose engraved portrait (Plate 12) shows him using a linear perspective machine, accompanied by appropriate symbols of precise mensuration and by a cluster of the kind of geometrical bodies upon which he worked such stunning variations in his *Perspectiva corporum regularium* of 1565 (Plate 13).[16] Not for nothing was Jamnitzer the maker of one of the most splendid astrolabes of the sixteenth century. If we wanted to follow this nexus, we could travel via the Rudolphine court at Prague, where instrument makers such as Erasmus Habermel satisfy the emperor's highly developed taste for wonders and curiosities in the worlds of nature, science and art.[17] This takes us into the world of Kepler's *Mysterium cosmographicum* (Plate 14), in which the cosmos is displayed as the work of a divine master-craftsman from the workshop of Jamnitzer. Kepler's correspondence shows that he planned a 'goblet' version of his scheme and, later, a fully geared planetarium.[18]

Kepler's plans to manufacture his model at considerable expense and for an aristocratic patron, Duke Friedrich of Wuttemberg, reminds us that what we would call aesthetic delight can play a conspicuous role in scientific projects. I think this is no less true of the scientific revolution of Galileo in Florence than that of Kepler in Prague. Indeed, Galileo's intellectual, aesthetic and social links with the tradition we have been examining are very close. There are clear associations with the visual sciences of Guidobaldo, with the astronomy of Santucci, with the military science of Lanci – all within a world in which most scientists depended in large measure on powerful patronage for their ability to pursue science at a high leel, and indeed for their very living. Galileo's links with Ludovico Cigoli, the greatest of all the perspective machinists of his era, are equally strong.[19] Cigoli, the most respected Florentine painter of the period, was a confidant of the great scientist. When Cigoli was working in Rome he passed a regular supply of information to Galileo concerning the news from the Papal Court, particularly the latest gossip about the sunspot controversy. Cigoli's *Prospettiva pratica*, left unpublished on his death in 1613, contains an extended discussion of a variety of machines, including his own 'universal instrument', which he shows in its dismantled components (Plate 15) and in a variety of uses (Plate 16).[20] Not only could it be used to record the appearance of forms on a drawing surface but it could also be used in 'reverse', that is to say to project pre-existing drawings onto distant and larger surfaces, such as the curved surface of the dome he was painting in the Pauline Chapel in S. Maria Maggiore.[21] We are still inhabiting the same visual and intellectual world of Danti and his Bolognese colleagues. It may be worth noting – though I cannot elaborate this argument here – that Galileo's contemporaneous arguments in favour of the sunspots being located on the actual surface of the sun were framed in *'virtù di prospettiva'* as he put it. His interpretation relied upon the observation of the spots in perspectival foreshortening (*'in scorzio'*) as they progressed towards the edges of the sun's curvature.[22]

Although Cigoli shows how to use the machine, I think we may legitimately ask, as we may ask of any scientific instrument of this period, whether it really is a utilitarian object. It is unlikely to have been widely used for the depiction of complex forms, and its long-distance function in ceiling painting can hardly have achieved great precision. It appears to work best as an object of intellectual delectation, ingeniously demonstrating the basis of perspectival representation and showing the inventive genius of its maker. It certainly appeared in this kind of role on one of the occasions when we can document the actual existence of a Cigoli machine. This occurs in Jean-François Niceron's *Thaumaturgus opticus* (Plate 17) which illustrates an *instrumentum universale* owned by Ludovic Hesselin, counsellor to the King of France.[23] Hesselin's Château d'Essones was a treasure-trove of illusions and curiosities, exciting the admiration of even such a well-informed observer as Queen Christina of Sweden.

We should also remember that, in Catholic Europe during the Baroque era, such pieces of optical magic as perspective curiosities and anamorphic designs were not only items of entertainment but were also taken as manifestations of the ultimate mysteries of divine creation. Thus the pantograph invented by Galileo's adversary in the sunspot controversy, Christoph Scheiner, was set within a world of Christian devotion and magic, as witnessed by title-pages of his treatises on the pantograph (Plate 18) and on the eye.[24] The world of the Jesuit *magi*, Bettinus, Schott and Kircher is not far away. We are again dealing with a set of values specific to a certain style of intellectual and social context.

This is not to say, of course, that there are inherent qualities in an instrument like a pantograph that dictate this kind of intellectual and social context. Related devices, such as Christopher Wren's perspective machine (Plate 19) could appear in the distinctly different context of the Royal Society in Britain, which was (notwithstanding some recent suggestions) hardly a hot-bed of Jesuit mysticism.[25] In fact it is the translation of a pantographic device into a very different social and intellectual context that introduces the second area of focus in this paper, namely the second golden age of the optical devices in art during the late eighteenth and early nineteenth centuries.

In 1786, a musician turned portrait-engraver, Gilles-Louis Chrétien, devised an instrument for the capturing of portraits' likenesses.[26] It was called a physionotrace (Plate 20), and was dedicated to the production of profile portraits, akin to the popular silhouettes and much in tune with the widely discussed notions of physiognomics advocated by Lavater. Physiognotrace studios like that of Bouchardy (Plate 21) sprang up in Paris, producing small-scale portrait engravings in a way that obviously grants them the status of the forerunners of photographers' studios. The art was practised in America, where the most notable sitter was Thomas Jefferson. It is not surprising that Jefferson, lover and practitioner of gadgetry, should have been attracted to the new device. One of the instruments which had attracted the attention of this supreme democrat was the writing machine (Plate 22), which he strove to perfect as a way of making multiple copies of his letters.[27] I think it is not unfair to say that the style of Jefferson's machine breathes the air of the democratisation of such devices, which are no longer fancy pieces of goldsmithery associated with the mathematical magic of Baroque courts but are now fabricated for the daily business of a bureaucrat and man-of-the-world. I would not wish to push this too far in the case of Jefferson, who is an intellectually exceptional figure, but it is noticeable that the physionotrace was taken up with particular avidity in the new society of America and that the leaders of independence queued up to be snapped by Saint-Mémin in his studio.

We can also look to other optical instruments of this period to confirm the new social context in which their production could flourish. The devices of which I am thinking are the many patent machines designed to assist the amateur in the achieving of professional results in landscape painting and portraiture. Groups of such instruments are illustrated in encyclopaedias and hand-books of optical and mechanical devices.[28] Perhaps the most viable of the devices was the camera lucida (Plate 23), patented in 1806 by William Hyde Wollastone.[29] Although it was far from easy to use – even in its many later variants and improvements – it provided the growing ranks of lady and gentlemen amateurs with a portable camera which enabled them to capture picturesque scenes and images of their loved ones with a proficiency which would elude their unaided eye and hand. To illustrate the kind of context in which it was used, I will look at two relatively unfamiliar incidents in what is becoming a reasonably well-documented story.

The first concerns an amateur scientist and artist, Captain Basil Hall, who not only used the camera lucida for topographical sketches on his travels – and which he subsequently published – but also to take an image of Sir Walter Scott (Plate 24). The somewhat unsatisfactory drawing of Scott was made by Hall in 1830 to aid his brother James, who was hoping to make his name as an artist by painting a full-length portrait of the great Scottish author.[30] His hopes were disappointed.

The second episode concerns a scientist of an altogether diffe-rent callibre, Sir John Herschel (Plate 25). On his many drawings with an Amici camera lucida he invariably noted not only such information as the place and date but also recorded technical details of the optical co-ordinates.[31] Herschel's involvement stresses an element of intellectual continuity with the era of Danti in as much as the history of such instruments is still closely associated with astronomy and related disciplines. However the institutional and social contexts are quite different. We are dealing with a world in which high-level science is not linked so intimately with private patronage, but rather with a technological explosion which radically affected both the material aspects of life and what we may call the leisure industries. A camera lucida was hardly the working-class equivalent of a Box Brownie, but it was a relatively affordable device, manufactured in considerable numbers and widely advertised to the public. It was precisely geared to those classes who had sufficient education and leisure to enjoy some genteel arts and sciences. Paul Sandby's charming watercolour of Rosslyn Castle (Plate 26) makes this point succinctly, showing a well-attired young lady using a camera obscura (akin to Storer's Delineator) to take a 'snap' of an admired view.[32]

The style and manufacture of such devices provides evidence for an as yet unwritten social history of optical instruments. However we should not assume that all or even the majority of the devices were made and marketed on a widespread basis. William Storer's 'Royal Delineator', patented in 1778, was produced in two limited editions and sold within a relatively narrow circle of cognoscenti.[33] By contrast, the nineteenth-century devices appear to have been manufactured in relatively large numbers, although some of the more elaborate of the instruments, most notably Cornelius Varley's graphic Telescope (Plate 27), patented in 1811, were almost certainly expensive and highly specialised objects.[34] The great watercolourist, John Sell Cotman, was an admirer of Varley's device once he had trained his eye in its efficient use. He used it both for portraiture and to take views for his published collection of *Architectural Antiquities of Normandy* in 1822 (Plate 28).[35] It is an indication of the relatively high cost and exclusivity of the Graphic Telescope that Cotman was presented with his example by a wealthy patron. However the purposes for which it was used went beyond this exclusive context. The topographical images were printed in a 'travel book' which could enjoy a reasonably wide circulation. A comparably 'popular' use for the Graphic Telescope was Hornor's exploitation of it for his great panorama of London, taken from an 'observatory' on the Dome of St Paul's.[36]

In contrast to the popular demand – then as now – for works displaying verisimilitude, there existed a continuous strain of resistance to the imitation of nature in the raw. Even scientists, who were utterly dedicated to the direct investigation of nature in their own work, were inclined to acknowledge that 'artistry' demanded more than mechanical imitation. The machine devised by Sir Francis Ronalds (Plate 29), pioneer of the electric telegraph, provides a good case in point. In 1825, he patented an 'Instrument for sketching from nature'.[37] Its line of descent from Cigoli's perspectograph is obvious, though the technological advances in Ronalds's day have permitted the design of a machine for one-handed operation with a minimum of ropes and pulleys. An improved machine, in full-scale and pocket versions, was developed by the Garards in Paris, and one example by Adrien Garard featured at the Great Exhibition in 1851.[38] Efficient though such machines were, Ronalds feels compelled to warn that his device cannot on its own aspire to produce the highest ideas of 'picturesque' beauty or obey the high principles of 'composition', and can certainly never rival the responsiveness of the eye.[39]

By this time we have long since entered a world in which optical entertainments had developed into a considerable industry, with respect both to home entertainments and to great public spectacles such as panoramas and dioramas. We should remind ourselves that, just as there was a continuity in the seventeenth century between optical curiosities and the highest levels of philosophical science, so in the nineteenth there was an unbroken spectrum between popular devices and the most serious observational sciences. The activities of Sir David Brewster will serve to illustrate this point. A considerable scientist in his own right, his commercial activities extended to the invention of the kaleidoscope and the lenticular stereoscope (Plate 30).[40] By 1856, about half a million stereoscopes had been sold. It does not require much analysis of the qualities of a Brewster stereoscope, or of the even simpler Holmes-Bates version, to show that we are not dealing with a luxury item for a small aristocratic market. It was not exactly a cheap object – in the same sense that a television is not cheap – but it was aimed successfully at the mass market of the rising middle classes.

The natural environment for such devices can be illustrated by looking at the Zograscope or 'optical diagonal machine' (Plate 31).[41] Invented in France in the early eighteenth century, it reached the height of its popularity in the nineteenth. It was designed as a viewing device to enhance the magic illusion of perspectival views, most typically prints of buildings showing pronounced vistas. The painting by Frère (Plate 32) perfectly captures the context in which it and the stereoscope were used. The style of such instruments, in turned and polished mahogany, bears evocative witness to the world of the Victorian middle classes who were their consumers. It is perhaps significant that Zograscopes occasionally appear in antique shops as Victorian shaving mirrors – a misidentification, but one which recognises their domestic context. We are obviously worlds away from the use of perspective in the theologically and socially exclusive context of the ceiling of the Papal apartments in Gregorian Rome, Such contrasts involve questions of style in its broadest senses – styles of life and styles of intellectual endeavour – and in the more narrow sense of the style of design of particular artefacts. My contention is that it is possible to read the broad questions of style from the narrower ones. Style, in the broad sense, can be applied with profit to a range of artefacts not normally considered from a stylistic point of view because they are usually assigned to a non-artistic category. I suggest that a new role for style history lies less with the internalised histories of branches of art, but in an endeavour which seriously questions the categories on which internalised histories depend.

I would wish, in conclusion, to return to an earlier point. I am not saying that we simply need a regrouping of artefacts and ideas according to new perceptions of their stylistic affinities in order to achieve a correct understanding in the right context. A true cultural history, to my mind, would recognise that this kind of monolithic 'rightness' is neither desirable nor possible. Causal explanation in any kind of historical endeavour is a complex business, and in cultural history I believe that explanation should always exhibit a *necessary* untidiness and open-endedness. It should remain continually responsive to the wilful nature of individual creativity and taste. This may seem like a very old-fashioned, Whiggish formulation – and indeed it is – but, as someone trained initially as a scientist, I remain convinced that the search for a formula to grant historical explanation some kind of 'scientific' resolution is futile. The role I see for cultural history is a form of continuous taxonomic anarchy, grouping and regrouping concepts, texts and objects in such a way that we are never content with the categories and evolutionary formulas with which we are operating.

Notes

1. For two recent approaches to scientific instruments within the standard classifications, see J. A. Bennett, *The Divided Circle. A History of Instruments for Astronomy, Navigation and Surveying*, Oxford, 1987, and A. Turner, *Early Scientific Instruments, Europe 1400–1780*, London, 1987. The present chapter is a reorientated version of talk given at a conference on 'Museums, Artifacts and the History of Science' organised jointly by the British Society for the History of Science and the Group for Scientific, Technological and Medical Collections at the Science Museum in London on 29 November 1986.

2. M. L. Ringhini Bonelli and T. Settle, *The Antique Instruments at the Museum of History of Science in Florence*, Florence, n.d., pp. 16–17.

3. J. V. Field, 'What is Scientific about a Scientific Instrument? *Nuncius*, 111, pt. 2, 1988, pp. 3–26.

4. N. Pastore and C. Rosen, 'Alberti and the Camera Obscura', *Physis*, xxv, 1984, pp. 259–69.

5. *Leon Battista Alberti 'On Painting' and 'On Sculpture'*, ed. C. Grayson, London and New York, 1972 pp. 69–79. A fuller account of the various kinds of instrument for the imitation of nature is in this author's *The Science of Art. Optical Themes in Western Art from Brunelleschi to Seurat*, London and New Haven, 1990. For architectural drawing devices, see M. Hambly, *Drawing Instruments*, London, 1982.

6. *The Literary Works of Leonardo da Vinci*, ed. J. P. Richter, 3rd edn, 2 vols, New York and London, 1970, para. 523 (MS. B.N.2038 f.24r; Codex Urbinas f.41r–v).

7. M. Kemp, 'Geometrical Perspective from Brunelleschi to Desargues: A Pictorial Means or an Intellectual End', *Proceedings of the British Academy*, lxx, 1984, pp. 89–132.

8. J. Barozzi da Vignola, *Le due regole della prospettiva pratica*, ed. I Danti, Rome, 1583, pp. 61–2. See C. Maltese, 'La prospettiva curva di Leonardo da Vinci e uno strumento di Baldassare Lanci', *La Propspettiva rinascimentale,* ed. M. Dalai Emiliani, Florence, 1980, pp. 417–25.

9. M. L. Ringhini Bonelli, *Il Museo di storia della scienza*, Florence, 1968, no. 313.

10. S. Pepper and N. Adams, *Firearms and Fortification. Military Architecture and Seige Warfare in Sixteenth-Century Siena*, Chicago and London, 1986, pp. 66, 77, 88–9 and 157–9.

11. *Gabinetto disegni e stampe degli Uffizi, XXXI. Feste e apparati Medicei da Cosimo I a Cosimo II*, Florence, 1969, no. 9.

12. L. Berti, *Il Principe dello studiolo*, Florence, 1967, and T. S. R. Boase, *Giorgio Vasari, The Man and the Book*, Princeton, 1979, pp. 314ff.

13. T. Settle, 'Antonio Santucci, his "New Tractatus on Comets" and Galileo', *Novità celesti e crisi del sapere*, ed. P. Galuzzi, Florence, 1983, pp. 229–38.

14. F. Mancinelli and J. Casanovas, *La Torre dei Venti*, Vatican, 1980.

15.   For the Bolognese illusionistic painters, see E. Sjöstrom, *Quadratura, Studies in Italian Ceiling Painting*, Stockholm, 1978.

16.   W. Jamnitzer, *Perspectiva corporum regularium* Nuremberg, 1568; I. Franke, 'Wenzel Jamnitzers Zeichnungen zur Perspektive', *Münchner Jahrbuch der bildenden Kunst*, 1972, pp. 165–86; and J. Hayward, *Virtuoso Goldsmiths and the Triumph of Mannerism*, London and New York, 1976, pp. 203–6.

17.   For Rudolph's tastes, see *Prag um 1600*, exhibition catalogue, Villa Hügel, Freren, 1988

18.   *Johannes Kepler gesammelte Werke*, ed. M. Caspar *et al.*, Munich, 1938, xiii. pp. 50–4; and F. D. Prager, 'Kepler als Erfinder', *Internationales Kepler Symposium, Weil der Stadt 1971*, ed. F. Krafft *et al.*, Hildesheim, 1973, pp. 385–405. Also M. Kemp, 'Geometrical Bodies as Exemplary Forms in Renaissance Space', *World Art. Acts of the XVII International Congress for the History of Art (1986)*, ed. I. Lavin, 3 vols., Pennsylvania and London, 1986, vol. 1, pp. 237–42.

19.   *Macchie di sole e pittura. Carteggio L. Cigoli–G. Galilei*, ed. A. M. Matteoli, *Bolletino della Accademia degli Euteleti*, xxxii, San Miniato, 1959; and M. Chappell, 'Cigoli, Galileo and Invidia', *Art Bulletin*, lvii, 1975, pp. 91–8.

20.   L. Cigoli, *Prospettiva pratica . . . demostrata con tre regole, e la descrizione di sue strumenti . . .* Gabinetto disegni e stampe degli Uffizi, Codice 2660A. An edition is planned by Filippo Camerota, Miles Chappell and myself. Also Camerota's unpublished doctoral thesis, 'Dalla Finestra allo specchio: la "Prospettiva practica" di Ludovico Cigoli alle origini di una nuova concezione spatiale', Florence, Università degli Studi, Faccoltà di Architettura, 1987.

21.   F. Faranda, *Ludovico Cardi detto il Cigoli*, Rome, 1986, tav. xliii and no. 83.

22.   Galileo Galilei, *Istoria e dimostrazioni intorno alle macchie solari e loro accidenti*, Rome, 1613, p. 52.

23.   J. F. Niceron, *La Perspective curieuse ou magie artificielle*, Paris, 1638, p. 77, and *Thaumaturgus opticus*, Paris, 1646, p. 191.

24.   C. Scheiner, *Pantographice, seu ars delineandi*, Rome 1631, and *Rosa ursina sive sol*, Rome, 1630. For the context, see J. Baltrušaitis, *Anamorphic Art*, Cambridge, 1977, p. 79 ff.

25.   'An instrument invented diverse years ago by Dr. Christopher Wren, for drawing the Out-Lines of an object in Perspective', *Philosphical Transactions of the Royal Society*, iv, 1669, pp. 898–9.

26.   See J. Freund, *Photography and Society*, London, 1980, pp. 8–17; and P. Jay, *Lumières et images. La photographie*, Musée Nicéphore Niépce, Chalon-sur-Saône, nd.

27.   S. Bedini, *Thomas Jefferson and his Copying Machines*, Charlottesville, 1984.

28.   Eg. A. Rees, *The Cyclopeadia or Universal Dictionary of Arts, Science and Literature*, 39 vols, London, 1819–20, xi, 'Delineators'; and J. Smith, *The Mechanic*, 2 vols, London, 1825, ii, pp. 71ff.

29.   See C. Varley, *A Treatise on Optical Drawing Instruments*, London, 1845, p. 27; and J. H. Hammond and J. Austin, *The Camera Lucida in*

Art and Science, Bristol, 1987.

30. H. Smailes, 'Sir Walter Scott in Camera', *Bulletin of the Scottish Society for the History of Photography*, Spring 1986, pp. 2–5.

31. L. Schaaf, *Tracings of Light, Sir John Herschel and the Camera Lucida* San Francisco, 1989.

32. For a 'camera' drawing by Thomas Sandby, Paul's brother, see A. P. Oppé, *The Drawings of Paul and Thomas Sandby in the Collection of His Majesty the King at Windsor Castle*, London, 1947, no. 14729.

33. *Storer's Syllabus . . . or the New Optical Principles of the Royal Delineator Analysed*, London, 1845; for this and camera obscuras generally, see J. H. Hammond, *The Camera Obscura. A Chronicle*, Bristol, 1981.

34. Varley, *Optical Drawing Instruments*, for illustrations and analysis.

35. M. Pidgeley, 'Cornelius Varley, Cotman and the Graphic Telescope', *Burlington Magazine*, cxiv, 1972, p. 785.

36. A. T. Storey, *The Life of John Linnel*, 2 vols, London, 1829, ii, p. 222. Lithographs of Honor's panorama were published by R. Ackermann, *Graphic Illustrations of the Colosseum*, London, 1829. See D. Altick, *The Shows of London*, Cambridge, Mass. and London, 1978.

37. F. Ronalds, *Mechanical Perspective or, Description and Uses of an Instrument for Sketching From Nature*, 2nd edn, London, 1838.

38. See the *Jury Report* of the 1852 exhibition, p. 306.

39. Ronalds, *Mechanical Perspective*, introduction.

40. D. Brewster, *A Treatise on the Kaleidoscope*, Edinburgh, 1819, *The Kaleidoscope: its history, Theory and Construction with its Application to the Fine and Useful Arts*, Edinburgh, 1858 and *The Stereoscope: its History, Theory and Construction . . .*, London, 1856. See *'Martyr of Science': Sir David Brewster, 178–1868*, ed. A. Morrison-Lowe and J. R. R. Christie, Edinburgh, 1984.

41. See C. J. Kaldenback, 'Perspective Views', *Print Quarterly*, ii, 1985, pp. 86–103; and J. A. Chaldecotte, 'The Zograscope or Optical Diagonal Machine', *Annals of Science*, ix, 1953, pp. 315–22.

7

Inventing the Common Reader: Samuel Johnson and the Canon

Lawrence Lipking

Culture is subject to selection and appreciation, perhaps no more so than in the world of books where critics create canons of what to read for the 'common reader'. This is the topic of Lawrence Lipking's contribution. Since the proliferation of books in the eighteenth century to meet the needs of a heterogeneous mass of readers, society has drowned in books. From the point of view of our own age's preoccupation with ideologies, the comments of Foucault ring true – that the organisation of knowledge inevitably obeys the dictates of history and power and consequently those without power are denied the right to define knowledge for themselves. The organisation of knowledge is a privileged area in more ways than one. The question of what is excluded lies at the heart of the interpretation of culture.

A rather different predicament is that of the expert who is keenly aware of his ignorance, of the limitations of his expertise. Faced with the need to establish priorities, the understanding of knowledge as power can be subsumed to an urgent sense in the cultivated mind of reading as education – arguably a less harmful, even if a more insidious priority. Lipking demonstrates a continuity of concern here from Diderot, whose preoccupation with organising knowledge resulted in the *Encyclopédie* (whatever the consequences) to Virginia Woolf whose responsibilities as a reviewer were, like those of Lipking's subject, Dr Johnson, to the hypothetical yet all-important audience of all print, the common reader.

A canon can only exist in terms of a concurrence of readers: that can only be achieved by readers being sufficiently involved with the books they read, emotionally, intellectually and imaginatively, to agree in their priorities.

In 1755, in the brilliant article on 'The Encyclopedia' that he contributed to his own *Encyclopedia*, Denis Diderot looked into the future of learning and saw there a sort of science-fiction nightmare, the end of civilisation as he knew it. What he saw turned out to be true; and it is, in fact, the nightmare in which we still live. There would be, in a word, too many books – *many* too many books.

> As long as the centuries continue to unfold, the number of books will grow continually, and one can predict that a time will come when it will be almost as difficult to learn anything from books as from the direct study of the whole universe. It will be almost as convenient to search for some bit of truth concealed in nature as it will be to find it hidden away in an immense multitude of bound volumes.

Once upon a time, Diderot continues, a small number of gifted men composed manuscripts for scribes to copy for other gifted men. Now things have changed. 'If you look ahead to a future age, and consider the state of literature after the printing press, which never rests, has filled huge buildings with books,' you will see another division of labour.

> Some will not do very much reading, but will instead devote themselves to investigations which will be new, or which they will believe to be new (for if we are even now ignorant of a part of what is contained in so many volumes published in all sorts of languages, they will know still less of what is contained in those same books, augmented as they be by a hundred – a thousand – times as many more). The others, day laborers incapable of producing anything of their own, will be busy night and day leafing through these books, taking out of them the fragments they consider worthy of being collected and preserved. Has not this prediction already begun to be fulfilled? And are not several of our literary men already engaged in reducing all big books to little ones, among which there are still to be found many that are superfluous?[1]

Even the specialists in digestion belch forth new printed matter. And eventually the world of learning – our world – may drown in books.

Diderot's analysis tends to be self-serving. His remedy for the illness is, by a contrived coincidence, the book in which we are reading about its symptoms – the *Encyclopedia* itself: 'Thus we have now undertaken, in the interests of learning and for the sake of the human race, a task to which our grandsons would have had to devote themselves; but we have done so under more favorable circumstances, before a superabundance of books should have accumulated to make its execution extremely laborious.'[2] At the moment, in 1755, the situation is still under control; a small group of intelligent scholars can master everything worth knowing from books and distil learning into an orderly, alphabetical series of authoritative volumes, the one book that everyone has to own. Or so at least the editor would like us to believe. But we the grandsons, and the granddaughters, may have our doubts. For us the *Encyclopedia* has become not the end-product of learning but the source of still more books, a part of history – Diderot's nightmare, from which we are trying, and failing, to escape.

Yet the enterprise still haunts us. Few eighteenth-century legacies have been more persistent and decisive than the effort to organise learning. The results of that quest are around us. They are embodied in our universities, in the divisions and departments and curricula and degree requirements that seem identical, in our unreflective moments, with learning itself; in the card-catalogues of our libraries as well as in their books, and the footnotes and indexes of those books; in museums and newspapers and airline schedules and television guides and all the institutions that collectively make up what we call culture. When we want to find something out we seldom look, like Diderot's imaginary seeker for truth, directly at nature. Instead we finger the yellow pages of learning, that vast encyclopedia of print where every bit of information can be retrieved, so long as one knows the proper code or cubby-hole from which to extract it. It all begins with knowing where to look. What Diderot's century discovered, from this point of view, was that control of learning belongs to those who have the power of organising it. And so for us. Confronted by too many books, we do not play Caesar or the pope and burn them. Our form of control is more subtle: we put them in their places.

Much recent thought has been devoted to this process. In an age when many people think that print culture itself may be coming to an end, what could be more logical than to examine the underlying assumptions of that culture, its organisation of knowledge, in order to show how arbitrarily and adventitiously they came into being, whose purposes they serve, and how they might be replaced? Thus Robert Darnton, a leading scholar of the *Encyclopedia*, stresses above all its 'epistemological strategy', the shaping of a modern *Summa* 'when the Encyclopedists recognized that knowledge was power and, by mapping the world of knowledge, set out to conquer it.'[3] Darnton describes the *philosophes'* 'Tree of Knowledge' without polemics. But behind him one may hear the influential voice of Michel Foucault, whose 'archaeology of knowledge' pays homage to the *Encyclopedia* largely by trying to unwrite it. The organisation of knowledge, Foucault spent his lifetime in showing, obeys the dictates of history and power. It is never neutral, it is always a means by which someone exerts domination over the 'outsider', the ignorant, the 'criminal', the 'mad' – in short, over everyone denied the right to define knowledge for themselves. Even the university might thus be considered a conspiracy against anyone outside its walls. Each book enforces a bookish mode of thought, constraining its readers to accept its table of contents and rules of evidence as if they somehow represented the nature of truth. And books beget more books. Only those who carefully scrutinise the margins – who study what books *leave out* – will fully grasp their power of exclusion. For knowledge is only another name for power.

What happens when there are too *many* books? Few scholars have taken up this part of Diderot's argument. The subject is just too personal and painful. To observe how those in power profit from the organisation of knowledge, how canons of learning exclude the disenfranchised and the dispossessed, how a revolution in thought might change forever the grounds of the rulers' support – all this is stimulating and often rather pleasant.Most scholars like, at times, to imagine new curricula, especially those that would put their own interests at the centre. But what is not pleasant, not pleasant at all, is to remember how many books, how many many books one simply has not read. Even those who agree with Foucault on all the important things – like the structure of Western civilisation, say. or the meaning of history – have sometimes been troubled by noting that on some little matter, the treatment of mad *women*, for instance, he did not always know what he was talking about. And Foucault himself became quite testy at such accusations. All of us do, of course. For every learned person is well acquainted with the limitations of learning in the most personal way: the holes in what each of us knows. We try to forget them. We do not like to be reminded of them. We try to catch up; we quickly fall further behind. Meanwhile the books keep coming. There are always too many books.

To put this another way: when it comes to the organisation of knowledge, each of our minds less resembles a library than a neighbourhood bookstore. Alvin Kernan has elegantly formulated the problems of print culture in terms of 'the imaginary library', that vast but ordered set of shelves which 'focuses the intellectual world and provides a paradigm of consciousness, what a society knows and how it knows it'.[4] But the consciousness of an individual is rather different. As readers, the children of print, we seldom follow the Dewey decimal system. Instead, our reading tends to clump in categories as irrational but as decisive as those of a not-very-good bookshop: fiction and non-fiction, best-sellers (what everyone else is reading) and discounted stuff for browsing. When we search the shelves of our minds for classics, or for the genuinely learned book that allows us to understand all sides of an issue, we almost always find that they are not in stock. Even the best academic mind has plenty of empty spaces – in the sciences, in history, in the oriental collection. We waste our time glancing through the magazines. Diderot knew this would happen, and he gave us the *Encyclopedia*. But how many of us have read very far in that?

We are also reluctant to face the situation. No question stirs more passion and debate in literary studies, these days, than the question of the canon: what works must we read? What works must our students read? It surely deserves our attention. Defining the canon, in Diderot's terms or Foucault's, lays bare the most basic issues of knowledge and power, and the institutions that control them. Whoever rules the reading lists rules the future. Yet in one respect the debate often seems oddly at cross-purposes: many of the disputants have not read the writings that they are arguing argainst. In an age of specialists, when theorists read theory and medievalists read Gower, it is not surprising that they should disagree about which is more important. But who is to decide the issue? Often someone who has read neither theory nor Gower. That is the way it happens. Nor do many of the debaters squarely face the other consequence of their competition for limited resources in an expanding universe of print, the grim ecology of Spaceship English: in order to put something into the canon, you must first take something out. Goodbye to Edmund Burke; Mary Astell, hello.

Not even the most enlightened of canon breakers can avoid this predicament. Consider, for instance, the admirable, enthusiastically reviewed *New Oxford Book of Eighteenth-Century Verse*. Roger Lonsdale has sifted tirelessly through the rubble of forgotten verse in chap-books, miscellanies, and journals, and his selections are wonderfully fresh. The crucial difference from the earlier *Oxford Book* emerges clearly in letter A of the Index of Authors. I do not refer to the reduction of Addison from six poems to three, of Akenside from nine poems to three, nor even to the addition of two women, Jean Adams and Mary Alcock. These are significant, but they are quite overshadowed by the new star of the book, Anonymous, whose six entries (in Nichol Smith) have swollen to 46 in Lonsdale. Anonymous may not have high poetic ambitions, but she does pay attention to the daily life around her. The *New Oxford Book* is much bulkier than the old one (almost half again more space), and it uses the extra pages to put in 'the vigorous, humorous, idiosyncratic verse of authors, many of them anonymous, who felt impelled at least to try to describe with some immediacy and colloquial directness the changing world they lived in, often for anything but a polite readership'.[5] Cricket, golf and boxing; the kitchen, the bedroom, the prison; slavery, war and the poor; drink, tobacco, opium. This book is fun to read.

What then gets left out? So-called 'major' poets, of course, have been trimmed, to be left to other anthologies. Pope, as Lonsdale notes, will 'survive my attentions', and presumably so will Burns (cut 50 per cent). This seems reasonable enough, though it may be worth remarking that not a single good anthology of standard eighteenth-century British poetry remains in print. But what of Sir John Henry Moore, whose hilarious *Duke of Benevento* was one of Nichol Smith's discoveries? He too goes out through the hatch of Spaceship English. I think that I know why. Lonsdale cannot abide one sort of later eighteenth-century poem, the 'evasive, escapist' work of poets 'turning their backs on public experience, and losing any capacity or desire to observe the actualities of contemporary life with any precision or immediacy.' Evidently 'actuality', an eye, for example, for 'the harsh realities of rural life',[6] assumes a canonical power in this book. The witty, aristocratic attitudes of Moore, in contrast, have no redeeming social significance; and he prefers the Orient, or never-never land, to the rich social tensions of Britain. So out he goes; and with him goes the strain of poetry that, in the next generation, in the hands of Byron, would become the most popular in Europe.

My point is not that Lonsdale's canon is wrong. It is only that his choices, fresh and unstereotyped as they are, function to make in effect another canon. There is no help for this situation. Lonsdale's knowledge is power, and he has earned this power by reading a great many poems that the rest of us do not want to read, selecting the ones he likes, and discarding the others. We pay him for that. At the same time, however, we may feel resentful. Who has given him the power of life and death over forgotten poems? One answer is 'Oxford'; but a better answer is '*we* have' – we the readers, or we who have not read enough. Too little time, too many poems, too many books. *Someone* must make the decisions. And the cumulative effect of such decisions, collaborated on by all of us who do not spend the time and effort to put together a unique anthology of our own, is just what we mean by a 'canon'.

No author can teach us more about the literary canon than Samuel Johnson. Johnson lived at just the moment when Diderot's nightmare, the deluge of books, become a central issue in European culture; and in the same year that Diderot published his article on 'The Encyclopedia', Johnson brought forth his *Dictionary*, which (as Robert DeMaria has recently argued at length, must itself be viewed as a sort of encyclopedia.)[7] The rest of Johnson's career, from the early catalogue of the Harleian library through the edition of Shakespeare to the culminating *Lives of the English Poets*, is similarly involved with the work of discriminating and sorting, the choice of books in balance with the choice of life, that helps define a culture to itself. But Johnson was not only the maker of the canon but a prominent figure within it – *Dictionary* Johnson, as if he were not only the author of that canonical book but an ambulatory folio himself, well-stuffed with words. The election of Johnson to stand for authorship in his age reveals how much the idea of the author was changing. Not the greatest of playwrights, of poets, of novelists, he made his name instead by telling others what to read. This was a new sort of qualification for canonical status – St Peter at the gate, whose keys allow him to keep some people out and let himself in. Yet, as this image shows, another lesson Johnson can teach us about the canon is how much uneasiness or hostility it attracts to those who guard it. The charge of tyranny was entered against Johnson early in his career, rose to a mighty cry by the end of his life, and for following generations threatened to be the main way he would be remembered. Dictator, the Great Cham, King Critic, above all and forever *Doctor* – each of these labels perches on Johnson like a top hat at which every schoolboy would like to throw a brick. Indeed, much of Johnson's canonical function depends on the well-defined target he offers. Hardly a critic can write about 'Lycidas' without rebutting its one great adversary. Yet Johnson himself was no stranger to the spirit of resistance to authority or defiance of the tyrant. An intellectual Jacobite (and perhaps a political one as well), he understood the satisfaction of saying 'no' to a Lord or patron of letters. If Johnson invented the modern canon of English, he also saw clearly the flaws of canonical thinking.

It all began, however, with reading. Johnson is the Hero as Reader. Kernan has recently discussed the legendary quality of this reading, immortalised in Reynolds's marvellous portrait, the book held closely to the one good eye, the face almost frightening in its intensity, as if to illustrate the well-known comment of Mary Knowles: 'He knows how to read better than anyone; he gets at the substance of a book directly; he tears out the heart of it.'[8] Ravenous, crude, devouring – a picture of Johnson reading. This is the stuff of legends, and it is not hard to observe myth-making at work in the frequent contemporary references to Johnson's omnivorous learning. Boswell picks up the theme again and again. 'Dr. Adam Smith, than whom few were better judges on this subject, once observed to me that "Johnson knew more books than any man alive." '[9] By their nature such claims are unprovable. We might recall that another acquaintance of Boswell, William Temple, called Thomas Gray 'the most learned man in Europe'; and I never hear these superlatives without speculating about some unknown, a certain Pécuchet, let us say, assistant librarian at Lyon, who by dint of constant study and no writing at all has read more books than Johnson and Gray together. But the legend of Johnson as universal reader has not only a factual basis; it fulfils a deep cultural need. England expects it (and Scotland too). *Someone* must do the reading.

What Johnson had read, in short, was everything worth reading; and the definition of what was worth reading was what Johnson had read. We may watch this circle at work, for instance, in his casual remark at the end of a discussion of Fielding: 'I, indeed, never read *Joseph Andrews*'[10] If someone else had said this, it would be a confession of weakness, or at any rate a lacuna. On Johnson's lips, however, it serves to condemn the book (just as his later comment that 'he read Fielding's *Amelia* through without stopping' confers the ultimate praise).[11] Whatever Johnson reads has entered, if not the canon, then at least the first stage of candidacy for inclusion. Whatever Johnson does not read remains in limbo, or at best in the maiden chamber of canonicity. I do not say this cynically. A critic does not command such authority for long unless he is thought to deserve it by a great many people; and among the many forms of power, the power born of reading, and devoted to reading, is one of the more benign. It was not the king, nor even the booksellers, who gave Johnson his power, but the public, and he served the public well as its surrogate reader. Yet even those who rely on others to sort, extract and judge books for them as most of us rely on reviewers, may hesitate to acknowledge their submission. Surely we ought to be reading for ourselves. Why then must we first let Johnson cut the pages?

The answer may be put in historical form. Before the invention of printing in Europe, only a very few scholars seem to have worried about the number of books they had not read. When books were precious and few, a literate person read what he could, often re-read the same book, and tended to use what might be called reading-intensive techniques, for instance, parsing the grammar word by word. We do not have to subscribe to Walter Benjamin's sentimental notion of the *aura*, the cult value of the unique work of art, to perceive that a limited supply of books is likely to result in a small community of like-minded readers. More pretentiously, one might argue that for many centuries, the individual minds of a group of scholars – Thomas Aquinas, say, or William of Baskerville – were identical with the Mind of Europe. That is to say, a single learned reader might still be acquainted with virtually every text thought worth reading. This circle of completeness depends, of course, on principles of exclusion; Aquinas's universe did not contain the *Gilgamesh*, the *Bhagavad-Gita* or *The Tale of Genji*. Yet the value of knowing everything there is to know should not be underestimated. Even during the first era of the Age of Print, Anno Gutenbergi, or what we used to call the Renaissance, many humanists still filled the role of universal reader; and the greatness of an Erasmus or a Scaliger depends on their confidence in the possibility of scholarly comprehensiveness. They are men with no lacuna. But during the seventeenth century, as the printing presses hummed, vast rents began to appear in the Mind of Europe. In France, the last man reputed to have read everything seems to have been Pierre Bayle; and by the mid-eighteenth century even the optimistic Diderot, who was ready to jettison all books based on mere authority, thought that a large team of *philosophes* would be needed to encompass everything that a man of reason had to know.

'Sir, thus it is. This is the proportion . . . As three to sixteen hundred, so is the proportion of an Englishman to a Frenchman.'[12] Johnson's notorious gibe compares his work on the *Dictionary* to that of the French Academy. But most of his labour consisted of reading, as he culled illustrative quotations from the classic texts of English; and British readers prized him as their champion, the competitive gold-medal reader. Only an English mind was large enough to hold the Mind of Europe. Thus, after Johnson's death, when Samuel Parr set out to write his life, he prepared by reading shelves of books in imitation of the hero, and died before he was ready to start writing. The task was too much for Parr, or any one man. 'It would have contained a view of the literature of Europe.'[13] After Johnson, no one in Europe or anywhere else could claim to be the universal reader. 'Let us go to the next best: – there is nobody; – no man can be said to put you in mind of Johnson.'[14]

Yet reading is not, of course, an absolute term. It describes many different sorts of activity, many different levels of comprehension. The schoolboy who traverses Virgil word by word, the priest who chants from the prayer book, the addict of romances who gulps down a long one in an hour, the philosopher who wrestles with each phrase and shde of meaning, have nothing in common but the word that names them all readers. Nor do we have a good history of reading, despite a few pregnant remarks by Father Ong.[15] Evidently Johnson was an uncommon reader, unusual enough for his habits to attract a good deal of attention from his contemporaries. The Hero as Reader stands out in a crowd (not least because Johnson often read while literally standing in a crowd). But what we demand from him is not only conspicuous consumption but quality control: the ability both to concentrate on the book in hand and to judge it by comparison with others. The 'Tree of Knowledge' does not matter much to Johnson. Most of the time he is content to equate the word 'literature' with all kinds of reading and writing, as in his nod to Horne Tooke: 'I hope they did not put the dog in the pillory for his libel; he has too much literature for that.'[16] Despite his allegiance to hierarchies and principles of subordination, Johnson has the curiosity of a polymath, and never assumes that a bad epic poet is worth more than a good honest hack. But he does pass judgement, on both the lord and the hack. To read like a Turk (in his phrase), to tear out the heart of a book, implies a fierce punitive side to reading; the hand that cuts the pages wields an executioner's blade. Johnson is not a harsh reader. He takes pleasure in books for what they have to offer, gives credit where it is due, and finds a great deal to praise. Yet he rarely praises without also spying some fault, in Shakespeare as well as in Jenyns. In reading begin responsibilities, and Johnson's duty is judging.

In fact we might say that two types of reader coexist in Johnson, and that sometimes the two types seem to be at war. One is the reader who utterly immerses himself in a book, who enters its world so completely that he loses all sense of company and time, suffering the death of Cordelia or Desdemona so personally that he cannot endure it, and startled to wake from that world and find himself back among the living. The other is the reader who picks and chooses from books, who gleans a few facts and tosses the book aside, who refuses to submit to Fielding's spell, who holds himself aloof like a judge on the bench. This is, in brief, the fully *professional* reader – that reader who went through English literature, while compiling the *Dictionary*, not with an eye to the art of argument, but underlining suitable words for amanuenses to copy. Such reading requires a highly developed power of attention. But it also demands suppressing the amateur reader, who might become too interested in the book and forget to do his job. If Johnson was a great amateur reader, he was also a great professional; and the two were at odds.

To some extent this conflict may define a problem that is not merely Johnson's but deeply a part of his era. In so far as we do have a history of reading in the later eighteenth century, it focuses on what seems to be a new sort of reader, what Darnton calls 'the Rousseauistic reader'.

> Something happened to the way that readers responded to texts in the late eighteenth century. . . . Rousseau taught his readers to 'digest' books so thoroughly that literature became absorbed in life. The Rousseauistic readers fell in love, married, and raised children by steeping themselves in print. . . . [They]

threw themselves into texts with a passion that we can barely imagine.[17]

Darnton probably gives Rousseau too much credit. The passionate reader, so personally involved with the Text that it seems more real than life, already existed in England in Richardson's time; and we see the species fully developed in responses to *The Man of Feeling*, in Diderot's emphasis on absorption (as Michael Fried calls it),[18] in which the audience is drawn into the work of art so completely as to be held enchanted in its world, or in those literal-minded readers who identified with Werther to the point of killing themselves. Moreover we cannot leave religion (especially Evangelicalism) out of account. The art of the sermon depends on breaking down the reader's aesthetic distance, converting mere understanding to passionate belief. That was what happened to Johnson when he picked up Law's *Serious Call to a Holy Life*, expecting to laugh at it but discovering his soul; henceforward he would have to change his life. Such books assume a reader who will lose himself in them. And Johnson no less than Rousseau was that kind of reader.

The history of late eighteenth-century reading may also be written, however, in just the opposite way. According to German scholars of 'bourgeois' reading, the period marks a radical shift from 'intensive' reading, in which a few books are deeply absorbed and studied again and again, to 'extensive' reading, in which educated people 'ran through a great deal of printed matter, especially novels and journals . . . read each item only once, for amusement, then raced on to the next.'[19] Darnton cites this analysis only in order to disagree with it. But a heavy weight of evidence supports it; and not the least is the proliferation of such volumes as the *Encyclopaedia* itself, meant to be scanned or consulted rather than slowly read through. Even Rousseau's own constant insistence that his books are not to be treated like others, to pass a casual hour or furnish materials for some entertaining public squabble, but rather to be taken to heart, suggests that he viewed 'extensive reading' as the norm of his time. A similar defensiveness has often been noted in Wordsworth – 'O reader! had you in your mind/ Such stores as silent thought can bring,/ O gentle reader! you would find/ A tale in every thing'[20] – whose ironic tone implies that the poet expects his actual readers to be anything but gentle. The public cannot be trusted. Corrupted by superficial modern styles of reading, by frivolous and sensational reading matter, and above all by the easy availability of books, too many books, it will not take the time to read intensively. Instead it skims the surface.

The two main historical accounts of the special character of late eighteenth-century reading, then, are not merely different but totally contradictory. Readers were deep or shallow, intensive or extensive, passionate or uninvolved. What are we to conclude? In the face of so dramatic a split, a prudent historian might suspect that something is wrong with the formulation of the problem. Perhaps the two kinds of reading are not so different after all; perhaps they are no more than two hemispheres of a single brain, two aspects or interpretations of the same set of events. I think that is the case. We have already seen, in glancing at Rousseau and Wordsworth, the coexistence of a high ideal of intensive reading with a culture devoted to extensiveness; and everywhere we look at models of reading, in the period, a similar doubleness makes itself felt. Consider, for instance, the reader implied in Sterne's *Sentimental Journey*. Ideally that reader, like Parson Yorick himself, will clasp the text to her bosom, linger on every sentimental occasion, be ready to drop a tear, surrender herself to the author. 'My Journey shall make you cry,' Sterne told one susceptible reader, 'as much as ever it made me laugh.'[21] But many readers laugh along with Sterne and refuse to be taken in; they see *through* the text. They too are model readers. For such duplicity is just the point of sentiment. Sterne lures his readers into personal, unself-conscious engagement, precisely in order to play self-conscious tricks, to catch us while letting us know that we are caught. Hence the book may be equally understood as grossly sentimental or as a devastating critique of sentiment. These two effects are hardly opposite. They constitute the two sides of Sternean reading, in which perfect unconsciousness and perfect self-consciousness blend as the yolk and white in the one shell.

A similar analysis may help to clarify the split in Johnson's reading: what I have called the conflict of the amateur and professional reader or, in the terms of German historians, the most intensive reader with the most extensive. To stay closer to Johnson's own language, one might observe that this most uncommon of readers was the critic who invented and popularised that great eighteenth-century discovery, the common reader. What has Johnson in common with that hypothetical person? Very little, it seems. For one mark of that reader is not to have read very much, and another is a tendency to prefer mediocrity to greatness. In a long and thoughtful study of Johnson's term,[22] Clarence Tracy compares the common reader to Yeats's 'Fisherman', in that moving poem where the poet tries to imagine his ideal audience, 'A man who does not exist,/ A man who is but a dream', a reader whose independence and simplicity would be worthy of 'one/ Poem maybe as cold/ And passionate as the dawn.' But Yeats's fisherman was not of course common, and perhaps not even a reader. The poet imagines him specifically in opposition to his actual audience of knaves and fools, 'The witty man and his joke/ Aimed at the commonest ear.' Yeats took revenge on such common readers in *The Oxford Book of Modern Verse*, which bars the way to any author who does not catch his own high aristocratic tone. But Johnson, uncommon as he is, respects the common reader even while looking down on him. His imagined audience consists not of an idealised and purified version of himself but of a lowest common denominator.

When Johnson undertook his prefaces to the English poets, to accompany an anthology, he added only five names, among them John Pomfret, 'the favourite of that class of readers who, without vanity or criticism, seek only their own amusement'. Is Pomfret a favourite of Johnson? Evidently not. 'His *Choice* exhibits a system of life adapted to common notions and equal to common expectations', and 'perhaps no composition in our language has been oftener perused.' Yet when Johnson turns his own critical eye on Pomfret, he can manage nothing more convincing than this: 'He pleases many, and he who pleases many must have some species of merit.'[23] This is a handsome concession, but it also implies that Johnson is not among the many who are pleased and that he does not understand Pomfret's species of merit. Instead he surrenders his judgement to the public, as if to disappear amidst that class of readers 'without vanity or criticism.' The critic disarms himself. Many of Johnson's references to the common reader strike the same note of selfless capitulation, as in the famous conclusion of *The Lives of the Poets*: 'In the character of [Gray's] *Elegy* I rejoice to concur with the common reader; for by the common sense of readers uncorrupted with literary prejudices, after all the refinements of subtilty and the dogmatism of learning, must be finally decided all claim to poetical honours.'[24] Perhaps a drop of poison clings to this sentiment, since (as I have argued elsewhere) the

'Life of Gray' has taught the reader to think of Gray himself as the personification of 'the refinements of subtilty and the dogmatism of learning.' But Johnson is also relieving a painful suspense, by showing that his hostility to Gray does not extend to the one work most favoured by the public. Indeed, he probably contrived this effect deliberately, saving the 'Elegy' for the end (against chronology) in order to associate himself with the general will. Johnson concurs, at last, with all the unsubtle and unlearned, the semi-literate students who are also his masters. Yet this submission to the common reader would not work unless we knew that Johnson did not find it easy. It takes a large man to stoop so far. Or to paraphrase T. S. Eliot, only those who read with personality and emotion know what it means to want to read like a common person.

Yet is not *everyone*, at last, a common reader? The sense of doubleness I have been exploring, the perilous adjustment between an individual, passionately involved consciousness like that of Rousseau or Johnson and the common denominator of ordinary understanding, might be considered less dramatically as a description of the normal experience of any reading. To read at all, one has to be able to think like someone else. Reading is a social activity. We learn the codes and idioms, we learn the language, by submitting to the common inheritance of shared conventions and institutions implicit in the text. There are no private languages, as Wittgenstein said, and in the same sense there are no private readings. Only an age of perverse and deluded individualism, an age when the practice of misreading, unsupported by any norm of true or accurate reading, can be regarded as a positive value for critics who want to be strong, would think that any reader could be unconstrained by a community. Nor do we lose our individuality by learning how to read as others do. On the contrary, assuming that set of social roles, understanding our own involvement in the processes of human life and language, is how we become ourselves. Or so the argument goes. And as it applies to reading, so to canons. The expert who compiles anthologies cannot indulge his private taste too far. Even while reading, he must reserve a part of his mind for the larger audience, those he instructs by accommodating to their needs. Canons are social constructs. Significantly, for all their differences, Nichol Smith and Lonsdale begin their volumes with the same selection. I doubt that it is a favourite of either; but each editor evidently thinks that popular suffrage has chosen it, and therefore it must have some species of merit. The poem is, of course, Pomfret's 'The Choice'.

Johnson made many such choices. Both as a reader and as a guide to reading, he took his orders from the booksellers and public, and managed to think as they did most of the time. Of all the great British authors, he is the one most *commissioned* to greatness; he very seldom wrote as a volunteer. Hence Johnson's authority derives from his compliance, as in, defining a word, one tries to replicate and acquiesce in everyone else's usage. At his best, such an authority catches the essence of common understanding so well that we feel it with the force of an original insight – yes, that is what the word *does* mean; yes, that is why I *do* like Shakespeare. No one doubts Johnson's force. But the condition of his authority is to choose Pomfret's 'Choice', to true his reading with the public mind.

The identification of Johnson's interests with those of the common reader is not merely the end-product of his writing. It is part of the process of reading. We may see this process at work, for example, in the well-known passage where Johnson discusses the painful ending of *Lear*.

> In the present case the publick has decided. Cordelia, from the time of Tate, has always retired with victory and felicity. And, if my sensations could add any thing to the general suffrage, I might relate, that I was many years ago so shocked by Cordelia's death, that I know not whether I ever endured to read again the last scenes of the play till I undertook to revise them as an editor.[25]

More than one element of this paragraph might be singled out for attention. Once again the intensity and vividness of Johnson's response remind us that he was no casual reader. It is not clear whether Cordelia's death shocked him, years before, in a theatre or in his study; but Johnson's imagination could bring scenes to life from the barest words on a page. At the same time, he acknowledges that he will read for pay (even against his will). A scene beyond the amateur's endurance becomes just one more task for the professional. But the brunt of the paragraph falls elsewhere, on the relation of the critic's 'sensations' to the 'general suffrage.' Johnson introduces the point with characteristic modesty. The public has settled the issue, and his own experience merely confirms the justice of that choice. Yet, for a modern reader, what is most striking is the critic's assumption that his own violent reaction – so personal; so rich with psychological implications, so insistent on the first person singular – duplicates that of every other reader. Those of us who do not prefer Tate's ending to Shakespeare's will not concede that Johnson's choice is 'natural'; and some of us might even argue that the strength of his repulsion testifies to the success of the tragedy in producing a strong artistic effect (so that Johnson was of Shakespeare's party without knowing it). But that is *our* way of reading. Johnson read differently. He measured his judgement by that of the common reader, and knew that he read best when that reader was part of himself.

I conclude with two more questions. The first is historical. Is Johnson's relation to the common reader typical of his age, its modes of reading and canon formation, or is it rather the product of his own particular critical position? My whole analysis suggests the former; but since most scholars of Johnson, ever since Boswell, have favoured the latter, there is still some room for scepticism. The question may be clarified by asking it in a slightly different way: to what extent is Johnson's notion of the common reader a private fantasy, the necessary fiction that allows him to project his own opinions onto the vast, uninterested masses, rather than the image of any social or cultural reality? In this form the question may look harder to answer than it is in fact. For the common reader can easily prove his unreality by not buying books, by refusing to read what he is supposed to, or like Yeats's fisherman casting his flies alone. Johnson's common reader was more concrete. He or she kept the *Dictionary* on a handy shelf, tended to read the plays and poets Johnson recommended, quoted his judgements often, hungered for anecdotes about his personality, and to a surprising extent even managed to imitate certain features of his style (no book is more important than *The Rambler* in sponsoring the weighty locutions of Victorian prose). I do not mean to exaggerate Johnson's ability to identify with his readers. Plenty of readers, some of them common, hated his writing or, worse yet, found it too boring to read. Nevertheless it does seem true that no British critic (not even Addison) has ever been thought more representative of canonical taste by those best qualified to judge, the public that buys the canon.

So much for material causes. More speculatively, however, it might be argued that not only Johnson's critical authority but even his intimate habits of reading reflect the pressing social conflicts of his era. To put this schematically: he assumed the task of making the literary heritage of England – a set of works composed for a small, often aristocratic audience – available to a large public of middle-class (and sometimes lower-class) readers. Such labour can never be free from implicit tensions. The lower-class reader who owns a good dictionary can find out the meaning of words that people like him had never used before, a vocabulary previously owned only by those who had been born or educated to it; and when that lower-class reader tries out such words, he inevitably disturbs the upper classes, not only by making mistakes, but by intruding on their linguistic prerogatives. Eliza Doolittle is charming in the singular but threatening as a cohort, let alone as a spouse. And so it is with literary canons. When anyone can be familiar with the best of poetry, and even know the right things to say about it, the cultivated or aristocratic reader may begin to lose his taste for poetry. That situation had never occurred before in Britain. In Johnson's time, with Johnson's aid, it did. And one of the names we give to this social climber, who thinks her right to language as good as anyone else's, is the common reader.

But Johnson did not only instigate this inter-class competition; he represented it in his very self. Despite his belief in social subordination, through reading he rose and rose. A doctor only by courtesy, at first barely hanging on to the bottom rung of the middle class, eventually he turned into King Critic, the embodiment of the learned reader, if not the Mind of Europe. But people who travel so far tend to carry the baggage with which they started. In Johnson's time, his enemies liked to note the incongruity between the man of principle, that Jacobite and scorner of patrons, and the comfortable pensioner. Yet a deeper conflict inhabited his own mind. All the ways in which I have already characterised the tensions of late eighteenth-century reading – intensive and extensive reading, the amateur and the professional, the uncommon and common readers, the learned and unlearned, the aristocrat and bourgeois, the encyclopedist and the browser – help to form Johnson's habits of reading. For to read in his time, in his way, meant to be of two minds, just as reading itself is both a private and a public experience. The place where the two join is a struggle of classes that may also be described as a process of thought. We call it the Age of Johnson.

My second question moves from the eighteenth century to our own, oppressed by two more centuries of books, too many books. How can Johnson help us to think about the canon? Is the notion of the common reader still useful at all? We might call in to testify one critic, Virginia Woolf, who could not do without the common reader. In the book-ends of her collected essays, the little title piece that opens the first series of *The Common Reader* and 'How Should One Read a Book?', which closes the second, Woolf reveals how much Johnson's term means to her. Perhaps it even means more to her than to him. The tide of books has swamped her, not least because her criticism is that of a reviewer for the weeklies, always bombarded by a new shipment of volumes she barely has time to sort and assess and she clings to the common reader as if to a spar. Hence she identifies more than Johnson does with the figure, imagining herself half-educated or utterly amateurish.

> When books pass in review like the procession of animals in a shooting gallery, and the critic has only one second in which to load and aim and shoot [he] may well be pardoned if he mistakes rabbits for tigers, eagles for barndoor fowls, or misses altogether and wastes his shot upon some peaceful cow grazing in a further field.[26]

This critic clearly has nightmares, Diderot's nightmares. Yet she has not given up Diderot's hope of making sense out of all this confusion. Indeed what most appeals to her about Johnson's common reader is his ability to decide 'all claim to poetical honours.' Though 'hazy, inaccurate, and superficial,' this reader never stops judging and choosing a canon. 'Above all, he is guided by an instinct to create for himself, out of whatever odds and ends he can come by, some kind of whole – a portrait of a man, a sketch of an age, a theory of the art of writing.'[27] In this respect, too, Woolf identifies with the figure. She wants to distil the best of books into a whole, the definitive book of books.

Yet Woolf is also a twentieth-century reader, and will not bend to anyone else's canon. 'To admit authorities, however heavily furred and gowned, into our libraries and let them tell us how to read, what to read, what value to place upon what we read, is to destroy the spirit of freedom which is the breath of those sanctuaries. Everywhere else we may be bound by laws and conventions – there we have none.'[28] Every common reader must judge for herself. Woolf hardly seems to recognise the inconsistency of this principle with her hope for some scale of reading or 'poetical honours'. When she advises her own readers to 'be severe in our judgments; let us compare each book with the greatest of its kind,' she assumes that 'we' will somehow have read the 'greatest' without being told what it is. Nor does she note the disparity between her warning against authorities who would tell us what to read and her own practice of reviewing. These problems are certainly not Woolf's alone. To some extent they trouble almost every modern reader, who thinks of reading as a private sanctuary where authorities cannot tread and prefers not to notice the long train of social assumptions and manipulations that have put this reading matter in her hand. We teachers ought to be troubled most, who ask students for a personal response to books they have been assigned. That is our 'spirit of freedom'. Nor do we share Johnson's confidence, or Woolf's faint hope, that we would know a common reader when we found her.

Nevertheless we need canons more than ever. Not even the passing of print culture now seems able to stanch the flow of books, or whatever book-substitutes may exist in the future. In fact anthologies accumulate; and so many encyclopedias compete for space that expert guides must tell us which to choose. Meanwhile facsimiles of the common reader are simulated from opinion polls and marketing research. Surely Johnson's canon is obsolete. But not the idea of the canon. For without some authority to think about, to start the conversation, or even to *resist*, we would not learn to read as moderns do. Once again Virginia Woolf may be called to the stand. The great authorities on reading, she says – Coleridge, Dryden and Johnson – can help us find ourselves. 'But they are only able to help us if we come to them laden with questions and suggestions won honestly in the course of our own reading. . . . We can only understand their ruling when it comes in conflict with our own and vanquishes it.[29] The adversarial canon, like the adversary culture, may seem to be a contradiction in terms. Yet even Johnson's common reader, we ought to remember, acquires his power largely through resistance; he will read Pomfret's 'Choice' no matter what scholars say. Woolf's common reader – *our* common reader – serves the same function.

He would not exist without Johnson and Woolf and Lonsdale and others who invent him as the imaginary auditor whom every writer needs to address, in the Age of Print. Yet, even though imaginary, he exerts a pressure on the canon and the authorities that keeps them in motion. Diderot's *Encyclopedia* did not last. Johnson's common reader did, for good or ill. Our task is still imagining what he is, and what he might become.

Notes

1. Tr. Ralph H. Bowen, in *Rameau's Nephew and Other Works*, Indianapolis, 1964, pp. 299–300.
2. Ibid., p. 300.
3. 'Philosophers Trim the Tree of Knowledge: The Epistemological Strategy of the Encyclopédie', in *The Great Cat Massacre*, New York, 1984, p. 209.
4. *Printing Technology, Letters & Samuel Johnson*, Princeton, 1987, p. 246.
5. *The New Oxford Book of Eighteenth-Century Verse*, Oxford, 1984, p. xxxvii.
6. Ibid., p. xxv.
7. *Johnson's Dictionary and the language of Learning*, Chapel Hill, 1986.
8. *Boswell's Life of Johnson*, ed. G. B. Hill and L. F. Powell, Oxford, 1934, iii, pp. 284–5.
9. *Life of Johnson*, i, p. 71.
10. *Life of Johnson*, ii, p. 174.
11. *Life of Johnson*, iii, p. 43.
12. *Life of Johnson*, i, p. 186.
13. William Field, *Memoirs of the Life, Writings, and Opinions of the Rev. Samuel Parr*, London, 1828, i, p 164.
14. William Gerard Hamilton, in the *Life of Johnson*, iv, p. 421.
15. 'Reading, Technology, and the Nature of Man: An Interpretation', *Yearbook of English Studies*, x, 1980, pp. 132–49.
16. *Life of Johnson*, iii, p. 354.
17. 'Readers Respond to Rousseau: The Fabrication of Romantic Sensitivity', in *The Great Cat Massacre*, p. 251.
18. *Absorption and Theatricality: Painting & Beholder in the Age of Diderot*, Berkeley, 1980.
19. *The Great Cat Massacre*, p. 249. The views summarised are principally those of Rolf Engelsing, *Der Bürger als Leser*, 1974.
20. 'Simon Lee', 1798, lines 65–8.
21. Letter to 'Hannah', quoted by Ian Jack in his edition of *A Sentimental Journey*, London, 1972, p. xv.
22. Clarence Tracy, 'Johnson and the Common Reader', *Dalhousie Review*, lvii, 1977, pp. 405–23.

23. *Lives of the English Poets*, ed. G. B. Hill, Oxford, 1905, i, p. 302.
24. *Lives of the English Poets*, iii, p. 441.
25. *Johnson on Shakespeare*, ed. Arthur Sherbo, New Haven, 1968, ii, p. 704.
26. *The Common Reader*, New York, 1948, ii, p. 294.
27. *The Common Reader*, i, p. 11.
28. *The Common Reader*, ii, p. 281.
29. *The Common Reader*, ii, pp. 293–4.

8

Rewriting the Caribbean Past: Cultural History in the Colonial Context

Peter Hulme

Lipking focused on a central issue within the Eurocentric framework of culture, yet the ramifications of culture are wide. Peter Hulme reminds us that the roots of culture have to do with the senses of cultivation and colonialisation: senses which involve nature and power, core and periphery.

Hulme shares with Jordanova a close and subtle reading of 'texts' (understood in the widest sense) which is informed by a critical social awareness of culture. He uses this approach to analyse how different texts about the Caribbean can be read. *The Tempest* which in the seventeenth and eighteenth centuries was not read by anyone as a play about the New World, is now seen by some as concerned with the central themes of colonialism. Hulme argues that who defines the meaning of our culture is not unproblematic, and that readers situated away from the centre, for instance in Madagascar or Barbados, with different interests and perspectives from an English critic, are able to show that 'Prospero's behaviour towards Ariel and Caliban is indefensible' and to overturn the canonical judgements about who are the heroes and villains of the play.

Hulme goes on to use two accounts of the Caribbean, one written at the beginning of the seventeenth century, the other the end of the eighteenth century. From these texts Hulme illustrates his point, taken from Walter Benjamin, that 'there is no document of culture that is not at the same time a record of barbarism'. In the Caribbean the early settlers' own account shows how they both denied and described native Carib culture. The Amerindians or Caribs were depicted as cultivating plants and fruits, and tending animals; they had a culture, yet they were perceived as 'cruel Cannibals' without any civilised feelings. This mass blindness of one

175

culture for another, mediated by the need to colonise (to cultivate, to culture) was, believes Hulme, a type of collective psychosis, reflecting the nature, not of individuals, but of 'the colonial project as a whole'. The later text, Alexander Anderson's *Geography and History of St. Vincent*, shows that this blindness continued but that, in Anderson, an Enlightenment intellectual outside the establishment plantocracy, it was lightened by a limited appreciation of the original inhabitants' culture, and by a perception of the damage that colonial cultivation was doing to the environment of the island. Hulme's chapter reminds us that culture has not always been the vehicle of light and emancipation, inevitably, given its semantic roots, and that the way culture is interpreted, indeed whether a people are allowed to be seen to possess culture, is often a matter of power and force.

Leopold von Ranke once spoke of the historian's calling as divine, and in this context, one can perhaps see why. In a secular age, one might better characterize it as colossally presumptuous.

(George Stocking)

The entry on 'culture' in Raymond Williams's book *Keywords* reads in part as follows:

Culture is one of the two or three most complicated words in the English language. This is so partly because of its intricate historical development, in several European languages, but mainly because it has now come to be used for important concepts in several distinct intellectual disciplines and in several distinct and incompatible systems of thought.

The fw is *cultura*, L, from rw *colere*, L. *Colere* had a range of meanings: inhabit, cultivate, protect, honour with worship. Some of these meanings eventually separated, though still with occasional overlapping, in the derived nouns. Thus 'inhabit' developed through *colonus*, L to *colony*. 'Honour with worship' developed through *cultus*, L to *cult*. *Cultura* took on the main meaning of cultivation or tending, though with subsidiary medieval meanings of honour and worship . . . The French forms of *cultura* were *couture*, oF, which has since developed its own specialized meaning, and later *culture*, which by eC15 had passed into English. The primary meaning was then in husbandry, the tending of natural growth.[2]

The area I wanted to explore at the 1987 Aberdeen conference was the 'occasional overlapping' that Williams refers to, particularly the residual overlap between the 'separated' meanings of 'colony' and 'culture' – and I was thinking of the material roots of 'culture': the growth of crops as a prerequisite for the growth of minds and, behind this, the possession of land as a prerequisite for the growth of crops. My intention was to address this nexus through some 'Caribbean' texts, a focus that might open up a discussion of the meanings and usages of the notion of 'culture', and provide an oblique angle of approach to Europe, so often regarded as its single location.

But as well as focusing the culture/colony nexus, looking at these texts was also a way of raising some of the broader methodological and theoretical questions which I imagined the conference would be debating. My presumption was that one of the unquestioned gains of new critical theory over the last twenty years or so has been a much subtler awareness of quite what might be involved in 'reading texts'. Literary critics, for example, are today much less likely to get away with building walls around texts so as not to be confused by what lies 'beyond' them, and historians are more chary of referring airily to 'documentary evidence' as if the problem of interpreting such evidence did not exist. We all should now be reading more alertly, more suspiciously. In particular, the readings offered here present themselves as, in Louis Althusser's term, 'symptomatic'; in other words they are undertaken with the aim of making the texts reveal more than they claim to know, tracing the play of history to be found on the margins of the texts. If, however – extending the metaphor – the 'text' is taken to be something like 'European cultural history', then the essay that follows is primarily concerned with the ways in which such a self-evidently *central* agenda might be understood through attending to what its very centralising gesture has established as peripheral. There are, then, two analogous topographies involved here: a textual topography in which the 'marginal' is read as the locus of a textual unconscious; and a physical topography in which the peripheral space of the colony is read as the repressed of the metropolitan centre.[3]

The period addressed by the conference – 1600–1800 – was roughly that usually referred to as the 'First British Empire', from the early English settlements in the New World to the loss of the thirteen colonies.[4] The relevant Caribbean parameters would be

Raleigh's first expedition to Guiana in 1595 and the so-called Brigands' Wars of the 1790s. I chose as my principal reference points two little-known texts, one from each end of the period. John Nicholl's 'An Houre Glasse of Indian News . . .' tells of a disastrous expedition to Guiana in 1605 which ended in shipwreck on the coast of a Caribbean island. It was published in 1607, collected in abbreviated form in *Purchas His Pilgrimes* in 1625, and reprinted, almost complete, in 1966. Alexander Anderson's *Geography and History of St. Vincent, West Indies* was written right at the end of the eighteenth century (possibly in 1798), bequeathed on his death in 1811 to the Linnaean Society, and finally edited and published in 1983.[5] Both texts therefore presented the opportunity to address the problems of 'insertion', in other words to look at how a 'new' text might be placed within existing generic and discursive regimes, and at what kinds of effect it might have there.

Writing about the Caribbean makes that perspective impossible to ignore. The past is constantly, and necessarily, being rewritten. There is still in place a colonial historiography which has read documents and written texts; and there is a post-colonial historiography which is rewriting history, in part because it is re-reading both the documents and the colonial historiography differently. Quite what 'differently' might, and should, mean in such circumstances is a fascinating but difficult question. As a way of introducing the themes of my paper I wanted to approach that question through Goerge Lamming's essay on *The Tempest* from his book *The Pleasures of Exile*, written in 1960, thereby bringing into direct contact one of the single most potent signifiers of European 'culture' and a characteristically ambivalent view from the margins.[6]

I

The Tempest was written before there were any English colonies in the Caribbean. And the play itself makes no explicit reference to 'the Caribbean' or indeed to any of its component islands. The nearest place referred to is Bermuda, and that in such a way as to make it clear that the setting of the play is *not* Bermuda. It is worth making this literal point because it raises at the start the question of reading, which ought to be central to any discussion of cultural

history. For many readers such absence of reference would disqualify *The Tempest* from having anything to say about the
Caribbean. The play clearly does not speak openly about that part
of the world; indeed the overt geography of the play, gauged by
place-names, appears resolutely Mediterranean. And, if you look
at the ways in which *The Tempest* was read during the seventeenth
and eighteenth centuries, there is little to suggest that any reader,
performer, editor or adapter saw anything in the play that would
relate its concerns to the New World in general or to the Caribbean
in particular.[7]

All of which makes it even more remarkable that, over the last
forty years or so, there has developed a powerful counter-reading
of the play which asserts the centrality of questions of colonialism
for *The Tempest*, and often argues that the Old World topography
works as a displacement of the play's genuinely New World
concerns. By common consent the first significant reading along
these lines was given in a book entitled *Psychologie de la colonisation* and written in Madagascar by a French social scientist, Octave
Mannoni, in the aftermath of the Madagascan uprising of 1947.
The genesis of this work is of the utmost interest. What now, from
the perspective of the 1980s, seems like a breakthrough in the
reading of *The Tempest* came from a site all of whose key terms –
French, social scientist, Madagascar – differ from the attributes of
whose who have conventionally been endowed with the authority
to 'read' Shakespeare and interpret anew the supposedly eternal
verities of his plays.

Mannoni's psychological theory of colonialism was based on the
idea of the mutual support of the coloniser's inferiority complex
and the colonised's dependency complex. Prospero and Caliban
stood as immediate archetypes while Mannoni developed his
more detailed analysis of colonial Madagascar. In 1952, Frantz
Fanon wrote a devastating critique of the notion of a dependency
complex within colonised societies, but Mannoni's brief remarks
on Prospero still stand as an acute pointer to the sceptical readings
of the play that have followed.[8]

In 1960, before Mannoni's work was translated into English, the
Barbadian writer George Lamming published a book of loosely-
linked essays called *The Pleasures of Exile*. The whole book is to
some extent a dialogue with *The Tempest*, which is after all, in one
of its most frequent readings, a play about exile. But one essay in
particular offers a trenchant re-reading of the play in terms even

more unconventional – and rather less difficult to ignore – than those deployed by Mannoni. I will give just one example. Lamming quotes the exchange between Prospero and Caliban in which Prospero claims to have used Caliban 'with human care; and lodg'd thee / In mine own cell, till thou didst seek to violate / The honour of my child' (I.ii.348–50). Caliban responds: '. . . would't had been done! / Thou didst prevent me; I had peopled else / This isle with Calibans' (I.ii.351–3). Lamming then comments:

> What an extraordinary way for a slave to speak to his master and in the daughter's presence. But there is a limit to accepting lies and it was the Lie contained in the charge which the man in Caliban could not allow. 'I wish it were so.' But he does not wish it for the mere experiment of mounting a piece of white pussy. He goes further and imagines that the consequence of such intercourse would be a fabulous increase of the population . . . Is there a political intention at work? Does he mean that he would have numbers on his side; that he could organise resistance against this obscene, and selfish monster . . . Did Caliban really try to lay her? This is a case where the body, in its consequences, is our only guide. Only the body could establish the truth; for if Miranda were made pregnant, we would know that someone had penetrated her. We might also know whether or no it was Caliban's child; for it is most unlikely that Prospero and his daughter could produce a brown skin baby . . .[9]

Of special interest here is Lamming's chosen angle of address to the play. In his 'Introduction' to *The Pleasures of Exile*, Lamming anticipates the charge of blasphemy, and you can see why. In the Caribbean, 'Shakespeare' signified – and of course continues, somewhat ironically, to signify – 'culture' in the most limited and iniquitous of that word's meanings. For Lamming, 'Shakespeare' is the pinnacle of a colonial education system that taught West Indians to denigrate, if not totally to deny, their place of birth. As he says, 'for all the books [West Indian writers] had read, their whole introduction to something called culture, all of it, in the form of words, came from outside: Dickens, Jane Austen, Kipling and that sacred gang.' To speculate about Caliban 'mounting a piece of white pussy' is a quite calculated desecration of what he calls 'the whole tabernacle of dead names',[10] the very altar of

British culture. No doubt, thirty years on, we wish that Lamming had found a different way of making the gesture.

Yet, even more significantly, the raising of that spectre of incest opens up the political dimensions of the play in a genuinely novel way. For the 'new' readings, of which Lamming's can be taken as an early and representative example, the centre of the play is to be found in the question of the rights to territorial possession, raised in perfectly straightforward fashion by Caliban when he says to Prospero: 'This island's mine by Sycorax my mother / Which thou tak'st from me' (I.ii.333–4). Questions of law and inheritance are of supreme importance, to Prospero as well as to Caliban; and yet, strangely, such matters, especially as they relate to the play's women – Prospero's wife, Sycorax, Claribel, Miranda – cannot be discussed, particularly by Prospero, without an anxiety which always has sexual undertones.

From a theoretical point of view the crux of the matter is the status of readings such as Lamming's. There are, broadly speaking, four possible positions on the matter. The first would say that Lamming's reading is a distortion of *The Tempest*, that the play has been subjected to a deliberately provocative *mis*reading, but that 'we' should not be diverted from directing 'our' attention to the text itself. A second position would turn this desecration into a virtue. Lamming himself offers something of a hostage to fortune when he says that, even if it is 'wrong', his reading 'proves the positive value of error'.[11] In this way Lamming's reading of *The Tempest* could be coupled with, for example, Aimé Césaire's play *Une tempête*, which is subtitled as being *after The Tempest*, an 'adaptation for a black theatre'.[12] Both would be what have recently been called 'transgressive appropriations' of *The Tempest*.[13] A third position – the most permissive – would reject any distinction between so-called 'readings' and 'misreadings', and argue that Lamming's *Tempest* should merely take its place alongside Coleridge's and Kermode's and whoever else's. A fourth position would simply say that Lamming's reading of the play is right and the others wrong.[14] These positions cannot be analysed in detail here, but the one point should at least be made that there is an important line to be drawn between 'reading' and 'transgressive appropriation'. This might seem just common sense, yet in practice and in theory the distinction is an extremely difficult one to make, especially when dealing with drama where every production is an interpretation, and where the 'text' may well be a hypostatisation of an 'original' performance. None the less, Lamming's 'reading' and Césaire's are different in kind, not least because Lamming's, unlike Césaire's, openly contests earlier, and supposedly authoritative, readings. It is for this reason that Lamming's *Tempest* cannot simply be placed *alongside* Coleridge's and Kermode's. It offers an implicit critique of its forerunners, and would wish to displace them from their authoritative positions within, for example, the educational apparatus.[15]

A brief look at the history of productions of *The Tempest* would bear out this argument. It is widely accepted that, of all Shakespeare's plays, *The Tempest* suffered most from the free adaptations that were common in the seventeenth and eighteenth centuries. Adaptation here, though, means something different from the example of Césaire. In Césaire's case his *Tempest* exists *alongside* Shakespeare's – however much philosophical difficulty we might have with a notion of Shakespeare's 'original' text. But from its first production in 1667 until the middle of the nineteenth century, Dryden and Davenant's *Tempest* was, at least as far as audiences were concerned, synonymous with Shakespeare's *Tempest*. The play was in fact much more of a musical, indeed sometimes a comic opera, with the possibly troubling figure of Caliban partially displaced by the presence on the island of a new character, Hippolito, who usurps Caliban's role as 'natural man', and Prospero's political conflicts with the other characters considerably toned down. Why was it that *The Tempest* suffered more than the other plays from these travesties, and why were these particular alterations made? As long as the New World was at the centre of the British Empire, a world which, according to colonial ideology was 'virgin' and 'empty', then perhaps a play which dealt, in however oblique and fraught a fashion, with questions of the legality of territorial acquisition and the reliance of European colonists on native agriculture needed to be contained and neutralised, the troubling issues of power and domination replaced by comic intrigue and sexual pantomime.[16]

When pressures of another kind led to the restoration of the text of the First Folio, subsequent readings of the play tended to see Prospero as a central Shakespearean hero, perhaps the closest thing in the canon to a self-portrait, and a character to be admired without reservation, especially for his commitment to the values of 'culture': his 'Art' and the 'nurture' he is so selflessly willing to extend, even if thanklessly and without ultimate fruit, on the recalcitrant nature of Caliban. Consequently *The Tempest* was consistently read as if through Prospero's eyes. Mannoni, Lamming and others – notably Roberto Fernández Retamar – were able to see from their particular vantage points what has only dawned very slowly, if at all, on English literary critics, that Prospero's behaviour towards Ariel and Caliban is indefensible, that his determination to inflict humiliation on Alonso is, to say the least, unpleasant, and that his exchanges with Miranda and Caliban reveal a whole series of psychic anxieties.[17] Lamming and the others have been able, because of their particular geographical and political angles upon *The Tempest*, to read the play not just in a new way, but in a way which is decisively *better*, in the sense of more powerful and more complete, than the readings previously available.

II

Four years before Shakespeare wrote *The Tempest*, an account was published in London of a disastrous voyage to Guiana which ended in shipwreck on the coast of St Lucia, a Caribbean island without European settlements, and where the only inhabitants were the native Caribs. Since the same Amerindian word gives both 'carib' and 'canibal' – both in fact used in John Nicholl's text – and since Caliban is a simple anagram of 'canibal', it is perhaps surprising that 'An Houre Glasse of Indian News' has never been taken seriously as a possible 'source' for *The Tempest*. The stories they tell are not dissimilar.

The central point to be drawn from 'An Houre Glasse of Indian News' can be gauged from the single sentence describing the landing on the island:

And so having been seventeen weeks at sea, instead of our hopeful expectations of attaining to a pleasant, rich and golden Country, and the comfortable company of our friends and Country-men, there as we supposed them resident, we were brought to an Island in the West India somewhat distant from the main, called Santa Lucia, having about twelve degrees of North latitude, inhabited only with a company of the most cruel Cannibals, and man-eaters, where we had no sooner landed anchored, but the Carebyes came in their Periagoes or Boats aboard us with great store of Tobacco, Plantains, Potatoes, Pines, Sugar Canes, and divers other fruits, with Hens, chickens, Turtles, & Iguanas: for all which we contented and pleased them well. (pp. 49–50)

A symptomatic reading of that sentence could begin to unpick the textual practices of colonialism in several different registers. There is here, for example, important early evidence of the English form of the ethnic name by which the surviving Amerindians of the Caribbean came to be known, a resonant name, but one which was in all probability, and in despite of anthropological insouciance, first deployed by the European colonists to designate those natives hesitant enough about the advantages of European 'culture' to wish to defend their own way of life by force. In other words what has come down to us as an observed ethnic designation in fact already marks a *reaction* to European presence.[18]

Alternatively – and this is the register of most interest here – the sentence could be seen as brief but potent evidence of the extremely effective 'culture' of the St Lucian Amerindians: tobacco, plantains, potatoes, pineapples, sugar cane, to which 'divers other fruits', including cassava, guavas, papaya and mamey apples, can be added from a subsequent paragraph (p. 51). All these cultigens required a sophisticated horticulture, and the majority of them were first developed in America by Amerindians.[19]

Nicholl goes on to describe the characteristic Amerindian *conuco*, 'made round like a Bower, encompassed with a green Bank, so equally' as he puts it, 'that made us think some Christians had made it for a strength to save them from the Indians' (p. 53). Nicholl's difficulty in comprehending the very idea of Amerindian horticulture, despite the multitude of evidence, could be analysed as a common trope within this kind of discourse, speaking, against the grain of the text, of the extraordinary commitment shown by European colonists to their expectations, almost irrespective of their experience, a blindness to 'see' intellectually even what they report as seeing physically.

The story Nicholl tells is not unpredictable. Initial Carib hospitality gives way to increasing suspicion in the face of boorish behaviour on the part of the colonists, and soon to loss of patience with a hostile drain on the economy that shows little inclination to shift for itself. Finally the Caribs fail to supply food, the English start to steal it, and a violent conflict ensues. Here Nicholl has to confront the strangest mystery of all. The handful of surviving English sailors and adventurers is surrounded, hopelessly outnumbered, and without food. Nicholl recounts the series of 'miseries' that have plunged them into perplexity, very much like Alonso and the court party bewailing their fate in *The Tempest*. Yet – and this is a frequent pattern in these narratives, which are, after all, at least for the writer, narratives of survival – the dénouement proves providential: 'it pleased God . . . to relieve us'. But not only that: the instrument of God's pleasure is 'our enemies', who choose (although Nicholl obviously cannot think of it as *their* choice) to bring food and drink every day for the English sailors (p. 59).

There is, in other words, an internal distance perceptible within Nicholl's text between the events that he describes and the explanation that he can offer for them. That breach can only be closed by a reassertion of the initial ethnic stereotype. At the beginning St Lucia is inhabited 'only with a company of the most cruel Cannibals, and maneaters' (p. 49). And at the end the company is happy to leave the island of the Caribs, 'who thirsted for nothing but to eat our flesh, and drink our blood' (p. 59). The evidence to the contrary is, so to speak, swallowed. Ironically, the final prayer, to 'guide us safely to some Christian Harbour' (p. 59) is answered, only for the Spaniards in Venezuela to give Nicholl and his companions an even harder time than the Caribs had done.

So one of the central features of Nicholl's text is that Amerindian culture is at the same time described and denied. It is marvelled over, and yet such descriptions prove unable to penetrate the closed categories which define the Amerindians as 'without culture', as – classically – living in a 'state of nature'. This phenomenon is not comprehensible within the terms of 'perception'. It is not just the case that the colonists were prevented from 'seeing' certain things by the perceptual framework which they carried with them across the Atlantic. It is not simply a question of a mismatch between 'expectation' and 'reality'. The 'blindness' of the colonists is only a metaphor. Nicholl's description of Carib horticulture is in fact quite detailed; and a few years previously

John White had drawn and painted the culture of the coastal Algonquian of North America in even greater detail.[20] The only explanation that makes any sense, as far as I can see, is one which draws on the language of psychoanalysis. To say this does not imply embracing psychohistory, at least in any unproblematic sense. But it would suggest an attempt to think through the kind of relationships that might obtain between psychoanalytic categories and written texts.

There are three levels upon which the categories of psychoanalysis could conceivably have some purchase. Least interesting, though most commonly essayed, is the psychoanalytic reading of an author, the attempt to use the text as raw material analogous to, say, the dream in Freudian analysis. The analogy is exceedingly hazardous because for Freud the language of dreams is inherently private and can only therefore be elucidated through the kind of associative exercise impossible outside a consulting room. The second level takes as its object of analysis the character within a fiction. This is open to something of the same objection – strictly speaking, a character cannot be psychoanalysed; but fictional characters are arguably quite closely analogous to the subject of psychoanalysis. It is certainly on this second level that many recent psychoanalytical readings of *The Tempest* have operated. Mannoni takes Prospero as the type of a colonialist psyche; Lamming says that Prospero's imperialism 'is like an illness' and begins to diagnose some of the symptoms.[21]

The third level at which the language of psychoanalysis can work is the social. This is the most rewarding level, and the most pertinent here, but also the most problematic since the address of psychoanalysis is so determinedly towards the level of the individual psyche that it is very difficult indeed to apply its concepts at a broader and more collective level. Obviously I can give no extended theoretical justification for such a move. But I will give an example of what I mean. If you take as object of study the colonial narratives of the period, then they are marked by the persistence of that internal distance noted within Nicholl's text, a distance which is quite properly and necessarily called psychotic, to indicate both its immunity to contradictory evidence and its tendencies to disavow its own failures and project them onto its opponents. But at this level the 'unconscious' is social rather than individual: the object of analysis is less Nicholl's own psyche (in any case unavailable to us) than the colonial project as a whole.

And that colonial project is analysed as something like a discursive formation with, as its unconscious, its own morphological features, its own architecture and, especially, its own rhetorical tropes and strategies.[22]

III

To move to Alexander Anderson's *Geography and History of St Vincent* allows us to gauge, however approximately, some of the changes in the ways Carib culture was represented in European discourse and, perhaps even more importantly, some of the very signal continuities with the tropes characteristic of the earlier part of the period.

Any full analysis of Anderson's manuscript would need to give proper attention to a number of facts I can mention only briefly. Clearly the text has its place within the genre of the 'natural history' which often functioned within the colonial enterprise as the textbook of natural resources, those 'resources' including the native inhabitants. But the *Geography and History of St Vincent* is anomalous within that genre to the extent that its notion of natural history is far less instrumental than earlier examples from the Caribbean. This might in part be explained by Anderson's position as director of the island's botanical garden, famous as the first Caribbean home of the breadfruit tree which Captain Bligh brought from the South Seas to provide cheap food for the slaves; a fact that serves as a perpetual reminder that botany is not divorced from the realities of colonial exploitation. Nevertheless, Anderson's point of view in his *Geography and History* is by no means identical to that of the colonial plantocracy, and the subsequent analysis will look in more detail at some of the moments when that divergence becomes apparent, when Anderson seems to deploy a vocabulary belonging in part to an emergent discourse which can be recognised as 'romantic', and in part to a discourse of environmental concern which may owe something to Anderson's time in North America in the 1770s.[23]

Perhaps the most interesting feature of Anderson's manuscript is the extent to which it is a text marked, almost despite its author's intentions, by the historical circumstances of its composition; in other words the way in which the interests of the geographer and historian are constantly inflected by those of the participant in the recent 'troubles' that wracked the island in 1795 and 1796, and ended with the forced exile of the infamous Black Caribs. So, for example, the imaginative descriptive tour offered by Anderson in the early part of the manuscript, which presumably compresses his own tours on horseback around the island, is broken off at one point because the particular spot he has reached on the north coast functions as a mnemonic for the landing of the French 'incendiaries' in 1795.

The rhetoric of the manuscript establishes the writer in general terms as an independently-minded 'concerned resident': 'Who was to blame', he says at one point, 'is not my affair to investigate, but one thing is evident . . .' (p. 16). At various points he distances himself from the plantocracy whose sole interest is in profit:

> On account of commerce all West India towns are built in the lowest and swampiest parts of the islands at [end] of valley and inlets of the sea, consequently the most unhealthy spots in the West Indies. But what will not man do for money? (p. 25)

A little later the planters are described as 'inconsiderate' and 'improvident', because of their 'extirpation' of more of the woods and trees than was strictly necessary (pp. 36–7). Overall the planters' attitude is seen as self-defeating and philistine. 'Even to a savage', Anderson says, clumps of trees and woods are more pleasing than bare and bleak hills (p. 38).

But Anderson's dislocation from the centre of official ideology leads the text into some uncertainty. Take, for example, his attitude towards the French. They are principally, of course, the incendiaries of the 1790s who have, particularly in the person of the despised Victor Hugues, fomented rebellion in the English colonies. Yet Anderson recognises that their successes in this endeavour have been due to their ability to get on with the native inhabitants. He talks of their 'insinuating address and ready mode of adopting the habits and customs of savages' (p. 45), with the clear implication that they too easily 'go native' and become indistinguishable from the Caribs; yet at the same time he cannot help but admire the kind of conciliation that was so lacking in the English address to the natives, and which might, he suggests, have prevented the war which eventually ensued.

Anderson's attitude to the Black Caribs themselves is almost 'coherent', in the sense that he roughly shares the official view of plantocracy, administration and military – the three major spheres of English interest on the island. And even when his position is more nuanced than theirs his vocabulary is inevitably drawn from those terms, like banditti, savages, outlaw, forest, which inscribe an otherness without the pale of culture and law.

But despite – or almost, on some occasions, because of – his enthusiastic support for the colonial line, his text always reveals rather more than the official ideology. There is a kind of textual excess, a luxuriance of metaphoric vegetation which spills over the usually well-tended borders of official discourse.

The Black Caribs make their first appearance alongside their French allies, accumulating – in a spectacularly inappropriate metaphor – 'like a snow ball', before issuing from the thickets 'like the clouds of locusts on Syria and Egypt' to reduce English cultivation to ashes (p. 15). The official line on the Black Caribs is evident when Anderson repeats some of the stories about Black Carib origins put forward in the account given by Sir William Young, who was an English commissioner in the 1760s and who owned two of the largest sugar plantations on the island:

> From the traditions that can be gathered from authority of this tribe of Africans getting a foothold in the island, it is ascertained that about a century ago . . . a ship from Africa with slaves for some of the islands was wrecked on the windward coast of St. Vincent or one of the neighboring Grenadines . . . At that period St. Vincent was the rendezvous of the yellow Carribs or aborigines from all the other islands settled by the English and French, nor had Europeans made encroachments on them . . . . By them the blacks were received with their wonted hospitality and kindness . . . For some time they remained one people and joined interest . . . but the cunning and daring Africans soon found themselves an overmatch . . . for the simple and unsuspecting Carribs and powerful enough to dispossess them of their lands and women. (pp. 43–4)[24]

The key move within this official ideology was to distinguish the Black Caribs from the 'original' inhabitants of St Vincent, who were usually referred to as 'Yellow' Caribs. For Anderson 'no two tribes of men are more distinct', which immediately seems a rather over-enthusiastic endorsement of the official position since the next phrase has to admit the similarity of their 'modes of existence' (p. 42) – a fairly major concession to similarity, one would have thought. It finally becomes clear that Anderson's anxiety on this matter is due to the possibility of charges of 'inhumanity' or 'tyranny' being laid at the door of the colonists or of the English ministers who had sanctioned what Anderson rather openly calls the 'extermination' of the Black Caribs (p. 43).

The Caribs 'properly so-called' (p. 43) now offer no threat, Anderson says, indeed 'deserve hardly to be mentioned as constituting part of the inhabitants' (p. 69). They can therefore be allowed 'true' proprietorship 'by God and nature' (p. 69), a rather more generous allowance than any of the official ideologists felt able to make. The text actually gives quite substantial play to the language of compassion which had triumphed in the 1770s, turning opinion in England decisively against the earlier war in St Vincent. The 'mind susceptible to humanity', 'the melancholy reflection', 'harmless but brave race of man' (p. 69): this language had always had some hold in England – at least from the time of the first translation of Las Casas's *Brief History* into English in the late sixteenth century – because its thrust was aimed principally at the Spaniards.[25] In this context it could be brought into play without dangerous ambivalence because it was the Black Caribs who were responsible for the extirpation of the 'innocent' original Caribs.

The acutest contrast with Nicholl's text from nearly two centuries earlier is that the fearful and man-eating Caribs, a byword for ferocity in the early seventeenth century, have been miraculously transformed into 'this yellow, inoffensive race, the original and lawful owners of the land', overmatched by the 'cunning and daring Africans' who managed to dispossess the 'unsuspecting' Caribs (p. 44). The 'true' story of Black Carib origins can never be known: there is now no possible access to it, but the blatant contradictions between different parts of the official picture make it clear that it was in the English interest to play up the 'blackness' of the Black Caribs, and to play down their 'caribness'. In this way their right to the land they occupied, at least under natural law, would appear less firm than Anderson clearly fears it might actually be. They would be, under this account of their origins, newcomers whose violence towards the 'original' inhabitants could be rectified by the English settlers. In turn these settlers would be rewarded for their knight errantry by legal possession of the Black Carib territories – the most fertile parts of the island. This, at any rate, was the somewhat optimistic narrative that the English settlers constructed for themselves.

But a quite different story gradually emerges from the margins of Anderson's account. A key sentence reads: 'At that time the island was an entire forest to the sea except some detached spots near the bays the French had cultivated in ground provisions and small plantations of coffee and cocoa' (p. 46). As in Nicholl's earlier text, the force of an ideological position – that the Amerindians live in a 'state of nature' – prevents recognition of their agricultural practices: 'cultivation' is European and antithetical to the notion of 'forest', which is where the natives live. This is the central plank of colonial ideology and, as it happens, one of its chief ideologists during this period, John Locke, glossing the concept of the 'state of nature', referred directly to the inhabitants of the West Indies 'to whom the rivers and woods afforded the spontaneous provisions of life'.[26] Interestingly enough, the only real recognition Anderson's text gives to the *idea* of Carib agriculture – as opposed to descriptions of its practices – comes when a few of the chiefs purchase slaves: this, it seems, is the true mark of 'cultured' behaviour.

But perhaps the most significant possibility that *History and Geography* opens up, beyond the bounds of its conscious narrative, is that the true nature of the conflict known as the Brigands' War was the incompatability between two different agricultural practices. Throughout the text Anderson, as an Enlightenment intellectual, shows himself suspicious of monopolies of landed property and of huge engrossments, and therefore fundamentally out of sympathy with the monocultural island economy of the sugar barons. Those who suffered from the engrossment, in the years between 1763 and 1795, were the French smallholders as much as the Black Caribs, or to put it in a slightly different and more telling way: those who suffered were the smallholders. In other words, the war fought in 1795 might, from a different perspective, and one for which there is evidence in Anderson's manuscript, be seen almost as much as a war between two economies as a war between native inhabitants and colonial oppressors.[27]

As Anderson gets closer to the terrible events of 1795, his critical remarks about the planters get more pointed:

> . . . the planters set themselves down in self-security, clearing, planting and building on to the very boundary, John Bull-like, thinking of no interruption to the calm until the storm bursts upon him, the too general prevailing idea with West Indians interest for the present moment only, without any regard to the future. Possessing a fertile soil which amply repaid their labour and expense, they dreamed of no accident or danger, the only object who should have the most land in canes and send the greatest number of hogsheads of sugar to market, forgetting they were surrounded with mortal enemies. (p. 58)

At moments like this Anderson seems on the point of empathising more easily with the Caribs than with the English. Certainly the planters' complete disregard for anything other than economic calculation is painted by Anderson in terms not far short of psychosis: 'forgetting they were surrounded with mortal enemies' sounds like a more than random aberration. A phrase he uses a little later, 'yet with the savage as well as with the civilized' (p. 59) threatens to blur one of the most crucial eighteenth-century dichotomies. And, for somebody whose interests are, in the last analysis, irretrievably tied to the success of the colonial enterprise, Anderson gives unusual play to a kind of philosophical discourse which comes close to condoning Black Carib behaviour – albeit by positing savage ignorance of civilised legality:

> The savage knows the laws of nature for his own interest and preservation and those under which his tribe avenges from tradition and the protection of his wife and children. What can he know more? He can commit no crime if he complies with these or can he with justice be punished for transgressing the civil laws of his neighbor when he knows not what civilization is nor sensible of a crime by the transgression. And whatever bounds may be set him, he can conceive himself under no laws or obligations to them but those handed down by his ancestors and of simple nature . . . (p. 61)

Their final exile evokes a compassionate response ('yet who can avoid melancholy sensations on a whole race of mankind transported forever from their native land inhabited by them for many generations') and Anderson leaves the open question of 'something radically wrong in the principles of [the] government necessitated to that act' of extirpation (p. 97).

But the rhetorical thrust of these colonial narratives is inevitably towards closure, towards the suturing of any breach that may have been opened during the process of composition. For Anderson's manuscript this closure comes when he addresses the question of the remarkable decline of Black Carib numbers during their imprisonment on the island of Balliceaux, a decline from 5200 to 2700 in the matter of a few months. These are the most fraught paragraphs of the manuscript, where Anderson clearly shows his anxiety that criticisms of the colony might be voiced to the effect that the Caribs were deliberately starved. Far from it, he says, they were provided with an 'abundance of nourishment', vessels were 'in constant employ' taking food and water to the island, in fact the large number of deaths can probably be ascribed to 'overabundance of food during their stay on Balliceaux' (pp. 94–5). It is difficult to resist the conclusion that, having offered so many criticisms of the colony during the course of his narrative, Anderson is trying rather too hard to redress the balance.

Ironically his attempt backfires. Far from the 'pen of the historian' (pp. 94–5) addressing any imputation of inhuman treatment, the cover-up was remarkably successful. The only full contemporary account of the second Carib war is Charles Shephard's *An Historical Account of the Island of St. Vincent*, commissioned by the Vincentian planters to present their story and published in 1831. Here the number of Caribs embarked for Ruatán in 1797 is listed as 5080, the same number as taken prisoner. The historical debate has always been conducted in terms of how many Caribs embarked for Central America. The Central American evidence suggests 2700, therefore that figure has sometimes been given as the number taken prisoner and kept on Balliceaux – through Shephard's figure could only be assimilated to *this* account by assuming that the planters had deliberately exaggerated the figure in order to increase compensation. Anderson's is the first contemporary evidence that, for whatever reason, there was a loss of 2500 Carib lives in the concentration camp of Balliceaux.[28]

IV

The respective fates of *The Tempest* and the *History and Geography of St Vincent* could hardly be more different. *The Tempest* has had an almost unbroken history of productions since 1611, with its central character becoming an emblem of the colonial venture which, inasmuch as it saw itself as a *cultural* enterprise, took Shakespeare as the signifier of its mission to civilise. The *History and Geography* lay unpublished and unread for over 150 years. Yet a new set of circumstances has brought their respective histories together in ways which would have been inconceivable even ten years ago. Anderson is not exactly Prospero, but he has to explain the presence of his culture on a foreign island and justify the harshness of white behaviour towards those who were there first. He also repeats, as I have tried to show, Prospero's blindness towards the culture of the island, a failure to recognise which was always, in the interests of a clean conscience, a necessary forerunner to the felt need to destroy. If we remember that, then we are perhaps in a better position to understand why Walter Benjamin, in his critique of historicism, should suggest an attitude of 'cautious detachment' towards the 'cultural treasures' carried aloft by our present rulers. As he says, there is no document of culture that is not at the same time a record of barbarism.[29]

Notes

I would like to acknowledge the assistance given me in writing this essay by Jonathan Barry, Nancie L. Gonzalez, Richard A. Howard and, especially, Ludmilla Jordanova.

1. *Race, Culture, and Evolution: Essays in the History of Anthropology,* Chicago, 1982, p. 197.
2. Raymond Williams, *Keywords: A Vocabulary of Culture and Society,* Glasgow, 1976, p. 77.
3. For 'symptomatic', see Louis Althusser (with Etienne Balibar), *Reading Capital,* trans. Ben Brewster, London, 1970, pp. 11–69; for the play of history as the textual unconscious, Pierre Macherey, *A Theory of Literary Production,* trans. Geoffrey Wall, London, 1978, p. 94. On the relationship between centre and periphery within the capitalist system see Immanuel Wallerstein, *The Modern World-System II,* New York, 1980, pp. 157–75, and Eric Williams, *Capitalism and Slavery,* New York, 1960. For elaboration of these necessarily condensed remarks on marginality see the essays on 'subalternity' in Gayatri Chakravorty Spivak, *In Other Worlds: Essays in Cultural Politics,* New York, 1987, especially p. 210. For further references see n. 22 below.
4. James Williamson, *A Short History of British Expansion,* 2 vols, London, 1930, divides his narrative between 'The Old Colonial Empire' and 'The Modern Empire'.

5.   John Nicholl, 'An Houre Glasse of Indian News . . .' 1607, ed. Rev.
      Charles Jesse, *Caribbean Quarterly*, xii, 1966, pp. 46–67 (it appeared
      in shortened form as John Nicol, 'A true relation of the traiterous
      massacre . . .', in Samuel Purchas, *Hakluytus Postumus, or Purchas
      His Pilgrimes*, 1625, 20 vols, Glasgow, 1905–7, xvi, pp. 324–37); and
      Alexander Anderson, *Geography and History of St. Vincent, West
      Indies*, 1798?, ed. Richard A. and Elizabeth S. Howard, Cambridge,
      Mass., 1983. Further references to these two books appear
      parenthetically in the text.
6.   William Shakespeare, *The Tempest*, 1611, ed. Frank Kermode,
      London, 1958; George Lamming, *The Pleasures of Exile*, 1960,
      London, 1984, pp. 95–117.
7.   For a more detailed discussion see Peter Hulme, *Colonial
      Encounters: Europe and the Native Caribbean, 1492–1797*, London,
      1986, pp. 89–134.
8.   Octave Mannoni, *Psychologie de la colonisation*, 1950; *Prospero and
      Caliban: The Psychology of Colonization*, trans. Pamela Powesland,
      New York, 1964. Frantz Fanon, *Peau noir, masques blancs*, 1952; *Black
      Skin, White Masks*, trans. Charles Lam Markmann, London, 1986,
      pp. 83–108.
9.   Lamming, *The Pleasures of Exile*, p. 102.
10.   Ibid., p. 27.
11.   Ibid., p. 13.
12.   Aimé Césaire, *Une tempête: d'après 'La Tempête' de Shakespeare.
      Adaptation pour un théâtre nègre*, Paris, 1969.
13.   Rob Nixon, 'Caribbean and African Appropriations of *The Tempest*',
      Critical Inquiry, xiii, 1987, pp. 557–78 (at 558).
14.   On some of the issues involved here, see 'The "Text in Itself": A
      Symposium', *Southern Review*, no. 17, 1984, pp. 115–46.
15.   See, for example, the two pieces by Derek Longhurst: 'Reproducing
      a National Culture: Shakespeare in Education', *Red Letters*, no. 11,
      1981, pp. 3–14; and ' "Not for all time, but for an Age": An
      Approach to Shakespeare Studies', in *Re-Reading English*, ed. Peter
      Widdowson, London, 1982, pp. 150–63.
16.   See Maximiliam Novak, 'The Tempest', in *The Works of John Dryden*,
      Berkeley, 1970, x, 319–43; and George Robert Guffey, 'Introduction',
      in *After 'The Tempest'*, Los Angeles, 1969. The Dryden/Davenant
      version, with its later operatic elaborations by Shadwell and
      Garrick, was only replaced on the English stage in 1838 when
      Macready went back to the early text.
17.   Roberto Fernández Retamar, *Calibán: Apuntes sobre la cultura de
      nuestra América*, Buenos Aires, 1973. On the post-colonialist
      readings of the figure of Prospero see Nixon (n. 13 above), and
      Thomas Cartelli, 'Prospero in Africa: *The Tempest* as Colonialist
      Text and Pretext', in *Shakespeare Reproduced: The Text in History and
      Ideology*, ed. Jean E. Howard and Marion F. O'Connor, New York,
      1987, pp. 99–115; and cf. Hulme, *Colonial Encounters*, pp. 125–7,
      202–3.
18.   See Hulme, *Colonial Encounters*, pp. 46–73.

19. For a brief account see Carl Ortwin Sauer, *The Early Spanish Main*, Berkeley, 1966, pp. 37–69.

20. For example, as reproduced in Theodor de Bry's 1590 edition of Thomas Harriot, *A Briefe and True Report of the New Found Land of Virginia*, rpt. New York, 1972.

21. Mannoni, *Prospero and Caliban*, pp. 97–109; Lamming, *The Pleasures of Exile*, p. 113.

22. The idea of the 'textual unconscious' goes back to the Althusserian deployment of a Freudian vocabulary, clearly mediated through Lacan's 'linguistic' reading of Freud. The unconscious is not, in this reading, *somewhere else*, not behind or beneath the text, not even latent within the manifest surface, but right there, both within and without, or – in Macherey's fine trope – 'on the margins of the text' (*A Theory of Literary Production*, pp. 90–4). Cf. n.3 above.

23. Very little is known about Anderson's background. He attended the University of Edinburgh and emigrated to New York in 1774. He became director of the St Vincent Botanic Garden in 1785. By a 'discourse of environmental concern' I refer to the North American debates about environmental change, particularly with respect to forestry: see Gilbert Chinard's two articles, 'Eighteenth-Century Theories on America as Human Habitat', *Proceedings of the American Philosophical Society*, sci, 1947, pp. 27–57; and 'The Americal Philosophical Society and the Early History of Forestry in America', *Proceedings of the American Philosopical Society*, xxxix, 1945, pp. 444–88. A broad context to this discourse is provided by Clarence J. Glacken, *Traces on the Rhodian Shore: Nature and Culture in Western Thought from Ancient Times to the End of the Eighteenth Century* Berkeley, 1967. For a more particular study of the relationship between the development of the botanic garden and the colonial enterprise, see Lucile H. Brockway, *Science and Colonial Expansion: The Role of the British Royal Botanic Gardens*, London, 1969.

24. Cf. William Young, *An Account of the Black Charaibs of St Vincent*, London, 1795, pp. 6–8.

25. Bartolomé de Las Casas, *The Spanish Colonie . . .*, trans. M.M.S., London, 1583; William S. Maltby, *The Black Legend in England: The Development of Anti-Spanish Sentiment, 1558–1660*, Durham, NC, 1971. On the earlier war, see Hulme, *Colonial Encounters*, pp. 242–9.

26. John Locke, 'A Third Letter for Toleration', 1692, in *The Works of John Locke*, London, 1801, vi, p. 225.

27. See I. E. Kirby and C. I. Martin, *The Rise and Fall of the Black Caribs of St Vincent*, 2nd edn, Kingstown, St Vincent, 1986; Charles Gullick, 'The Ecological Background to the Carib Wars', *Journal of Belizean Affairs*, vi, 1978, pp. 51–60; Michael Craton, *Testing the Chains: Resistance to Slavery in the British West Indies*, Ithaca, 1982, pp. 161–238; and Michael Craton, 'From Caribs to Black Caribs: The Amerindian Roots of Servile Resistance in the Caribbean', in *In Resistance: Studies in African, Caribbean, and Afro-American History*, ed. Gary Y. Okihiro, Amherst, 1986, pp. 96–116.

28.   Charles Shephard, *An Historical Account of the Island of St Vincent*, London, 1831. The definitive study of these events is now Nancie L. Gonzalez, *Sojourners of the Caribbean: Ethnogenesis and Ethnohistory of the Garifuna*, Chicago, 1988, pp. 39–50.
29.   Walter Benjamin, *Illuminationem*, Frankfurt, 1961, pp. 271–2.

9

Provincial Town Culture, 1640–1780: Urbane or Civic?

Jonathan Barry

The transmission of culture from place to place is a significant issue in the relationship between a capital and its provincial towns. As Jonathan Barry points out, French towns from the Middle Ages retained their economic and cultural importance, whereas England, unlike France, became increasingly centralised, with the population of London showing a huge increase over the period 1500–1750. Barry argues that, despite the power of London, historians have been wrong in denying provincial towns like Bristol any culture of their own and seeing them as the receptacles of culture trickling down from London's newly developing commercial-consumer society. Provincial town culture did not have to wait for the Industrial Revolution to come into its own. As Barry suggests, historiographical trends in English history have meant that English towns in the first half of the seventeenth century have been studied in terms of their political and economic structures, whilst in the period following what study there has been of *mentalité* and culture is limited to London. Using the example of the self-awareness that Bristolians had of the history of their town, Barry is able to point to an indigenous social and political culture for Bristol. Its histories evoke a sense of common civic purpose where there is a continuity of values and a merging of the past with the present. They also indicate that local and national history was seen as one piece, and that Bristol was not perceived as a mere consumer of London culture. Barry's study of civic consciousness is significant because it shows that historical lacunae are liable to occur when economic and social historians omit culture from their focus, or deny it to particular groups of places because of the dictates of their interpretative frameworks. Historians as well as people in the past can be blind to the culture of others.

This chapter attempts a critical review of the historiography of provincial urban culture in England between 1640 and 1780. The reasons for the neglect of town culture in early modern England are identified and shown to be unjustified in the light of recent evidence on the importance and character of provincial towns. A re-evaluation of the topic, however, requires a questioning of the dominant models, not just in urban history but also in the cultural history of the period, which have discouraged the development of suitable frameworks in which to analyse urban mentality. In order to illustrate the possibilities of an alternative approach, the second half of the chapter considers the ways in which perceptions of the past held by early modern Bristolians can help us to identify important themes in civic consciousness. The Bristol evidence suggests a different picture of how the past provided 'visions of the urban community' than has emerged from work conducted within the dominant model, which raises doubts about the assumptions and methodology of such studies, if Bristol's experience can be regarded as a guide to provincial town culture in general.

Given this last caveat, it may be helpful to begin with a brief description of Bristol's development in this period, compared to that of provincial towns generally. Until the end of the eighteenth century, when it was finally outstripped by several northern and Midland towns, Bristol vied for second place in the urban hierarchy with Norwich. Like most of the regional capitals before 1750, Bristol had a long tradition of importance and civic autonomy, with corporate and then county status. Unlike other leading towns, however, Bristol had not become a cathedral city until 1542, and even then did not act as the heart of a proper diocese, since Bristol and its immediate hinterland were yoked uneasily with the county of Dorset, fifty or more miles away. Nor was Bristol the seat of county government for a surrounding shire, because it lay on the boundary of Somerset and Gloucestershire, both heavily urbanised counties in this period, with several important county towns. In both civil and ecclesiastical administration therefore, Bristol was unusually distinct from the countryside around.[1]

Economically, however, the city was clearly, in Minchinton's phrase, the 'metropolis of the west'. Bristol's own role in the production of cloth had greatly declined, but it remained the chief market and port for what was still the heartland of England's main industry. Bristol was also the premier port for imports into the

West Country. By 1650, the character of this trade was beginning to shift, from European goods such as wine to colonial goods, notably tobacco and sugar, although sherry, or Bristol milk, remained an important item. Through its colonial trade Bristol also became involved in the slave trade, especially in the early eighteenth century. The expansion of trade in colonial goods and their re-export to southern Europe provided the basis for a great growth in the port industries of the city and in manufacturing such as sugar-refining. Cheap local coal also encouraged the growth of glass and pottery industries.[2] It was these economic factors which enabled the city to grow steadily in population through our period from about 12 000 in 1600 (below its medieval peak) up to about 21 000 by 1700, 40 000 or so by 1750, and more than 60 000 by 1800.[3] By then Bristol's steady growth was being overshadowed by the massive expansion of the new cities, but this should not be interpreted too readily as a sign of failure. Bristol did not share the absolute decline of some of the other traditional cities, and its unspectacular growth chiefly reflects the declining prosperity of its hinterland, which suffered deindustrialisation after 1750 in the face of northern competition.

Meanwhile, Bristol was also developing as a leisure and services centre. Bristol had always fulfilled the latter role, particularly through its two great annual fairs in January and July. During our period, however, the range of professional and skilled people in the town grew steadily. Bristol also emerged as a leisure resort with the development of the Hotwells, based on a medicinal spring by the river, close to where the Suspension Bridge now spans the gorge. After gradual development in the seventeenth century, this expanded rapidly in the early eighteenth century until it became almost as fashionable for summer visitors as nearby Bath. Like Bath it was losing its elite appeal by the end of the century, but by then the neighbouring village of Clifton had begun to grow as a place to visit or retire, and was becoming one of several elegant suburbs on the hills surrounding the ever-expanding city. Before the Lake District was discovered, it was the Avon, Severn and Wye valleys of the Bristol Channel which benefited from the rage for the picturesque and romantic. Symbolically, Wordsworth and Coleridge's *Lyrical Ballads* were to a large extent composed around Bristol and first published by a Bristol bookseller.[4]

The significance of some of these brief points about Bristol will become clear later. The main point I wish to make here is that Bristol, while no more typical than any other town in England's very varied urban landscape, was involved in most of the major developments that affected the towns during this period. Obviously its experience reflects that of the major towns, and not the much more numerous market or small county towns. Undoubtedly Bristol had more autonomy and greater civic tradition than most of the newly expanding towns, such as Leeds, Liverpool or Manchester, but was less integrated into the traditions of the church and landed society than other regional capitals such as Norwich or York. The closest parallels may be Newcastle and Hull.[5] But I believe that my observations are not based on a hopelessly unrepresentative example of provincial urban culture.

Until recently, not much attention had been paid to the cultural life of English provincial towns before the Industrial Revolution. In part this reflected the emergence of English urban history, above all at Leicester, out of a local history tradition, which had its roots in economic and agrarian studies. Towns have primarily been studied as centres of economic activity, and within the context of the rural economies which they serviced, or as ports or manufacturing centres involved in international or coasting trade.[6] This perspective has not encouraged examination of what is distinctive about the character of urban life, except perhaps in the rather sterile debate about the role of guilds and civic protectionism in the economic fortunes of towns. Studies which have attempted a 'total history' of towns, almost all of them before 1640, have tended to deal with political and especially administrative history when they stray from the economic dimension, and to deal with culture as a side-issue, at best. It is indicative that David Palliser's thesis on Tudor York was published with the section on civic mentality and the environment excluded on grounds of space, although fortunately this excellent piece has since been published as an article.[7]

There is a clear contrast between this English situation and the position in France where the major French towns have been the subjects of excellent studies which include *mentalité*, while the work of Daniel Roche and others has illuminated other aspects of the provincial cultural scene.[8] It is tempting to explain this purely in historiographical terms, in particular the *Annales* influence and the importance of cultural explanations of the French Revolution. But underlying this contrast is undoubtedly a very obvious and real difference between the position and history of English and French provincial towns in this period. French urban history, like that of much of western Europe, is marked by the emergence in medieval times of a network of major provincial centres which, despite the growth of Paris, retained both economic and governmental importance within a nation that remained relatively decentralised and culturally diverse. Continued importance was combined with relative stagnation of population and economic activity throughout the early modern period. In England, on the other hand, the broad sweep looks very different. The medieval provincial towns, though not yet dominated by London, did not develop control over the countryside around. The chief feature of the period 1500–1750 was the incredible growth of London as the centre not only of a strong national government, but also of a national market economy based on agrarian capitalism. A more general trend of urbanisation was occurring, from 1600 at least, but it was only in the eighteenth century that London's expansion began to be outstripped, in relative terms, by the growth of other urban centres. This growth, moreover, was concentrated in the north and Midlands, not previously the most urbanised parts of the country, and in towns which, though hardly the villages of legend, had never been major regional centres before, such as Birmingham, Manchester and Liverpool.[9]

Studies of urban culture in England have reflected these fundamental facts. Some attention has been paid to the cultural life of medieval towns, most notably Charles Phythian-Adams's fascinating portrait of Coventry in decline.[10] During the early modern period, however, the focus has naturally been on London. Study of the arts both by historians and by those in particular disciplines such as drama, music or art, have focused on the major figures and the mechanisms of production and distribution, almost exclusively in London. The broader investigation of *mentalité* through such media as popular literature or customs has again gone furthest in London.[11] Interest in the culture of the provinces has generally been restricted to those 'provinces' in the contemporary sense, namely Wales, Ireland, Scotland and the American colonies. Particularly fine work has been done on the last two of these, examining the extent of their dependence on the metropolis and their efforts at cultural autonomy.[12] For similar work on English provincial towns and their relation to London, however, one has to wait until the later eighteenth century. Donald Read's influential book on the provinces took the period from 1760 to 1790 as its starting-point and most subsequent authors have echoed his contention that the new industrial conurbations of the north created for the first time the conditions in England for a provincial consciousness separate from, indeed antagonistic to, the influence of London, and also independent of the values of the countryside around. Jack Langton has recently taken this further, in suggesting that our modern conception of regional cultures can only be dated back to the regions defined by the new industrial cities of that period.[13]

There has, of course, been considerable debate about provincial attitudes in early modern England, associated with the theory of localism and the county community in relation to the origins and course of the Civil War, which was dubbed by John Morrill 'the revolt of the provinces'. But very little attention was paid to the towns in what became essentially an analysis of the gentry class.[14] The main exception, Roger Howell, from his work on Newcastle in particular, has been closely aligned with Morrill in emphasising the neutralism of the towns in the civil war, reflecting their concern for local affairs rather than national issues.[15] Similar analysis of what is usually, and significantly, called 'court–*country*' tension after 1650 has largely been carried on at the level of national politics rather than local, let alone urban, studies, although there have been some developments here, to which I shall return.[16]

There would be little point in writing this essay, however, unless I believed that, despite these general truths, there was an important sense in which provincial towns, and their culture in particular, influenced English history in the early modern period. Let us look again at some of the points that I have just made in my summary contrast between the continental and English situations. Tony Wrigley, commenting on De Vries's work, has recently stressed that the unusual aspect of English urban history was not so much the growth of London, for most metropolises were expanding through our period, but rather the continued vitality of the rest of the English urban system. If there is an English variable which can explain its economic strength and industrial take-off, the broad basis of urban growth may be as important as the impact of London. This point gains added strength given the recent emphasis in economic history on the long-term trends underlying the industrial revolution, and the importance of the development of a skilled workforce and a consumer society in generating economic growth. Less attention is now paid to the new manufacturing centres and more to the growth of the retail, service and financial sectors and the less spectacular expansion in traditional industries.[17]

In relation to government, the debates about court and country have generated an awareness that the relationship between the centre and the provinces was a complex one. Continental towns may have had more autonomy in many local affairs, while acting as centres of government officialdom in the countryside. But the precocious centralisation of the English state encouraged the provincials of England to take a great interest in national affairs, leading in turn to the growth of party politics. As this developed, through elections, organisation by churches and clubs, and the growth of the press, the towns became the centres of provincial politics. From the mid-seventeenth century, moreover, the state did begin to establish a greater presence in English towns, through tax officials and military men, while the hold of the centre on less contentious areas of local government, especially in the socioeconomic sphere, weakened. The unusual English combination after 1688 of a state strong militarily and financially but weak at home, in terms of policing and socioeconomic control, gave the provincial towns considerably more influence than first appearances would suggest.[18]

Finally, even if one accepts the predominance of London during the early modern period, the provincial towns of England must still be seen as having an important role in mediating between London and the countryside. They organised the movement of goods in both directions, and it was through them that the modes of life characteristic of the capital spread through the country. The evidence we have on migration, admittedly imperfect, suggests that most country people moved only within the orbit of their county town, and that long-distance migration to London from outside the Home Counties, heavy in the sixteenth century, declined thereafter as the provincial towns became more attractive.[19] Although the improvements in transport undoubtedly made London ever more accessible to the affluent, for most people the chief effect was probably to encourage ties to the local towns. Indeed Alan Everitt has run contrary to the general trend by claiming that the emergence of a national economy, which implied regional specialisation in production, created a whole series of regional societies firmly based on the towns central to the region, which offered a specialised level of skill in crafts, marketing and services. Langton's argument about the great industrial centres, by this account, would merely provide the latest example of towns creating regions, admittedly on a larger and more permanent scale.[20] The 'impact of towns' has become established as a major issue in the history of early modern England.

If the attitudes of provincial townspeople are worthy of study, within what kind of conceptual framework are we going to conceive that study? How appropriate are the prevailing interpretations of cultural history? None of the models currently in favour seems to me very suitable. Over the past decade accounts of cultural change in England have been dominated by variants of a dualistic theory of culture, most often referred to as elite and popular, but sometimes as patrician and plebeian, or polite and popular. A major stimulus behind this way of thinking has undoubtedly been Peter Burke's masterly overview of European developments; many disciples have not perhaps been as careful as him to question the firmness of elite–popular distinctions and to urge the study of the intermediaries between the two.[21] On a more ideological front, polar theories of culture have found champions, perhaps unexpectedly, on both the left and the right. Socialist historians, attracted to the themes of crime and popular behaviour, and wearied perhaps by the attempt to prove that England experienced a bourgeois revolution, have tended to neglect Marxian analysis for accounts of the growing division between rich and poor in early modern England. The first and most important account of this kind emerged from E. P. Thompson, who coined the distinction of patrician and plebeian, and offered a series of highly persuasive cameos of the clash of cultures in eighteenth-century rural society.[22] *Mutatis mutandis*, his account has been extended back into the late sixteenth and seventeenth centuries by Keith Wrightson's brilliant synthesis with its highly persuasive analysis of how economic and social differentiation were combined with growing differences in literacy and in religious and cultural attitudes to create the dichotomy from which Thompson's account proceeds.[23] Even Christopher Hill, so long the champion of the middling sort as a third force in English history, appears to have accepted that this is the best approximation to class consciousness and conflict which he is likely to find as a long-term explanation for the English Revolution and what ensued.[24]

In the meantime, the resurgence of the right has seen a growth of interest in the culture of the aristocracy, most flamboyantly in the work of J. C. D. Clark, but also in other studies, synthesised in scholarly works by Beckett, Bush and Cannon. They have found a perhaps unexpected ally in the shape of Lawrence Stone, and his monumental effort to disprove the existence of 'an open elite'.[25] A common theme to this work has been an emphasis on the cultural hegemony of the aristocracy and their values over the middling orders of English society, which was, if anything, strengthened during the century after 1660. In this respect, despite all Clark's jeers and challenges to old hat and the like, the aristocratic school are in many ways closely aligned with the Thompsonite interpretation, although obviously miles apart in their evaluation of the naturalness and desirability of such a patrician society.[26]

Some accounts of the patrician–plebeian relationship, notably J. C. D. Clark's, have tended to portray it as an inevitable and static characteristic of a pre-industrial *ancien régime*. Others, however, have been more sensitive to the way in which such a cultural stability may have been manufactured from the crisis of the mid-seventeenth century. A number of accounts have portrayed how a ruling class, shocked by the social and intellectual upheavals of the Civil War, turned to a culture of order and stability, based on property and propriety. Although the religious and political strife of the years to 1688 or 1715 is seen as delaying the establishment of stability, by the early eighteenth century a united elite shared the cultural and social heritage of the English Enlightenment, distanced from the culture of the lower classes.[27] As Jenkins has shown for the Glamorgan gentry, this process owed some of its success to economic prosperity and demographic change, but it was primarily a cultural movement.[28] The very essence of the development is seen to be the dissociation of elite and popular cultures, for it was only through a new polite culture that the religious and political divisions of the elite could be healed. The polite culture was one of negatives, of moderation, designed to avoid the twin evils of absolutism and anarchy, of popery and enthusiasm, and to prevent any alliance of the disaffected elite with the lower orders. The moral and magical economy of popular culture was rejected as vulgar and unrefined in favour of Augustan values whose essence was their distance from the local and popular.

The problem for the urban historian lies in establishing the position that town-dwellers, and in particular the middling sort so prominent in towns, can be ascribed within these models of culture based on a twofold division in rural society. In many accounts they are ignored, but a substantial body of research is now emerging in which the role of towns in the growth of polite culture is studied. It would be fair to say, however, that these studies view the town-dwellers as largely passive in this process, the receivers of a culture created by their superiors. Or perhaps it would be more accurate to say that townspeople are considered not as the makers of culture but as its salespeople, and as its consumers. The upper class created a society which could only be entered through status and wealth, gained and displayed in an increasingly urban setting, and invited the urban middle classes to compete for entry in this world, and to leave behind them any associations with the popular culture of the lower orders.

The most detailed chronicling of this process has been in the work of Peter Borsay, and he has been most responsible for highlighting the growing importance of towns as social spaces in which elite culture, including such apparently rural pursuits as horse-racing, could be organised and serviced.[29] The guiding vision of this approach, however, has been provided by Jack Plumb. Having pioneered the notion of stability in the political sphere, Plumb has moved on to study the commercialisation of leisure and the modernisation of eighteenth-century England, and although he has not himself explicitly drawn the link between the two, Geoffrey Holmes and Roy Porter have made the necessary connections.[30] Peter Clark has given this approach his imprimatur, and provided a series of case-studies in the two volumes he has edited on county towns, in particular, and on provincial towns generally.[31]

A number of key common themes underlie this work, although there are obviously differences of weighting and interpretation. The first is the emphasis on a break in urban history at some point in the mid- to late-seventeenth century. Before then the traditional cultural role of the towns had been weakened by Reformation, economic and social problems, and the disruption of Civil War. Thereafter an 'urban renaissance' occurred, but one based on towns as service centres for the upper classes in general. Most study has been directed at spas, leisure resorts and county towns, and the demand for cultural provision is traced to the country gentry and their cousins, the pseudo-gentry and the professions, living in the towns but linked by kin, occupation and life-style to the gentry around.[32] Although it has been assumed that the merchant class, at least, within the towns would participate in such culture, less attention has been given to how far down the social scale these developments permeated, and most townsmen are seen as the salespeople more than the consumers of such culture.

The second and third themes are suggested by the language of this last point, namely the language of consumption and of permeation. In contrast to cultural activity based on the public, communal, non-commercialised world of the church, corporation, guild or neighbourhood, the forms of culture now seen as dominating town life were essentially there to be purchased by consumers. Their emergence reflected the expansion of surplus wealth in the English economy, and increasing attention is being paid to the way this culture was marketed, and the implications for the economy and such intangible issues as leisure preference. The establishment of such cultural facilities as theatres, squares and assembly rooms has been seen in the wider context of increased urban investment in street improvement, lighting, drainage and public building.[33] This reflects the strong tradition, mentioned earlier, of giving economic explanations of urban history priority, and emphasising the economic ties between the town and its countryside. Much less attention has been paid to unravelling *why* surplus wealth should be spent on cultural activity, or on particular forms of culture in preference to others. Plumb has certainly set a bad example here by his own description of the process as 'the pursuit of happiness', which begs rather more questions than it answers.[34]

When an explanation has been offered, it has generally been that through cultural consumption wealth could be transmuted into social status. As manners and cultural possessions established social position, particularly in the open world of the towns, so social emulation was pursued through culture. Here the notion of permeation becomes crucial. The seal of social approval was set on cultural activity by its association with the aristocracy, and the imitation of fashions set by this elite in London. The metropolitan basis of these trends is constantly reiterated, and the success of the provincial towns seen as that of regional entrepots for the spread of metropolitan products and ideas. London was undoubtedly the only English city with the concentration of demand necessary to support a commercial scale of production and distribution in most areas of culture, and it naturally attracted the best specialists in these areas.[35]

The cumulative effect of these generalisations is to justify a situation in which, although cultural activity in provincial towns is considered an important topic of research, little challenge is actually offered to the traditional view that the culture of the townspeople themselves, their distinctive values and lifestyles, was of little intrinsic importance. The dominance of London is reaffirmed, cultural activity is analysed primarily in economic terms, and the existence of a distinctive urban, bourgeois or civic consciousness within English provincial towns is, by implication, denied. Indeed a heightened contrast is sometimes drawn between the introverted, increasingly inappropriate, civic identity of town life before the Civil War, and the newly extrovert and successful adaptation made by town culture after 1660.[36] The key to town culture in the years 1660 to 1780 is urbanity in the sense of *urbaneness*, rather than any distinct urban or civic consciousness. It is still left to the new provincial centres of the late eighteenth century to establish a genuinely bourgeois culture independent of aristocratic and metropolitan hegemony.[37]

As will no doubt have become clear, I am not satisfied that this new consensus offers a satisfactory basis on which to erect a study of urban provincial culture. There are many aspects of urban mentality that cannot be explored properly within such a model and, by implication, explanations are being proposed for the character of cultural change within towns which my work on Bristol suggest are, if not incorrect, then at least only partially true. A fuller appreciation of urban provincial culture would actually make the cultural history of such towns appear a more important ingredient in English history than is currently appreciated. Crucial to such a development, I will suggest, is a greater awareness of the civic consciousness of towns such as Bristol, of the ties between local factors and national cultural developments, and of the role of

the provincial townspeople themselves in *making* their own culture. I am not going to propose that we resurrect the autonomous,
introverted local community of Everitt or Morrill. Rather I want to
suggest that England was *such* a unified nation that, rather than
simply imitating national cultural changes among the elite caused
by social, religious and political developments, the inhabitants of
places like Bristol felt the same pressures directly within their own
community and, allowing for the unique set of circumstances of
each town, responded directly to these in their changing patterns
of culture. Moreover the open character of English society and
politics made the way in which townspeople thought and behaved
important to the fate of the nation. Just because they did not
behave according to some abstract model of middle-class provincial consciousness, reified by Marx from early nineteenth-century
Manchester, does not mean that their responses were not a
genuine expression of a civic, or bourgeois, outlook independent
from, though obviously related to, the culture of the landed upper
classes.

Up to now the debate on the values of the middling sort, and the
existence of a bourgeois identity, has largely centred around the
behaviour of the merchant elites of the town, and in particular
whether they were inclined to move away from trade and set
themselves up within the landed gentry. I do not intend to enter
this controversy, which is rendered complex by the economic, as
well as social, implications of land ownership, and the problem of
defining when purchases of land involved withdrawal from active
participation in urban affairs. The distinction appears increasingly
meaningless with the growth in suburban residences and weekly
commuting by the richer townspeople, and of prolonged urban
residence by the landed.[38] In any case, it is far from clear that the
rich merchants usually studied in this context offer a typical
example of the 'middling sort' in towns. Only if we *assume* that a
merchant oligarchy dominated town life and that other citizens
imitated their values does a study of this group act as a suitable
surrogate for deeper analysis of urban life. But we shall not know
if this assumption is correct until such analysis has been made!

There is obviously not space here for such an analysis over the
whole range of urban culture, even for one town. I have analysed
elsewhere the problems involved in locating a separate sphere of
'popular culture' in early modern Bristol, and I have tried to
delineate the main characteristics of Bristol's 'civic consciousness'.

Responding to Keith Thomas's influential suggestion that the 'decline of magic' is related to cultural polarisation, I have explored this hypothesis for eighteenth-century Bristol, and suggested some qualifications.[39] In this essay I will attempt a similar revision of one of the few studies which has tackled directly the 'exploration of urban mentality', namely Peter Clark's overview of the civic annals and antiquarian histories produced in English towns before 1800.[40] In particular I wish to challenge Clark's contention that the chronology of urban antiquarianism reinforces the view of provincial urban culture criticised above. Clark sees urban historiography before the Civil War as lively but old-fashioned, typified by the keeping of civic annals, and thus essentially introverted and concerned with 'the shoring up and reassertion of the values of the civic community in a time of instability'. After the Restoration the character of urban histories changed, as professional men and the gentry took over from the merchant elite, and concentrated on antiquarian scholarship and publications, which were often stimulated by, and aimed at, 'London and county society'. Even these stimuli, however, were only capable of producing a small range of published work. But, after 1750, 'a boom in urban antiquarian activity' occurred, produced by a broad range of 'new' groups, confident in their towns as 'dynamos of commercial and industrial expansion' and celebrating 'a rediscovered communal consciousness and pride . . . determined to reassert the urban voice in the regional and national arena'. This was manifested in a 'surge of published histories'.

It should be clear how close a correlation there is between Clark's account of urban historiography and the general consensus on the course of urban culture which I have described and criticised. An alternative reading of this particular theme will, I hope, suggest how urban culture could be studied and understood differently. It would also take further than Clark the claim that understanding how people viewed the past offers an excellent method to explore their thought in general. As Keith Thomas has recently indicated, perceptions of the past played a vital role in early modern consciousness, rooted as it was in reverence for tradition. Even the radicals of this period tended to challenge the *status quo* through rival visions of the past, while every aspect of life was permeated by the influence of precedent, through the omnipresence of the law. This made 'antiquarian studies' far from academic in their significance, while, as I shall suggest, there was no clear boundary between the exploration of the past through historical scholarship and its evocation in the public life of the early modern town.[41]

To criticise Clark's analysis on the evidence of one town is dangerous, as he rightly stresses the diversity of urban experience. There will always be exceptions to any generalisation, yet general patterns must be searched for. However there are equally grave dangers in relying on necessarily sketchy surveys of many towns, which may mislead concerning the state of affairs in all of them. Clark's pioneering study had to rely on meagre secondary work of very varied quality, plus quantitative work of his own based largely on the urban histories that were published. In the case of Bristol this would mean relying on a single secondary study, which completely fails to cover most of the antiquarian work of this particular period,[42] and also judging the quantity of historical interest from the single complete work published, namely William Barrett's *History and Antiquities of the City of Bristol* (Bristol, 1789). From manuscript sources, however, I have established the survival of a vigorous tradition of annals-keeping in Bristol throughout our period (at least twenty examples survive), although the only example of this genre that has been published subsequently is an early seventeenth-century chronicle kept by William Adams. It is also clear that Barrett's *History* was the product of more than a hundred years of scholarly effort by various individuals and groups in the city, whose work was passed down and built upon until brought to fruition by Barrett. Andrew Hooke had begun publication of a serial history in 1748, while Barrett's research was largely completed by the early 1770s.[43] In short, to judge from Bristol, quantitative approaches which rely on publications can give a most misleading chronological picture.

If we examine the social background of those interested in Bristol's history, the evidence certainly supports Clark's view that antiquarian scholarship was almost exclusively pursued by schoolmasters, medical men, lawyers, clergymen or gentlemen, or by others of similar background, such as heralds and accountants. The common quality of such people, however, may not have been their social status, as Clark suggests, but their occupations, which made them familiar with old documents, as these were important precedents in their work, or brought them into contact with the leading families who often held old records. Moreover annals-keeping was maintained by a much wider social group until the later eighteenth century, when the spread of newspapers seems to have eroded the practice. During the early and mid-eighteenth century annals were kept by a tobacconist, a peruke-maker, an ironfounder, a wine-cooper and an apothecary, as well as a merchant, a schoolmaster and several clergymen and town officials, if anything a broader social range than is recorded for earlier chroniclers.[44] These annals were passed down in manuscript, and clearly not intended for publication, but they were certainly lent out to, and copied by, other interested citizens.

The antiquarian scholars, on the other hand, did, in some cases, intend to publish. Does their failure to do so suggest that the Bristol public were not interested until 1789? There is certainly evidence to suggest this. Antiquarians were conscious of being isolated and figures of fun. When Hooke's serial publication failed to win sufficient subscribers, he lamented that 'the taste of the town' was not ready for such a work.[45] Much of the problem with publication, however, lay with the antiquarians themselves, and the kind of history they felt that they should produce, rather than with a general lack of interest in Bristol's history. In the first place, the vocations which made professional men interested in antiquities kept them so busy that they lacked the leisure to complete their studies.[46] The sensitive character of much of the material, to which I shall return, also led to problems of access to vital corporate and church records.[47] As yet very few national records had been published to supplement the local sources. Yet Bristol's antiquarians were interested, above all, in a series of very complex historical issues concerning the origins and early development of Bristol which would have required very elaborate archival work, as well as pioneering work in archaeology, to answer. These centred around the question of whether Bristol had existed before its first clear mention in published chronicles (in the eleventh century), and the chronology of its town government and church-building. Traditionally these questions had been answered by reference to the Brut legend, in which Bristol was founded by Brennus and Belinus, and by various other stories about the early city.[48] Annalists and antiquarians knew that such stories could no longer count as decent history, but they had no coherent account with which to replace them. The result was a variety of strategies, designed to fill in the missing pieces. Greatest attention has been paid to the forgeries of Thomas Chatterton, who claimed to have discovered works by Thomas Rowley and others. These provided 'documentary' evidence on most of the issues Barrett and others wished to settle. Chatterton's brilliance, however, was not merely literary, but that he created a history wholly consistent with the picture which the antiquarians were beginning to build up by other means, including important archaeological and architectural work, as well as the accumulation of genuine documents. In a similar way Andrew Hooke combined some very dubious 'conjectural history', in Scottish style, designed to prove Bristol's early importance, with some intensive research into medieval documentary sources.[49] Viewing such figures as 'fifth-rate' mythmakers underestimates the intellectual challenge facing the local historian of that period.[50] No wonder those with less leisure and expertise stuck to the relatively simple form of annals-keeping, which started in the thirteenth century and repeated well-established local and national events, within a time-honoured form. No wonder, too, that the antiquarians all lamented their inability to complete their task, and dreamed of a rich, leisured and multi-talented Renaissance gentleman to come along and complete 'the great work of the History of Bristol'.[51]

Equally different problems arose concerning the format of any published history. Since the 'historical revolution' of late Tudor and Stuart times, history, and especially local history, had become an affair of great folios, partly from fashion, and partly to contain the mass of documentation which such histories were now meant to include. But such publications were massively expensive and totally different from the publishing ventures that provincial printers or booksellers were prepared to risk, in *any* field, until the late eighteenth century. County histories had also established a topographical format as standard, and in many ways the Bristol antiquarians, with their deep interest in parish history and the growing structure of the city, found this a natural model to adopt. Yet they were equally keen to preserve the annalistic approach of earlier civic history. Variants and combinations of these two models were each proposed, and the two can be seen uneasily combined in Barrett. Even more difficult to solve, as Momigliano has highlighted, was how to combine antiquarian standards of scholarship with the rhetorical intentions of the historian. Bristol's historians wanted to use their history to teach various lessons, as discussed below, and they needed to attract ordinary readers.

Hooke's *Bristollia*, published in serial form to avoid the expense and risk of a single bulky publication, nevertheless offered an indigestible mass of facts (though its Whig flavour was also perhaps unpalatable to many Bristolians). In 1729 another antiquarian group, despairing of publishing their researches, prefaced a 1629 sermon that they reprinted with an elegant summary of the lessons their history *would* teach, if ever published. Barrett did manage to publish most of his material, but only in English translation, and without citing all his authorities. The reviewer in the *Gentleman's Magazine*, criticising this decision, admitted that it made Barrett's account 'readable'.[52]

Meanwhile the main findings of such research were being published in the various guide-books and directories that began to proliferate, while the local newspapers carried many short items on local history. To look for evidence of the general consciousness of urban history through specialised publications on local history is fundamentally misleading, unless we set such specific work in a much broader context, namely how local history, and indeed history in general, was perceived and exploited within the civic community. The rest of this essay will attempt to sketch this broader picture, within which the specific annalistic and antiquarian studies become comprehensible as the work of particular interest-groups, rather than representative of the city as a whole.

There is ample evidence, from contemporary comment, from educational treatises, and from the titles used to attract local readers, that Bristolians were enthusiastic for history, or perhaps we should say 'histories', for they had a broad sense of history, encompassing any subject with a narrative or descriptive element. Evidence from the past was seen as relevant to many subjects, and many of those interested in, for example, economics, medicine or natural history, saw historical studies as integral to such work.[53] The annals of Bristol were often composed of national and local history in equal proportion, and with no clear sense of distinction, at least until the eighteenth century, when the greater availability of published accounts of national events may explain a greater concentration on purely Bristolian events.[54] Bristol's antiquarians rarely restricted their interests to local affairs. Andrew Hooke lectured and published on geography and economics, while Barrett was one of many interested in church history. Arthur Bedford's work on his parish church must be seen in the context of his elaborate historical studies of ancient music, drama and chronology.[55]

It was therefore natural, as well as perhaps inevitable, that those trying to conceptualise Bristol's history did so in language which drew heavily on national and indeed international history. Parallels with Rome are frequent, while Jerusalem and Babylon also sprang to the mind of groups steeped in the Bible.[56] Accounts of Bristol's origins depended very heavily on models of an 'ancient constitution', although tastes varied as to whether Trojans, Celts, Romans or Saxons provided the most noble founders of English and Bristolian society.[57] As indicated earlier, many of the problems in composing and publishing a Bristol history flowed from an obsession with establishing a suitable early origin for the town, and there is no sign of change in this fundamental respect.

Paradoxically this attitude coexisted with a reiterated conviction that commercial success lay at the heart of Bristol's distinctive character. To Barrett 'this reflected greater honour on Bristol than anything we have said or can say in its praise for its antiquity, the only thing many places more extolled in chronicles or old histories have now left to boast of whilst this, like a well-cultivated spot, has been continually flourishing with renewed vigour'.[58] As might be expected the keen Whig Andrew Hooke took this furthest, constructing a conjectural commercial history of the town and reinforcing the contrast between cities based on military and ecclesiastical settlement, and so noticed by 'monkish chroniclers', and a commercial town like Bristol, first described by geographers. To him Bristol was 'a natural growth that like a single acorn, planted by a skilful hand. in a fertile soil, soon unfolds its innate beauties, and by due care and culture grows up into a stately oak, whose widespreading branches in process of time become a solace and shelter for all the people of the neighbourhood'.[59] Clearly such language could lead to careless history, and Bristol's historians were often guilty of anachronism in attributing, for example, Bristol's success to its location in a place favourable for contemporary trading patterns, without proving that these had been important factors at the time.[60]

But set against this was the considerable historical content given, not only to the 'skilful planting', but also to the 'due care and culture' needed for urban growth. Bristol's historians all assumed that commerce only grew in a favourable historical matrix, and here again they drew on a vision which encompassed both local and national history. Hooke was typical in emphasising 'the successive favour of princes', especially in granting the city rights of self-government.[61] The links between civic government and commercial advance were implicit in the annalistic approach, which generally commenced with the establishment of civic offices, based its notes upon the mayoral year and the succession of its officers, and emphasised the growth of civic privileges. The historians were more explicit. Thomas Ford gave as the primary value of a city history, in a work dedicated to the magistrates, that 'in the annals of your predecessors you will, with pleasure, recognize a Magistracy always renowned for inviolable loyalty, for wise conduct in government, for courage tempered with discretion in the administration of justice, for a provident care for the necessities of the poor in times of scarcity and distress, and especially for a magnificent economy in entertaining princes graciously accepted and rewarded by royal grants of more extended liberties'.[62] Bristolians knew that they were operating in a 'corporate state' where influence with central government mattered, and that local and national history could not be distinguished. Barrett was no doubt typical in thinking that national progress depended largely on commerce, and that therefore the history of towns like Bristol was more important than county histories.[63] But, vice versa, Bristolians saw the growth in Bristol's privileges depending on the accretion of national liberties within an ancient constitution properly governed. The same dangers, of civil war, invasion and popery, were identified by successive generations as threatening both nation and city, while loyalty and legality were lauded as the means to prosperity.[64]

It was not, of course, merely in historical writing that these ideas were spread. Indeed these were probably minor vehicles of such propaganda compared to other areas of civic culture. These messages about the past were conveyed to most people, for example, through civic ritual. Mayoral elections or the annual assizes, together with royal visits, were replete with historical symbolism to heighten the sense of a local magistracy integrated with royal government. Even more spectacular were the anniversaries celebrated every year, starting with 5 November and followed by 30 January and 29 May, all of these turned into occasions when civic government and solidarity were, at least in theory, affirmed alongside the commemoration of the national authority of crown and parliament. After 1685, each successive monarch was celebrated by further anniversaries. These occasions attracted large crowds of spectators but also involved many of the middling orders as guild members, processing behind the leading merchants who formed the Corporation.[65] This should remind us that many of the leading figures in commerce, far from seeing themselves as modern entrepreneurs, tended rather to emphasise their honour and antiquity, either personally through heraldic displays, or collectively through association. Both guilds and their successors, the Freemasons' Lodges and charitable societies, associated themselves with an ancient and honourable past.[66]

Bristol's buildings also conveyed messages about the city's past and present character. At the city's heart, where its merchants gathered, stood the High Cross, with its statues of the monarchs who had granted the city privileges. Four statues were added in 1633 and the Cross was often repaired and regilded, as befitted the focal point of civic ritual. Bristol's annalists and historians, like its visitors, paid great attention to the churches, civic buildings, walls, gates, crosses, pumps, sewers and water-pipes which constituted the city's fabric.[67] The opening of the new Exchange in 1743 was marked by lavish ceremony and the keynote speech emphasised that such edifices were 'at all times held in esteem and considered as manifestations of the wisdom and grandeur of a state'.[68] In such buildings utility and honour went together. So to Barrett Bristol's greatness began with the construction of the first stone bridge and the new quay in 1240–7. The spirit of improvement that had marked such past efforts should animate present Bristolians to yet further advances.[69] It is true that, in the eighteenth century, heritage and improvement increasingly clashed, as new traffic requirements and new aesthetic standards prompted rebuilding and the removal of old structures such as the High Cross, town gates and the like. There was considerable opposition to this from admirers of 'the Gothic', but with little success. Opponents of such structures could themselves appeal to history, arguing that any veneration for the antiquity of the High Cross should be offset by the inappropriateness to civic life of such a 'relic of popish superstition'. Ironically those, like Barrett, who saw old structures such as the Cross as part of the living fabric of the town, to be recast as needed, were less able to object to change than outsiders like Pope who merely admired the Cross as a piece of Gothic, and regretted the regilding which had spoilt its 'venerable antiquity'.[70]

Attitudes to Bristol's architectural heritage confirm the observation that a fully 'historicist' attitude is slow to develop amongst those for whom the past merges indistinguishably into the present. One manifestation of this was the indiscriminate way in which Bristol's antiquarians recorded epitaphs and inscriptions from monuments past and present.[71] Since they wished to emphasise the continuity of urban values, the distinctions we might make were not relevant. History was particularly treasured as a storehouse of moral lessons, of ancestral wisdom.[72] Three key ingredients were constantly reiterated as characterising the values embodied by past Bristolians, which their successors had to emulate. These were virtue, industry and charity. The past was plundered for exemplars of the first two values, while charity could easily be documented, in the endless records of bequests which filled the annals and histories.[73] Needless to say, these values from the past were also brought to people's attention visually, for example in the tables of bequests on church walls, and through parish and civic ritual. From 1658, four county societies held annual feasts in aid of charity, and their numbers grew in the eighteenth century. The eighteenth century also saw the raising to mythical status of one local philanthropist, Edward Colston, whose birthday became an annual day of celebration after his death in 1721, and Thomas Chatterton's efforts to raise the medieval merchant Canynges to a similar position.[74]

In all of these areas the past was being used, with very little variation over time, to create an image of Bristol which simultaneously reinforced a sense of civic community, based on a hierarchical but morally just society, and yet also tied in all of these values to an image of the national community. Although the ingredients of that image might seem mythical and old-fashioned, there is little evidence that they appeared inappropriate to a commercially dynamic city like Bristol. A few Bristolians did deny the relevance of this civic past to contemporary Bristol, notably Dean Tucker, a thorough-going historicist who loathed civic ritual and the like, but he was well aware of his isolated status and the popularity of the traditional approach.[75]

The greatest tribute to the power of the past in conveying models of the city was its role in the conflicts which racked Bristol during this period. So far I have stressed those elements of the civic image which could be agreed, or seemed open to appropriation, by all parties in the city. But views of the significance of such historical events could vary, while there were other aspects of the town's history that were of importance only to one particular group. For much of our period it is possible, although obviously simplistic, to reduce this to a distinction between Whig and Tory uses of history, which dominate the story from the Exclusion Crisis to the American Revolution.

History was important to the rival sides both as propaganda and in very practical terms. The Bible and church history were ransacked by the rival religious groups to justify their stances.[76] The balance of the ancient constitution could be interpreted very differently to stress liberty or authority, to exalt the monarch above the rest of government or stress his role within it.[77] Not only were these issues the constant theme of sermons and other publications, they were also raised by the major anniversaries of the period. The most partisan was 30 January, the date of Charles I's execution. In 1680, the moderate Anglican Samuel Crossman felt it necessary to defend the fast appointed for the day against suggestions that it was an unnecessary slur on England's past. Whigs can hardly have been encouraged by the use made of the occasion the previous year, when an extreme Anglican clergyman reportedly went beyond the usual message against rebellion and dissent to claim that there was no Popish Plot, rather a Presbyterian one, and for good measure denounced Henry VIII and Elizabeth for despoiling the church during the Reformation. For this he was taken to London and questioned by the Exclusion Parliament. The year before that, by contrast, punishment in London awaited the leaders of the carpenters' apprentices who had walked the streets on the fast day with sharpened axes. Their claim that they were merely taking them to be sharpened prior to Shrove Tuesday was rejected and they were imprisoned for several months.[78]

November 5 was an anti-popery celebration which both sides could join, but varying emphases could be placed on whether King, Church or Parliament had been saved. After 1688, Whigs exploited the coincidence of the day with the Torbay landing to celebrate a double deliverance from Popery, but in 1684 the Whig Soapboilers' Company had been reported to the Secretary of State for refusing to join the guild procession on Gunpowder Day, probably as a Whig gesture of defiance during Tory ascendancy.[79] After 1688, the Stuart associations of 29 May, Restoration day, rendered it an object of Whig suspicion. The largely Whig Corporation presented the day as a celebration of government as such, but many people saw Jacobite overtones in the symbolism of oaken boughs in doorways and oakleaves on clothing, and these may explain corporate efforts to restrain popular bonfires and tree-cutting.[80] Needless to say, anniversaries of reigning and deceased monarchs became equally contentious, as did other gestures of commemoration such as the equestrian statue of William III erected in Queen Square.[81] Jacobite groups matched royal anniversaries with those for the exiled Stuarts.[82] The cult of Edward Colston can also be seen as a Tory attempt to create a new hero, exploiting the civic passion for charity.[83] All parties sought to associate themselves with the civic traditions of virtue and charity, and the charitable societies became caught up in such partisan propaganda.

In many ways, therefore, Bristolians in their public life found themselves faced with interpretations of history, both national and local, which had strong propaganda implications in terms of current divisions within the city. The past was not just a source of propaganda, however. In many ways Bristol was still governed, as England was, by precedent, above all through the legal system. The notion of precedence was used to settle all kinds of disputes, from the order of guilds in civic processions to the selection of aldermen.[84] As political disputes deepened, appeal to precedents seemed a way to resolve conflict, yet the precedents were themselves many and contradictory, so encouraging rival historical research. In the 1690s, for example, the radical Whig John Cary investigated the nature of medieval Bristol government in order to justify the open election of the Council by all freemen. He never made his researches public, perhaps because his friends gained control of the closed Corporation.[85] Throughout the next century there was a series of public disputes over the powers of various elements in town government, and over the electoral franchise, all of which raised major historical issues. The city archives were often searched, while the various city charters were key documents.[86] During a dispute over harbour dues in the 1730s the Tory printer Felix Farley published an edition of the city charters in 6*d* serial numbers so that ordinary freemen could decide the precedents for themselves. The outraged Corporation promptly paid for the translation of the latest charter and distributed a thousand free printed copies.[87] Not surprisingly, historians who wished to consult the official archives were carefully vetted for political suitability by the authorities. The Whig Andrew Hooke was naturally given free access for his studies, whilst the Tory Barrett was initially refused in the 1760s, though later he became acceptable to an increasingly conservative Corporation.[88]

Generally speaking it was Tory historians who had the greatest problems with civic history; they were particularly sorry when one of their number, Richard Haynes, who was himself a member of the Corporation and so had unrivalled access, never completed his historical work.[89] This reinforced the innate tendency of Tory historians to devote more attention to ecclesiastical and, in particular, parish records. These records were also of course sensitive documents, since quarrels between clergymen and parishioners, or about the powers of the church in the city, were themselves dependent on precedent. Arthur Bedford was refused access to the records of his own church.[90] Bristol historians also faced problems caused by the fact that Bristol had, until 1542, been part of the vast Worcester diocese. Even the subsequent Cathedral records were lamentably deficient on vital points.[91]

Nevertheless antiquarians gave priority to uncovering Bristol's ecclesiastical inheritance, because most of them were clergymen or lay supporters of the Church party. They hoped that, by publicising the former rights and powers of the Church, and showing how integral it was to the city, they could uphold its contemporary claims.[92] Ford and Barrett, for example, both aimed to show that Bristolians traditionally augmented 'the maintenance of a learned and laborious clergy', since the issue of civic payments to the Anglican clergy was an issue of lively contemporary controversy.[93] In many cities the Cathedral would have been the natural focus for such an alternative approach, but this was a relatively minor theme in Bristol, owing to its late foundation and marginal position in the city. Much more impressive, both physically and in medieval heritage, was St Mary Redcliffe, and it was appropriate that it was from this parish, and its supposed records, that Chatterton launched his historical assault on the establishment of his day, recreating a medieval city of pious, generous and cultured clergy and merchants to set against the corruption of modern times.[94] No other historian was as alienated from the present as Chatterton, but Tories generally came to focus on the histories of the parishes rather than the city, just as they came to lean more heavily on parish ritual once they lost control of Corporation affairs.

One of the distinguishing characteristics of the antiquarians was also that they either ignored or were deeply critical of the dissenting presence in the city. Dissent was written out of Bristol's past, or viewed as the offshoot of the disasters of Civil War.[95] This contrasts with the annals, where, although some annalists are hostile to dissent, others give a fuller, even sympathetic, account of religious persecution.[96] Groups such as the Quakers and Baptists, who had largely withdrawn from civic life in any case, made little effort to claim a share in the city's past, concentrating instead on their own history of persecution and purification. Their relation to the civic heritage was largely a negative one, refusing as they did to participate in public holidays, although they might occasionally take on a prophetic mantle and treat Bristol as an Old Testament city.[97] Only the Presbyterians retained an active presence across the full range of civic life, and there were a minority of antiquarians sympathetic to the Presbyterians.[98]

In this essay it has only been possible to sketch some of the themes involved in exploring urban mentality through town histories. I hope that this has suggested the need to consider urban mentality as a complex subject with its own agenda of issues. Many of the trends identified by Clark from the published material can be explained in an alternative fashion. I have emphasised the complex mixture of practical difficulties and ideological aims which shaped the writing of civic history, rather than national fashions or social changes. I have stressed the continuity well beyond the Civil War of attitudes which might be considered expressions of an old-fashioned and introverted civic community, but also how these were able to offer articulation to a complex and shifting cultural scene. The major strand in the published works undoubtedly represented a 'conservative' ideology, closely associated with the Toryism of many county historians and antiquarians, while a figure like Hooke could clearly be linked with a Whig Enlightenment. But I see no great advantage in reducing these urban historians to mere emulators of rival trends in metropolitan or aristocratic culture. Rather we should take them seriously as members of a civic community trying to make sense, through history as in many other ways, of the problems common both to the nation and to their particular community. Some of these were perennial issues concerning the maintenance of order and identity in society, but, during much of our period, these were aggravated by the political and religious conflicts which grew up around many of the institutions which had traditionally been the pillars of the establishment. We may find it easier to understand the national debate on these issues when we have more case-studies of how they were conceived in the provinces.

Notes

1. J. Latimer, *Annals of Bristol in the Seventeenth Century*, n.p., 1900; J. Latimer, *Annals of Bristol in the Eighteenth Century*, n.p., 1893; C. M. MacInnes, *Bristol : A Gateway of Empire*, new edn, Newton Abbot, 1968; B. Little, *The City and County of Bristol*, London, 1954; *Bristol in the Eighteenth Century*, ed. P. McGrath, Newton Abbot, 1972; E. Ralph, *The Government of Bristol 1373–1973*, Bristol, 1973.
2. W. Minchinton, 'Bristol – Metropolis of the West in the Eighteenth Century', in P. Clark, ed., *The Early Modern Town*, London, 1976, pp. 297–313; D. H. Sacks, 'Trade, Society and Politics in Bristol 1500–1640', Univ. of Harvard PhD thesis, 1977; P. V. McGrath, *The Merchant Venturers of Bristol*, Bristol, 1975; K. Morgan, 'Bristol Merchants and the Colonial Trades', Univ. of Oxford D.Phil. thesis, 1983.
3. Sacks, 'Trade, Society and Politics', pp. 205–54; J. R. Holman, 'Apprenticeship as a Factor in Migration: Bristol 1675–1726', *Transactions of the Bristol and Gloucestershire Archaeological Society* (hereafter *TBGAS*), xcvii, 1979, pp. 85–92; *The Inhabitants of Bristol in 1696*, ed. E. Ralph and M. Williams, Bristol Record Society, xxv, 1968; W. R. Savadge, 'The West Country and the American Mainland Colonies', Univ. of Oxford D.Phil. thesis, 1973, Appendix F.
4. E. Baigent, 'Bristol Society in the Later Eighteenth Century', Univ. of Oxford D.Phil. thesis, 1985; V. Waite, 'Bristol Hotwells', in McGrath, ed., *Bristol in the Eighteenth Century*, pp. 109–26; A. Gomme, M. Jenner and B. Little, *Bristol: An Architectural History*, Bristol, 1979; G. Lamoine, *La Vie Littéraire de Bath et de Bristol*, 2 vols, Lille, 1978.
5. J. Ellis, 'A Dynamic Society: Social Relations in Newcastle-upon-Tyne, 1660–1760', in P. Clark, ed., *The Transformation of English Provincial Towns 1600–1800* (hereafter *Transformations*), London, 1984, pp. 190–227; G. Jackson, *Hull in the Eighteenth Century*, Oxford, 1972.
6. W. G. Hoskins, *Provincial England*, London, 1965; W. G. Hoskins, *Industry, Trade and People in Exeter 1688–1800*, 2nd edn, Exeter, 1968; A. Everitt, *Landscape and Community*, London, 1985; A. Everitt, ed., *Perspectives in English Urban History*, London, 1973. For a perceptive review of the Leicester school from within, and suggestions for change which link closely with some of the ideas suggested here,

see C. Phythian-Adams, *Re-Thinking English Local History*, Leicester, 1987.

7. W. MacCaffrey, *Exeter 1540–1640*, 2nd edn, Cambridge, Mass., 1976; A. Dyer, *The City of Worcester in the Sixteenth Century*, Leicester, 1973; J. F. Pound, 'Tudor and Stuart Norwich 1525–1676', Univ. of Leicester PhD thesis, 1974; D. M. Palliser, *Tudor York*, Oxford, 1979; D. M. Palliser, 'Civic Mentality and the Environment in Tudor York', *Northern History*, xviii, 1982, pp. 78–115.

8. For instance: J. Queniart, *Culture et Société Urbaine dans la France de l'Ouest au 18ᵉ Siècle*, Paris, 1978; D. Roche, *Le Siècle des Lumières en Province*, Paris, 1978.

9. J. De Vries, *European Urbanization 1500–1800*, London, 1984; P. Clark and P. Slack, *English Towns in Transition 1500–1700*, Oxford, 1976; P. Corfield, 'Urban Development in England and Wales', in D. C. Coleman and A. H. John, eds, *Trade, Government and Economy in Pre-Industrial England*, London, 1976, pp. 214–47; P. Corfield, *The Impact of English Towns 1700–1800*, Oxford, 1982;L. Stone, 'Residential Development in the West End of London', in B. C. Malament, ed., *After the Reformation*, Manchester, 1980, pp. 167–212; E. A. Wrigley, 'A Simple Model of London's Importance in Changing English Society and Economy 1676–1750', *Past and Present*, 37, 1967, pp. 45–70.

10. C. Phythian-Adams, *The Decline of a City*, Cambridge, 1979; M. James, 'Ritual, Drama and Social Body in the Late Medieval English Town', *Past and Present*, 98, 1983, pp. 3–29; S. Reynolds, *An Introduction to the History of English Medieval Towns*, Oxford, 1977.

11. M. Foss, *The Age of Patronage*, 1972; R. Paulson, *Popular and Polite Art in the Age of Hogarth and Fielding*, London, 1979; R. D. Altick, *The Shows of London*, London, 1978; P. Burke, 'Popular Culture in Seventeenth-Century London', in B. Reay, ed., *Popular Culture in Seventeenth-Century England* (hereafter *Popular Culture*), London, 1985, pp. 31–58; M. D. George, *London Life in the Eighteenth Century*, new edn, London, 1966; C. Phythian-Adams, 'Milk and Soot: the Changing Vocabulary of a Popular Ritual', in D. Fraser and A. Sutcliffe, eds, *The Pursuit of Urban History*, London, 1983, pp. 83–104.

12. J. G. A. Pocock, 'The Limits and Divisions of British History', *American Historical Review*, 87, 1982, pp. 311–36; G. H. Jenkins, *Literature, Religion and Society in Wales 1660–1730*, Cardiff, 1978; P. Morgan, *The Eighteenth-Century Renaissance*, Llandybie, 1981; J. Simms, *Colonial Nationalism 1698–1776*, Cork, 1976; N. T. Phillipson, 'Culture and Society in the Eighteenth-Century Province', in L. Stone, ed., *Universities in Society*, 2 vols, Princeton, 1975, ii, pp. 407–48; N. T. Phillipson, 'The Scottish Enlightenment', in R. Porter and M. Teich, eds, *The Enlightenment in National Context*, Cambridge, 1981, pp. 19–40; J. P. Greene and J. R. Pole, eds, *Colonial British America*, Baltimore, 1984. For a useful comparative typology see R. Emerson, 'The Enlightenment and Social Structures', in P.

Fritz and D. Williams, eds, *City and Society in the Eighteenth Century*, Toronto, 1973, pp. 99–124.

13. D. Read. *The English Provinces*, London, 1964; I. Inkster and J. Morrell, eds, *Metropolis and Province: Science in British Culture 1780–1850*, London, 1983; J. Money, *Experience and Identity: Birmingham and the West Midlands 1760–1800*, Manchester, 1977; J. Langton, 'The Industrial Revolution and the Regional Geography of England', *Transactions of the Institute of British Geographers*, 9, 1984, pp.145–67.

14. J. Morrill, *The Revolt of the Provinces*, London, 1976; A. Everitt, 'The County Community', in E. W. Ives, ed., *The English Revolution*, London, 1968, pp. 48–63; P. Zagorin, *The Court and the Country*, London, 1969; C. Holmes, 'The County Community in Stuart Historiography', *Journal of British Studies*, 19, 1980, pp. 54–73; C. Herrup, 'The Counties and the Country', *Social History*, 8, 1983, pp. 169–82.

15. R. Howell, *Newcastle-upon-Tyne and the Puritan Revolution*, Oxford, 1967; R. Howell, 'Neutralism, Conservatism and Political Alignment in the English Revolution: The Case of the Towns 1642–9', in J. Morrill, ed., *Reactions to the English Civil War 1642–9*, London, 1982, pp. 67–87. He gives greater emphasis to national involvement, however, in his 'Newcastle and the Nation: the Seventeenth-Century Experience', *Archaeologia Aeliana*, vii, 1980, pp. 17–34.

16. J. J. Murrin, 'The Great Inversion or Court Versus Country 1688–1776', in J. G. A. Pocock, ed., *Three British Revolutions*, Princeton, 1980, pp. 368–453; J. G. A. Pocock, *Virtue, Commerce and History*, Cambridge, 1985.

17. E. A. Wrigley, 'Urban Growth and Agricultural Change', *Journal of Interdisciplinary History*, 15, 1985; P. Mathias, *The Transformation of England*, London, 1979; N. McKendrick, J. Brewer and J. H. Plumb, *The Birth of A Consumer Society*, London, 1982.

18. D. H. Sacks, ' "Bristol's Little Businesses": The Corporate Town and the English State 1603–40', *Past and Present*, 110, 1986, pp. 69–105; J. T. Evans, *Seventeenth-Century Norwich*, Oxford, 1979; J. H. Plumb, 'The Growth of the Electorate 1600–1715', *Past and Present*, 45, 1969, pp. 90–116; W. Speck, 'The Electorate in the First Age of Party', in C. Jones, ed., *Britain in the First Age of Party*, London, 1987, pp. 45–62; H. T. Dickinson, 'The Precursors of Political Radicalism', in *ibid*, pp. 63–82; L. Colley, 'Eighteenth-Century English Radicalism before Wilkes', *Transactions of the Royal Historical Society*, 5th ser., xxxi, 1981, pp. 1–20; J. Brewer, 'The Commercialization of Politics', in McKendrick *et al. Birth of a Consumer Society*, pp. 197–262; J. A. Phillips, *Electoral Behaviour in Unreformed England*, Princeton, 1982. Most of these writers, however, would probably still emphasise the limitations of provincial political independence, as does N. Rogers, 'Urban Opposition to Whig Oligarchy', in M. C. and J. Jacob, eds, *The Origins of Anglo-American Radicalism*, London, 1984, pp. 132–48.

19. P. Clark 'Migration in the Late Seventeenth- and Early Eighteenth-Century England', *Past and Present*, 83, 1979, pp. 57–90; J. Wareing,

'Geographical Distribution of Apprenticeship Recruitment to London 1486–1750', *Journal of Historical Geography*, 6, 1980, pp. 241–50; D. Souden, 'Migrants and Population Structure in the Later Seventeenth Century', in Clark, ed., *Transformation*, pp. 133–68.

20.   A. Everitt, 'Country, County and Town', *Transactions of the Royal Historical Society*, 5th ser., xxix, 1979, pp. 79–108.

21.   P. Burke, *Popular Culture in Early Modern Europe*, London, 1978; Reay, ed., *Popular Culture*; E. and S. Yeo eds, *Popular Culture and Class Conflict 1590–1914*, Hassocks, 1981; H. C. Payne, 'Elite versus Popular Mentality in the Eighteenth Century', *Studies in Eighteenth-Century Culture*, viii, 1979, pp. 3–32; H. Medick, 'Plebeian Culture in the Transition to Capitalism', in R. Samuel and G. S. Jones, eds, *Culture, Ideology and Politics*, London, 1982, pp. 84–113; S. Clark, 'French Historians and Early Modern Popular Culture', *Past and Present*, 100, 1983, pp. 62–99.

22.   E. P. Thompson, 'Patrician Society, Plebeian Culture', *Journal of Social History*, vii, 1974, pp. 382–405; E. P. Thompson, 'Eighteenth-Century Society: Class Struggle without Class?', *Social History*, iii, 1978, pp. 133–65.

23.   K. Wrightson, *English Society 1580–1680*, London, 1982.

24.   C. Hill, 'Parliament and the People in Seventeenth-Century England' *Past and Present*, 92, 1981, 100–24.

25.   J. C. D. Clark, *English Society 1688–1832*, Cambridge, 1985; J. V. Beckett, *The Aristocracy in England 1660–1914*, Oxford, 1986; M. L. Bush, *The English Aristocracy*, Manchester, 1984; J. Cannon, *The Aristocratic Century*, Cambridge, 1984; L. and J. C. F. Stone, *An Open Elite? England 1540–1880*, Oxford, 1984.

26.   As Clark has recently admitted in his exchange with Joanna Innes in *Past and Present*, 117, 1987, p. 198.

27.   M. Heyd, 'The Reaction to Enthusiasm in the Seventeenth Century', *Journal of Modern History*, liii, 1981, pp. 258–80; G. Holmes, 'The Achievement of Stability', in J. Cannon, ed., *The Whig Ascendancy*, 1981, pp. 1–23; R. Porter, 'The Enlightenment in England', in Porter and Teich, eds, *The Enlightenment in National Context*, pp. 1–18; M. MacDonald, 'Religion, Social Change and Psychological Healing', *Studies in Church History*, xx, 1982, pp. 101–26.

28.   J. P. Jenkins, *The Making of a Ruling Class: The Glamorgan Gentry 1640–1790*, Cambridge, 1983.

29.   P. Borsay, 'The English Urban Renaissance', *Social History*, ii, 1977, pp. 581–603; P. Borsay, 'Culture, Status and the English Urban Landscape', *History*, lxvii, 219, 1982, pp. 1–12; P. Borsay, ' "All the Town's a Stage": Urban Ritual and Ceremony 1660–1800', in Clark ed., *Transformation*, pp. 228–58; P. Borsay, *The English Urban Renaissance: Culture and Society in the Provincial Town, 1660–1770*, Oxford, 1989. I am very grateful to Dr Borsay for many cordial disputes on these themes.

30.   J. H. Plumb, *The Growth of Political Stability*, London, 1967; McKendrick *et al.*, *Birth of a Consumer Society*, pp. 265–334; Holmes, 'Achievement of Stability'; Porter, 'Enlightenment in England'.

31.   P. Clark, ed., *Country Towns in Pre-Industrial England*,Leicester, 1982; Clark, ed., *Transformation*.

32.   A. Everitt, *Change in the Provinces*, Leicester, 1969; G. Holmes, 'The Professions and Social Change', *Proceedings of the British Academy*, lxv, 1979, pp. 313–54. The first major case-study of this kind was Penelope Corfield, 'A Provincial Capital in the Late Seventeenth Century: Norwich' reprinted in Clark, ed., *Early Modern Town*, pp. 233–72. A very different perspective on such developments is offered by R. S. Neale, *Bath: A Social History*, London, 1981.

33.   P. Abrams and E. A. Wrigley, eds, *Towns in Societies*, Cambridge, 1978; M. E. Falkus and E. L. Jones, 'Urban Improvement and the English Economy', *Researches in Economic History*, iv, 1979, pp. 193–233; C. W. Chalklin, 'Capital Expenditure on Building for Cultural Purposes', *Business History*, xxii, 1980, pp. 51–70.

34.   J. H. Plumb, *Georgian Delights*, London, 1980. A similar criticism can be made of the work of R. M. Wiles: 'Provincial Culture in Early Georgian England', in P. Fritz and D. Williams, eds, *The Triumph of Culture*, Toronto, 1972, pp. 49–68; 'Crowd-Pleasing Spectacles in Eighteenth-Century England, *Journal of Popular Culture*, i, 1967, pp. 90–105.

35.   Borsay, 'Culture, Status and English Urban Landscape'; R. Porter, 'Science, Provincial Culture and Public Opinion in Enlightenment England', *British Journal for Eighteenth-Century Studies*, iii, 1980, pp. 20–46.

36.   For example in P. Clark, 'Visions of the Urban Community: Antiquarians and the English City before 1800', in Fraser and Sutcliffe, eds, *The Pursuit of Urban History*, pp. 105–24.

37.   M. Billinge, 'Hegemony, Class and Power in Late Georgian and Early Victorian England', in A. R. H. Baker and D. Gregory, eds, *Explorations in Historical Geography*, Cambridge, 1984, pp. 28–67.

38.   Stone, *An Open Elite?*; R. Grassby, 'Social Mobility and Business Enterprise in Seventeenth-Century England', in D. Pennington and K. Thomas, eds, *Puritans and Revolutionaries*, Oxford, 1978, pp. 355–81; N. Rogers, 'Money, Land and Lineage in Hanoverian London', *Social History*, iv, 1979, pp. 437–54 and vi, 1981, pp. 359–69; H. Horwitz, 'The Mess of the Middle Class Revisited', *Continuity and Change*, 2, 1987, pp. 263–96; R. G. Wilson, *Gentlemen Merchants: The Merchant Community in Leeds 1700–1830*, Manchester, 1971.

39.   J. Barry, 'Popular Culture in Seventeenth-Century Bristol', in Reay, ed., *Popular Culture*, pp. 59–90; J. Barry, *Bristol Pride: Civic Consciousness in the Seventeenth and Eighteenth Centuries*, Bristol Branch of the Historical Association, in preparation; J. Barry, 'Piety and the Patient: Medicine and Religion in Eighteenth-Century Bristol', in R. Porter, ed., *Patients and Practitioners: Lay Perceptions of Medicine in Pre-Industrial Society*, Cambridge, 1985, pp. 145–76. All these studies are based on the research behind my 'Cultural Life of Bristol 1640–1775', Univ. of Oxford D.Phil. thesis, 1985.

40.   P. Clark, 'Visions of the Urban Community'.

41.   K. V. Thomas, *The Perception of the Past in Early Modern England*,

Creighton Lecture, 1984; D. C. Douglas, *English Scholars*, 2nd edn, London, 1951; E. Hobsbawm and T. Ranger, eds, *The Invention of Tradition*, Cambridge, 1983.

42. I. Gray. *Antiquaries of Bristol and Gloucestershire*, Gloucester, 1981.

43. *Adams' Chronicle*, ed. F. F. Fox, Bristol, 1910; this version was started in 1623; a later version running to 1644 is in manuscript in Bristol Archives Office (hereafter BAO) 13748(4); A. Hooke, *Bristollia*, 1748; A. Hooke, *A Dissertation on the Antiquity of Bristol*, 1748. Unique copies of both Hooke's works, with manuscript notes by his friend and advisor Charles Godwyn of Balliol College, are bound together in Bodleian Library, G. A. Som. 8 12. The chain of transmission of material can be traced through Brit. Lib., Additional MS. 5811, fo. 84; *The Complete Works of Thomas Chatterton*, ed. D. S. Taylor with B. S. Hoover, 2 vols, Oxford, 1971, i, p. 667; W. Barrett, *Proposals for Publishing a History of Bristol*, Bristol, 1788; S. Seyer, *Memoirs, Historical and Topographic, of Bristol and its Neighbourhood*, Bristol, 1821, pp. v–vi. *Felix Farley's Bristol Journal*, 29, Oct. 1771, 'A Sojourner at Hotwells' and 21 Mar. 1772, 'Mercator' both contain puffs for Barrett's *History*, envisaged as near to publication.

44. Comments on annalists can be found in Bodl. Lib., Gough Somerset MS. 2, fos. 13–17; Seyer, *Memoirs*, pp. x–xiii; Bristol Central Library, Bristol Collection (hereafter BCL), 12196, fo. 335 and 7950, fo. 90. A complete list of annals will be found in the bibliography of Barry, 'Cultural Life of Bristol'.

45. Bodl. Lib., Wood MS. F41, fos. 260, 263; Bodl. Lib., Gough Somerset MS. 2, fo. ix; Bodl. Lib., Willis MS. 43, fos. 113–14; BAO, Infirmary Memoirs MS. 1, fo. 79; Barrett, *History*, pp. v, 22; *Felix Farley's Bristol Journal*, 22 Mar. 1755; J. Thistlethwaite, *The Consultation*, Bristol, 1775, p. 66; notice in front of Bodleian copy of Hooke, *Bristollia*.

46. Bodl. Lib., Aubrey MS. 13, fo. 83; Bodl. Lib., Willis MS. 64, fos. 144–6, 150–11, 159; J. Whitson, *Farewell to the World* ed. T. Ford, London, 1729, pp. iv–v; *Gentleman's Magazine*, 56, 1786, pp. 460, 544–5; BAO, Infirmary Memoirs MS. 1, fos. 76–9.

47. See below, nn. 87–9.

48. BCL, 21917, fos. 111–18 and 22477, fos. 54–60; *Life of Marmaduke Rawdon*, ed. R. Davies, Camden Soc., 1863, p.173; J. Dryden, *Poems and Fables*, ed. J. Kinsley, Oxford, 1967, p. 697; D. Defoe, *Tour through the Whole Island of Great Britain* (hereafter Defoe, *Tour*) new edn, London, 1778, ii, p. 241.

49. *Adams' Chronicle*, pp. 1–5, 12, 15–20; BAO, 13748(4) e.g. 'Large and Honourable Evidences for Antiquity' in summary annals under 1603' Bodl. Lib., Gough Som, MS. 2, fos. 1–3 and appendix; E. H. W. Meyerstein, *The Life of Thomas Chatterton*, London, 1930; pp. 109–11, 189–90; D. S. Taylor, *Thomas Chatterton's Art*, Princeton, 1978; Hooke, *Dissertation*; Hooke, *Bristollia*; BCL, 4504–5, 5009.

50. Clark, 'Visions of the Urban Community', p. 124.

51. Bodl. Lib., Wood MS. F41, fos. 249–51, Aubrey MS. 13, fos. 64–7, Willis MS. 43, fos. 93–4; Barrett, *Proposals*; Whitson, *Farewell*, p. iv.

52. A. D. Momigliano, *Studies in Historiography,* new edn, London,

1969, pp. 1–55; Bodl. Lib., Willis MS 43, fo. 87; *Oracle* (Hooke's newspaper), 23 Oct. 1742; Whitson, *Farewell*, p. v; *Gentleman's Magazine*, 59, 1789, pp. 921–4.

53.   J. Cary, *An Essay on Coyn and Credit*, London, 1696; G. Randolph, *An Enquiry into the Medical Virtues of Bristol Water*, 2 edns, Oxford, 1745 and 1750; A. Catcott, *A Treatise upon the Deluge*, London, 1768. For a typical survey of local historical writing, mingling natural and civil histories, see J. Rawlinson, *The English Topographer*, London, 1720, pp. 52–7, 215–21.

54.   Annals with much general history include: *Adams' Chronicle*; BAO, 22156; BCL, 4502, 10161, 10163 (3), 10166 (1); Brit. Lib., Egmont MS. 2044. Bristol-only annals include: BAO, 09594 (1), 37541; BCL, 10162, 10163 (2 and 4).

55.   For Hooke see above n. 42; Latimer, *18C Annals*, pp. 51–2, 240, 279; BCL, 4504–5, 5009; A. Hooke, *An Essay on the National Debt and National Capital*, London, 1750. For Bedford see *Dictionary of National Biography*. The theological scholar and musicologist Arthur Broughton (see *Dictionary of National Biography* and Meyerstein, *Life of Chatterton*, pp. 9–11) kept annals (BCL, 10162 and 4533 fo. 119), as did the Quaker Richard Champion, author of *Considerations on the Present Situation of Great Britain and Ireland*, 2nd edn, London, 1784; BAO, 38083 (7).

56.   Rome: *An Historical and Poetical Description of Bristol*, Bristol, 1729; Defoe, *Tour*, new edn, London, 1769, ii, p. 237; Barrett, *History*, p. 57. Jerusalem: T. Speed, *Reason versus Rage*, London, 1691, p. 28; below, n. 96.

57.   See above n. 47; *Adams' Chronicle*; BAO 13748 (4); Hooke, *Dissertation*, pp. 36, 49–52; Bodl. Lib., Gough Somerset MS. 2, fos. 1–3; 'Civis' in *Felix Farley's Bristol Journal*, 12 Sept. 1772; Meyerstein, *Life of Chatterton*, p. 265; Barrett, *History*, pp. 2–8, 28–30; J. Collinson, *History and Antiquities of Somerset*, London, 1791, preface.

58.   Barrett, *History*, pp. 1, 66–7, 164–90.

59.   Hooke, *Dissertation*, pp. 1–2, 5, 10, 41, 49; Hooke, *Bristollia*, p. 1.

60.   *Historical and Poetical Description*; excerpts from Anderson's *History of Commerce* in *Felix Farley's Bristol Journal*, 5–26 May 1764 and 'A Plebeian', 2 May 1772; BCL, 12196 fo. 2; Champion, *Considerations*, pp. 208–9; Barrett, *History*, pp. 2–37, 54, 57–8, 81–2, 182–4; E. Shiercliff, *Bristol and Hotwell Guide*, Bristol, 1789, ch. 1; G. Heath, *A New History, Survey and Description of Bristol*, Bristol, 1794, pp. 4, 37.

61.   Hooke, *Dissertation*, pp. iii–iv; notes at the end of BCL, 4505 on 'the Antiquity of the Corporation'; his Prospectus for *Bristollia* in Bodl. Lib., Willis MS. 43, fo. 87.

62.   Whitson, *Farewell*, pp. v–vi. See also *The Maire of Bristow Is Kalendar*, ed. L. Toulmin Smith, Camden Soc., n.s., v, 1872, pp. 1, 4; *Adams' Chronicle*, p. 241; BAO, 13748 (4), 'To the Reader'; Brit. Lib., Egmont MS. 2044; Bodl. Lib., Top. Gloucs. MS. c.2, fo. 350b; *Sketchley's Bristol Directory*, Bristol, 1775, pp. 117–18; Barrett, *History*, pp. 82–4, 114–26.

63.   Barrett, *Proposals*; Whitson, *Farewell*, p. vi; Hooke, *Bristollia*,

preface; speech during visit of Prince of Wales in 1738 reported in *Gentleman's Magazine*, viii, 1738, pp. 603–4.

64.   *Adams' Chronicle*, pp. 34, 50, 106; BAO, 13748 (4) statement of purpose; Hooke, *Dissertation*, pp. iii–iv.

65.   The best introduction to Bristol's civic ritual is the civic sword-bearer's diary for the 1720s, edited in *TBGAS*, lxi, 1939, pp. 224–68. For examples see *Bristol Journal*, 7 Oct. 1748 and 6 April 1771; Barrett, *History*, pp. 120–1, 493.

66.   For heraldry, see E. Gander and F. Ware, 'The Heraldry of some of the Citizens of Bristol between 1662 and 1683', *TBGAS*, xxx, 1907, pp. 273–82, together with many reports on heraldic devices found in homes reported in the same journal; T. F. Fenwick and W. C. Metcalfe, *Visitation of the County of Gloucestershire 1682–3*, Exeter, 1884. Although the last herald-painters locally are recorded just after 1700, interest did not die out (e.g. R. Arding's heraldic book collection in BCL., 14799, fos. 77–8). In 1744 A. S. Catcott preached to the Society of Merchant Venturers on *The Antiquity and Honourableness of the Practice of Merchandize*, Bristol, 1744. For the 'Ancient and Honourable Society of Free and Accepted Masons', see A. C. Powell and J. Littleton, *History of Freemasonry in Bristol*, Bristol, 1910; J. Price, *The Advantages of Unity Considered*, Bristol, 1748. Price also preached on *The Antiquity of the Festival of Saint David's Day*, Bristol, 1754, to the 'Society of Ancient Britons', that is Welsh settlers in Bristol, one of many charitable societies for immigrants in the town. For about 50 years from 1658 there was a similar society for native Bristolians and in his *Sermon preached before the Free-born Citizens of Bristol*, Oxford, 1703, S. Chapman apologised (pp. 20–1) for his inability to comment on the city's history on such an occasion.

67.   M. H. J. Liversidge, *Bristol High Cross*, Bristol Branch of the Historical Association, 1978; C. Fiennes, *Journeys*, ed. J. Hillaby, London, 1983, p. 266; W. Goldwin, *A Poetical Description of Bristol*, Bristol, 1712, p. 13; *Narrative of the Journey of an Irish Gentleman*, ed. H. Huth, London, 1869, pp. 143–4; Defoe, *Tour*, new edn, 1748, ii, pp. 308–9. Maps and drawings of the city often contained historical remarks: these are brought together in *TBGAS.*, xlviii, 1926, pp. 325–53. James Stewart began studying Bristol history after an enquiry from the Buck Brothers about the buildings they were engraving, and he combined his history with a plan to draw all the notable buildings in the city: Bodl. Lib., Gough Somerset MSS. 2 and 8.

68.   *Gentleman's Magazine*, xiii, 1743, pp. 496–7; J. Wood, *A Description of the Exchange of Bristol*, Bath, 1743; Barrett, *History*, pp. 461–4.

69.   Barrett, *History*, pp. 66–7, 73–80, 95–7; 'A Citizen', *A Short Historical Account of Bristol Bridge*, Bristol, 1759; 'A. Y' in *Felix Farley's Bristol Journal*, 19 Apr, 1760; poem on port improvement in *Bristol Journal*, 26 Sept. 1767. Chatterton's first Rowley poem concerned the building of the first bridge.

70.   The architectural changes are described in Gomme, Jenner and

Little, *Bristol: An Architectural History*, and a full account of the reactions will appear in my 'Bristol Pride'. See Liversidge, *Bristol High Cross*; BAO, Common Council Proceedings, July 1733; Barrett, *History*, pp. 82–113, 294; Latimer, *18C Annals*, p. 223.

71.   Whitson, *Farewell*, p. viii; Bodl. Lib., Willis MS. 64, fos. 150–1; Brit. Lib., Additional MS. 5811, fos. 56, 91; *Felix Farley's Bristol Journal*, 12 Oct. 1754 and 24 Jan. 1761; Barrett, *History*, pp. 294–5.

72.   J. Chetwynd, *Anthologia Historica*, London, 1674; J. Jones, *Steps towards an English Education*, 2nd edn, Bristol, 1740, pp. 2–5; J. Brooks, *Antiquity or the Wise Instructor*, Bristol, 1770. The reprinting of Whitson's *Farewell* a hundred years after his death was intended to have the same admonitory effect, and it was further reprinted in 1759 and 1789. In 1757, debate over the new militia prompted a letter to the *Bristol Weekly Intelligencer* (29 Oct.) quoting a Bristol militia sermon of 1635.

73.   Whitson, *Farewell*, p. vii; Hooke, *Dissertation*, pp. iii–iv; Barrett, *History*, pp. 66–7, 82, 184, 610–23; *An Account of the Hospitals, Almshouses and Public Schools in Bristol*, Bristol 1775 (probably compiled together with the historical guide to Bristol in BCL, 12196 by Macaulay's grandfather, the pietist bookseller Thomas Mills). Annals stressing bequests are: Brit. Lib., Egmont MS. 2044; BCL, 4946, 10095, 10161–2, 10166 (3), 15861.

74.   *Farley's Bristol Newspaper*, 4 Nov. 1727; *Felix Farley's Bristol Journal*, 18 Nov. 1752, 17 Nov. 1753; *Several Charitable Settlements of Edward Colston*, Bristol, 1760.

75.   J. Tucker, *Two Dissertations*, Bristol, 1749, pp. 5, 48; J. Tucker, *Reflections on the Expedience of a Law for the Naturalisation of French Protestants*, London, 1751, p. 3; J. Tucker, *Second Letter to a Friend concerning Naturalisation*, London, 1753, pp. 5, 7, 9, 12, 17, 25; and his letters in *Memoirs of Lord Kames*, ed. A. F. Tytler, London, 1814, i, pp. 172, 176–7, 183. His attitude stands in vivid contrast to the use of ancestral wisdom by the Tory MP, Sir John Knight, in his notorious attack on the naturalisation of foreigners in his *Speech to the House of Commons*, London, 1694, p. 8.

76.   G. Bishop, *A Looking-Glass for the Times*, London, 1668; E. Harwood, *A New Introduction to the Study and Knowledge of the New Testament*, London, 1767; see below, nn. 94, 96.

77.   *Adams' Chronicle*; R. Towgood, *Disloyalty of Language Questioned*, Bristol, 1643, pp. 69–77, 85; 'T. D.' in *Bristol Weekly Intelligencer*, 2 Aug. 1750; E. Gardner, *Liberty: A Poem*, Bristol, 1776; M. Frampton, *A Sermon to the Wiltshire Society*, Bristol, 1776, pp. 8–10; R. Jenkins, *Historical Law Essays*, Bristol, 1779.

78.   T. Jekyll, *Peace and Love Recommended*, London, 1675; C. Reynell, *Two Sermons*, London, 1730; *Bristol Chronicle*, 2 Feb. 1760; S. Crossman, *Two Sermons*, London, 1681, p. 3; *Report of the Committee of the Commons concerning Richard Thompson*, London, 1680; *The Vizar Pluck't off from Richard Thompson*, London, 1680; *The Bristol Riot*, London, 1714, p. 9; Bodl. Lib., Gough Somerset MS. 2, fo. 99; *Correspondence of John Locke*, ed. E. S. De Beer, Oxford, 1976, ii, pp.

160–1. For two 'calves-head' festivals on the day see Brit. Lib., Additional MS. 5540, fo. 26; *H.M.C. 29 Portland IV*, p. 287.

79.   *Calendar of State Papers Domestic 1684*, pp. 240–1; J. Chetwynd, *Eben-Ezer*, London, 1682; *Oracle*, 6 Nov. 1742; J. Needham, *National Deliverances*, Bristol, 1753; *Bristol Chronicle*, 7 Nov. 1761; C. Evans, *British Constitutional Liberty*, Bristol, 1775; BCL, 26064, fo. 180.

80.   J. Gibb, *Mutual Duties of Magistrates and People*, Bristol, 1721, pp. 19–21; Bodl. Lib., Gough Somerset MS. 2, fo. 174; Huth, ed., *Narrative*, pp. 144–5; J. Curwen, *Journals and Letters*, New York, 1845, p. 241; Latimer, *18C Annals*, pp. 110, 164, 483; *Bristol Journal*, 24 May 1766, 26 May 1770.

81.   *Michael Rysbrack*, ed. K. Eustace, Bristol, 1982, pp. 24–34. While the Corporation celebrated events concerned with William and George I, most of the parishes ignored these monarchs in favour of Elizabeth and above all Anne, whose memory was ostentatiously recalled when George III ascended.

82.   *The Bristol Contest*, Bristol, 1754, pp. 43–4; *Bristol Weekly Intelligencer*, 16 June 1750; Latimer, *18C Annals*, pp. 19, 112, 113, 164, 196–7, 319. Admittedly both sides in Bristol denounced the '45 and two editions of J. Ray, *Complete History of the Rebellion* were printed in Bristol, 1750 and 1752.

83.   *An Occasional Poem on the Meeting of the Loyal Society*, Bristol, 1711; J. Harcourt, *A Sermon at the Funeral of Edward Colston*, London, 1721; *Felix Farley's Bristol Journal*, 25 Nov. 1752, 16 Nov. 1754; W. Hawkins, *Nature, Extent and Excellence of Christian Charity*, Bristol, 1755, p. 25; Barrett, *History*, pp. 377, 654–6.

84.   *Calendar of State Papers Domestic 1663–4*, pp. 472–84, 498, 622, 545 and *1689–90*, p. 241 show the political importance of civic precedence.

85.   Brit. Lib., Additional MS. 5540, fo. 37. At the same period Cary was also using precedent in a trade dispute with the Irish: J. Cary, *A Vindication of the Parliament of England*, London, 1698.

86.   *Bristol Charters*, ed. R. C. Latham, Bristol Record Soc., xii, 1947; *The Case of the Bristol Election*, London, 1735; BCL, 11161 (Hooke letter of 27 July 1747); Bodl. Lib., Willis MS. 43, fos. 90, 93–4; *Bristol Contest*, pp. 54–6; J. Thistlethwaite, *Tories in the Dumps*, Bristol, 1775, p. 23; Barrett, *History*, pp. 141–63; N. D. Harding, 'The Archives of the Corporation of Bristol', *TBGAS*, xlviii, 1925, pp. 227–50.

87.   BAO, Common Council Proceedings, Jan. 1736 and Corporation Vouchers 1736–7; *Bristol: The City Charters*, Bristol, 1736; *Sam Farley's Bristol Newspaper*, 10 Oct. 1735, 3 July 1736; BCL, 4504 (under 1163), 4502, fo. 129; Barrett, *History*, pp. 121–2, 656; S. Seyer, *Charters and Letters Patent of Bristol*, Bristol, 1812, pp. viii–x; BAO, JS/53/59(1); Latimer, *18C Annals*, pp. 194–5; copy of 1710 charter in Bodl. Lib., Gough Somerset 1.

88.   BAO, Common Council Proceedings, Feb. 1747; Hooke, *Dissertation*, p. iii; Barrett, *Proposals*; Bodl. Lib., Top. Gloucs. MS. c.9, letter of 30 Jan. 1761; BCL, Braikenridge Colelction I, fo. 17.

89.   Bodl. Lib., Willis MS. 43, fos. 1–2, 83, 93–7, 106–114, MS. 60, fos.

108–10 and MS. 64, fos, 150–1.; Barrett, *Proposals*. For the Haynes circle see: F. J. Poynton, *Pedigree of Haynes*, Bristol, 1885; BAO, 09701 (1–24), Temple E4 letters, 8019 (4), HA/W.10.

90. BCL, 4904, 5494; BAO, Temple FA (1, 9), EP/V/3 1705 Temple presentment.

91. The Willis MSS. in the Bodleian contain endless complaints about this. See also BAO, CD/A/6/6; *Gentleman's Magazine*, lvi, 1786, pp. 450–3, 544–6.

92. Before the Haynes group the most active Tories were linked to Andrew Paschall, a friend of Aubrey: Bodl. Lib., Aubrey MSS. 12 and 13.

93. *An Apology for the Clergy of the City of Bristol*, Bristol, 1712; Whitson, *Farewell*, p. vii; Barrett, *History*, pp. 83, 130; Bodl. Lib., G. A. Glos B4a, no. 858.

94. *Complete Works of Thomas Chatterton*; Taylor, *Thomas Chatterton's Art*.

95. S. Crossman, *A Sermon to the Artillery Company*, London, 1680, pp. 8, 20, 24–30; R. Kingston, *Vivat Rex*, London, 1683, pp. 3, 6–9, 18, 23–7, 34–9, 42–3; H. Jones, *Clifton: A Poem*, Bristol, 1768, pp. 27–8, 35–6; Barrett, *History*, pp. 58, 243, 278–9, 295, 339, 387–8, 449, 579–80.

96. Only the 1680s persecutions are covered in any detail: BCL, 10166 (1–3), 10163 (2, 4), 4502 offer a range of attitudes.

97. *Records of a Church of Christ in Bristol 1640–87*, ed. R. Hayden, Bristol Record Soc., xxvii, 1974, pp. 81–3, 114–15, 371, 389; *Minutes of the Men's Meeting of Bristol*, ed. R. S. Mortimer, Bristol Record Soc., xxx, 1977, p. 116; J. Whiting, *Persecution Exposed*, London, 1715; 'Amicus Veritatis' in *Bristol Weekly Intelligencer*, 2 June 1750; J. Besse, *A Collection of Sufferings*, 2 vols, London, 1753, i, pp. 41, 43, 63, 65; *Felix Farley's Bristol Journal*, 29 June 1754, 17–24 Feb. 1759; J.Gough, *Britannia: a Poem*, London, 1767, pp. 12, 30; J. Toulmin, *The Observation of Festivals and Holydays considered*, Bristol, 1771; BCL, 20095 under 1 Mar. and 21 Sept. 1780.

98. Anthony Wood was in contact with two Bristol historians sympathetic to Presbyterianism, Nathaniel Freind (Bodl. Lib., Top. Oxon MS. F 31, fo. 293) and John Chetwynd (see *Dictionary of National Biography*): Bodl. Lib., Wood MSS. D4, fo. 65 and F41, fos. 249 et seq. Arthur Bedford was an Anglican Whig, though with many High Church interests. Andrew Hooke, a passionate Whig who approved of 'a primitive episcopate', and his friend Alexander Morgan, another Whig (see *Felix Farley's Bristol Journal*, 22 Mar. 1755), both contacted the Tory Browne Willis (Bodl. Lib., Willis MS. 43, fo. 90; BCL, 5009, fos. 9, 13, and letters at end) but the relationship was not close. Barrett bought Morgan's notes from his widow, and obtained Bedford's through a later Tory vicar of Temple, but never had access to Hooke's materials (Barrett, *Proposals*).

10

Ignorance and Revolution: Perceptions of Social Reality in Revolutionary Marseilles, 1789–92

William Scott

It is not surprising that France's national anthem is the 'Marseillaise'. Though in origins foreign to Marseilles, its adoption by the 'five hundred men who know how to die', who marched in the summer of 1792 from the Midi to Paris to overthrow the king, assured its immortality. This expedition symbolised the élan of Marseilles's contribution to the Revolution.

Marseilles had its own revolution in 1789, before that of Paris – its own popular insurrection, destroying its own local 'tyrants', and its own revolutionary guard, as early as March 1789. Most Marseillais welcomed subsequent events at Paris with enthusiasm. This early commitment is partly a reflection of the city's dynamism. Since the halving of its population by the plague of 1720, Marseilles had recovered strongly. In 1789, it was France's third city. Despite difficulties, producing social tensions, it was economically vigorous. Its leading citizens, the principal merchants, were particularly enlightened. Thus, from the outset, Marseilles accepted many of the fundamental changes of 1789 and did not, as it were, waste time in struggling against a nobility which was locally insignificant. Already struggles were within the third estate, with artisans, manufacturers and sometimes workers putting forward radical demands which alarmed the rich, complacent in their belief that a moderate, constitutional revolution would suit themselves. Thus phases which, elsewhere, were often successive, were 'telescoped' at Marseilles, giving the city a reputation for turbulence and extremism.

Marseilles had been a Greek republic and had preserved republican traditions. Far from Paris, a feeling of separatist superiority was rekindled

235

in 1789. Provence was backward. It was Marseilles's revolutionary mission to spread the new principles throughout the Midi, to 'export' them to Aix, Nîmes, Arles and Avignon – or even to Paris, if the capital faltered. Marseilles was the Revolution's southern bastion. Its Jacobin Club was second only to that of the capital, and sometimes more resolute and more advanced. The city's revolutionary task, undertaken by committed clubists backed by a ruthless national guard, was facilitated by the great port's economic role: it distributed imported grain throughout the south. By mid-1792, the Jacobins of Marseilles were masters of the Midi.

Inevitably, resistance developed. Social struggles within the city, attacks on the 'aristocracy of wealth', were paralleled in the countryside, with the 'missionaries' from Marseilles being widely feared. When, in the spring of 1793, the Marseilles Jacobins proposed measures of terror, the rule of the 'anarchists' was overturned and Marseilles rebelled against the Jacobin 'dictatorship'. But Marseilles's attempts, with other cities, to organise an armed expedition against Paris failed. Marseilles, reconquered by the Convention, was subjected to the Terror. For having betrayed its revolutionary destiny, it suffered the ultimate indignity of being rebaptised, in the cultural revolution of the Year II, *Ville Sans Nom*.

What a marvellous revolution in attitudes and in circumstances! It would be fascinating to know all the causes which produced it.

(Dominique Audibert)[1]

Ignorance has been massively present throughout history, yet few historians, cultural or otherwise, have given it much direct attention. Here we wish, taking one locality and a short time-span, to look at varieties of ignorance in order to contextualise the writings, decisions and acts of participants in the French Revolution. For many historians, that Revolution, with its intense politicisation of most aspects of life, initiated modern political culture,[2] making a significant break with a situation in which 'ignorance of the principles of politics' and, still more, an absence of political practice, were frequently deplored by educated, patriotic would-be citizens. We wish to consider some of the forces and influences which stimulated or, conversely, weighed upon, revolutionaries, especially certain negative ones which made for a shortfall between aims and achievements, a shortfall often attributed then, and now by historians such as François Furet, to the resistance of a complex, recalcitrant reality.[3] This frustrated extravagant hopes, over-rational schemes and naive desires for a total knowledge assuring mastery over events and circumstances and led inexorably, but no less sadly for a revolution of *'lumières'*, to illusory solutions which brought not just violence but terror. Moreover most participants in the Revolution were afforded little leisure for consoling thoughts that hard-won lessons and a deeper knowledge might be acquired through the very failure of endeavours to solve problems whose scope had been only dimly discerned. Many doubted if they would live long enough to benefit.

With the stakes so high, revolutionaries were torn between exhilaration at the chance to realise an immense historical task, and anxiety lest failure cast the world back into ignorance and barbarism. To declare everything to need making anew was to make everything problematical – history, existing structures of power, modes of thought, forms of discourse. As the realm of choice was vastly extended, the possibilities of failure were multiplied. Embarking on a voyage of discovery, yet bearing aspects of the past which had not been specifically chosen for the expedition, a cargo of uncertain provenance and composition, they could not be confident that 'knowledge' had been safely stowed on board. Yet to attain knowledge was also an *objective* of the trip. The progress of civilisation in the future, as in the past, depended – as contestants in Marseilles Academy's *concours* in praise of James Cook the explorer were arguing[4] – on the acquisition and use of knowledge. Yet to advance was often to open out new vistas of ignorance, at best encouraging further exploration, but daunting even so.

Traversing different areas of concern to the cultural historian – *mentalités*, attitudes, problems of public opinion and political consciousness, participation and manipulation, the limits of systems of thought, the role of 'impersonal forces' of which participants were ignorant – and perhaps sounding areas of silence too often neglected by historians (though the noisy clash of rival discourses in the Revolution left few depths for silence), the study of ignorance may illuminate different areas of social activity. Ideas of ignorance were influential, if often implicit, in 1789. At worst mere insults, at best they informed a subversive but argued critique of viewpoints often more restricted, of positions often-

more exposed, than their holders realised. Accusations of ignorance – partly because of their somewhat indiscriminate nature,
which needs to be unscrambled – opened out new areas of
discussion and dispute, to a *choc* of opinions from which not only
truth and knowledge emerged. The reality of ignorance, as well as
its invocation, were part of a praxis which cut across artificial
boundaries between social, economic, political or ideological
history and which is therefore a fitting object for cultural analysis.
Ignorance links different areas of struggle, crossing any frontier
between 'popular' and 'elite' culture, since in certain respects the
educated could be most ignorant (and therefore easily outwitted),
while the ignorance of one class could be a resource for another.
The historian's pursuit of ignorance can therefore penetrate
deeply into the heart of social relationships. Ignorance disrupts
the historian's ready-made categories, just as it was often disrupt-
ive in history, though occasionally, perhaps, a sense of common
ignorance has united rather than divided. Above all, the definition
of ignorance is clearly socially-determined. Which individuals or
collective persons are seen as ignorant obviously varies with the
social context, as does actual, 'demonstrable' ignorance. This last
concept however – perhaps measured to an unprecedented degree
from the period of the Revolution, with its impulse to the collection of statistics and towards categorisation – was itself, in its
professed objectivity, open to challenge from the dissident or the
disparaged.

Consideration of ignorance by the historian may also break
down the too-rigid distinctions of the *Annales* school between the
'longue durée' and 'l'histoire événementielle'. Certain ignorances
were almost structural to an old regime which was certainly not
'immobile' in the area of attitudes (as Vovelle's work on wills at
Marseilles has shown, however ambiguously)[5] but which evolved
comparatively slowly. But they might also contribute to short-term
events, to be examined in close analyses of riot and revolt. Certain
ignorances can remain secure for centuries during which some
things may be 'unthinkable' – or they may suddenly collapse.
Attention to ignorance may therefore help to discriminate between what was new in the Revolution and what was carried over
from the old regime. For, though concepts of ignorance changed,
some underlying phenomena remained comparatively unscathed.
The 'ignorance' of the masses, for example, could not be remedied
overnight, despite crash efforts, though this ignorance might be

appreciated differently after 1789. The dialectic between the long and the short term is exceedingly complex.[6]

Sudden feelings of ignorance perhaps threaten to overwhelm participants in a vast upheaval such as the French Revolution, often likened to an immense force of nature, but alternating rapidly between the liberating and the catastrophic. Yet rarely can thought about social relationships, and the means to represent them in words, figures and symbols, have been as intense and widespread. Such was the Revolution's undoubted boost to the search for a knowledge not necessarily exploitable in the short term that we, as its heirs, can easily fail to comprehend the problems caused by the lack of, for example, social statistics. It needs imagination to evaluate perceptions so differently based from those of our own age. However this too makes what we say here all the more speculative or conjectural – or, at best, exploratory.

Today, when it is once more academically respectable to speak (without discrimination) of the revolutionaries as ignorant – as *'imbéciles'* or *'nullités'* who, in the opinion of Pierre Chaunu, declared war on 'French intelligence'[7] – we need a balanced and accurate understanding of the difficulties inherent in the revolutionary venture and of the odds stacked against it. While we might conclude that the voyage was itself foolhardy and presumptuous, serious consideration of the ignorance, real or alleged, of the revolutionaries might help to rescue *us* from the false and ignorant alternative of denigration or celebration. The Revolution needs to be seen as a period of intense and fairly sophisticated self-reflection.

Yet what was not known might seem as important as what was known. The future, of course, though this could be 'tamed' by the projection forward of trends ruthlessly extrapolated from the past. At Marseilles, the linkage of commerce, freedom and *lumières*, from the Phocaean republic onwards, provided an ideal myth of origins, not totally obscured by long periods of ignorance and barbarism, which themselves deserved to be ignored by the enlightened.[8] However the future was still a barrier (and if its trials and tribulations had been known, would anyone have begun 'the Revolution'?. This was a question posed early in the revolutionary period, and not just by malcontents). Luckily, perhaps, ignorance helps to define the context, as experienced by the actors of history who cannot, presumably, see beyond the barrier of their own ignorance, even if they are ignorant of where this barrier lies.

Ignorance, however, was rarely pure, except perhaps when cited patronisingly by revolutionaries as an excuse for the sincere misdeeds of the lower classes. It was frequently linked, as cause or result, with inexperience and incompetence. It might also serve as a mask for *mauvaise volonté* or for a perhaps preventable lack of foresight. Often revolutionaries, as was pointed out by defenders of the old regime at Marseilles, had been 'hommes ignorés', who would normally, and justly, have remained unknown. They were certainly in no position 'to know'. At best, or, some said, worst, they were *'demi-savants'*. Lacking 'real' experience, they revealed ignorance and incompetence when in power. Clearly the absence of an active politics in the *ancien régime* was itself a powerful factor in this unpreparedness, especially at Marseilles where the Intendant was all-powerful. The municipality was a narrow oligarchy of men concerned only with their own businesses or property, who lacked public spirit and wanted a quiet life, having shown no zeal to serve in a body devoid of initiative, treated contemptuously by the government and its agents, with derision and insubordination by the populace.[9] But precisely how men could acquire experience of revolution, or competence in its management, was not convincingly explained: ignorance of Revolution in its modern sense – of the future – was inevitable. Moreover revolutionary rhetoric maintained, not therefore without some justification, that experience acquired in the old regime, and intimate knowledge of its labyrinthine workings, was a disqualification for loyal and effective service in the new.

Revolutionaries might accept that types of knowledge undervalued by the ruling classes of the old regime, but nevertheless developed and displayed there, given some prestige (if sometimes only locally) and bringing their possessors certain advantages would get enhanced status in the new order. The knowledge of the merchants (*négociants*), the group exercising economic and cultural hegemony at Marseilles and responsible for the remarkable economic growth of the city from the terrible plague of 1720 to the war in 1793 and cultural heroes of Montesquieu and Raynal,[10] would now be more salient, to be deployed to even greater effect and more widely, for the benefit of the *nation*. Even here, however, changes would be required. The arrogant, complacent habits of an 'aristo-cracy of wealth', which set the tone of Marseilles society as nobles did elsewhere, would need to give way to a greater regard for the contribution to economic progress of other classes – artisans, manufacturers, peasants. Then merchants' own knowledge would expand. While merchants used their claims to knowledge to promote themselves effectively enough in 1789 (all four of Marseil-les's third estate deputies to the States General were *négociants*) they did this brutally, to the detriment of other classes, thus exposing themselves to accusations that, though self-interested, they did not recognise that their own best interests lay in co-operation, not confrontation.[11]

In such conflictual situations, control of the definition of igno-rance was a crucial resource, entailing the capacity credibly to claim knowledge for oneself, or consciously to claim ignorance if it suited one's purpose, or the ability to brand others as ignorant and thereby disqualify them from a voice in the affairs of the city and a right to participate rationally, condemning them to inarticulate outbursts of fury (and further condemning them for this sign of ignorance). To assert possession of knowledge, or knowledge as possession, was often to condemn others, perhaps the vast major-ity, to passivity, to the need for tutelage. Their superiors would assume the burdens of office, would even relieve them of the chore of voting, would become spokesmen, representatives and decision-makers. To make others, especially those in a situation of rivalry, feel ignorant is to disarm them. But to make *le peuple* feel ignorant (and despised as such) might, conversely, be a factor in making them fight back with the only arms they had, physical force, as when, for example, the despised *journaliers* (or casual day-labourers) marched to Aix in July 1789 to effect the release of workers and peasants arrested after riots the previous spring – after a riot at Aix provoked when a nobleman told a hungry crowd, composed mainly of women, that they could eat the droppings of his horse.[12]

Of course, when competing groups can, with some mutually recognised justification, lay claim to knowledge, albeit perhaps different types of knowledge, the ignorance of the masses can make them an easy prey to the propaganda of rivals and so the situation becomes complex. Then it may be in the interests of one faction to 'open the eyes of the people' – in the revolutionary cliché – but in ways which approach indoctrination, often not dispelling popular ignorance directly, and often using non-verbal means (*fêtes*, dress, emblems, symbols) as short-cuts, appealing mainly to the senses and not presupposing, still less encouraging, an intellectual 'capacity' which the educated considered a prerequisite of good judgement and therefore participation. In old regime Marseilles, the populace was to be impressed *only* via the senses (the mayor and aldermen called on the government for a pay rise to buy robes which would magically impress the people with their authority).[13] In the Revolution, appeals to the people's reason, rather than their passions, appeals to them to 'reflect seriously on their own interests', were attempted but they became increasingly desperate as the actual people increasingly failed to live up to the image of them entertained by the more idealistic revolutionaries. At the outset, at least, the people were often regarded (ignorantly) as ignorant, therefore 'good', like children, but gullible. For others to enlighten them, in *their* way, was the worst of crimes: better to leave them steeped in *préjugés*. After all, *préjugés* which suited the politician or pamphleteer were popular 'good sense'. And if the people did become turbulent, but again in ways convenient to the writer, they could, in the hot climate of Marseilles, so unconducive to thought, be excused as 'gay' and 'vivacious', though this too, while attractive, also showed them as prone to be misled.

One strategy, an almost structural feature of the old regime with its corporative framework but used tactically in the Revolution, was to divide knowledge: to recognise that certain people, especially among the popular classes, have specific types of knowledge but to use this to disqualify them from a wider competence. Indeed the more knowledge one might have in one field, the less one might be assumed to have of general, therefore important, knowledge. Artisans could be lavishly praised for their craft skills but it would be alleged that, outside the guild, their voice was worthless. This was a common argument in the old regime. The municipality, in increasing the wine tax, complained:

The poor artisans are being seduced, flattered by the imaginary hope of being freed from a necessary and endurable yoke. They are being aroused by the description of injustices in matters which they themselves would hardly be able to explain if they were asked about the affairs of the city.[14]

It was an argument used in 1789, by diehard upholders of the old regime, against 'empty heads' who dared intervene in politics, by taking part in assemblies or signing petitions when they should have been confined to working, eating and sleeping (thus one official condemned an artisan for being out at dusk in August 1789 and was nonplussed when the prisoner answered that he had been out getting fresh air; he asked another, who earned his living mending chairs, if 'he could prove that he was constantly at work').[15]

Political life at Marseilles in the spring and summer of 1789 was probably more intense than in any other city (Paris not necessarily excluded). The meetings of the guilds in March to draw up grievance–lists and elect deputies to the States General involved not just master-artisans but their workers too and spilled over into an insurrection which rendered almost powerless both the agents of royal government and the old municipality. Artisans joined the new municipality, guild meetings continued and were themselves politicised. Elections were frequent and time-consuming. Marseilles was the first city in France to establish, in March, a national guard and this too demanded commitment. Not surprisingly, therefore, moderates frequently deplored the working time wasted by artisans in political activity. Even patriots joined this chorus, stressing the need to keep the wheels of commerce turning.[16]

Yet patriots in 1789, always anxious to get the artisans on their side, could also reverse the argument. Precisely because a man showed competence in the mechanical arts, even managing a small business, he had the right to share in at least municipal decision-making. Thus in June–July, Mathieu Blanc-Gilly, the most articulate of the patriots, championed the right of artisans to enter the municipality (an enlarged municipality, to multiply *'les lumières'*) by condemning their detractors as vile and contemptible men who believed themselves to live still 'in those ignorant ages when the poor swooned at the sight of the stupid rich. Don't they know that geniuses of the first order generally come from the ranks of the poor?' In fact, either as citizens or men exercising the mechanical arts, having acquired a spirit of method and purpose, artisans were worthy to participate in town affairs. Stupidity, equated with a lack of patriotism, resided in not seeing the sagacity of the artisans: in turn, *their* penetration was confirmed by their ability to comprehend instantaneously (but instinctively rather than intellectually) Blanc-Gilly's own lengthy pamphlets. In January 1790, another patriot, Charles Barbaroux, successfully urged the election of artisans to the new, revolutionary municipality.[17] Naturally artisans themselves often rejected any attribution of ignorance. When in the Revolution corporative organisation was swept away and the guilds abolished, artisans *en masse* were theoretically freed to become entrepreneurs: middle-class Jacobin politicians rejoiced that, clearly, their minds were going to expand with their businesses.

Others crudely vituperated 'the ignorant populace' or showed bogus commiseration with 'an unfortunate people' abused by unscrupulous patriots who translated their speeches into the language of the fishwives.[18] Attempts were made to define the degree of ignorance of the people. In the words of an anti-patriot, they were sufficiently enlightened to realise that they had been wronged in the old regime but not knowledgeable enough to recognise suitable remedies, far less choose hands capable of administering them.[19]

Yet the division of knowledge did not affect only the people. On 25 August 1785, a rich and famous merchant, Dominique Bertrand, welcoming into the Academy a fellow *négociant*, complained of those who regarded merchants as fit only to concern themselves with professional matters and not to participate in the general philosophic culture of *les lumières*.[20] Hence even merchants, who dominated the Academy, where the most wide-ranging values associated with trade were 'ennobled' by praise from *confrères* drawn from the nobility and the learned, legal and healing professions – even they had to prove their cultural credentials and combat allegations that they were obsessed with and totally preoccupied by making money.[21] Their *positive* claim to wide knowledge, of history, of foreign countries and their cultures, of matters of government and international relations, hardly concerns us here,[22] yet it was basic to their push in 1789 for a strong voice in politics both locally and nationally. To win elections, they elbowed aside guildsmen whom they condemned as 'mostly illiterate' and ignorant of the interests of the city and the third estate.[23] The merchants' claims were based on a fundamental identification of the growth of trade (since the sixteenth century) and the decline of ignorance. Local *érudits* supplied a history of the city – and of civilisation – in which the rise of trade was prominent.[24] Capitalism was knowledge-intensive, if selectively, and knowledge-extensive, breaking down divisions. To a degree, this was itself widely recognised. Blanc-Gilly, though critical of the wealthiest merchants, affirmed that any man desiring a reputation in society needed commercial knowledge, without which he should remain silent on public ills and possible remedies. Here knowledge of trade was somewhat dissociated from actual traders.[25] Divisions remained. Jacques Seimandy, complaining of the old regime's failure to consult knowledgeable merchants, to alleviate governmental ignorance, regretted that the foremost *négociants* entered the nobility, thus decapitating the profession, depriving it of a 'luminous body of knowledge', stripping the remaining merchants of knowledge as well as prestige.[26] The divisive, wasteful organisation of society into Orders was deplored by merchants in 1789.

The government had undervalued merchants' knowledge, complained Seimandy, in a pamphlet adopted and adapted by the Chamber of Commerce when trying to ensure adequate merchant representation in the forthcoming States General.[27] The Chamber, deleting as too sharp references to 'a financial administration without principles, thoughtless, inconsequential' – that is, ignorant – asked the government rhetorically (but deleting from Seimandy's original the words here italicised): 'Does it realise the vast range of knowledge which a leading merchant must have *in jurisprudence, in politics, in geography*, and all the elements from which the science of commerce is composed?' Seimandy thus condemned 'merchants of the second rank', often the most active in the Revolution, to at least relative ignorance.[28] Economic divisions within professions were very marked at Marseilles.

The old regime was a fragmented system, its already divisive corporate structure (not including the merchants, however, who belonged to a 'free' profession) being further fissured by strains imposed by commercial growth and an increase in the population.[29] Knowledge too was hoarded, or distributed parsimoniously. Secrecy was of its essence. The spread of knowledge of public affairs was minimal. The government was often itself ignorant – indeed the king was protected by a mythical and symbolic ignorance, to enable him to be absolved of responsibility for the misdeeds of his entourage. But, on a more mundane level, the government was ignorant even of its own workings, of its financial situation. Assuredly its evident ignorance of Marseilles could be advantageous to a city fearful lest bad news, of violent strikes for example, reached Versailles. But government policy also often threatened the privileges of the city. However, since even the municipality was ignorant of the precise nature of its privileges (regarding taxation, the administration of justice), disputes arose frequently and were tediously and destructively prolonged.[30] When the government summoned the city to produce accounts, the blind called to the blind. Moreover the city's highly ambiguous status as a 'free port' which was not free in every respect produced complaints of government violations mainly on behalf of the fisc. Indignant memoranda were despatched.[31] They did not resolve problems, but Marseilles educated the capital in economics, a thankless task continued in the Revolution. Marseilles produced no accounts, however, and was ignorant of the extent of its debts. This provided a convenient excuse for inactivity. At Marseilles, too, secrecy prevailed. When, in 1779, Ferréol Beaugeard proposed establishing a newspaper, to include reports on the deliberations of the Chamber of Commerce (significantly not of the municipality), he got a frosty reception from the authorities.[32] A campaign for a public library failed, partly for lack of municipal support.[33] Just as national laws were uncollected, so the 'laws and statutes' of Marseilles were dispersed. The city archives were a shambles.[34]

The demand in 1789 for accountability was a demand for the diffusion of knowledge, to dispel ignorance, especially perhaps the ignorance of the educated, though there would always be specialisation in expertise, to parallel the division of labour. But in 1789 a 'transparent' system of government – and nothing was more transparent than clear accounts – was one where all forms of knowledge were quickly communicated, though not necessarily to everyone. To go any significant way towards this objective would require the overthrow of the existing regime. Not for nothing did merchants, influenced by Montesquieu, admire Westminster, where conflicting viewpoints were argued out before an informed opinion and where knowledge of trade was a qualification for, not a bar to, political participation.[35] Almost by definition, a representative regime dispelled ignorance and collected facts, providing a focus for discussions hitherto ineffective, since dispersed. As each element in the old regime replicated the vices of the larger whole, especially in their secrecy, the whole system was dysfunctional. The claims of the third estate, the 'nothing' that wished to be 'everything', burst through the bonds of corporate ignorance.

Based on knowledge and the right to greater knowledge, patriotism considered that enlightenment, like trade, was now destined for a much more conscious development and dissemination.

If the Revolution redefined everything – notions of history, of change, of politics, of social hierarchy, of family relationships – knowledge and ignorance could not escape this process and were, indeed, constituents of it. Concern with the way knowledge was produced and broadcast, or not, had preoccupied those who spoke at, or wrote for, the city's vigorous Academy. Now, in 1789, a new, qualitatively different era opened.

In social terms, and speaking schematically, one might argue that a type of 'aristocratic' or noble knowledge had been honoured in the old regime, while concomitantly a type of aristocratic ignorance appeared praiseworthy. Knowledge of precedents, ancestors or charters was fine. Mirabeau, a maverick nobleman, when challenged on 8 February 1789 to state whether he owned any 'noble' land, which alone would entitle him to enter the assembly of Provençal (*not* Marseillais) nobility and hence give access to political power, answered: 'I do not carry my archives in my pocket.' So he was excluded and forged a political career at the head of the third estate. Accusing the nobility of an ignorance and inconstancy which disqualified them from politics, praising the merchants of Marseille – *'le négociant seul connaît l'univers'* – Mirabeau, though elected for Aix, was indeed an excellent spokesman for Marseilles's patriotic and commercial interests, relaying arguments and information provided by the Marseillais.[36]

Yet Mirabeau was an exception. Ignorance of mundane matters, such as those of bank and *maison de commerce*, might, for others less gifted for a career as transfuge, be a sign of true nobility: let our servants do our counting – or even thinking – for us. Certainly movement within sections of the French nobility from one type of knowledge to another has been highlighted, perhaps excessively,[37] on a national scale; but it was not very apparent among the intransigent backwoods nobility of Provence, either cut off from access to knowledge, disinclined to face the ardours of its acquisition, or understandably loyal to old forms of thought.[38] Yet in 1789, petty lawyers from the smallest Provençal townships expatiated on the seven or eight centuries of 'feudal' ignorance from which they were escaping, thanks to knowledge of natural rights. The knowledge of the nobility was obsolete and inappropriate, dating from before the existence of a merchant navy, from a time before trade had aided the development of printing, geometry, surveying, philosophy and all the other sciences pioneered by men of talent rather than of birth.[39] Some members of the nobility conceded the superiority of the third estate, in wielding abstract ideas, in the use – or rather abuse – of talents. Boisgelin, conceited archbishop of Aix, trying to dominate the political scene in Provence, deplored the injustice of its third estate, the nullity of its clergy, the stupidity (*bêtise*) of its nobility.[40] However, the nobility *within Marseilles* was ideologically (as well as numerically) weak, precisely because it was linked closely with the trading community and had largely espoused its values. In 1789, Seimandy jokingly pretended not to know if there were any 'real' nobles at Marseilles, so unobtrusive was their presence. Thus Marseilles merchants, feeling locally secure, felt all the more able to scorn the noblemen of Provence as ignorant.[41]

Merchant claims to knowledge – modern knowledge – were based on professional expertise, accusations of whose alleged 'narrowness' were eloquently and eruditely refuted. With regard to the nobility, social rank and the classification of knowledge into useless/useful did not coincide, perhaps a sign of a society in crisis or in need of change, a general realignment, for within each social group (but these were increasingly difficult to define according to traditional criteria) divisions were appearing which were at least partially related to divisions between, and attitudes to, ignorance and knowledge. The commercial classes had tried, within the old regime, to create a space for their activities and resented constant intrusions, especially from an ill-informed government unduly influenced by the privileged Orders. In disrupting the merchants' activities, the government destroyed future confidence, creating a distrust and suspicion which 'shrank' ideas and discouraged enterprise.[42] Thus, if trade were to expand, not only would noble values, and the tendency of some merchants to seek nobility and perhaps quit commerce, have to be overcome, but government interference be reduced. Both government and merchants were entangled in a multitude of incomprehensible laws and regulations, not only confusing but encouraging dishonesty and fraud. For Blanc-Gilly, in 1789, and he was at least a part-time merchant, 'whenever there is neither exact weight nor measurement, there is nothing just, constant or true'.[43] This was perhaps a move towards a redefinition of knowledge, which condemned whole areas of past knowledge to the realm of obscurantism, anecdote and ignorance.

But new areas of ignorance were also being uncovered. Certain assumptions of knowledge were called into question, or turned into *préjugé*, so that even the enlightened classes might have their confidence shaken. Of course a realisation of one's ignorance might be the first step to doing something to remedy it. A new recognition of certain ignorances at least, and a demand for more knowledge, might unite those who wanted change, especially if it was felt that crucial types of knowledge had been deliberately denied them. If ignorance was not their fault and could be blamed on someone else, the desire for knowledge might encourage acts – the writing of pamphlets, the fiery declamation of speeches – which boosted confidence. One could also delight in classifying as ignorant men, groups or classes hitherto seen as invulnerable and superior. Many patriots 'opened their eyes' only in 1789. They bitterly condemned those who had kept them in the dark.

Perhaps long acceptance of the *status quo* had derived from ignorance of the possibility of anything better, of the very possibility of men radically changing their world, or from ignorance that others wanted this too (despite the emergence of new forms of sociability at Marseilles, as elsewhere). But in 1789, what had seemed natural, even rational, often suddenly appeared time-bound and expedient. For example, at Marseilles, taxes were almost exclusively placed on basic foodstuffs – bread, meat and wine. In 1789 this system was attacked, first of all in Blanc-Gilly's pamphlet *Plan de révolution*, for a multitude of not always well-integrated reasons: humanitarian, in that it oppressed the poor labouring man with many mouths to feed; economic, in that it pushed up prices, including (allegedly) wages, thus pricing Marseilles goods out of world markets. The fact that revenue raised was not accounted for was an aggravating factor. With unusual frankness, the merchant Jacques Seimandy confessed that he had always considered this tax system just and appropriate to Marseilles, indeed part of the city's constitution (dating back to republican, even Greek, times). But now that he had been forced really to think about it he confessed his former ignorance and acknowledged the tax's disadvantages (possibly to himself, as merchant and employer of labour).[44]

The debate on taxation was a breakthrough, pushing forward the Revolution rapidly at Marseilles. From being *chasse gardée*, the city's finances stimulated fierce and wide-ranging debate, producing arguments both sophisticated and sophistical. Among the proliferation of words, statistics and pseudo-statistics, some fairly convincing knowledge emerged, but acres of ignorance were exposed. On 23 March, a popular insurrection swept the old tax away.[45] This was partly provoked by objective hardship – real dearth – but the crisis was made to appear worse by allegations of huge profiteering by the municipality. Rumours, such as allegations that the Intendant had banned the 'export' of potatoes to the free port, were easily spread in a climate of ignorance.[46] Moreover the municipality, urged a month earlier to cut food prices, refused, saying that this would be an avowal (either of immoderate profits or of too-high food prices) which would risk encouraging popular insubordination.[47] Detailed analysis of events suggests that a least some men of the educated and propertied classes were quite happy that the physical force of the 'ignorant multitude' had done so quickly what rational reasoning could not easily have achieved; others – or the same, for attitudes fluctuated with events – blamed the disturbances on patriotic pamphlets. The patriots, embarrassed, sometimes distanced themselves, blaming troubles not on 'the good people of Marseilles' but on foreign sailors and vagabonds, the flotsam and jetsam of the Mediterranean, but sometimes even justified the riots and acknowledged their own role.

Perhaps the people hardly needed to be told that they were exploited, and were saying so in their *cahiers*[48] in March, but before Blanc-Gilly's pamphlet (of January 1789) there is little evidence of protest. Anyway the old municipality would have turned a blind eye, for it tried to ignore abuses out of pusillanimity, contempt for the people and an acute sense of impotence. (To draw attention to abuses, yet fail to eradicate them was to be disastrous for the government.)

Whether the abuses concerned the city's main industry, soap-making, labour disputes or the 'plague' of gambling and the crime wave of the late 1780s, a 'see no evil' policy was resolutely maintained, ultimately provoking the patriotic pamphlets of 1789 which at least revealed abuses. But the secrecy and restricted politics of the old regime made the patriots vulnerable to the accusation that, ignorant themselves, they led the still more ignorant: Blanc-Gilly was 'the hero of the market place and street', idolised by the illiterate. However contacts between the patriots and the people were varied and would be a fascinating object of analysis. A single incident may be cited here. One aspect of the old tax system had been praised by the city's assessor on 29 December 1788: it involved no special summons to payment, so the poor paid it gladly and unaware (this argument had 'taken in' Seimandy). However to test this, one patriot appealed directly to experience. He had gone down to the port and questioned the dock workers (*portefaix*), one of whom had answered, 'in these remarkable words: *I wish that each penny extra which they make us pay cost them a pound of blood*'.[49]

To introduce a fair and rational tax required a lot of factual evidence. If it was to be a poll tax, what was the population of Marseilles? C. F. Achard wrote: 'There are 120 000 people at Marseilles, though the last count found only 75 000.'[50] If it was to be a graduated income tax, how to measure the income of different persons or collectivities? If a tax on houses, how many were there? (Houses were not numbered, though patriotic masons hastened to do this free, to the alarm of their occupants.) If house size was to be considered, this was still more complex. To divide the burden between owner–occupiers, tenants and so on would be a nightmare (or a bureaucrat's paradise). If industry was to be taxed, how many guilds were there? Even this was not known until the guilds were made the basis for the States General elections. The different size of the guilds and vast discrepancies of wealth between them – but even more strikingly within them – made comparison difficult. If trade was to be taxed, what about commercial fortunes and profits? Merchants, keen on openness in other respects, were frightened of it here: for all too many, their fortunes were only known, if at all, at the bankruptcy court.

Even more dubious were speculations about the effects of certain tax proposals on rents, house prices, jobs, exports, and on the consumption of various goods. A tax on luxuries, carriages for instance, might hit workers and artisans; this revived one of the most famous academic controversies in a practical, political context. A tax on male domestics might halt the (alleged) depopulation of the countryside. One on celibate males (over 30) might curb prostitution and would penalise the selfish rich, since, according to mythology rather than fact, only the poorer classes, influenced by *préjugés* or yielding to instinct, married and procreated freely.[51] A tax on wine might improve health and morality but might also weaken the dock labourer, kept strong only by liquor. Too great a tax burden on the poor might stunt mental as well as physical development at a time when the hospital of the Insensés was said to be offering shelter to more and more unfortunates from the lower classes.[52] Other taxes might attain footloose 'capitalists', foreigners, or entrap marginals, like the Catalan fishermen, in a new web of bureaucratic control. For censuses were begun, proposals made for a *cadastre*, for the registration of property transactions and capital transfers. The tentacles of a fiscal bureaucracy threatened the newly-emancipated citizenry with a permanent inquisition, an oppressive *quadrillage*, aimed, in a would-be scientific manner, at social stereotypes (the rich property-owner, the capitalist, the *célibataire*), victims of a vindictiveness which, from fiscal, might become fatal. Many acute points were raised regarding social, political and moral economy, as society became an object of increasingly detailed but often unwelcome scrutiny.

Though local tax plans were mostly abortive, national taxes, aiming for social justice, were placed on property, income and profession, providing historians with copious information. They were the formal basis for much revolutionary policy. Since political citizenship was now theoretically based on tax-paying capacity, crucial questions were involved here. At Marseilles, however, virtually everyone above the rank of vagabond had to be allowed to vote because no one knew how many 'active citizens' there were.[53] This local 'decision' seemed to the *modérés* lawless, allowing *gens sans aveu* into the primary assemblies, threatening complete anarchy, intensifying social conflict. This non-implementation of national laws of citizenship revealed both national and local bureaucratic weakness but also Marseilles's *mauvaise volonté*. It shows Marseilles, in the democratic Revolution as in the autocratic old regime, taking advantage of distance to mislead the government, exaggerating its ignorance of French legislation for its own purposes. This, and other instances of ignorance real or feigned, branded Marseilles in government circles as a lawless, recalcitrant city, aiming for independence, perhaps for a republic. This image of rebellion, sometimes magnified by the city's opulent disaffected, always ready to speak of 'streets running with blood', encouraged pre-emptive acts of extremism. These, in turn, helped to produce a reaction, the serious anti-Paris, anti-Jacobin revolt of the summer of 1793, bloodily crushed in the Terror.[54]

Taxation was a vexed question. Had the tax burden been increased or decreased by the Revolution? No one really knew, though the revolutionaries, arguing that property and commercial fortunes were now taxed, deployed statistics to show a lower burden on the lower classes. The counter-revolutionaries disputed this, and built up an extensive popular clientèle which took part in the 1793 revolt. In fact, despite a wishful thinking which equated patriotism and a willingness to pay taxes, evasion was rife. Non-payers swelled the lists of suspects and a bankrupt Revolution's *fuite en avant* into counter-productive ideological extremism was based at least partly on fiscal incompetence, inexperience and ignorance.[55]

Another question was crucially involved here. Was trade booming or collapsing in the first years of the Revolution? The new regime of liberty in trade and industry was acclaimed, since former restrictions had held back 'intelligence' as well as economic expansion. The guilds, for example, had preserved ignorance from the bracing winds of competition. Revolutionaries affirmed the prosperity of trade, whereas their opponents argued that political disturbances were having disastrous consequences, that merchants were exporting capital or emigrating, so that the labouring population would soon lose their jobs and starve. In a rare appeal to incontrovertible facts, the mayor hurried down to the Vieux Port and asked the customs authorities for figures of harbour movements. He was able to show that trade, in November 1790, was booming.[56] This did not end polemics but it might have steadied merchant support for the Revolution at this stage – complain though merchants invariably did – and it may have temporarily reduced antagonism to them from extremists among the Jacobins and the lower classes. With the war against Britain, however, the collapse of trade in the spring of 1793 was incontrovertible. Hence, again, popular support for the counter-revolution.

In the feverish atmosphere of revolution, evidence had indeed to be overwhelming before being – if at all – accepted. Ignorance, or a reputation for ignorance, could be a resource, to be cultivated, even hoarded, before being exploited. Moreover ignorance could be convenient: Dominique Bertrand referred to the 'voluntary' ignorance of those who did not wish to know how hard the old tax had hit the poor and who therefore wished to restore it, still feeling that the people would not notice it.[57] Revolutionaries accused their opponents, blinded by egoism and particular interests, of deliberately remaining ignorant of the tribulations of the lower classes. An unwillingness to face unwelcome facts was not, of course, the monopoly of any party, though the revolutionaries prided themselves on their openness, publishing budgets, accounts and explaining at length the new taxes. Yet historians can easily show that the Jacobins, once in power, often just did not want to know about the profound causes of popular discontent, preferring to blame the rich and educated for misleading the poor and ignorant.

Conversely, those of the lower classes who could plead ignorance of the new laws which they transgressed sometimes found this effective, especially if they could indeed prove that they had been led astray, especially by priests, who often knew much more about the plight of the poor than careerist politicians. If men, or especially women, were of a social group – peasants or fisherfolk, for example – thought by their superiors to be 'naturally' ignorant (and even for the self-appointed *amis du peuple* there was an ignorance 'appropriate' for certain classes) they could win an indulgence which, in the Terror, might save lives. Usually the implied lesson was that the ignorant should keep out of politics, even the new democratic politics, at least before benefiting from decades of *instruction* by their new political masters, unless, of course, their help was immediately wanted, in emergencies, where physical force or mass intimidation hardly needed knowledge. However, popular manpower – in the National Guard – was essential and political praxis was itself a political pedagogy. But one group to whom the more timid revolutionaries would dearly have loved to deny such pedagogy were the soldiers, to be kept in ignorance through isolation. The more radical patriots, however, saw the soldiers as having been blind automata in the old regime. Now they were to think for themselves, even to question orders. Their presence in political meetings was therefore encouraged.

Yet the *instruction* imparted by the Revolution was not very effective, despite the catechisms and dialogues putting points simply, for the unsophisticated, as well as numerous festivals and ceremonies. Interminable electoral meetings alienated many workers from a Revolution 'whose benefits they were too ignorant to see'. Some well-meaning patriots suggested over-ingenious means whereby the illiterate could get others to register their votes. Even the most committed revolutionaries, however, despaired of a people so easy to seduce. But others affirmed that patriotism transcended ignorance while the municipality, in its battle against the Chamber of Commerce, maintained, in December 1791, that the Revolution had indeed enlightened the people. Freed from servitude, their ideas now went beyond concern for merely physical existence. Today the people reasoned on all sorts of crucial questions, with justice and discernment. They, unlike the merchants of the Chamber, could tell the difference between honest trade and harmful speculation in goods and *assignats*. Such self-serving optimism was, however, short-lived. The incident tells us more about Jacobin attitudes to the merchants than to the actual people, who were merely ciphers.[58]

Attitudes to social groups of a more definable configuration than 'the people', 'the poor' or 'the rich' (though these labels were common), are a rewarding subject for cultural historians confronting the years of Revolution. The attitudes of different groups to each other, including problems as to how they were defined in discourse, ritual or by symbol; their place in the 'social imaginary' of the revolutionaries; their self-image, with their perception of their own histories and traditions, their aspirations for the future – these topics allow the cultural historian to cut through some of the rather artificial barriers between different types of history. Of course, in a situation of prevalent ignorance, stereotypes were tempting, easily drawn from the moralistic literature of eighteenth-century sensibility: the miser; the employer who seduced his female servant as the first stage on her road to prostitution; or the clever but unscrupulous creditor entangling the modest merchant in webs of indebtedness, getting him thrown into prison, there to mix with the dregs of society (but released, to general patriotic rejoicing, in 1789); or the dissolute and preferably aristocratic gambler tempting the honest but somewhat limited artisan with prospects of sudden wealth, with similarly disastrous consequences.

We might, however, wonder if, among the insults flying around revolutionary Marseilles, and among the panegyrics too, some were not more accurate than others, approaching more nearly 'reality', that reality perhaps approached more nearly by subsequent historians, perhaps able to draw on a wider range or even a different type of evidence and doubtless posing rather different questions. Perhaps both contemporaries and historians could extract a pattern or patterns from the mass of discursive material produced in 1789, patterns revealed by specific arguments, but also by changes in image, perspective, language – as definitions and attitudes were altered in the heat of controversy? And would patterns discerned by contemporaries resemble those which might be imposed by historians? Would their sense or meaning be the same?

Here only the briefest comments may be ventured, though voluminous attempts were made at accurate definitions. Yet even the merchant was difficult to define in a city where everyone, somehow, traded and where the merchant *was* the person who was seen as such. However, perceptions of the merchant varied greatly. He could be regarded, and not just by himself, as a cultural hero of the Enlightenment (and now his libraries can be examined;[59] his paintings catalogued; his attempts at versification admired; his attendance at the theatre noted; his presence in masonic lodges, *confréries* and other forms of sociability chronicled;[60] his philanthropy praised; his mismanagement of hospitals criticised; his contributions to knowledge at the Academy appreciated; his frequentations and residences mapped;[61] his testaments computerised).[62] The eminent merchant, at least, carried an impressive cultural cargo, which could be exploited but which, in the choppy seas of the Terror, might have to be jettisoned. More happily, trade was the basis of civilisation; each ship, it was said, carried its cargo of ideas. Merchants 'liked' liberty, as Montesquieu, thinking of Marseilles, had argued. They exhibited an independent outlook. Self-made men who created so much of the nation's wealth should have some say in how that wealth was used. Keeping their own affairs in order, they might do the same for those of the *patrie*. Men who gave employment to the lower classes deserved their support and that of the country as a whole. Indeed they might 'represent' all who toiled in trade and industry.[63]

Sometimes, however, such attitudes seemed arrogant and the merchant appeared avaricious and egotistical, aping the nobility. He might also appear complacent or, conversely, as restless, insatiable, unstable, always spawning new needs and uncomfortable desires (though these too could be given a favourable connotation).

The *bourgeois* often saw trade as bringing to Marseilles inflation, over-population, attracting a floating population, the 'scum of the Mediterranean', threatening life, property and tranquillity, propagating disease, increasing crime, threatening *mœurs* – and participating in the most dangerous episodes of the Revolution. But this was perhaps a defensive, defeatist reaction from a timid, unimaginative sector of society to a group whose dynamism cannot really be dismissed. Sometimes the old municipality, made up mainly of *bourgeois* and *propriétaires*, showed hostility to the merchants.[64] A clash between proprietary and mobile wealth may have underlain this antagonism. And, indeed, the historian may read from such evidence of the way different groups perceived each other – through a penumbra of ignorance and misinformation – not only a pattern but a sense of direction. In *ancien régime* Marseilles, where there was a property qualification for municipal office, the bourgeois property-owners regarded themselves as the true citizens, alone committed fully to the city. Retired merchants could join the group. In 1789, however, the *active*, wealth-creating, employment-providing merchant became the hero of the hour.

However, as early as 1789, patriots accused at least the richest merchants of wishing to replace an aristocracy of birth by one of wealth, of consuming the wealth won by their fathers, of not investing enough in trade. Trade itself was a lottery with rewards for the most unscrupulous. The rich merchants, unpatriotic themselves, punished their dependants (sea-captains, clerks) for showing an interest in politics.[65] Nor did they endear themselves to the more extreme revolutionaries by using their knowledge and experience to warn against 'excessive' issues of *assignats*. In these circumstances it was natural that the patriots should woo the artisans. By a well-established tradition, they were invariably 'interesting', 'respectable', 'honest', industrious, content with their mediocre lot, living exemplary family lives. It was only with difficulty that the Jacobins could bring themselves to recognise their all too human tendency to stay away from political meetings, to shirk guard service and avoid paying the new tax upon their industry. Yet they did show an impressive commitment to the Revolution and deserved their reputation as its 'solid bulwark'. They formed a stratum in which the cracks appearing under the pressure of merchant capitalism were a powerful dissolvant force but were ignored as much as possible in Jacobin rhetoric.

But some evidence shows that the well-off and enterprising

artisan or *fabricant*, now sometimes termed a *manufacturier*, was becoming more assertive, assuming a more positive image, defining a more independent interest. This assertiveness naturally involved a claim to knowledge and a repudiation of ignorance. Some artisans in 1789, when drafting their *cahiers*, did confess ignorance of 'political' matters, outside their corporative concerns, and some were aided by patriotic ideologues (distrusted by the merchants for their ignorance of practical matters, unforgivable in a trading city). But others affirmed that *'nous les manufacturiers'* alone knew of, and could therefore speak of, the conditions of the majority of the city's population, a clear rejection of merchant hegemony.[66] In 1790 and 1791, backed by a municipality claiming a wider view of trade than the merchants, because more appreciative of the contribution of agriculture and manufacturing, the Chamber of Commerce was forced to admit manufacturers, sea-captains and retail merchants (*marchands*). Maintaining that Marseilles had become a manufacturing a well as a commercial city, they tried to get their grievances directly to Paris, where Pierre Peloux, a deputy at the National Assembly, championed the interests of *'la classe manufacturière'*[67], rather than via the Chamber. They struggled with the merchants over control of raw materials in a blatantly economic conflict, accusing *négociants* of exporting materials needed in local industry and of speculating in them as the *assignat* fell in value. Merchants also restricted the importation of certain raw materials, yet imported cheap and nasty foreign manufactured goods, such as ropes, thus throwing Marseilles firms out of business and endangering sailors' lives. Championing – very selectively – 'free trade', the merchants claimed that any momentary dearth of goods at Marseilles would soon be made up as merchants hurried to import them to benefit from higher prices. They accused the manufacturers of ignorance of the true principles of political economy, manifested by their petty protectionism. However the manufacturers, sea-captains – and the municipality – attacked the concentration of wealth at Marseilles and argued that many small profits were better than huge speculative *coups*, that a large number of small fortunes was better for the State than a few grotesquely bloated ones.[68] Often a more modest economic status was equated by the revolutionaries with greater economic and political dynamism. The negative image of the really rich merchant, outlined above, could be 'sans-culotticised', forcing many to emigrate, and bringing some to the guillotine.

Yet most sectors of the city's active population could also unite, often behind the Chamber of Commerce, when arguing for the general commercial *and* industrial interests of the city, not invariably or even mainly conflicting, in the face of the ignorance or hostility of government, rival ports or towns of the interior. The sea-captains, often resentful of merchant control, could also join the Chamber in deploring the ignorance of noble naval officers, of noble consuls in the Levant, ex-*militaires* who disdained defending France's commercial interests and whose attitudes to the Turks had been formed at Paris by exaggerated tales from travellers such as Volney, 'spinner of pretty phrases'.[69] Extremely militant in many ways, they might also attack the patriots as 'négrophiles', recklessly ignorant of how millions of Frenchmen depended on the continuance of slavery and the slave trade.[70]

However, despite this belated introduction of certain complications into our analysis, (and, in the complex and fluctuating situation at Marseilles, many more could be added), we may perhaps be accused of having imposed something which looks suspiciously like a vulgar Marxist schema, postulating change from feudalism to proprietorial capitalism, to commercial capitalism and, finally, to manufacturing capitalism, thus compressing centuries of an already crude version of history into a few years. However, we can at least refer to the 'uneven development' of a thrusting cosmopolitan world port 'affixed' to a peripheral, particularist province, home of some of the most notoriously reactionary feudalists in France. Concepts of 'culture clash' seem relevant here. Moreover we would argue that concepts of interest were frequently debated by revolutionaries, P. L. Roederer of Metz, for example, bringing an industrial interest into theoretical existence.[71] Various economic interests had been discussed in essay competitions for the Academy of Marseilles. In revolutionary debate and struggle, interests became somewhat better defined and perhaps more outward-looking. Certainly Blanc-Gilly, attacking the most opulent merchants for forming 'a snobbish, stupid, ignorant and ferocious aristocracy', contemptuous of the people, condemned them for being ignorant of even their own interests, in their obsession with distinctions and privileges, their refusal to welcome the regime of liberty.[72] But the reform of the

Chamber of Commerce aimed at uniting more varied 'knowledges' and reconciling a wider spectrum of interests.

It is not therefore the case that in drawing attention to interests, a literal-minded historian, desperately seeking evidence of a firm, simplistic underlying 'reality', has extracted from a bewildering variety of sources, mostly of a literary (that is, non-quantitative) nature, a few stray indications, giving them undue prominence as a key to complex struggles going on 'overhead' in the realm of consciousness. Certainly, even with the evidence we have used, our impression of a discernible socio-economic evolution is supported, more or less clearly, by only a small proportion of our sources, many of which, moreover, are polemical pamphlets, marked not only by ignorance but sometimes by deceit, exploiting ignorance rather than dissipating it. But some of our most interesting sources are documents, often no less combative in tone, which come directly from the economic sphere, from the guilds and the excellent Chamber of Commerce archives.

We have been 'culturalist' in our approach, starting from the superstructure, rather than reading this off from the base. The revolutionaries engaging in polemics sensed only dimly the nature of the antagonisms which they articulated or the interests for which they fought. It is perhaps not for historians to say what the *real* significance of the issues was. Yet, if only because we have access to sources of which most of them were ignorant, we can make some quite definite points. Commercial correspondence shows, for example, many merchants not only committing the sins they were accused of – using raw materials speculatively – but privately boasting of it, while still fearing retribution.[73] But further exploration might usefully attempt to measure the extent to which a 'harder' history would confirm or undermine impressions gained from our survey of attitudes and perceptions. The powerful rise of Marseilles's commercial bourgeoisie has been brilliantly analysed by the late Charles Carrière, using all the resources of economic history allied to a keen feeling for his city's traditions.[74] The emergence of manufacturers likewise needs to be documented with statistics on specifically industrial growth, on the number and size of workshops and so on, statistics, however, hardly available at Marseilles for the brief, disrupted period of the Revolution. Sources which combine economic data and material throwing light on attitudes, include bankruptcy records and inventories of the possessions of *émigrés* and *guillotinés*. Even a subject as apparently arid as the debts of Marseilles's 'collectivités publiques' – the city itself, its hospitals, charitable institutions – has been made to illuminate the far from edifying attitudes of Marseilles's leading citizens.[75] Despite gaps, the revolutionaries, asserting the power of Knowledge and crusading against Ignorance, produced statistical surveys which historians can use in ways which their originators hardly envisaged. Perhaps in some contexts historians can even measure ignorance as a key element of the circumstances which historical actors had to face or a dimension of the structuration which constrains but also stimulates all activity, including thought.

Numerous areas of experience are amenable to a statistical treatment which should cast light on aspects of the problem of ignorance. Literacy rates and statistics on educational provision; participation rates in various forms of sociability, or in religious observance; data on electoral sociology – these, and many other sources, can provide useful indications regarding the implantation of the 'new' political culture.[76] The analysis of discourse, as practised at Marseilles by Jacques Guilhaumou, likewise illuminates political attitudes and *mentalités*.[77] However, where wide contexts are concerned, methods need to be varied and eclectic. Probably little that is precise and clear-cut can be said, for example, about the command of language in a city where a brand (or brands) of Provençal formed the habitual speech medium of most citizens for most of the time, without that necessarily implying an ignorance of French, at least in any very clear way. The educated elite's attitudes to Provençal were extraordinarily ambivalent. By 1789, the pure and noble language of the troubadours had become mixed, in the towns, with all the languages and dialects of the Mediterranean, including Turkish, yet – some considered – was not so debased as to be beyond retrieval or regeneration. In 1789, Provençal became suspect to the old authorities when used by patriots to address the peasants. Subsequently, 'l'idiome provençal' or 'le jargon provençal' became suspect to the patriots, potentially subversive of a revolutionary order embodied in a standardised (and impoverished?) French. However, types of pidgin Provençal or mickey-mouse Marseillais might be put into the mouths of 'the people' – peasants, artisans, sailors – saying how happy they were under the Revolution. Clearly there are differences of register here which the outsider cannot easily comprehend. But it is only remarkably recently that problems of language have been studied seriously by historians of Provence and Languedoc. They, however, are affected by the very delicate political issues involved in studying, or rehabilitating, as the *renaissantistes* desire, the various *langues d'oc*.[78] Yet access to language resources (or even a positive non-access, as when the local newspaper carried an advert for a domestic who spoke *only* French) was a key element in access to political culture, as was mastery of acceptable or respectable idioms (in the sense of modes of discourse), if the voices of 'the ignorant', of for example women,[79] are to make themselves heard directly rather than – all too often for the historian – through lawyers or other spokesmen.

In the scientific field too, quantitative methods can only supply a bit of the story. In the soap industry, we know, from statistics, that the largest producers were merchants. But the whole industry was split by conflicts with complex ramifications. These *négociants* were accused of trying to squeeze out the 'real' manufacturers by monopolising raw materials and by enforcing a summer closure period; for in the hot sun, they alleged, only poor-quality soap could be made. The more modest *fabricants*, who could not easily survive this inactivity, resisted a so-called scientific test designed to detect sub-standard soap, proposed by their richer colleagues backed by the municipality. Upholding a concept of knowledge as *savoir-faire*, closely tied to experience, silent and inarticulate, the *fabricants* denied that laboratory tests could be applied in the workshop, while the proponents of regulations and 'scientific' inspections argued that the more empirically skilled the *fabricant*, the more easily he was able to cheat the consumer (naturally the poor and ignorant consumer) by the artful presentation of a fraudulent product. While the small producers, or rather their lawyers, quoted Raynal to maintain that consumer interest would best be protected by freedom and competition, the whole matter was sent to Paris, with scientists such as Guyton de Morveau involved in adjudicating the rival claims of competing types of knowledge. Language was involved here too, for if soap was a *'denrée'* – as *my* dictionary suggests it is – then the municipality was correct in claiming a bitterly-contested right to enforce inspection.[80] In other matters concerning health – urban hygiene, health care on board ship, the reform of medical education, conditions in the city's hospitals – fraud, malpractice and ignorance were challenged by reform plans purportedly based on higher forms of knowledge. In this area, too, the concept of ignorance would be worth exploring.[81]

Thus, perhaps, the historian can hope to dispel some of the ignorances of the agents of history, while taking account of ignorance when assessing and analysing their actions and perceptions. It is fascinating to follow the correspondence between Versailles and Marseilles relating to the troubles of the spring and summer of 1789 and to note the dissensions between ministers which undermined their collective resolve, to see which agents in Provence – themselves at sixes and sevens – had lost the confidence of their superiors or, like the Intendant, had early given up the struggle to maintain the old regime. It is instructive to see how the government, in June 1789, could perspicaciously 'deconstruct' a would-be reassuring report by the military commander of Provence, having perhaps learned the lesson of a previous complacency born at least partly from unavoidable ignorance. On 29 March they had written to the commander that a revolt at Manosque on the eighteenth would be unlikely to have consequences elsewhere. We know, however, that this was a trigger for a wave of insurrections affecting much of Provence (with Marseilles plunged into turmoil on 23 March), producing a volatile situation in which no one incident could be isolated.[82] To have the text of a secret appeal, on 19 August 1789, by some of the richest citizens of Marseilles to obtain the entry of royal troops into the city to repress revolt rather supports patriotic allegations of the 'conspiracies' of their enemies which are now often derided as paranoiac.[83] And to read the minutes of committees of merchants and municipal officers concerned with food supplies is not only to acquire knowledge of purchases and stocks, prices and exchange rates, but also to feel the intense anxieties and dreads, to appreciate the good judgement or sheer luck involved in trying to buy gradually, without triggering panic purchases by others or reactivating the atavistic fears aroused by dearth, culminating in apocalyptic visions of the firing of the port in the frenzied violence of the dispossessed.[84]

Whether any progress was made on the road towards the eradication of ignorance, the assertion of mastery, the elimination of unintended consequences, may be doubted. Perhaps after 1789 the future became more unpredictable rather than less. Perhaps the Terror did attempt a draconian repression of a new uncertainty, only to plunge France and the world into experiences which proved how illusory, how dangerous, reliance on reason, or on certain concepts of reason, might be, experiences in which men and women's notions of knowledge and ignorance were deepened and strengthened, though not their control of the forces newly unleashed. Or perhaps we might conclude cynically: was it not Voltaire who said that the sum total of ignorance – or the crimes and follies of mankind – never varies much through the ages?

Notes

I would like to express my gratitude to Arnaud Ramière de Fortanier, and to his family, who have made my frequent visits to Marseilles so rewarding and enjoyable.

1. Besançon, Bibliothèque municipale, Correspondence of Dominique Audibert, MS 1413, letter to Abbé Bignon, 25 July 1789. Audibert, a leading merchant of Marseilles, was a friend of Voltaire, with whom he had exchanged an interesting correspondence.
2. Lynn Hunt, *Politics, Culture and Class in the French Revolution*, Berkeley, California, 1984.
3. François Furet, *Interpreting the French Revolution*, Cambridge, 1981.
4. The *concours* on Cook was being competed for at the start of the Revolution. L. T. Dassy, *L'Académie de Marseille*, Marseilles, 1877, provides an inventory of the Academy's archives.
5. Michel Vovelle, *Piété baroque et déchristianisation*, Paris, 1973.
6. For stimulating discussions of such problems, see Michel Vovelle, *Idéologies et mentalités*, Paris, 1982, and *La mentalité révolutionnaire*, Paris, 1985.
7. See, for example, P. Chaunu, *Au cœur religieux de l'histoire*, Paris, 1986, pp. 384ff and p. 540, and J. Baechler's introduction to A. Cochin, *L'esprit du jacobinisme*, Paris, 1979.
8. This sort of interpretation was fostered in the Academy of Marseilles. As well as its own Archives, see its *Recueil* of memoirs, Bibliothèque municipale of Marseilles, Fonds de Provence, 7911.
9. This characterisation of the Municipality of Marseilles is derived from a study of its deliberations, correspondence etc., mainly in Série BB of the Archives communales, Marseilles, (henceforth ACM).
10. The famous Book XX of *L'Esprit des lois*, praising the union of liberty and commerce, was held to have been inspired by Marseilles. The abbé Raynal enjoyed close relations with some of the city's leading merchants. He resided at Marseilles at the start of the Revolution. This claim as to cultural hegemony could be substantiated with reference to the position of merchants in the Academy of Marseilles. See also J. P. Ferran, *La haute bourgeoisie protestante marseillaise à la veille de la Révolution*, (D.E.S. mémoire, Faculté des Lettres, Aix,

n.d.) and Charles Carrière, *Les négociants marseillais au xviii* siècle, 2 vols, Marseilles, 1973.

11. Archives of the Chamber of Commerce, Marseilles, henceforth ACC, A24 and A25. Archives nationales, Paris, Ba 50.

12. For the march to Aix on 27 July, see Mathieu Blanc-Gilly, *Le Triomphe de l'humanité*, 29 July 1789, Bibliothèque municipale of Marseilles, Fonds de Provence, 5041. (Note: all documents cited from the Municipal Library – henceforth B. Mun. – are from the Fonds de Provence.) For the riot at Aix on 25 March, see, Archives nationales, H1453, *procès-verbal* of an anonymous *bourgeois*, 27 March 1789.

13. ACM, BB289, petition to Versailles, 16 May 1788.

14. ACM, CC2013B, *Observations pour les Sieurs Maire, Echevins . . .*, n.d., 1784?

15. Archives nationales, Paris, AD xvi 26, reports on interrogations of those arrested subsequent to disturbances on 19 August 1789.

16. By 'patriots' I refer to the men most active politically in the years 1789–92, in the Jacobin Club, the District Assemblies, administrative bodies, including the municipality. Socially they were drawn mainly from the intellectual and liberal professions, the less eminent merchants (but still *négociants*), retail merchants (*marchands*), artisans and *fabricants* (manufacturers, often hardly, if at all, distinguishable from artisans).

17. The pamphlets of Mathieu Blanc-Gilly, future member of the Legislative Assembly, are numerous. See, for the above quotations, B.Mun., 4717, *Très respectueuses représentations* and *Défense, apologie . . .*, 27 June and 7 July 1789 respectively. And B. Mun., 4717., Charles Barbaroux, *Réflexions*, 11 January 1790.

18. B. Mun., 4717, second of the two vols. on 'la justice prévôtale', report of J. S. Maury to National Assembly, 23 January 1790.

19. B.Mun., vol. 1, Méjan de Laboissière, *Mémoire adressé à l'Assemblée nationale*, Aix, 1790.

20. B. Mun., *Recueil* of Academy, 7911.

21. Several of the *concours* were concerned with commercial matters and the ethos of commerce. Especially interesting is one asking for educational reform plans suitable for a commercial city.

22. I am presently completing a study of political attitudes at Marseilles in the period 1785 to 1792 which gives considerable attention to the positive role of the merchants.

23. ACC, A24 (letter of 20 March 1789) and A25.

24. Among these were C. F. Achard and G. B. B. Grosson.

25. B. Mun., 4717, vol. 1 relating to tax reform, M. Blanc-Gilly, *Plan de révolution concernant les finances*, 1789.

26. ACC, A25, *Réflexions d'un négociant*, 1788, probably by Jacques Seimandy.

27. The printed original is in B. Mun., 4528 AM. It is one of the most wide-ranging justifications for merchants' claims to have a major political role, consistently emphasising their knowledge and experience. Some of the main points were adopted by the Chamber of Commerce on 23 January 1789, ACC, A25.

28.   The distinction between the richest merchants and their more modest colleagues – needless to say, based mainly on appearances and hearsay – was commonplace, with the less 'opulent' merchants being frequently cited as much more actively in favour of the Revolution in 1789. See Archives nationales, BB 30 14, etc.

29.   This appears from documents in the series HH in the Archives communales. There is precious little evidence of artisan 'solidarity' in the guild records.

30.   M. Zarb, *Histoire d'une autonomie communale: Les privilèges de la ville de Marseille*, Paris, 1961 In the Archives communales, the Série BB, *passim*.

31.   They fill numerous dossiers in ACC and in the F^{12} series of the Archives nationales.

32.   Archives départementales des Bouches-du-Rhône, Marseilles (henceforth ABR), C3339. Beaugeard did, however, establish a newspaper; see R. Gérard, *Le 'Journal de Marseille' de Ferréol Beaugeard, 1781–1797*, Paris, 1964.

33.   See Beaugeard's Journal, B. Mun., 4223, 28 December 1786.

34.   In searches for documents on the city's privileges and in preparation for the States General, any finds were largely due to luck. See, for example the relief expressed in ACM, BB 222, 17 December 1787. The revolutionary municipality accorded – in theory – great significance to its archives, to enable it to avoid the ignorance which had led the city to servitude. See, ACM, 1D8, 24 April 1790.

35.   Jacques Seimandy, *Mémoire d'un négociant de Marseille*.

36.   ABR, C111, 21 January and 8 February 1789. For his praise of merchants, British Library, F291(3), *Lettres au comte de Mirabeau*, Mirabeau's reply of 7 April 1789.

37.   By, for example, William Doyle, *The Origins of the French Revolution*, Oxford, 1980, ch. 6, and G. Chaussinand-Nogaret, *The French Nobility in the Eighteenth Century*, Cambridge, 1985.

38.   This is not meant to be a considered judgement on the Provençal nobility as a whole.

39.   B. Mun., 4717, 4 vols on the Provençal Estates. See, for example, vol. 2, *Réflexions philosophiques*, n.d.

40.   Archives nationales, M788, correspondence of Boisgelin, 7 April 1789, to Madame de Gramont.

41.   ACC, A25, J. Seimandy (?), *Réflexions d'un négociant*, 1788, and the work more convincingly attributed to him, *Observations impartiales*, 1789, in B. Mun., 4717, Deliberations of the municipality, vol. 1.

42.   B. Mun., 2236, *Mémoire et consultation pour le corps des marchands . . .*, Marseilles, 1786.

43.   B. Mun., 4717, Impositions, vol. 1, *Plan de révolution concernant les finances*, 1789.

44.   See his *Observations impartiales*.

45.   See, most recently, Monique Cubells, 'Marseille au printemps de 1789', *Annales du Midi*, 98, no. 173, Jan.–Mar. 1986, pp. 67–91.

46.   ABR, C4471, C2625, etc.

47. ACM, BB290, letter of 21 February 1789 from Municipality to Intendant.
48. J. Fournier, *Cahiers de doléances de la Sénéchaussée de Marseilles pour les Etats-Généraux de 1789*, Marseilles, 1908. A detailed examination of these relative to concepts of ignorance would be most rewarding.
49. B. Mun., 4717, *Non alligabis os bovi trituranti*, January 1789, attributed to Brémond, *avocat*.
50. C. F. Achard, *Tableau historique de Marseille*, Lausanne, 1789, p. 326.
51. B. Mun., 4717, Impositions, 2, *Réflexions sur l'impôt*, 1789, attributed to Eymar *aîné*.
52. ACM, 4D1, on 9 June 1791 the municipality confesses that it can produce no list of active citizens. Nor did it find it easy to effect a census of the poor for the National Assembly's Comité de mendicité.
54. William Scott, *Terror and Repression in Revolutionary Marseilles*, London, 1973.
55. The issue of *assignats* naturally intensified the problems of officials, who complained of their ignorance in monetary matters. For a recent, if ideologically monetarist, interpretation, see Florin Aftalion, *L'économie de la Révolution française*, Paris, 1987.
56. B. Mun., 4717, *Lettre détaillée de M. Martin*, (Mayor), 5 November 1790.
57. ABR, 16F34, *Mémoire*, 1789.
58. ACM, 4D5, Municipality to Chamber of Commerce, 26 December 1791.
59. Mireille Ferrières and Monique Yaiche, *Les bibliothèques des négociants marseillais au xviiie siècle*, Université de Provence, Centre Aix, Mémoire de maîtrise, 1974.
60. M. Agulhon, *Pénitents et francs-maçons de l'ancienne Provence*, Paris, 1968; René Verrier, *La mère loge écossaise de France à l'Orient de Marseille*, Marseilles, 1950; Bibliothèque nationale, FM^2 282–92.
61. *Atlas historique. Provence, Comtat-Venaissin . . .*, ed. E. Baratier *et al.*, Paris, 1969, Map 281, commentary p. 89.
62. Michel Vovelle, *Piété baroque et déchristianisation*, Paris, 1973.
63. B. Mun., 4528 AM, J. Seimandy, *Mémoire d'un négociant*, 1789. Seimandy, like others at the Academy was fond of citing Montesquieu.
64. ACM, BB289, 7 and 27 June 1788, Municipality to Intendant and government respectively, complaining of the merchants, a doleful theme of much municipal correspondence.
65. B. Mun., 4528 F, *Détail historique*, 1789.
66. J. Fournier, *Les cahiers de doléances de la sénéchausseé de Marseille*, Marseilles, 1908. Among those who professed some degree of ignorance were the *arquebusiers*, p. 7; the box-makers (*caissiers*), p. 33; the tailors, p. 273; and the glaziers, p. 307. It was the hatters who spoke for the '*manufacturiers*', p. 61, but many others did so in slightly less explicit terms. Barbaroux, E. J. Lejourdan and Blanc-Gilly – and the abbé Raynal – were among those alleged to have helped the artisans draft their grievances.

67.   ACM, BB360, letter from P. Peloux to municipality, 30 November 1790. He was a silk manufacturer.
68.   The struggle between Chamber and Municipality had many dimensions and its outcome was not clear-cut. Série H of the Chamber of Commerce Archives provides much information on the aspirations of manufacturers, while the grievances of the sea-captains of the Levant trade are expressed in E 107.
69.   Musée Arbaud, Aix, Liasse 207, for *mémoires* of sea-captains. The comment on Volney s from *Observations d'un capitaine marchand* n.d. Among captains' proposals for naval reform: British Library, R593(12), *Réflexions sur la nouvelle organisation de la marine militaire*, 1791.
70.   For petitions to the National Assembly regarding the slave trade and troubles in the colonies, ACC, H21, etc.
71.   Archives départementales de la Moselle, Metz, 18J299, *De la députation aux Etats-Généraux*, 1788.
72.   Brit. Lib., 1029(4), *Mémoire à consulter pour le Sieur Blanc-Gilly*, 1790.
73.   For example, Archives nationales, Fonds Greffulhe, especially 61 AQ 151 and 152 (I express my gratitude to the duc de Gramont for permission to consult this revealing correspondence); Archives départementales de l'Aube, Troyes, Fonds Fromageot, 3F 159–73; Arch. dépt. Aveyron, Rodez, fonds Solier de Camarès.
74.   C. Carrière, *Négociants marseillais au xviiie siècle*, 2 vols, Marseilles, 1973.
75.   Marcel Courdurié, *La dette des collectivités publiques de Marseille au xviiie siècle*, Marseilles, 1975.
76.   I do not mean to suggest that statistical sources on all these topics are abundant at Marseille.
77.   The *Dictionnaire des usages socio-politiques (1770–1815)*, Klincksieck, Paris, 1985, gives examples of the work of J. Guilhaumou and colleagues.
78.   *Cahiers critiques du patrimoine*, no. 2, 1986, *Révolution–Contre-Révolution. Le texte dialectal de la période révolutionnaire*, Marseilles, 1986. This collection of essays reviews much of the fairly scant 'political' literature in 'dialect'. C. F. Achard's *Dictionnaire de la Provence . . .*, vol. 1, Marseilles, 1785, with its fascinating y contradictory introduction, has been reprinted by Slatkine.
79.   See the stimulating article of Dorinda Outram, *Le langage mâle de la vertu . . .*, in *The Social History of Language*, eds Peter Burke and Roy Porter, Cambridge, 1987, pp. 120–35.
80.   See, for instance, ACC, H143 and H146; ACM, especially HH 428–9; B. Mun., 002950 and 2147.
81.   G. Mauran, *Avis aux gens de mer sur leur santé*, 2nd edn, Marseilles, 1786; also, ABR, 15E65, papers of Dr Raymond.
82.   Archives nationales, Maison du Roi, 0'485 for the letter of 29 March 1789 and 0'486 for that of 6 June 1789.
83.   ACM, AA 7, *Comparant*.
84.   ACM, 44F1A, 47F7 etc.

11

The Emergence of a Modern Vernacular Culture in North-East Scotland

Paul Dukes

Before the nineteenth century, the North-East was cut off from the rest of Scotland to a considerable degree. Through many hundreds of years, it had developed its own remarkable culture under the influence of a distinctive lie of the land, aspect of the sea and cast of climate. Thus the University of Aberdeen, founded in 1495, was something of an interloper, and the hopes of its founder, that 'the ignorant would acquire knowledge and the rude erudition', did not perhaps take full cognisance of this basic circumstance. On the other hand, in some ways, the gap between elite and vernacular culture was not yet fully formed: up to the sixteenth century, such local writers as John Barbour and Alexander Arbuthnot used 'gude braid Scotch' without self-consciousness, while their illiterate fellow North-Easterners carried on a whole range of cultural activities even more regardless. After the decline of Latin and the arrival of English throughout the seventeenth century, associates of the university made something of a 'rediscovery' of the vernacular culture as they distanced themselves from it in the eighteenth century. Without their intercession, what was still largely an oral culture might not have been transmitted to us, yet the process of percolation refined it and therefore distorted it, perhaps.

While a description and analysis of this process form the centrepiece of this chapter, a brief mention is made of nineteenth-century develop-

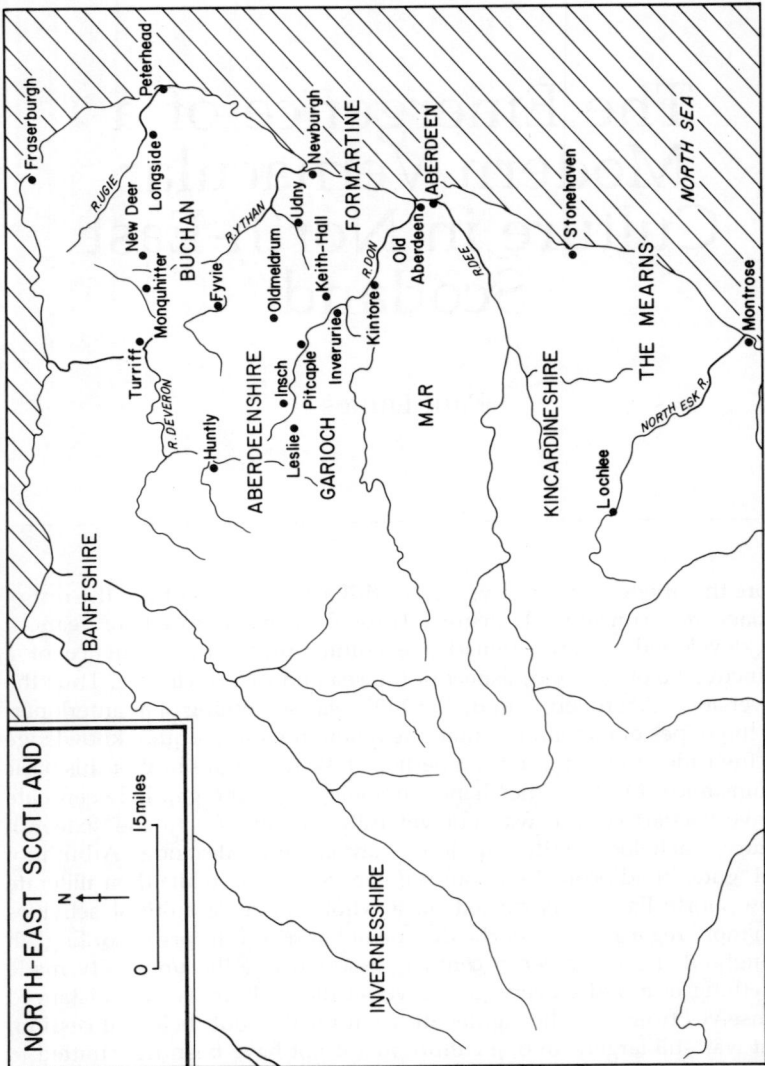

NORTH-EAST SCOTLAND

N

0   15 miles

NORTH SEA

Fraserburgh
Peterhead
Longside
New Deer
R. UGIE
BUCHAN
Monquhitter
Fyvie
Turriff
R. DEVERON
Huntly
ABERDEENSHIRE
Leslie
Insch
GARIOCH
Pitcaple
Inverurie
Oldmeldrum
Keith-Hall
R. YTHAN
Udny
Newburgh
FORMARTINE
Kintore
R. DON
Old
Aberdeen
ABERDEEN
MAR
R. DEE
Stonehaven
THE MEARNS
KINCARDINESHIRE
Lochlee
NORTH ESK R.
Montrose
BANFFSHIRE
INVERNESSSHIRE

ments, for example the composition and collection of bothy ballads, the transmission of vernacular culture through such novels as *Johnny Gibb of Gushetneuk*, before a twentieth-century coda. The gap that had opened up between elite and people was revealed by Hugh MacDiarmid, especially in his 'Synthetic Scots'. But, while he was 'headlong in dewy dallops or a moon-spairged fernshaw or caught in a dark dumosity', a more successful attempt at forming a literary vehicle out of the vernacular language was made in the North-East by Lewis Grassic Gibbon. Building on his breakthrough, former farm workers David Toulmin and Jessie Kesson completed the reunion of land and letters, an achievement recognised by the University of Aberdeen with its award to them of honorary degrees in the years 1986 and 1987 respectively. While associations of the University might still have a part to play in the continued prosperity of its latter-day embodiments, the resilience and essential independence of North-East vernacular culture in its most recent phase are indicated by giving the last word to David Toulmin.

Scotland, like most other countries, is far from uniform in its culture. If Braudel is right to emphasise the diversity of France,[1] British observers are justified in pointing out that the United Kingdom possesses the same quality. This basic fact will not go unobserved by alert travellers to Aberdeen from London by rail or road. In particular, the Borders from Berwick-upon-Tweed to Edinburgh and the Lothians, the Kingdom of Fife across the Firth of Forth and then beyond the Tay, Angus and the Mearns through Dundee and Montrose, all present distinctive areas of Scotland before the arrival at Stonehaven, the gateway to the North-East. The variations in physical aspect have produced distinctive qualities in the character of local cultures, all well formed before the coming of the railway and the macadamised road. However the

---

The map is adapted from several eighteenth-century sources, one of which, James Anderson, *General View of the Agriculture of the County of Aberdeen*, Aberdeen, 1794, pp. 10–12, tells us: 'Aberdeenshire was formerly divided into four districts, the names of which are still preserved, although they are not recognised in any political sense. These are Mar, Formartine and Buchan . . . Buchan . . . has a bleak and cold aspect, owing to the total want of trees around the hamlets, or hedges of any sort, the frequent and sombre aspect of mosses, and the broken and marshy appearance of the low grounds, which are every where in want of surface draining.

recent arrival of the motorway, like the nineteenth-century construction of viaducts, has served to disguise almost completely the
manner in which the region now known as Grampian was for
centuries to a considerable extent cut off from the rest of the
country to the south by the mountain range from which it has
taken its name. Similarly, within that region, the spread of
suburbia and the commuter belt has distracted attention from the
earlier existence of a large number of separate communities, some
less, some more remote from the major city, Aberdeen, whose
primary hinterland has traditionally been considered to have been
within a twelve-mile radius of itself (or themselves, for until the
nineteenth century Old and New Aberdeen were as distinct as
their respective universities).

Many centuries before the coming of the iron and metalled
roads, the culture of the North-East was in process of formation in
the city and the country, under the influence of a distinctive lie of
the land, aspect of the sea and cast of climate.[2] Indeed those
centuries have been so numerous that the process defies conventional chronology. The timeless quality is caught by the local
writer Lewis Grassic Gibbon in his short story 'Clay', in which a
workaholic farmer Rob Gault becomes convinced that the land he
is clearing, now called Pittaulds, has been cultivated by other
hands long before. Not even his wife's mortal illness can break his
obsessive toil, until his daughter finds him exhausted on a wet,
windy November day, beckoning her in triumph:

> 'Come in by and look on this fairely, lass, I knew that some
> childe had once farmed up here.'
>
> And Rachel looked at the hole in the clay and the chamber
> behind it, dim in the light, where there gleamed a rickle of
> stone-grey sticks, the bones of a man of antique time. Amid the
> bones was a litter of flints and a crumbling stick in the shape of
> a heuch.
>
> She knew it was an eirde of olden time, an earth-house built
> by the early folk. Rob nodded, 'Ay, he was more than that. Look
> at the heuch, it once scythed Pittaulds. Losh, lass, I'd have liked
> to have kenned that childe, what a crack together we'd have had
> on the crops!'

That very night, Rob is taken ill with a cold, and because 'He'd
worked all his go into the ground', cannot resist its intensification.

After her father is dead, Rachel goes up to the earth-house and decides to have him buried by the bones of his ancient predecessor:

> . . . And she shivered sudden as she looked round about at the bare clay slopes that slept in the dusk, the whistle of the whins seemed to rise in a voice, the parks below to whisper and listen as the wind came up them out of the east.
>
> All life – just clay that awoke and strove to return again to its mother's breast. And she thought of the men who had made these rigs and the windy days of their toil and years, the daftness of toil that had been Rob Gault's, that had been that of many men long on the land, though seldom seen now, was it good, was it bad? What power had that been that woke once on this brae and was gone at last from the parks of Pittaulds?
>
> For she knew in that moment that no other would come to tend the ill rigs in the north wind's blow. This was finished and ended, a thing put by . . .[3]

The short story 'Clay' not only conveys the aeon of North-East regional culture, it also constitutes an elegy for a way of life now, like Rob Gault, departed. For, in this case, a perennial and on occasion ill-founded complaint seems completely appropriate: times are indeed not what they once were. The arrival of full mechanisation as well as government policies have done for traditional farming, just as their offshore variants have done for traditional fishing. We are now living in a new age, shared by other disrupted communities from Portugal to Siberia, and beyond.[4]

But when the old age itself began is difficult to say. Those of us who are traditional workers in another kind of trade, cultural history, are sometimes unhappy about the lack of attention paid to precise chronology and location by the creators of culture, especially the vernacular variety. We like to think that there is a time and a place for everything, while they sometimes in their exuberance, desolation or other mood omit to tell us when and where they are. For example, we know that, when Aberdeen's first university was founded in 1495, Bishop Elphinstone was hoping that, through his creation in a 'remote portion of Scotland and cut off from the rest of the kingdom by arms of the sea and very lofty mountains . . . in the renowned city of Aberdeen, the ignorant would acquire knowledge and the rude erudition'. On the other hand, we know far less about the kind of culture developed in the late fifteenth century by the 'rude and ignorant'.[5]

By the seventeenth century, the picture becomes less obscure, and the gap narrows somewhat. Both these tendencies are reflected in the work of the 'Scottish Ovid', Arthur Johnston, who was born in the parish of Leslie in 1577 and, after an education in Kintore and Aberdeen, went to Heidelberg and then Sedan, where he held the Chair of Logic and Metaphysics for nearly twenty years. On his return to Scotland, he became for a time a farmer back on his ancestral lands, from which he wrote an Epistle to Dr Robert Baron, one of the famous Aberdeen Doctors:

> I am not what I was. My looks would scare
> My lady mother and my peasant nurse;
> And even myself am frightened to behold
> Hair gray with dust, a countenance begrimed,
> And feet and legs all filth. My neck is bowed,
> And, from a ploughman habit, I fix my gaze
> Ever upon the ground like any ox.
> Temples and brow are shaggy, and my breast
> A fell of hair: my beard is coarse, unkempt;
> My hands are horny, and my once soft skin
> Is tough as leather with the sun and frost.
> Such loss of comeliness one might endure:
> The outer husk were little if the mind
> Knew no decay. But mind and body pair:
> My wits grow clownish and my manners coarse,
> Fit only for this highland wilderness
> Where learning wit, and every kind of grace
> Of noble intellect are all to seek.[6]

Johnston laments to his friend how he longs to be once again 'A citizen, not a savage, on the earth'. Such beginnings of rapprochement are taken further with the Enlightenment of the eighteenth century, when, arguably at least, Thomas Blackwell drew on his awareness of local popular culture to point the way forward to the formation of modern folklore studies in *An Enquiry into the Life and Writings of Homer*, first published in 1735. In the years following, as we shall see later, there was further progress.

However, it is not until more recent years that the University of Aberdeen has given North-East culture its full imprimatur. We can in this case give precise dates, since it was in 1986 and 1987 respectively that honorary degrees were awarded to two outstanding local writers, both worthy heirs of Lewis Grassic Gibbon, David Toulmin and Jessie Kesson.[7] In this chapter I shall be making use of their words, both written and spoken, in the effort to describe the nature of the emergence of the modern culture that they themselves have caught in its most recent phase with such expertise, reversing the experience of Arthur Johnston in their movement from the soil to letters, at the same time as attempting to illustrate the evolving relationship of gown, town and hinterland.

Let us turn first to Jessie Kesson for her description of the life of local farmworkers, who, for many years, bore an evocative name with a provenance stretching far back into medieval centuries – that of 'cottar'. Let us take in particular her novel *Glitter of Mica*, set somewhere in central Buchan, north of Aberdeen, and numbering among its characters several cottars. A discerning critic, William Donaldson, notes that, on one level, the novel is intended as a 'sardonic rebuttal' of the cloying sentimentality of *The Cottar's Saturday Night*, by Robert Burns,[8] and it is certainly noticeable that Burns and his works form a point of reference throughout the whole of Jessie Kesson's narrative. Thus, one of the greatest figures in the formation of modern Scottish vernacular culture looms large in a not inconsiderable analysis of that culture's disintegration.

While Grassic Gibbon has seen the First World War as the beginning of the end, Kesson places more emphasis on the Second (an interpretation supported by the works of David Toulmin).[9] As one of her characters reflects:

> The curious thing about wars was that you were born in the remembrance of your parents' wars, and grew up within their constant recollections of an age, alluring as myth, 'Before the War', so that you got the feeling that it were better never to have been born at all than to live in the dull eras 'After the War' when 'Times have changed', and always 'For the worst'.

Everybody in the village seems agreed that postwar prosperity has spread too far:

'The World is coming to a pretty fine pass when you can no longer tell whether it's the farmers or the tinkers that are driving round the countryside in brakes.'

Another kind of time, that of the human span, is placed across this historical setting. The novel's hero, Hugh Riddel, has intimations concerning his own life and of life beyond on hearing his father's drunken rendering of some of the old popular favourites during the inter-war period:

> That was another of the times when Hugh Riddel, the boy, had felt all the glamourie of manhood tugging at himself. The *Annie Lauries* and *Bonnie Peggies* of his father's songs had come across to him even then as something more than idylls of time gone past; they had become lush promises of his own future. Strange, though; strange that they should still have remained idylls when the future had become the present.

Burns has his place in these brief escapes from daily drudgery, but Hugh's mother is critical: 'The men just uses Burns as an excuse for theirselves', while Hugh himself complains: 'Oh, Burns was it to suit the fine sentiments of the Edinbro' Gentry, once cursed by you, and always half despised, that you wrote such smarm as *The Cottar's Saturday Night?'* He reflects:

> Far more true of their way of life were the songs of his father and his father's friends on Term Night. Songs of their own countryside, composed by themselves for themselves; and having their origins in the very farms they worked on.

In his own adulthood after the Second World War, Hugh Riddel takes the opportunity of an invitation to toast 'The Immortal Memory' at a local Burns' Supper for several purposes. He quotes *Holy Willie's Prayer* in criticism of a local yuppie who is forgetting his roots. He also makes use of his experience. 'One Ploughman Speaks of Another – Robert Burns' runs the headline in the local paper, while the wagging tongues at the WRI (Women's Rural Institute) a week later 'had not quite got beyond the fact that one of themselves had been allowed voice at last, and were inclined to warm themselves contentedly at the thought'. But then one of them scatters straws of doubt: 'Twas just the kind of thing could make a man go all above himself.'

Class and hypocrisy, then, present difficulties in the way of comment and celebration after the Second World War as they did before it. But were the predicaments for vernacular culture similar or different during Burns's own lifetime? We certainly know that Burns himself spoke with different voices rather than with a forked tongue, and that he cannot be held personally responsible for later misappropriation of 'The Immortal Memory'. We must now try to investigate the manner in which his contemporaries in North-East Scotland approached their heritage and developed it.[10]

A fundamental problem here is presented by the inaccessibility of what was largely an oral rather than written tradition. Is it therefore impossible to listen directly to the authentic voice of the people? And, as always, who are the people? Let us begin to attempt to answer these difficult questions by way of *The Statistical Account of Scotland*, drawn up at the end of the eighteenth century through the agency of the parish ministers of the Established Church. We will put ourselves first in the hands of the Rev. A. Johnstone, of the Parish of Monquhitter, not very far to the west of the putative locale for Jessie Kesson's novel *Glitter of Mica*. He begins:

Perhaps it may be agreeable to the succeeding age to receive a more particular account of our forefathers than has as yet been given, and to observe how rapidly the current century has advanced refinement in every rank. Circumstances, which at present are universally known, will, when oral tradition ceases, become objects of curiosity. The following attempt, to delineate some prominent features in the character and conduct of our fathers, may, as prudence shall direct, be appointed to meet the public eye, or to rest in oblivion.

Now that 'rational farming' had dawned, while 'manufacture and mechanism' were 'eagerly pursued and liberally rewarded', there were improvements in the life of the three principal ranks, the gentry, farmers and farm servants, in their housing, their diet and their dress.

Manners were becoming more refined: quarrels were extremely rare and confined to the very lowest of the people; funerals were conducted 'with due solemnity by people in their senses'; drunkenness was losing ground. If traditional holidays persisted – 'as the means of throwing off that languor which oppresses the mind, and of exerting their active powers' – for many people, their nature had changed. Wrestling, throwing the hammer and stone, football were all among the activities of the fathers, but now athletic amusements were confined to schoolboys. Fires at mid-summer and Hallowe'en, both 'relics of druidism', were now attended by children only. Magic ceremonies to ward off witches and demons, and to forecast matrimonial fortunes, had largely disappeared: 'the country girl, renouncing the rites of magic, endeavours to enchant her swain by the charms of dress and industry'. Before, 'The market place was to the peasant what the drawing-room is to the peer, the theatre of shew and conse-quence.' Every joy of an idle and illiterate age was to be found at the penny bridal, in which hundreds of guests would attend a wedding for a small charge and indulge for several days in celebrations affording 'Ample materials for rural mirth and rural scandal.' However, the penny bridal had been rejected as 'an index of want of money, and of want of taste'. As a consequence, 'Dancing, taught by itinerant masters, cards, and conversation, are the amusements now in vogue; and the pleasures of the table, enlivened by a moderate glass, are frequently enjoyed in a suitable degree by people of every class.' The market place was now used generally for business, with far less 'shew and consequence'.

The Rev. Johnstone pointed out that, to the illiterate of earlier ages, rules for the conduct of daily life were presented in proverbs, allegories, frets and songs. He continued:

The proverb in every mouth, and seemingly flowing from the blood of the Panchas in every vein, explained, frequently in a coarse, but always in an expressive manner, the laws of proprie-ty and prudence. The allegory shadowed forth, by the entertain-ment to be prepared for certain personages, what stores were to be allotted for the various seasons. The fret, enforcing the duty to the neighbour and friend, contained the code of vulgar good-breeding. Many frets, like the institutions of Brama, cannot now be traced to their origin; but the benevolent mind rejoices to perceive that some of them strongly enforce the dictates of humanity. The song conveyed the outline of a flattering chronicle, and enforced the dictates of patriotic virtue:

while it illustrated the manners of preceding generations, it not seldom fired the bosom with heroic ardour. But now, a company of country men, despising the proverb, may be ranked among the disciples of the sinical Chesterfield. The allegory, no longer necessary to illustrate the laws of economy is reserved for the amusement of the nursery. The fret presents its terrors to the weakest class of old women only. And the song, to my sorrow, no longer painting the character of antient times, may vie in inanity with the ordinary vehicles of Italian music.

As far as general outlook was concerned, 'a system of mythology full as absurd and amusing as the mythology of Homer obtained general belief'. But yet again, there had been great change: 'Books, trade, manufacture, foreign and domestic news, now engross the conversation; and the topic of the day is always warmly, if not ingeniously discussed.'[11]

The Rev. Johnstone's discovery of reason and politeness conquering all in Monquhitter was not equalled by his brethren in many other parishes, but there were further observations of interest, not least concerning Buchan's distinctive language. The Rev. George Skene Keith, of Keith-Hall and Kinkell, asserted that 'there is no a provincial dialect, in Britain, better understood, on the Royal Exchange of London, than that of Aberdeenshire, if it be used without affectation'. But the Rev. William Greig, of Longside, in the heart of Buchan, was not so sure, observing: 'The Buchan dialect has long been famous for the want of that neatness of articulation, and of that elegance of sound and accent, by which the Southern and more cultivated nations have characterised their respective languages.' If the degree of mental cultivation in a country were to be measured by the state in which its language was found, Buchan's pretensions could not be very high. On the other hand, for many minds, language would be a very imperfect index, and cultivated understanding was possible without cultivated taste. The parish contained 'a body of men very respectable for their knowledge and education, if their circumstances and pursuits in life be properly attended to'.

Moving on to the provincial character, the Rev. Greig expressed the opinion that the inhabitants of Buchan differed not only from the people of other countries, but even from those of the other districts of the same county, lacking both their liveliness of imagination and warmth of feeling. The closest comparison could be made not with Scots in general, but with the Dutch, and the reason for this was 'the constant uniformity in the appearances of nature', with 'no scope for that violent agitation, which so frequently takes place in the breasts of Swiss and Scotchmen, when they contemplate their mountains, their woods, and their precipices'. However, because knowledge and society brought the higher ranks to a similar level in all countries, the closest comparison was between the peasants of Buchan and the boors in Holland.[12]

The Statistical Account gave a general impression of change for the better, even if the Rev.Johnson stood out for his enthusiasm among the informants from North and East Aberdeenshire. Let us turn from it to a second kind of source, the publications of the academics in the two colleges of Old and New Aberdeen, King's and Marischal, and begin with the above-mentioned *An Enquiry into the Life and Writings of Homer*, by Thomas Blackwell, Professor of Greek, later Principal at Marischal, and first published in 1735. Blackwell put forward the argument that Homer was a great oral bard drawing his descriptions from observations of the traditional life of the Greek people and using for his epic narrative their modes of presentation of the heroic tale and myth. Blackwell thus described the circumstances that made men what they were:

> FIRST, The *State of the Country* where a Person is born and bred; in which I include the common *Manners* of the Inhabitants; their *Constitution* civil and religious, with its *Causes* and *Consequences*: – Their *Manners* are seen in the *ordinary* way of Living, as it happens to be polite or barbarous, luxurious or simple.
>
> NEXT, the *Manners* of the *Times*, or the prevalent Humours or Professions in vogue: – These two are publick, and have a common effect on the whole Generation. Of a more confined Nature is, first, *Private Education;* and after that, *the particular Way* of Life we chuse and pursue, with our *Fortunes* in it.

Unfortunately, although it is difficult to believe that Blackwell did not draw at least some of his argument from his own environment, he makes no reference in *An Enquiry* to any aspect of it. The nearest he comes to such a remark is in his assertion that the great oral bard had no modern equivalent, continuing: 'For I should be unwilling to admit the *Irish* or *Highland Rüners* to a share of that Honour; tho' their business, which is to entertain a company with the Recital of some Adventure, resembles a part of the other.' At the end of the eighteenth century, it will be recalled, the Rev. Johnstone had written of a traditional local system of mythology 'full as absurd and amusing as the mythology of Homer'. Blackwell must have had some awareness of this traditional local system in 1735, even if he might not have considered it, any more than he did the original Homeric system, absurd and amusing. Yet one of the fathers of modern folklore studies made no explicit reference to the rich variety flourishing around him as he looked back at the heritage of Ancient Greece.[13]

To some extent, perhaps, Blackwell himself resolved the paradox with a series of rhetorical questions posed in his *Letters concerning Mythology*, published in 1748: 'Because there are *Empirics*, wou'd you have no *Physicians?* Because there are *rhyming Dunces*, would you have no *Poets?* Or because there are *wicket Heretics*, would you have no *orthodox Divines?*'[14] Moreover, Blackwell's works were published in London, where observations concerning Aberdonian culture would probably have helped to give their author a reputation as a provincial, a label which Blackwell and his successors in the Aberdeen Enlightenment were anxious to avoid. On the other hand, it is remarkable that, in 1742, there was first printed in Aberdeen an epic narrative entitled *Ajax*, done in broad Buchan by one Robert Forbes, a native later settled as a hosier in London. The flavour may be caught by juxtaposing an excerpt with a literal translation:

> But neither does my talent lie in speaking, nor his in acting, and as great ability as I have in fierce warfare, so much has he in talking.

This is rendered:

> At threeps [arguments] I am na' see perquire, [expert]
> Nor auld-farren [old-fashioned] as he,
> Bat at banes-braking', it's well kent,
> He has na' maught [might] like me.
> For as far as I him excell
> In tolzies [fights] fierce an' strong,
> So far in chaft-task [jaw] he exceeds
> Me, wi' his sleeked [cunning] tongue.[15]

Appropriately enough, because of its Latin overtones, *Ajax* was taken from Ovid rather than Homer. Nevertheless Blackwell is not likely to have been so much of a purist that he would not have recognised the power of the Forbes version, even if he made no reference to it in his major publications.

Forbes's use of the vernacular was an indication of a rediscovery of it occurring during the eighteenth century in parallel with an adoption of English. The distinction might not have been clear in the medieval and early modern periods, when such local writers as John Barbour, in the fourteenth century, and Alexander Arbuthnot, in the sixteenth, used what was known as 'gude braid Scotch' without self-consciousness. Here, for example, is a not untopical stanza from *The Miseries of a Pure Scolar*, written by Alexander Arbuthnot in 1572:

> I wald travel; and ydleness I hait;
> Gif I cud find sum gud vocatioun.
> But all for nocht; in vain lang may I wait,
> Or I get honest occupatioun.
> Letters are lichtliet in our natioun.
> For lernying now is nother lyf nor rent –
> Quhat marvel is thoch I murne and lament?

In the seventeenth century, although English was moving into fashion after King James VI of Scotland and I of England had published some of his poems in that language, 'the recognised vehicle for all who aspired to the higher pinnacles of contemporary poetic fame' was Latin. (We have quoted above a translation of the most successful of these aspirants, the Scottish Ovid, Arthur Johnstone.) However, wrote the leading nineteenth-century authority on North-East Scotland verse, William Walker, 'Nay, it is as hopelessly foolish to expect Latin poetry to live in this country, as it would be to look for palm trees flourishing in the *habitat* of our Scotch fir.'[16]

In the eighteenth century, the departure of Latin, like the consolidation of the arrival of English and the rediscovery of the vernacular, reflected political developments such as the rise and fall of Jacobitism and socioeconomic changes such as the beginnings of agrarian and industrial revolution.[17] For the vernacular culture in particular, the expansion of printing was also of prime significance. The *Aberdeen Journal*, the direct ancestor of today's

Press and Journal, was first published with a dateline 29 December 1747–5 January 1748, and a chap-book market was perhaps arising by about this time, too, although its heyday was still to come, from about 1780 to 1830.

Against this background, there occurred some important developments concerning North-East vernacular culture both in the academic world and the world beyond. Not long before Thomas Blackwell was made Principal of Marischal College in New Aberdeen, in the same year that his *Letters concerning Mythology* were published in London – in 1748 – and just after the Battle of Culloden brought to an end the second and last major attempt of the Stewarts to win back their throne – in 1746 – a happy event occurred in the household of Thomas Gordon, who held the chair of Humanity (Latin) in King's College, Old Aberdeen. The birth of a daughter was to lead to the collection of the first major corpus of Anglo-Scottish ballads by Anna Gordon, later and better known as Mrs Brown of Falkland. The importance of the date of Anna's arrival has been pointed out by David Buchan:

Mrs Brown's life spans a crucial sixty years. When she was born in 1747 the Northeast had, in essentials, changed little in the previous four hundred years, but when she died in 1810 it had undergone an agrarian, an industrial, and a social revolution she learned her ballads just after mid-century, before general literacy destroyed the oral mode and before the revolutions transformed the country, but by the turn of the century antiquarians had already begun their search for relics and lore of the old untransformed Scotland. Born one generation earlier, she would probably have remained unrecorded: born one generation later, she would not have been able to compose her ballads by the old oral method.

Some other critics might say that David Buchan makes the revolutions appear more precipitate than they actually were, but there can be little doubt that he gives the fullest analysis to Mrs Brown's thirty-three ballad stories, all of which have settings distancing them from 'the everyday work of the plough and the byre'. As he puts it: 'The ambience is aristocratic and their characters noble; the queens and ladies, kings, knights and squires enact their roles in castles, halls and bowers shadowily peopled by the maries and porters and pageboys of the noble household.'[18]

Similarly distanced from the workaday world but of more recent provenance were pastoral poems, of which eighteenth-century Scotland has been held to have produced at least two distinctive examples: 'The Gentle Shepherd', written by Allan Ramsay in Edinburgh and published there in 1725; and 'Helenore, the Fortunate Shepherdess', written by Alexander Ross, at Lochlee, NorthEsk, separated by the Grampians from North-East Scotland, and published in Aberdeen in 1768. Ross, a graduate of Marischal College, was schoolmaster at Lochlee from 1732, but retained contact with his *alma mater* through the agency of the Professor of Moral Philosophy, James Beattie, whose father he had known some years before. Beattie responded to 'Helenore' not only through his patronage of its author but also with a response in kind to the doric in which it is largely couched. For example:

> Our country leed [language] is far frae barren,
> 'Tis even right pithy and auldfarren [old-fashioned],
> Oursels are neiper-like [equal], I warran,
> For sense and smergh [substance];
> In kittle [insecure] times, when faes [foes] are yarring,
> [troublesome]
> We're no thought ergh . . . [reluctant]
> Our fine new-fangle sparks, I grant ye,
> Gie poor Scotland mony a taunty;
> They're grown so ugertfu' [affected] and vaunty,
> And capernoited; [peevish]
> They guide her like a canker'd aunty
> That's deaf and doited. [enfeebled]

Sending a copy of his verse to a friend, Beattie wrote:

> . . . having never attempted to write anything in this way, I thought I could not have done it, and was not a little surprised to find it so easy. However, I fear I have exhausted my whole stock of Scotch words in these few lines, for I endeavoured to make the style as broad as possible, that it might be better adapted to the taste of those whose curiosity I wished to raise.[19]

There were others whose stock of Scotch words carried them further than Beattie, and whose inhibitions about using them were smaller. The outstanding figure was John Skinner, graduate of Marischal College, and later Episcopal minister at Longside, in Buchan. His 'Tullochgorum' was described by Burns as 'the best Scotch song ever Scotland saw', while William Walker considered it to be even better than 'The Ewie wi' the Crookit Horn'. The suggestion for the latter work is said to have come from none other than James Beattie, who, asked to compose a pastoral song, got no further than three lines:

> The ewie wi' the crookit horn,
> Sic a ewe was never born,
> Hereabout nor far awa' . . .,

and then handed the commission on to Skinner as 'the best qualified person in Scotland'.[20]

However, rather than singing at any further length the praises of Skinner, we should move on to at least a brief mention of the voice of North-East vernacular culture as it was delivered, not through Mrs Brown, Alexander Ross, John Skinner or any other intermediary, but direct. This was made possible by the expansion of the printing press, although difficulties remained regarding the presentation of a culture that was still largely oral. A characteristic figure here seems to be Charles Leslie, born in 1677, a natural son of Leslie of Pitcaple, widely known as 'Mussle-mou'd Charlie' and as a hawker and singer of ballads throughout the East of Scotland – 'a Jacobite Homer singing his own compositions' in the description of William Walker. Unfortunately, all that survives of what must have been an extensive repertoire are the twenty-nine items contained in *The Ballad Book*, privately printed in Edinburgh in 1827. Here is a brief excerpt from 'The Man in the Moon', which makes fun of the optical illusions confronting somebody 'fou' (full or drunk):

> I saw the man in the moon,
> Wha's fou, wha's fou?
> I saw the man in the moon,
> Wha's fou, my jo [dear]?
> I saw the man in the moon,
> Driving tackets [hobnails] in his shoon;
> And we're a' blind drunk, bousin' jolly fou, my jo . . .
> I saw an eel chase the deil,
> Wha's fou, wha's fou?

I saw an eel chase the deil
Roun' about the spinnin' wheel,
And we're a' blind drunk, bousin' jolly fou, my jo.

Obviously, we cannot recapture the impact that this and other songs would have made on audiences in towns, villages and smaller communities. We do not know the full range of Musslemou'd Charlie's inspiration, although we are certain that he drew on earlier ballads as well as on aspects of life in Eastern Scotland around him.[21]

Another significant, if eccentric, figure is James Fleming, alias Jamie Fleeman, the Laird o' Udny's fool. Born in 1713 at Longside, later the residence of John Skinner, he soon made a local reputation for himself for reasons well summarised by David Toulmin:

. . . we are told that Jamie Fleeman, because of his bluntness of manner and shrewd remarks, attracted the attention of his associates, and more especially of his betters, who, because of his peculiarities, indulged his humour and permitted him a sense of freedom and liberties which would have been sternly denied to any normal child.

Like Charles Leslie (who is said not to have died until 1782, at the age of 105), Fleming drew at least some of his inspiration from the Jacobite movement. Here, for example, is a description of his encounter with a local Hanoverian laird:

'Where are ye going, Jamie?'
'I'm gaun tae hell, sir.'
'What are they doing in hell, Jamie?'
'Juist what they're deein' here, sir, lattin in the rich fouk and keeping' oot the peer.'
'And what said the devil to you, Jamie?
'Ou, the devil said na muckle tae me, sir, but he was speerin' [asking] sair aboot you.'"

Under the protection of the Laird of Udny until impoverishment brought about his dismissal, Fleming wandered the countryside until his death in 1778. Like Skinner, he is buried in the graveyard at Longside, his last recorded words forming his epitaph: 'Dinna bury me like a beast.'[22]

Soon after the death of Leslie and Fleming, the way of life that they had variously celebrated was on its last legs, a valedictory to some of its peripheral aspects being given by their younger contemporary, James Macpherson, who attended King's and then Marischal from 1752 to 1755 before going on to produce his *Fragments of Ancient Poetry* by 1760. However, although Macpherson may have been influenced by Thomas Blackwell (who did not die until 1757) and may have met the young girl Anna Gordon, his concern was not the culture of Aberdeen and its hinterland but the more marginal to North-East Scotland 'Highland Rüners' (to quote Blackwell again), especially Ossian.[23]

Like the Gaelic culture of the Highlands, its doric counterpart in the lowlands of Buchan went through a considerable transformation in the nineteenth century. Yet, just as the examples of modern vernacular culture that we have considered in this chapter had earlier roots, so the bothy ballads of the agricultural revolution era drew on their predecessors. And so, to take another strand of development, the collection of local songs by such individuals as Peter Buchan, Gavin Greig and James Duncan showed clearly that an unbroken line of oral tradition stretched back to medieval times. Moreover, in the second half of the nineteenth century, it was joined by a more complete printed vernacular culture, of which arguably the outstanding example was William Alexander's novel, *Johnny Gibb of Gushetneuk*, first published in Aberdeen in 1871.[24]

Roughly speaking, the years 1890–1910 were those of the 'First Folksong Revival'. In England, Cecil Sharp defined folksong in 1907 as that 'created by the common people, in contradistinction to the song, popular or otherwise, which has been composed by the educated'. He hoped that: 'When every English child is, as a matter of course, made acquainted with the folksongs of his country, then, from whatever class the musician of the future may spring, he will speak in the national musical idiom.' Sharp went on to express the view that:

The discovery of English folk-song, therefore, places in the hands of the patriot, as well as of the educationalist, an instrument of great value. The introduction of folk-songs into our schools will not only affect the musical life of England; it will also tend to arouse that love of country and pride of race the absence of which we now deplore.[25]

In Scotland, in 1891, Professor John Stuart Blackie of St Andrews University had declared:

Next to reverence for the great Source of our being, love of country, or as the Germans more significantly call it, the Fatherland, presents itself as the natural steam power to set the machinery of elevated musical expression in motion . . . But it is not only in moments of great national uprising and historic achievement . . . that the Lyrical Muse finds a field for her ennobling inspirations; from the familiar drama of daily life she is cunning to pick up themes, which, when transmuted by her magic, if less brilliant, are sometimes more pleasing, more profitable, and more permanent than far more lofty odes. In this department, while all honour is due to the Germans, as the most musical of modern nations, perhaps the seat of honour must be given to the Scots, in whose popular songs dramatic point, picturesque scenery, passion, pathos, simplicity, nature, grace, humour, and practical wisdom unite with the most delicate music, and the most musical of all popular dialects, to form an artistic compound as perfect in its sphere as the Odes of Pindar or the Choral Songs of the Greek drama.

But the professor's Introduction to *the Scottish Students' Song-Book* was contraverted by the last known lecture of the village schoolmaster Gavin Greig in October 1912 to the Inverurie Mutual Improvement and Literary Association:

As far as the North-East is concerned, research has convinced us that in the main our peasantry do *not* sing the songs of the books – the songs of Burns and the rest, but that their minstrelsy has been in the main just this unrecorded kind of thing which we are calling folk-song . . . We have reached a transition stage, and what may evolve we cannot well say; but as far as the past history of our country is concerned we maintain that the true minstrelsy of the Scottish peasantry has always been in the main traditional – folk-song and not book-song.[26]

An even greater transition stage was marked by the First World War, which not only reduced the general admiration for songs of the Fatherland, especially of the German variety, but also contributed to the demise of the peasant culture which had provided

Gavin Greig with such a rich collection of song and ballad. Moreover, towards the end of the First World War, in 1917, the Russian Revolution first removed the Tsar and then brought to power Lenin. Cecil Sharp confessed to the 'constant fear' that the war and the revolution would merge to produce a 'general revolution' following the 'hideous example' of Russia. In 1919, he declared 'Nationalism in art which before the war was an academic subject, has become a vital one.' On the other hand, there were those who, far from being alarmed by the new internationalism proclaimed by the Soviet government of Lenin, were inspired to attempt to contribute to it.[27]

In Scotland, the leading figure was Hugh MacDiarmid, who wrote in 1926:

It is amusing to find a few Scots assessors at Musical Festivals and other self-regarded experts – none of them with any work in Scots of the slightest consequence to their own credit – laying down the law, in evident alarm at the new tendencies which are manifesting themselves in recent Vernacular [*sic*] literature, that 'there must be no mixing of different dialects' – i.e. (for this is what it amounts to), no working back from the bits to the whole, no effort to reintegrate the *disjecta membra* – but despite these stick-in-the-muds, and no matter how long it may take the great body of lovers of Scots to arrive at any conception of the new position, it is happily obvious that Scots has at last – and not too late – been committed to a synthetic process.

This was to be observed in most other European countries, MacDiarmid noted, and in Scotland was the only way to realise the pledge of the Burns Federation and other bodies for the revival of the Scottish language. The time was propitious: 'The peculiar relations now establishing themselves between literature and linguistics make it obvious that a speedy and successful use of synthetic Scots would give Scotland a short cut into the very forefront of contemporary creative experimentalism.'[28]

MacDiarmid illustrated his point with some references to recent Russian literature, in particular by way of a comparison of Burns and the experimental Russian poet Velimir Khlebnikov (1885–1922). MacDiarmid asserted that Burns did nothing for the restoration of Braid Scots, simply taking it as he found it, arresting its decline but giving a new lease of life to what was only a ghost of its former self. Burns used in a synthetic manner a number of words from different dialects, several of which were probably already obsolete. However:

> . . . . his whole attitude to words was literal and the reverse of that which must be consciously adopted and applied if the recreation of the tongue instead of its mere conservation at a given level of declinature is to be the objective – if that immensely greater achievement is to be accomplished.

In other words, Scottish literature could have taken a different direction if Burns had possessed the attitude to words of Khlebnikov, for whom words and forms had an existence of their own. The Russian poet wanted to use his deep feeling for the nature of his language to build up a new world of words. Although he would probably never be read except by other poets and philologists, he was true in his creative linguistics to the genuine spirit of the Russian language. Khlebnikov's *zaumny* or trans-sense language was held up by MacDiarmid as a model to follow, even though he himself could become familiar with it apparently only through the agency of Prince Mirsky's book, *Contemporary Russian Literature*, which also enabled Macdiarmid to hold up other Russian writers, Rozanov and Mayakovsky, for emulation.

MacDiarmid complained that 'The ridiculing and non-comprehension of the movement towards a Synthetic Scots . . . simply shows the grotesque ignorance of the history of Continental literature on the part of certain so-called Scottish "critics".' Yet he himself was guilty of ridicule and non-comprehension, even grotesque ignorance, concerning places nearer home, especially the North-East, whose own literary revival he attacked for 'a mental parochialism, a constitutional incomprehension and a hatred of culture', asserting: 'I certainly do not see how any reasonable person can make common cause in the interests of Scottish national culture with those to whom *Johnny Gibb o' Gushteneuk* is a classic, and the Bible and plenty of porridge the only other requisites to a perfect life.' For MacDiarmid:

> Aberdeenshire Scots is certainly the reverse of 'pure': anything further from the conceivable norm – anything more corrupt – it would be difficult to find in any dialect of any tongue . . . the

very reverse of rich in beauty-creating powers, in intellectual resource, in technical accomplishment.

Under heavy attack from a number of North-East correspondents, MacDiarmid made no concessions, talking of the North-East revival as 'the worst form of highbrowism inverted . . . indeed worse than any form of highbrowism, for highbrowism does make certain demands of its devotees.' He continued:

> It is natural, therefore, that the majority of Buchan vernacular enthusiasts should be successful London Scots who, under a guise of local patriotism, are glad to make a virtue of their constitutional capacity for culture of any kind, and so, in the company of their kind, get rid of the oppressive sense of spiritual inferiority, so galling to those who have been merely commercially successful, which afflicts them in the presence of those incomprehensible people they encounter on all hands who are really artistic. The strain of living in an educated world makes them glad to relapse from time to time to the levels of the ploughman or the fishwife. The accuracy of this diagnosis will be apparent when it is remembered that the stock argument of these people is that the desuetude of the vernacular is due to 'superior people who consider it vulgar'.[29]

A decade or so later, MacDiarmid the élitist internationalist had reverted towards popular nationalism, a trend also noticeable in the Soviet Union, where Futurism had become a thing of the past. In Scotland, perhaps in the United Kingdom and Europe more widely too, experimentalism was giving way before development on a traditional basis. In 1934, MacDiarmid and his fellow-editor of *Scottish Scene or the Intelligent Man's Guide to Albyn* expressed a shared belief that 'a distance from the Scottish Scene would lend them some clarity in viewing it'. MacDiarmid himself was in the 'sound of the running seas by the Shetlands' while his partner was 'in a pleasant village near London', the erstwhile haunt of the worse than inverted highbrows. Even more strikingly, perhaps, MacDiarmid's distant collaborator was none other than Lewis Grassic Gibbon, who did more than anybody else to put the previously excoriated North-East on the literary map of Scotland through inventive exploitation of the culture of the fishwife and the ploughman.

MacDiarmid had not completely given up his esoteric flights of fancy, but the mock-Jaberwocky of 'headlong in dewy dallops or a moon-spairged fernshaw or caught in a dark dumosity' sits uneasily on the opposite page to the beginning of a short story (Lewis Grassic Gibbon's 'Greenden', companion piece to 'Clay' described at the beginning of this chapter): 'Folk laughed when they heard of the creatures coming to sit them down in the farm of Greenden that lay west of Tulloch by Bervie Water.'[30]

North-East 'local patriots', in London or at home, would also probably have permitted themselves a laugh or two at MacDiarmid's expense as they saw his collaborator so specifically, if no doubt unwittingly, refuting the arguments for synthetic Scots with such references to a precise location for 'Greenden', 'Clay' and the other short stories in *Scottish Scene*. On the other hand, several of them might have drawn back as they became familiar with the overt political message of Grassic Gibbon's trilogy *A Scots Quair*. Certainly this description of rural life in the Mearns and urban life in 'Duncairn', succeeded in adapting local culture for a wider audience of novel readers. Grassic Gibbon described his own approach in the following manner:

> The technique . . . is to mould the English language into the rhythms and cadences of Scots spoken speech, and to inject into the vocabulary such minimum number of words from Braid Scots as that remodelling requires. His scene so far has been a comparatively uncrowded and simple one – the countryside and village of modern Scotland. Whether his technique is adequate to compass and express the life of an industrialized Scots town in all its complexity is yet to be demonstrated; whether his peculiar style may not become either intolerably mannered or degenerate, in the fashion of Joyce, into the unfortunate unintelligibilities of a literary second childhood, its also in question.[31]

For some critics, the first question is to be answered in the negative, since they have found 'Grey Granite' the least successful part of the trilogy, not so much for its explicit socialism as its inadequate creation of 'Duncairn', described by Grassic Gibbon himself as 'the city which the inhabitants of the Mearns . . . have hitherto failed to build'. Yet, for Raymond Williams, it is precisely the movement from the country to the city that gives *A Scots Quair* its essential strength. He sees the first volume, *Sunset Song*, as 'a classic statement of what is seen as the dissolution of the peasantry'. Then the 'spiritual feeling for the land and labour' is transmitted and transmuted through *Cloud Howe* and *Grey Granite* as 'the radical independence of small farmers, the craftsmen and the labourers is seen as transitional to the militancy of the industrial workers'. In such a manner, *A Scots Quair* is an effective counterblast against the rural retrospect which has become explicitly reactionary, since 'given the break of continuity there have been very few voices on the other side'.[32]

In more recent years, 'the other side' has been eloquently spoken for by a number of academic analysts, such as David Buchan and Ian Carter, and by inheritors of the modern vernacular culture of the North-East such as Jessie Kesson and David Toulmin, both of whom have acknowledged a literary debt to Lewis Grassic Gibbon, but also created their own distinctive approaches to the writing of the novel and the short story. To illustrate this point, let us look again at a description give by Lewis Grassic Gibbon of his method, this time in the prefatory Note to *Sunset Song*:

> If the great Dutch language disappeared from literary usage and a Dutchman wrote in German a story of the Lekside peasants, one may hazard he would ask and receive a certain latitude and forbearance in his usage of German. He might import into his pages some score or so untranslatable words and idioms – untranslatable except in their context and setting; he might mould in some fashion his German to the rhythms and cadence of the kindred speech that his peasants speak. Beyond that, in fairness to his hosts, he could hardly go – to seek effect by a spray of apostrophes would be both impertinence and mistranslation. The courtesy that the hypothetical Dutchman might receive from German a Scot may invoke from the great English tongue.

To effect such an aim, however, the score or so of words and idioms that Grassic Gibbon imported were not so much 'Braid Scots' as the North-Eastern dialect found so corrupt by Hugh MacDiarmid.[33]

However, while the characters in *A Scots Quair* are presented for the most part by Grassic Gibbon without condescension, they remain 'his peasants'. Kesson and Toulmin differ from him in that they *are* their own people. Moreover, rather than wanting to put over any message, they are both attempting simply to project life in Buchan as it has been in their own lifetime. This picks up the story, so to speak, where Grassic Gibbon left it off, roughly speaking in the 1930s. For if *A Scots Quair* bestrides the First World War, the work of Kesson and Toulmin leads up to and follows the Second. No doubt they were assisted by the passage of time as well as by their predecessor's stylistic pathfinding, since the Second World War did indeed bring about a further degree of general democratisation, as well as accelerating the demise of the 'traditional' way of farming life developed from the late eighteenth century onwards. Avoiding for the most part the mawkish senti-mentality of which MacDiarmid had been fully justified to comp-lain, they have achieved a truthful immediacy born of personal experience as much as acute observation, making adept use of the modern vernacular culture of North-East Scotland and its contem-porary manifestations. In such a manner, they have forged links between pre-industrial and post-industrial phases of develop-ment, and shown that the Buchan heritage is not stagnant and backward-looking, but vital and adapting itself to new challenges.

So let us give the last words to David Toulmin. In *Blown Seed* he writes:

> They even tried to scare the snipe from the Myreloch, piping ashore their maritime gas, but for the good folk of the Bogside who said Na faith ye! Gang further sooth, ayont the Battery Head wi' yer gas pipes, and the navvies laid them across the bents where the farming billies used to get the shell grit for their hens . . . But neither have they stopped the showers of willow-herb and burr thickening in the sunbeam and blowing across the howe; insecticide has failed in this as much as the hoe, and even worse when you look at the parks, where the blown seed has landed.[34]

Notes

For their comments on earlier drafts of this paper, I am grateful to David Buchan, William Donaldson, Peter Hall, Ian Olson and John Reid (David Toulmin).

1. Fernand Braudel, *L'identité de la France: espace et histoire*, Paris, 1986, p. 28.
2. The best introduction is John R. Allan, *North-East Lowlands of Scotland*, 2nd edn, London, 1974.
3. Lewis Grassic Gibbon, 'Clay', in Lewis Grassic Gibbon and Hugh MacDiarmid, eds, *Scottish Scene: or the Intelligent Man's Guide to Albyn*, London, 1934, pp. 277–9.
4. See, for example, John Berger, 'Historical Afterword', *Pig Earth*, London, 1979, pp. 195–7.
5. Rev. Henry Cowan, 'Bishop William Elphinstone', P. J. Anderson, ed. *Studies in the History and Development of the University of Aberdeen*, Aberdeen, 1906. See more generally Leslie J. Macfarlane, *William Elphinstone and the Kingdom of Scotland, 1431–1514: The Struggle for Order*, Aberdeen, 1985.
6. T. D. Robb, 'Arthur Johnston in his Poems', *Scottish Historical Review*, vol. 10, 1912–13, p. 291. For the original, see Sir William Duguid Geddes, ed., *Musa Latina Aberdonensis*, I, Aberdeen, 1892, pp. 249–54.
7. David Toulmin (John Reid) is the author of several collections of short stories and essays as well as a novel, *Blown Seed*. Jessie Kesson has produced three novels, *The White Bird Passes, Glitter of Mica* and *Another Time, Another Place*, as well as short stories, plays for radio and film scenarios.
8. William Donaldson, Introduction, Jessie Kesson, *Glitter of Mica*, Edinburgh, 1982, p. 4.
9. See, for example, David Toulmin, *A Chief Among Them*, Aberdeen, 1982, pp. 85–93; *The Clyack Sheaf*, Aberdeen, 1986, pp. 119–37.
10. Kesson, *Glitter of Mica*, pp. 69–70, 73, 30, 34–5, 55–8. See more generally Mary Ellen Brown, *Burns and Tradition*, London, 1984.
11. *The Statistical Account of Scotland, 1791–1799*, ed. Donald J. Withrington and Ian R. Grant, xv, *North and East Aberdeenshire*, Wakefield, 1982, pp. 324–5, 336–48.
12. *The Statistical Account*, xv, pp. 235, 298–301.
13. Thomas Blackwell, *An Enquiry into the Life and Writings of Homer*, 2nd edn, London, 1736, pp. 12, 146. I am grateful here for the suggestions of Neil R. Grobman.
14. Thomas Blackwell, *Letters concerning Mythology*, London, 1748, p. 20.
15. William Walker, *The Bards of Bon-Accord, 1375–1860*, Aberdeen, 1887, pp. 211–12.
16. Walker, *The Bards*, pp. 31, 55. See in general J. D. McClure and M. R. G. Spiller (eds.) *Bryght Lanternis*, Aberdeen, 1989.
17. See, for example, William Donaldson, *The Jacobite Song: Political Myth and National Identity*, Aberdeen, 1988.

18. David Buchan, *The Ballad and the Folk*, London, 1972, pp. 73, 76.
19. Walker, *The Bards*, pp. 217–18, 240.
20. Ibid., pp. 272–3.
21. Ibid., pp. 188–98.
22. David Toulmin, *A Chiel Amang Them*, pp. 142, 144, 153.
23. See, for example, Maurice Colgan, 'Ossian: Success or Failure for the Scottish Enlightenment?' and other contributions, ed. Jennifer J. Carter and Joan H. Pittock, *Aberdeen and the Enlightenment*, Aberdeen, 1987, pp. 344–431
24. William Donaldson, *Popular Literature in Victorian Scotland: Language, Fiction and the Press*, Aberdeen, 1986. See also William Donaldson, *The Language of the People: Scots Prose from the Victorian Revival*, Aberdeen, 1989.
25. Dave Harker, 'May Cecil Sharp be Praised?', *History Workshop*, no. 14, Autumn 1982, p. 59.
26. John Stuart Blackie, Introduction, *The Scottish Students' Song-Book*, Glasgow, 1891, pp. vi–vii; Ian A. Olson, 'Gavin Greig's Lecture to the Scottish National Song Society, November 1909. A failure of nerve?', *Northern Scotland*, vol. 7, no. 2, 1987.
27. Dave Harker, 'May Cecil Sharp', p. 60.
28. Hugh MacDiarmid, *Contemporary Scottish Studies*, Edinburgh, 1976, pp. 117–18.
29. MacDiarmid, *Contemporary Scottish Studies*, pp. 7, 10, 12–13, 53–4, 82, 117–20. See also Peter McCarey, *MacDiarmid and the Russians*, Edinburgh, 1987, and Charlotte Douglas, ed., Velimir Khlebnikov, *The King of Time: Poems, Fictions, Visions of the Future*, Cambridge, Mass., and London, 1985.
30. Gibbon and MacDiarmid, *Scottish Scene*, pp. 68–9.
31. Gibbon and MacDiarmid, *Scottish Scene*, p. 205.
32. Raymond Williams, *The Country and the City*, London, 1973, pp. 268–71.
33. Lewis Grassic Gibbon, *A Scots Quair*, 8th impression, London, 1969, p. 14. For a full discussion of the North-East setting, see Ian Carter, *Farm Life in Northeast Scotland 1940–1914: The Poor Man's Country*, Edinburgh, 1979.
34. David Toulmin, *Blown Seed*, Edinburgh, 1976, p. 289.